ABOUT THE AUTHOR
ipraywiththegospel.org

Rev. George Boronat M.D. S.T.D is a   of Opus Dei, working in the Archdiocese of Southwark in London. He is the Chaplain of The Cedars and The Laurels School in West Norwood, and of Kelston Club & Study Centre (Balham). He also works at Oakwood School (South Croydon). He has developed his pastoral ministry mainly with young people.

Discover the iPray app

Android   Apple

Scripture quotations are from The Revised Standard Version of the Bible: Catholic Edition, copyright © 1965, 1966 the Division of Christian Education of the National Council of the Churches of Christ in the United States of America. Used by permission. All rights reserved.

Copyright © 2022 by George Boronat. All rights reserved. This book or any portion thereof may not be reproduced or used in any manner whatsoever without the express written permission of the publisher except for the use of brief quotations. For permission requests, write to

ipraywiththegospel.org/contact-us/

HOW TO APPROACH YOUR PRAYER
Some ideas that might be useful before you start your prayer

— **Can I pray?** as in talk with God? Most certainly! God created you to be His friend; and friends talk to each other. To do mental prayer you don't need training. There is no standard method.

— **How do I begin?** You can begin with the Introductory prayer to tune in. Then… just start talking to Him. As St Josemaría teaches, it is all a matter of getting the conversation started: "You don't know how to pray? Put yourself in the presence of God, and as soon as you have said, "Lord, I don't know how to pray!" you can be sure you've already begun."

— **What should I do then?** You can read the Gospel and the comments of the iPray. They can trigger a topic for your prayer. But remember: the most important part of your prayer is not written in this booklet. The main part is what you say to Him and, especially, what He says to you.

— **What should I talk about?** About everything! "About Him, about yourself—joys, sorrows, successes and failures, noble ambitions, daily worries, weaknesses! And acts of thanksgiving and petitions—and Love and reparation" (St Josemaría).

— **How do I finish?** At the end of your prayer you can ask Our Lady for help; you should also give thanks to Our Lord for that dialogue. You can finish, if you want, with the Closing prayer.

January

Octave day of the Nativity
Mary, the Holy Mother of God
Wednesday 1st January
Lk 2:16-21

And they went with haste, and found Mary and Joseph, and the babe lying in a manger. And when they saw it they made known the saying which had been told them concerning this child; and all who heard it wondered at what the shepherds told them. But Mary kept all these things, pondering them in her heart. And the shepherds returned, glorifying and praising God for all they had heard and seen, as it had been told them. And at the end of eight days, when he was circumcised, he was called Jesus, the name given by the angel.

Mary, the Holy Mother of God, is the beginning. It just makes sense. She initiated our Redemption. She opens the New Year also. Is there any better way to kick off? You have heard that *a good start is half of the battle*. Let's make that good start today, with Our Lady.

We are still in the Christmas Season and we are reminded of Our Mother keeping all the memories of Jesus and "pondering" them in her Immaculate Heart. Christmas is a season to focus our sights on Jesus. There is no better way than to learn from Mary. To look at Him with the loving eyes of Our Lady. St John Paul II invites us to contemplate the Virgin's gaze on her Child: *"The contemplation of Christ has a remarkable model in Mary. In a unique way the face of the Son belongs to Mary. It was in her womb that Christ was formed, receiving from her a human resemblance which points to an even greater spiritual closeness. No one has ever devoted himself to the contemplation of the face of Christ as faithfully as Mary."*

We hurry like curious little children to the crib - and there we find Jesus, in the arms of His enraptured Mother. As you are little you can get really close; in the arms of Mary there is room for two, Jesus and you. There, in silence, you look at Him and smile at her; you contemplate them both and you learn to love.

And in the arms of Mary, beside that beautiful Baby, we promise for the New Year to struggle to be good children of Mary, to remain in her arms during the whole year, to try to grow in love with Jesus. Throughout this year that we begin today, with the Grace of God, may I keep my eyes on Jesus and, from your lap, Mary, my Mother, may I be like you, keeping a permanent dialogue with Jesus every single one of the 365 days of this year.

Saints Basil and Gregory, bishops and Doctors of the Church
Thursday 2nd January
Jn 1:19-28

The Pharisees asked John, "Then why are you baptising, if you are neither the Christ, nor Elijah, nor the prophet?" John answered them, "I baptise with water; but among you stands one whom you do not know, even he who comes after me, the thong of whose sandal I am not worthy to untie." This took place in Bethany beyond the Jordan.

The baptism of St John was a penitential rite that prepared the Jews to change their way of life. The Gospel says in another place that they were 'confessing' their sins to St John as well (*Mk* 1:5). These rites were not sacraments yet. They were a preparation for the real Sacraments that Jesus inaugurated with His Death and Resurrection. The Sacrament of Baptism does not 'prepare' us, as John's Baptism did. It 'transforms' us, makes us Christians.

Today we celebrate Saints Basil and Gregory. Theirs is a beautiful story of friendship. Both born in the year 330, they were good friends and they both had an excellent education. They weren't saints to begin with, though. St Basil writes about wasting time on frivolities and vanities. "*One day,*" he wrote, "*like a man roused from deep sleep, I turned my eyes to the marvellous light of the truth of the Gospel, and I wept many tears over my miserable life.*" They encouraged each other and were both baptised at the age of 28. Years later Basil was ordained bishop and fought against the Arian heresy. But when he needed help and support in that exhausting doctrinal battle, he called his friend Gregory who became a bishop as well and fought heresy at his side.

One of the most inspiring texts about friendship was written by St Gregory years later: "*We seemed to be two bodies with a single spirit. We became everything to each other: we shared the same lodging, the same table, the same desires, the same goal. Our love for each other grew daily warmer and deeper. The same hope inspired us. Our rivalry consisted, not in seeking the first place for oneself but in yielding it to the other. Our single object and ambition was virtue, and a life of hope in Heaven...In order to make a name for ourselves, the great name we wanted, was to be Christians: **to be called Christians.**"* Mary, my Mother, may I be that kind of friend to my friends so we can all go to Heaven together!

The Most Holy Name of Jesus
Friday 3rd January
Jn 1:29-34

The next day John saw Jesus coming toward him, and said, "Behold, the Lamb of God, who takes away the sin of the world! This is he of whom I said, 'After me comes a man who ranks before me, for he was before me.' I myself did not know him; but for this I came baptising with water, that he might be revealed to Israel...I saw the Spirit descend as a dove from heaven, and it remained on him...And I have seen and have borne witness that this is the Son of God."

Until then Jesus had been hidden in Nazareth, known only by His parents, some relatives and a few friends. But now the time had come to reveal to all nations that God had sent His Only-Begotten Son to save them. In our Baptism we were made Christians and were given our names, but there was another 'Name' that was given to us in Baptism: the Name of Jesus, so that in that Name we could ask for everything and receive everything through It.

In Harry Potter there are many powerful words (spells) - too many to memorise them all. Some are more useful than others: *Expelliarmus* is useful to disarm your opponent; *Accio* can summon objects at will to the caster; *Lumos* turns on your wand like a torch... and of course, *Avada Kedavra* supposedly destroys people. Well. Don't waste any time or memory space - they don't work in real life. Instead, the word that can be used for all purposes, especially in this battle against the enemy, is easy to memorise: the Name of Jesus.

Jesus is the Word. Those five letters are the shortest and mightiest prayer ever given to mankind, the most beautiful aspiration to praise God, the loveliest Word to give thanks, the most comforting in time of distress, the most effective in time of temptation; the most powerful to banish the darkness of the enemy, the mist of doubt, the lack of trust; the most invincible prayer against any challenge to our faith, the fire that can burn up the remains of our sins... *Jesus* is the most compelling Name to be heard from Heaven: "*If you ask the Father anything in my name he will give it you,*" Jesus said.

The Holy Name of Jesus has worked wonders in the past. Mary, Mother of Jesus, how lovely is the Name of your Son. What could be impossible for me if I have that Name on my lips, in my mind, in my heart?

Saturday 4th January
Jn 1:35-42

John was standing with two of his disciples; and he looked at Jesus as he walked, and said, "Behold, the Lamb of God!" The two disciples heard him say this, and they followed Jesus. Jesus turned, and saw them following, and said to them, "What do you seek?" And they said to him, "Rabbi...where are you staying?" He said to them, "Come and see." They came and saw where he was staying; and they stayed with him that day, for it was about the tenth hour.

What was He like? That day John the Baptist was with John "the Beloved" and Andrew. They saw Jesus. There was something magnetic in that Person. The Baptist smiled, looked at the two disciples and said, *'Behold, the Lamb of God! That's the One you should follow.'* They rose immediately and followed Jesus. Jesus turned, and laid His eyes on them. It was the first time He looked the Beloved in the eyes. God had loved him, created him, chosen him - and that day, He met him. How did John and Andrew feel when Jesus looked at them with His captivating Eyes, an irresistible smile on His Face? A memorable moment that none of them forgot! Then Jesus opened His mouth and they heard His charming Voice for the first time: *"What do you seek?"* Perplexed for an instant, they were momentarily dumbstruck with the echo of those words resounding in their ears: *"What do you seek?"*

O, Jesus! What do we seek?! We seek Someone who can fill our hearts with Love to the brim; we seek eternal happiness! We seek freedom from sin, we seek forgiveness; justice, redemption, hope; we seek Someone who is worth living with, Someone worth dying for. Jesus, we seek to quench the thirst for eternity that You put in our hearts. *"Where are You, Lord? Where are You staying?!"* *"Come and see,"* Jesus said. And they went; they followed Him; and they stayed with Him that day, and the following day and the next...and for ever. And many years later, when John was a blind old man, he could still remember precisely: *"it was about the tenth hour... how could I forget?!"* That was the memorable day when they met Jesus, when they decided to follow Him, with determination: for ever! Mary, Mother of Jesus, help me get to know your Son, follow Him... and stay with Him for ever. Today can be 'My Memorable Day'!

The Epiphany of Our Lord
Sunday 5th January
Mt 2:1-12

Now when Jesus was born in Bethlehem of Judea in the days of Herod the king, behold, wise men from the East came to Jerusalem, saying, "Where is he who has been born king of the Jews? For we have seen his star in the East, and have come to worship him."... they went their way; and lo, the star which they had seen in the East went before them, till it came to rest over the place where the child was. When they saw the star, they rejoiced exceedingly with great joy; and going into the house they saw the child with Mary his mother, and they fell down and worshipped him. Then, opening their treasures, they offered him gifts, gold and frankincense and myrrh.

These Wise Men set out in search of the Heavenly King. They left everything behind: the comfort of their homes, the security in their lives, their plans, families, friends, towns, belongings... They left everything and went in pursuit of Jesus. That's what they were looking for. When they found the King in a manger they were not disappointed. With immense joy, they adored Him and gave Him their gifts.

But the initiative wasn't theirs. God made the first move. To call them, He put a sign in the sky so they could discover it and seek Him. We often hear of men's search for God, but seldom, if ever, hear of God's search for us. The truth is that God first seeks *us* out, so that we might seek *Him*. He thirsts for us, so that we might thirst for Him. There is the story of a man who was running around looking for God. He never stopped for a second. He rushed from place to place asking others about God always and everywhere. But he couldn't find Him. When he died and met God in Heaven he asked, "*I looked for you everywhere... Where were You?*" And God replied, "*Chasing you; trying to catch up with you!*" God is seeking us out first.

These Men were not expecting illuminated signs saying '*King of the Jews*' and arrows pointing the way. A star in the sky was enough of a sign for them to leave everything and look for Jesus. Probably many of their neighbours thought they were crazy. But eventually they realised everything was worthwhile. They found Jesus and "*rejoiced **exceedingly** with **great joy**.*" They followed the star and ended up over the moon! Mary, Star of the Sea, may I learn to seek and find God in the signs He has prepared for me every day.

Second Sunday of Christmas
Sunday 5th January
Jn 1:1-18

In the beginning was the Word, and the Word was with God, and the Word was God. He was in the beginning with God; all things were made through him, and without him was not anything made that was made... He came to his own home, and his own people received him not. But to all who received him, who believed in his name, he gave power to become children of God.

We get used to read that "*He came to his own home, and his own people received him not.*" We tend to forget that it was You, Jesus, Who came to us. At times, we are more focused on what we *have to* do for God than what You, Lord, have done for us.

Fr Vincent Donovan went as a missionary to the Masai in Tanzania. He described a conversation he had with a Masai elder. The elder said that for a man *to believe*, is like a lion going after his prey. His nose and eyes and ears pick up the prey. His legs give him the speed to catch it. All the power of his body is involved in the final leap and single blow to the neck with the front paw. And as the animal goes down the lion envelops it, pulls it to himself and makes it part of himself. This is the way a lion kills. This is the way a man believes, the man explained.

Fr Donovan looked at the elder in silence and amazement. And the Masai elder continued: «*We did not search you out, Padri. We did not even want you to come to us. You searched us out. You followed us away from your house into the bush, into the plains, into the steppes where our cattle are, into the hills, into our villages, into our homes. You told us of the High God, how we must search for him, even leave our land and our people to find him. But we have not left our land. We have not searched for God. He has searched for us. God has searched us out and found us. All the time we think we are the lion. In the end, the lion is God.*» It is always You, Lord, who seek us out.

Mary, my Mother Immaculate, help me be taken by God.

Monday after Epiphany
Monday 6th January
Mt 4:12-17, 23-25

Jesus began to preach, saying, "Repent, for the kingdom of heaven is at hand." And he went about all Galilee, teaching in their synagogues and preaching the gospel of the kingdom and healing every disease and every infirmity among the people. So his fame spread throughout all Syria, and they brought him all the sick, those afflicted with various diseases and pains, demoniacs, epileptics, and paralytics, and he healed them.

This is a synopsis of the public life of Our Lord. *"He went about all Galilee"*. He *went*. He didn't wait for them to come. And He did it in a rather 'radical' way: He went about *all* Galilee teaching and healing *every* disease and *every* infirmity; His fame spread throughout *all* Syria; they brought Him *all* the sick… Nothing low-key, no half-measures… We could say that He took it *seriously*.

Christmas has reminded us that Jesus came to the world to fulfil that mission. His love for *everyone* was *total*. He wanted to reach *all* who had lost *everything* through sin, so as to give them back *everything*. Jesus can't act in a half-hearted way because He has given us His entire Heart. He loves each one of us so much!

Love is proved in trial. One of the most beautiful love stories is the one of Jacob and Rachel. From the moment Jacob saw her, he fell in love and soon after he asked Laban, Rachel's father, to marry her. Jacob loved her so much that he offered to work for Laban for 7 years in order to marry Rachel. *"So Jacob served seven years for Rachel,"* we read in the book of Genesis, *"and they seemed to him but a few days because of the love he had for her"* (Gen 29:20). But that wasn't the end of the story. After those 7 years Laban told Jacob that, in order to marry Rachel, he had to work 7 more years; and Jacob agreed! So, all in all, Jacob worked 14 years to marry the woman he loved. That is real love.

The love of God for souls is as serious as that. He never gives up on us, searching for us and bringing us to Him, to our happiness. One day, when Bl Angela of Foligno was meditating on the Passion of Jesus, she heard His voice saying: '*I did not love you as a joke.*' No. There is no love more serious than the Love of God for us. If only I could grasp how much God loves me! Mary, my Mother, help me to feel God's love for me.

The Epiphany of Our Lord
Monday 6th January
Mt 2:1-12

Now when Jesus was born in Bethlehem of Judea in the days of Herod the king, behold, wise men from the East came to Jerusalem, saying, "Where is he who has been born king of the Jews? For we have seen his star in the East, and have come to worship him."... they went their way; and lo, the star which they had seen in the East went before them, till it came to rest over the place where the child was. When they saw the star, they rejoiced exceedingly with great joy; and going into the house they saw the child with Mary his mother, and they fell down and worshipped him. Then, opening their treasures, they offered him gifts, gold and frankincense and myrrh.

These Wise Men set out in search of the Heavenly King. They left everything behind: the comfort of their homes, the security in their lives, their plans, families, friends, towns, belongings... They left everything and went in pursuit of Jesus. That's what they were looking for. When they found the King in a manger they were not disappointed. With immense joy, they adored Him and gave Him their gifts.

But the initiative wasn't theirs. God made the first move. To call them, He put a sign in the sky so they could discover it and seek Him. We often hear of men's search for God, but seldom, if ever, hear of God's search for us. The truth is that God first seeks *us* out, so that we might seek *Him*. He thirsts for us, so that we might thirst for Him. There is the story of a man who was running around looking for God. He never stopped for a second. He rushed from place to place asking others about God always and everywhere. But he couldn't find Him. When he died and met God in Heaven he asked, "*I looked for you everywhere... Where were You?*" And God replied, "*Chasing you; trying to catch up with you!*" God is seeking us out first.

These Men were not expecting illuminated signs saying '*King of the Jews*' and arrows pointing the way. A star in the sky was enough of a sign for them to leave everything and look for Jesus. Probably many of their neighbours thought they were crazy. But eventually they realised everything was worthwhile. They found Jesus and "*rejoiced **exceedingly** with **great joy**.*" They followed the star and ended up over the moon! Mary, Star of the Sea, may I learn to seek and find God in the signs He has prepared for me every day.

Tuesday after Epiphany
Tuesday 7th January
Mk 6:34-44

As he went ashore he saw a great throng, and he had compassion on them, because they were like sheep without a shepherd; and he began to teach them many things. And when it grew late, his disciples came to him and said, "This is a lonely place, and the hour is now late; send them away, to go into the country and villages round about and buy themselves something to eat." But he answered them, "You give them something to eat."

Jesus was moved with pity for those people and *"began to teach them many things."* Finally, it was growing late. It was time to call it a day, the disciples thought, or people wouldn't have time to *get* something to eat. 'They don't need to *get* anything'; Jesus said: "*You give them something to eat.*"

'But we have nothing!,' the Apostles thought. "*You give them!*", said Jesus, as if saying: 'I have taught them... now it's your turn! Give them from what I have given you.' Because every time God asks us to give, He wants us to give from what we have received. You remember the rest of the story. They brought Him five loaves and two fish. And Jesus arranged it so that 5,000 could eat and 12 basketfuls of leftovers were gathered.

But in order to give, we first need to receive. This is especially true of our spiritual formation. The Church offers so many means of formation that we are free to accept. When you have the chance to receive formation, remember that you have a duty to share it with others.

During his prayer a young student was struck by that command of Jesus: 'You give them'. He started feeding the poor in the streets but later understood that Jesus was asking him to share 'more'. He gave food, time, formation, help... but he still wasn't at peace. He wrote years later: "*'You give them,' said Jesus in my prayer. And I gave my time. That wasn't enough. Still He insisted, 'Give them!' And I decided to distribute food. But Our Lord kept saying to me, 'You give them!' I studied and gave them my knowledge and formation. It didn't bring peace to my soul. Still I could hear Him insisting in my heart, 'You give them!' And I never found peace until I gave MYSELF.*" He is now a young priest. Mary, my Mother, I know that your Son still needs generous people who know how to give themselves to others. I pray through your intercession, Virgin Most Admirable, that God may multiply our generosity.

Wednesday 8th January
Mk 6:45-52

Immediately he made his disciples get into the boat and go before him to the other side, to Bethsaida, while he dismissed the crowd...And he saw that they were making headway painfully, for the wind was against them. And about the fourth watch of the night he came to them, walking on the sea. He meant to pass by them, but when they saw him walking on the sea they thought it was a ghost, and cried out; for they all saw him, and were terrified. But immediately he spoke to them and said, "Take heart, it is I; have no fear." And he got into the boat with them and the wind ceased.

Do you realise that Jesus knew the forecast better than the Met Office? Jesus knew the speed of the wind, the height of the waves and even the temperature of the water... And nevertheless He *sent* His disciples out on to those waters at that particular time (evening) with that particular boat. Why did You do that, Lord?

Do you remember the story of Gideon? Whilst the Israelites were being oppressed by the Midianites, an angel appeared to this young man and said, "*The Lord is with you.*" "*If the Lord is with us,*" Gideon protested, "*why then has all this befallen us?*" As we read the story we discover why: so they might learn to trust God. The Lord asked Gideon to raise an army to fight against the Midianites. He managed to gather 32,000! But then God asked him to get rid of those who were afraid. Gideon saw his army reduced to 10,000. Then God asked him to choose 300 of them. Initially, they may well have thought the 300 were being chosen to be discarded, but actually it was just the opposite: those 300 men were to be the entire army!

Gideon couldn't understand why God would prefer a squad of 300 when He had an army of 32,000. But Our Lord knows what He is doing, He knows the *what*, the *who*, the *where*, the *when*, the *how*... Only He knows. In the end (spoiler alert) those 300 hundred won against thousands. Well, God did.

Like Gideon, that day the Apostles learned to trust. They never forgot Our Lord's words: "*Take heart, it is I; have no fear.*" Now they could weather any storm because they knew that Jesus would never leave them alone. Mary, my Mother, may I never forget that your Son will '*walk*' with me.

Thursday after Epiphany
Thursday 9th January
Lk 4:14-22

Jesus came to Nazareth, where he had been brought up; and he went to the synagogue, as his custom was, on the sabbath day. And he stood up to read; and there was given to him the book of the prophet Isaiah. He opened the book and found the place where it was written, "The Spirit of the Lord is upon me, because he has anointed me to preach good news to the poor..." And he closed the book, and gave it back to the attendant, and sat down; and the eyes of all in the synagogue were fixed on him. And he began to say to them, "Today this scripture has been fulfilled in your hearing."

We read that "*the eyes of all in the synagogue were fixed on him*". We can imagine the curious looks of those Jews in Nazareth who had seen Jesus as a Child running through their streets, as a Boy passing with Joseph in front of their houses, as a Teenager carrying furniture that He had made with His own Hands. Now they see the Man in front of them and they can't take their eyes off Him.

Sometimes in our prayer we spend time talking to Our Lord. But sometimes nothing comes to mind, we feel exhausted, our minds go blank. That shouldn't prevent us from doing our mental prayer. Prayer can lead us to the 'contemplation' of Jesus. This lesson has been taught by simple people to many priests. St. John Vianney once noticed a peasant come in to the church and stay for hours in front of Jesus in the Blessed Sacrament. The Saint asked this man, "*What do you say to Him?*" The peasant replied, "*Nothing, I look at Him and He looks at me.*"

Another priest found a woman praying intensely in front of the Tabernacle with the Gospel opened on her lap. The priest told the woman, "*I thought you didn't know how to read!*" "*And I don't,*" she replied, "*I open the Gospel and kiss a different page every day. Then I look at Him and wonder how He was... and try to see Him with the eyes of my soul.*" Throughout the Christmas season we have been contemplating Him in the Crib, with you, Mary, Mother of Jesus, my Mother, and with Joseph, my father and lord. In my prayer I want to fix my eyes on Him, convinced that He is looking back at me. "*I know Your Gaze well, Lord, when You rest Your Eyes on me serenely and firmly. That's probably why you allow the thick fog to remove all doubt. I always search for my answer in your eyes. And there I always find it*" (Francisca González).

Friday 10th January
Lk 5:12-16

There came a man full of leprosy; and when he saw Jesus, he fell on his face and besought him, "Lord, if you will, you can make me clean." And he stretched out his hand, and touched him, saying, "I will; be clean." And immediately the leprosy left him. And he charged him to tell no one; but "go and show yourself to the priest, and make an offering for your cleansing, as Moses commanded, for a proof to the people."

Do you see how simple the miracle is? "*If you will... I will: And immediately the leprosy left him.*" You know that in those days lepers had to cover themselves from the crown of their head to the soles of their feet. They were forbidden to show any skin at all, to avoid contaminating other people. This man fell on his face and asked for Mercy. Jesus touched him and his leprosy was gone for ever. So simple. But Jesus' miracle included the fulfilment of a commandment: "*go and show yourself to the priest.*"

We must learn to come to Jesus with that same simplicity, showing Him our leprosy (our sins) in Confession. In this Sacrament Jesus touches your wounds and heals them. But you need to "*show yourself to the priest.*" You have to unveil your wounds (your sins) as you do with the doctor. Don't cover up... show yourself without fear, because the Divine Doctor has to see the wound to heal it, and He has entrusted that mission to priests.

We should help people go to Confession more frequently, to show their 'wounds' before they get 'infected', not to wait too long. Like with doctors, regular checkups can prevent serious sickness. John Paul I tells the story of Jonathan Swift's servant, who refused to wash the mud off his master's boots after a long trip because he considered it a waste of time: "*They'll only get dirty again,*" he said. Swift said nothing until the next morning, when he announced he wanted to set out immediately. His servant protested he hadn't had breakfast. "*So what?*" Swift replied. "*You'll only be hungry again!*" Yes. If we go to Confession we will have more sins to confess in a while. But our soul is like the windscreen of a car. It gets dirty little by little with midges, gnats and bugs. If you don't clean it often you can't see properly and eventually you risk having a crash. Mary, Virgin Mother of Mercy, help me to proclaim the inexhaustible Mercy of God: all the sins of all men of all times together are but a *speck of dust* in the *ocean of His Mercy*.

Saturday after Epiphany
Saturday 11th January
Jn 3:22-30

They came to John, and said to him, "Rabbi, he who was with you beyond the Jordan, to whom you bore witness, here he is, baptising, and all are going to him." John answered, "No one can receive anything except what is given him from heaven. You yourselves bear me witness, that I said, I am not the Christ, but I have been sent before him. He who has the bride is the bridegroom; the friend of the bridegroom, who stands and hears him, rejoices greatly at the bridegroom's voice; therefore this joy of mine is now full. He must increase, but I must decrease."

The disciples of St John the Baptist thought that he would be concerned or upset about Jesus, but the saint was beaming with joy. Mission accomplished! His mission was to prepare everything for Jesus. Now Jesus was at work. No more preparations, no more waiting, no more uncertainty or confusion: 'Operation Redemption' had begun!

John's disciples may have wanted more prominence, more public recognition for him... but he just wanted to hide and disappear, so that only Jesus would shine: "*He must increase, but I must decrease,*" he said. His mission was to point out the light of Jesus, not to shine himself.

St John Henry Newman explains: "*God has created me to do Him some definite service; He has committed some work to me which He has not committed to another. I have my mission... He has not created me for naught.*" And He has risked a lot. God is like a good football coach who has chosen to train you. He helps you to develop your skills. He teaches you all you need. He invests His money, time and gifts in you. But you are free. You can turn your back on Him and decide to do synchronised swimming. You might be good at it and be famous. But your coach would feel disappointed... and your team will be missing a vital player.

"*Vocation does not come from a voice out there calling me to be something I am not.*" Thomas Merton explains. "*It comes from a voice in here calling me to be the person I was born to be, to fulfil the original selfhood given me at birth by God... For each one of us, there is only one thing necessary: to fulfil our own destiny, according to God's will, to be what God wants us to be.*" Mary, Virgin Most Faithful, may I be faithful to my vocation.

The Baptism of Our Lord
Sunday 12th January
Lk 3:15-16, 21-22

John answered them all, "I baptise you with water; but he who is mightier than I is coming, the thong of whose sandals I am not worthy to untie; he will baptise you with the Holy Spirit and with fire. Now when all the people were baptised, and when Jesus also had been baptised and was praying, the heavens were opened, and the Holy Spirit descended upon him in bodily form, as a dove, and a voice came from heaven, "Thou art my beloved Son; with thee I am well pleased."

"*The Lord was Baptised*", explains St. Ambrose of Milan, "*not to be cleansed Himself, but to cleanse the waters, so that those waters might have the power of Baptism*". During His Ascension, He told His disciples to go and baptise all people and they did exactly that.

Saints have greatly valued this Sacrament. St Vincent Ferrer always celebrated the anniversary of his baptism and often went to kiss the baptismal font in the church of St Stephen in Valencia. After many years of absence, St Francis Solano went back to his hometown. Before doing anything else he knelt and rested his forehead on the font of the church where he was baptised and sang the Creed. When St Josemaria found out that they were discarding the font where he was baptised, he arranged for it to be brought to his chapel and kissed it every time he passed by it. Do *you* know the date of your baptism?

A young woman came to see the parish priest to discuss what was needed for her conversion to the Catholic Church. She explained that she had been reading the Gospel, fell in love with Jesus, and wanted to be a Catholic. The priest was surprised that no one had instructed her or talked to her about our faith. "*No one has taught you anything about the faith?*" asked the astonished priest. "*That's strange! You must have had a bit of guidance from someone.*" The girl explained: "*No one, father. Nobody, since I was baptised as a baby...*" "*But you were baptised?!...*" the priest interrupted her, and with a smile he added: "*I rest my case!*" Of course Someone had been helping her. Baptism made her a temple of the Holy Spirit. He had been helping her for many years...from inside! Mary, my Mother, may I never forget to give thanks to God for my Baptism and to truly value it as the saints did.

Monday 1st week in ordinary time
Monday 13th January
Mk 1:14–20

Jesus came into Galilee, preaching the gospel of God, and saying, "The time is fulfilled, and the kingdom of God is at hand; repent, and believe in the gospel." And passing along by the Sea of Galilee, he saw Simon and Andrew the brother of Simon casting a net in the sea; for they were fishermen. And Jesus said to them, "Follow me and I will make you become fishers of men." And immediately they left their nets and followed him. And going on a little farther, he saw James the son of Zebedee and John his brother, who were in their boat mending the nets. And immediately he called them; and they left their father Zebedee in the boat with the hired servants, and followed him.

It is hard to imagine a simpler and quicker way to leave everything and follow Jesus: the Apostles didn't even answer Him. They just left *everything immediately*: nets, boat, profession, income, projects, home; even - in the case of James and John - their father! And they left it all to follow Jesus, without yet knowing Him very well, without knowing where they were going, what they were going to do, or with whom, nor knowing for how long... And we read the same about the other Apostles: St Matthew (*Mt* 9:9) and Nathanael (*Jn* 1:49)... It was immediate. They didn't hesitate, they didn't calculate.

Jesus didn't choose men with great talent, power or position. He counted on men who were quick to respond to His calling. They were not like Alexander the Great, Julius Caesar or Charlemagne, whose empires have disappeared. They were fishermen, tax collectors... normal people.

Blessed Alvaro del Portillo had met St Josemaria in the spring of 1935. On 7th July they met a second time. Bl Alvaro attended a day of recollection and at the end of it he asked to join Opus Dei. And from then on until the end of his life he was faithful to his calling. Saints who have changed the world didn't make God wait. A youngster asked his spiritual director about his vocation. He knew he had to give his life to God but wondered 'when' to take the step. The holy priest replied to him, *"If God needs you tomorrow, He will call you tomorrow. If He is calling you now: He needs you now!"* Holy Mary, Mother most Faithful, help me to respond quickly to whatever God asks of me.

Tuesday 1st week in ordinary time
Tuesday 14th January
Mk 1:21-28

And they went into Caperna-um; and immediately on the sabbath he entered the synagogue and taught. And they were astonished at his teaching, for he taught them as one who had authority, and not as the scribes. And immediately there was in their synagogue a man with an unclean spirit; and he cried out, "What have you to do with us, Jesus of Nazareth? Have you come to destroy us? I know who you are, the Holy One of God." But Jesus rebuked him, saying, "Be silent, and come out of him!" And the unclean spirit, convulsing him and crying with a loud voice, came out of him. And they were all amazed, so that they questioned among themselves, saying, "What is this? A new teaching! With authority he commands even the unclean spirits, and they obey him." And at once his fame spread everywhere throughout all the surrounding region of Galilee.

"*They were astonished at his teaching,*" today's Gospel tells us. And in St Luke's Gospel we read: "*all the people hung upon his words*" (19:48). People came from all over the region to listen to Him and to 'drink' from the Word. Can you imagine the crowd captivated by His teaching? That's the power of the Voice of God. And to this day, the Voice of God still remains 'recorded' in Sacred Scripture. Origen, one of the early Christian writers, said that "*we should reverence every word of Scripture in the same way we reverence every particle of the Consecrated Host.*"

A young priest entered the oratory one day and found a little girl sitting on the priest's chair on the Sanctuary. He went up and said to her, "*This is no place for children; you should go down and use the pews.*" The girl replied, "*But from down there I cannot hear Him!*" The priest took these words as a lesson: we should have that same eagerness to listen to Him, to read His Word, to talk to Him. We were made for it.

The Bible is like a series of letters written by God to you and me. For centuries Christians have been reading them and if they couldn't read they went to Church to have them read for them. Mary, Mother of the Word, teach me to read the Scriptures as you would; help me to *hang upon your Son's Words*. This is a good 'New Year's resolution': to read the Gospels every day; *a chapter a day keeps the devil away!*

Wednesday 1st week in ordinary time
Wednesday 15th January
Mk 1:29-39

And the whole city was gathered together about the door. And he healed many who were sick with various diseases, and cast out many demons; and he would not permit the demons to speak, because they knew him. And in the morning, a great while before day, he rose and went out to a lonely place, and there he prayed. And Simon and those who were with him pursued him, and they found him and said to him, "Everyone is searching for you."

"*Everyone is searching for you!*" Everyone is searching for happiness, searching for Truth, searching for Beauty... But if that is the case... why don't many souls find Him? Because some are searching for Him in the wrong places. C. S. Lewis says that "*nearly all that we call human history is the long terrible story of man trying to find **something other than God** which will make him happy*." But the truth is that there is *nothing other than Him* that can fill human hearts with happiness.

As soon as we make the effort to start looking for Him, He comes to meet us like the father of the prodigal son. A. J. Cronin, a famous writer and doctor, explained his conversion. He was spending a few days partying with some friends in Rome. One day he went for a walk and got lost. He entered a chapel to ask for directions. The chapel commemorated the tradition of Jesus' encounter with St Peter. When Nero was killing Christians, Peter's disciples urged him to run away. Jesus appeared to him and when Peter asked Him, "*Quo vadis, Domine?*" [Where are you going, Lord?] Jesus answered, "*I'm going to Rome to be crucified again.*" Peter understood that he had to go back to Rome... and there he died, crucified upside down. Cronin explains, "*I thought I heard a gentle whisper from over the centuries asking me: Quo vadis? (Where are you going?)*" He experienced an emptiness and unhappiness and wondered, like St Augustine, why he wasn't happy. Why he was so empty... And he found the answer there, in front of him, in the Tabernacle.

Mary, Mother of the Hidden Lord, everyone is searching for your Son. Help me, Mother, to encourage others with my prayer and apostolate not to give up in their search, because "*everyone who seeks, finds.*"

Thursday 16th January
Mk 1:40-45

And a leper came to him beseeching him, and kneeling said to him, "If you will, you can make me clean." Moved with pity, he stretched out his hand and touched him, and said to him, "I will; be clean." And immediately the leprosy left him, and he was made clean.

The 'Touch' of Jesus is like the spark of static electricity that we feel sometimes when we touch someone. But God's spark is almighty. It heals everything! The impossible happens when He touches us. In an instant, the Grace of God can do anything.

Paul Claudel (1868 – 1955) was a famous French poet, dramatist and diplomat, nominated six times for the Nobel Prize in Literature. He wrote: "*Catholic faith was for me a treasure of absurd anecdotes. I felt the same disgust and hatred for her priests and faithful.*" On December 25th 1886 a taxi dropped him off at the gate of the Cathedral of Notre Dame in Paris. From there he heard the hymns of the Christmas Vespers. Attracted also by the stained glass windows, he decided to go in. They were singing the '*Magnificat*'. "*I was standing amid the crowd,*" he explained later, "*next to the sacristy. In an instant, something touched my heart and I believed. I believed, with such force, with so much agitation in my being, with a conviction so strong, with so much certainty that there was no place for doubt. After this, all the books, all the reasoning, all the events of my complicated existence have been unable to shake my faith or, to be honest, touch it! Suddenly, I thought: 'How happy are the people who believe! And what if it is true? But it is true! God exists, He is there! He is **Someone**! And He loves me! He calls to me.' Tears and sobs came to me and the singing of the Adeste Fideles only increased my emotion.*" The Touch of God could change that man in an instant.

Such is the Almighty 'spark' of the Touch of Grace. If Jesus stretches out His Hand and touches me, my misery is over: the stains of my past sins, all the dirt of my bad habits, my lack of charity, my lack of obedience, my laziness, my stubbornness, my vanity, my pride, my critical thoughts, my selfishness, my cowardice to stand up for my faith... will all disappear, Lord, if You touch me! Mary, my Mother, keep me close to your Son, to touch Him and be healed.

Friday 1st week in ordinary time
Friday 17th January
Mk 2:1-12

Four men brought to him a paralytic. And when they could not get near him because of the crowd, they removed the roof above him; and when they had made an opening, they let down the pallet on which the paralytic lay. And when Jesus saw their faith, he said to the paralytic, "My son, your sins are forgiven." Now some of the scribes were sitting there, questioning in their hearts, "Why does this man speak thus? It is blasphemy! Who can forgive sins but God alone?"

The faith of the paralytic's friends helped them to overcome every difficulty in order to bring the man to Jesus. The great miracle was the forgiveness of his sins. His paralysis would last until his death if it wasn't healed. But if his sins weren't forgiven they would last for all eternity.

In August of 1917 Our Lady of Fatima told the children, "*pray much and make sacrifices for sinners.*" We are the apostles of the 21st Century. We have the mission of bringing souls to Jesus, with prayer, sacrifice and sometimes with our conversation. If we have faith, like these men, we will make the miracle of conversion possible. At the end of the day, all we have to do is to put them in front of Jesus and let them discover how much Christ paid for their sins.

A well-known artist in Paris was painting the Crucifixion of Jesus. The last character to be portrayed was Mary Magdalene. He looked for a woman of bad reputation to use as a model. As the woman was posing she saw the canvas and asked what it was all about. Over several portrait sittings the artist had time to explain to her the life and death of Jesus. "*Do you mean that He died for my sins and yours?*" asked the incredulous woman at the end. "*Then I should love Him... And you, how long have you known that?! How much you must love Him!*" The artist continued in silence, embarrassed, with those words echoing in his heart: *how much you must love Him!* And he changed his life that very day, going to Confession after many years of absence.

When Bl Alvaro was asked at the end of his fruitful life which were his happiest moments, he said, "*Those moments in which God forgave my sins in the sacrament of Confession.*" Mary, Mother of Mercy, may I help many to go to Confession.

Day 1 of the Unity Octave
Saturday 1st week in ordinary time
Saturday 18th January
Mk 2:13-17

And as he passed on, he saw Levi the son of Alphaeus sitting at the tax office, and he said to him, "Follow me." And he rose and followed him. And as he sat at table in his house, many tax collectors and sinners were sitting with Jesus and his disciples; for there were many who followed him.

Matthew "*rose and followed Him*." Just like that! Jesus had chosen him to be with Him, to be close to Him, to be sent by Him to preach. He had been asked to leave everything there: his money, his job, his projects and future... his sins as well. To leave all that behind and start a new life with Jesus, to stop changing money and start changing the world! God's plan is always far better than our own.

Pope Francis loves a painting by Caravaggio of this very moment in the life of Jesus. In it you find Jesus pointing at Matthew with his finger, like someone choosing a friend for his football team. "*That finger of Jesus, pointing at Matthew. That's me. I feel like him. Like Matthew,*" said the Pope. "*It is the gesture of Matthew that strikes me: he holds on to his money as if to say, 'No, not me! No, this money is mine.' Here, this is me, a sinner on whom the Lord has turned his gaze. And this is what I said when they asked me if I would accept my election as pontiff: 'I am a sinner, but I trust in the infinite mercy and patience of our Lord Jesus Christ, and I accept in a spirit of penance.'*" Matthew could be an instrument of God because he was sorry for his past life.

Saints are sinners who keep trying. All saints have experienced a conversion (except Our Lady). We, apostles of the 21st century, need to tell everyone that they have a place in Heaven and that, in order to begin their journey to Heaven, they don't need to be perfect... they just need to be sorry. It is no coincidence that the first one who received a promise of salvation (do you remember him? "*Today you will be with me in Paradise*") was a thief, a criminal condemned to death... but he was repentant, like Matthew.

I'm *a sinner on whom your Son has turned His gaze*, but with your help, Mary, my Mother, may I take up His invitation to become an apostle!

Day 2 of the Unity Octave
Second Sunday in Ordinary Time
Sunday 19th January
Jn 2:1-11

There was a marriage at Cana in Galilee, and the mother of Jesus was there; Jesus also was invited to the marriage, with his disciples. When the wine failed, the mother of Jesus said to him, "They have no wine." And Jesus said to her, "O woman, what have you to do with me? My hour has not yet come." His mother said to the servants, "Do whatever he tells you." Now six stone jars were standing there, for the Jewish rites of purification, each holding twenty or thirty gallons. Jesus said to them, "Fill the jars with water." And they filled them up to the brim. He said to them, "Now draw some out, and take it to the steward of the feast." So they took it. When the steward of the feast tasted the water now become wine, and did not know where it came from … [he] called the bridegroom and said to him, "Every man serves the good wine first; and when men have drunk freely, then the poor wine; but you have kept the good wine until now."

We never get tired meditating on the second Mystery of Light of the Holy Rosary. Our Lady discovered the problem long before anyone else. She didn't wait to be asked. She couldn't do anything but her Son could do everything. Jesus said, "*My hour has not yet come.*" And Mary changed God's plan and brought forward 'the hour'. That's the power of Mary's intercession.

The miracle happened because Mary interceded. But it didn't happen just through Jesus' power. It took something else: Mary said to them, "*Do whatever he tells you.*" And they did it. When Jesus asked them to fill the jars with water they didn't complain even if they couldn't understand it. They didn't need water, they needed wine! But they obeyed to perfection. The Gospel says, "*they filled them up to the brim.*" "***To the brim!***" Not three quarters; not 80%; not even 95%... "*they filled them up to the brim.*" And they received according to their obedience. That's how miracles happen. Jesus asks you to do your bit. And He transforms it. In Cana He didn't produce just any kind of wine. It was superb! Because their obedience was also superb. My Mother, I hear your voice: "*Do whatever he tells you.*" And I ask you to help me to do it generously: "***to the brim!***"

Day 3 of the Unity Octave
Monday 2nd week in ordinary time
Monday 20th January
Mk 2:18-22

Now John's disciples and the Pharisees were fasting; and people came and said to him, "Why do John's disciples and the disciples of the Pharisees fast, but your disciples do not fast?" And Jesus said to them, "Can the wedding guests fast while the bridegroom is with them? As long as they have the bridegroom with them, they cannot fast. The days will come, when the bridegroom is taken away from them, and then they will fast in that day."

Fasting is good. But it's not the most important thing. The Pharisees were convinced that those sacrifices were 'justifying' or 'sanctifying' them. But they forgot more important things, like charity, for instance. They offered all kinds of sacrifices but didn't love God or others. We could say that fasting is a complement. But love is the essence. Fasting is like a hat. Charity is the clothes. You can run around without your hat; but never without clothes!

There was a friar whose daily job was to collect wood. On his way back, after spending hours out in the scorching sun, he would get very thirsty. One day, he approached a well with fresh water to quench his thirst, but then he thought, '*What a great sacrifice it could be not to drink from this well.*' So he decided to deny himself the drink and offer it up. At night, before going to bed he looked at the sky and discovered a new star shining as an appreciative smile from God. Every day he offered that sacrifice and every night he was delighted to see the star ('his star'!) in the sky.

A young novice was once asked to accompany him. They walked together and suffered in the heat. When in the afternoon they passed by the well, the monk found himself in a dilemma. If he didn't drink, the poor young novice wouldn't quench his thirst either; but if he drank he wouldn't have his star in the sky. After a moment's hesitation, for the sake of the novice he decided to drink and so, his companion drank also. On his way back he remained silent, sad at the thought of not seeing the star that night. Just before going to bed with an attitude of resignation, he looked up to the sky and saw that in the clear night there was not one... but two stars. Charity was an even greater sacrifice! Mary, Mother of Fair Love, may I learn to put charity first; may I grow in love for God and for others every day.

Day 4 of the Unity Octave
Tuesday 2nd week in ordinary time
Tuesday 21st January
Mk 2:23-28

Jesus was going through the grainfields; and as they made their way his disciples began to pluck heads of grain. And the Pharisees said to him, "Look, why are they doing what is not lawful on the sabbath?" And he said to them, "Have you never read what David did, when he was in need and was hungry, he and those who were with him?...The sabbath was made for man, not man for the sabbath; so the Son of man is lord even of the sabbath."

That was the Pharisees' motto: 'this can't be done', 'this is forbidden', 'this is prohibited', 'this is against the law'... always ready to point out what was banned. It's a very dark view of religion, isn't it? Yet, when Jesus had to summarise the whole law, He didn't say, "*Thou shall not...*"; He said instead, "*Thou shall love...*" The Pharisees weren't wrong regarding the Sabbath. Their mistake was that they said what SHOULDN'T be done but didn't help to do what SHOULD be done. Instead of letting the disciples starve, they could have proposed other options or provided something else to eat.

The problem was the stiffness of the Pharisees. We could make the same mistake sometimes when we try to bring our friends closer to God. Consider the commandment of attending Mass on Sunday, for instance. Some people find it difficult to go to Mass for very different reasons. It doesn't seem very helpful to say, '*If you don't go to Mass you will go to hell!*' It isn't very persuasive, is it? We can call that '*The Pharisees' Approach*'. The Christian 'way' doesn't consist then in saying, '*You should go to Mass,*' but in saying, '*Why don't you come to Mass with me?*' Do you see the difference?

Saints didn't just point out what was forbidden or wrong. They helped people to do the right thing. And those souls followed them to Heaven. It's like the child who was asked by his mother why he always did his English homework and never finished his Maths. "*My English teacher helps us with instructions to do the homework;*" said the boy, "*the Maths teacher only gives us problems.*" And he added with indignation, "*Besides, he never gives any solution!*" The Pharisees were like the Maths teacher. We should be like the English one. Mary, Mother of Good Counsel, teach me not to lecture others but to help them do the right thing.

Day 5 of the Unity Octave
Wednesday 2nd week in ordinary time
Wednesday 22nd January
Mk 3:1-6

Again he entered the synagogue, and a man was there who had a withered hand. And they watched him, to see whether he would heal him on the sabbath, so that they might accuse him. And he said to the man who had the withered hand, "Come here." And he said to them, "Is it lawful on the sabbath to do good or to do harm, to save life or to kill?" But they were silent. And he looked around at them with anger, grieved at their hardness of heart, and said to the man, "Stretch out your hand." He stretched it out, and his hand was restored. The Pharisees went out, and immediately held counsel with the Herodi-ans against him, how to destroy him.

What a contrast between Jesus and the Pharisees. "*Again*" starts the Gospel today: 'again' those grouches show their absolute lack of concern towards people in need. You can hear them shouting, '*I don't care, the Sabbath is the Sabbath!*' But in the middle of the silence Jesus, saddened at their reaction, "*looked around at them with anger*"; how could they be so mean?

He looked at them but didn't say a word. He paused long enough to take a glance at each one of them. And He "*grieved*", says today's Gospel, at their egoistic lives, like a loving father disappointed with his children because they despise each other. But still in Jesus there was - and is - *more compassion than passion*. The man with the withered hand needed Him. His concern for souls who needed Him was greater than His grief over those who thought they didn't.

Saints have always had that zeal for souls. Unlike the Pharisees, they were ready to do 'anything' for them. Fr. Toccanier was the assistant priest of St John Vianney in his parish. One day, aware that the life of the holy priest was coming to a close, Toccanier asked him, "*If Our Lord gave you the possibility to choose between going straight to Heaven on the spot or staying a bit longer to keep working for the salvation of souls, what would you choose?*" St John Vianney answered without hesitation, "*I would stay. Saints are extremely happy, but... They can't gain souls for God like us, with their work and sufferings.*" St Josemaría explained that apostolic zeal always comes with a "*constant concern for souls.*" Mary, Queen of Apostles, help me to obtain that apostolic zeal, that real concern for my friends and for the salvation of their souls.

Day 6 of the Unity Octave
Thursday 2nd week in ordinary time
Thursday 23rd January
Mk 3:7-12

Jesus withdrew with his disciples to the sea, and a great multitude from Galilee followed; also from Judea and Jerusalem and Idumea and from beyond the Jordan and from about Tyre and Sidon a great multitude, hearing all that he did, came to him. And he told his disciples to have a boat ready for him because of the crowd, lest they should crush him; for he had healed many, so that all who had diseases pressed upon him to touch him.

"*A great multitude, hearing all that he did, came to him.*" In their desire to touch Him they were about to crush Him "*for he had healed many, so that all who had diseases pressed upon him to touch him.*" For a time, Jesus was very popular. But *where were they all on Good Friday?* one wonders. It seems that some of the crowd came to Him interested in what they could *get* from Him, but very few followed Him for what they could *give* to Him.

We see this all the time: people who pray because they need something, but when they receive it and are *fine*, they no longer pray, nor do they even thank God for it. Our Lord Himself complained once, "*you seek me, not because you saw signs, but because you ate your fill of the loaves*" (*Jn* 6:26). But when He needed them on Calvary, just a few women with Our Lady and the adolescent John were there for Him. It's very important to remember that we don't pray just because we need it, but also because Jesus loves it. Sometimes our prayer is easy, when, for example, we need to pray for an important intention... At other times, however, we don't feel urged to pray because everything is fine. It is important that we pray on those days as well, not out of duty, but out of love.

A school's chaplain entered the oratory and found four little girls praying there. He asked them, "*What are you praying for?*" "*For my aunty who is sick*", answered one; "*For dad's job*", said another; "*For my brother's exams*" replied the third. The priest smiled and asked the last one, "*What about you? What are you asking for?*" "*I'm not asking for anything,*" replied the girl, "*I just came because Jesus is my friend.*" Friendship: That's it! Mary, my Mother, Master of Prayer, may I learn to pray, not just to *get* but also to *give*. To pray not for my sake but *for God's sake*.

Day 7 of the Unity Octave
Friday 2nd week in ordinary time
Friday 24th January
Mk 3:13-19

And he went up on the mountain, and called to him those whom he desired; and they came to him. And he appointed twelve, to be with him, and to be sent out to preach and have authority to cast out demons: Simon whom he surnamed Peter; James the son of Zebedee and John the brother of James, whom he surnamed Boanerges, that is, sons of thunder; Andrew, and Philip, and Bartholomew, and Matthew, and Thomas, and James the son of Alphaeus, and Thaddaeus, and Simon the Cananaean, and Judas Iscariot, who betrayed him.

"*He called to Him those He desired*" for no other reason than that: He just wanted those and no others. This wasn't like 'The Voice' or 'X-Factor' where the winner is the most talented. Jesus didn't choose the best or the most charming, those who had more friends, more knowledge or a better position... He just chose those He wanted; because *He felt like it*. St Paul explained it to the Corinthians, "*consider your call, brethren; not many of you were wise according to worldly standards, not many were powerful, not many were of noble birth; but God chose what is foolish in the world to shame the wise, God chose what is weak in the world to shame the strong.*"

God has a certain inclination to choose very '*low profile*' instruments. Did you know, for instance, that Moses stuttered? And yet, among the thousands of Israelites that God could choose to negotiate with the Pharaoh, He wanted the stammerer! The biographies of many saints paint a similar picture. St Bernadette and St John Vianney are known for their learning difficulties. An online biography of St. Joseph of Cupertino (1603-1668) reads: "*he was an Italian mystic whose life is a wonderful combination of a complete lack of natural capacity and an extraordinary supernatural efficiency. He lacked every natural gift. He was incapable of passing a test, maintaining a conversation, taking care of a house, or even touching a dish without breaking it. He was called Brother Ass by his companions in the monastery.*" Wow! What a description! Yet by the end of his life his reputation for holiness was widespread and crowds would come to attend his Mass. The lesson is clear: God doesn't choose the best. He chooses those He wants. Mary, my Mother, may I learn to be a faithful instrument of God for whatever He has chosen me to do.

The Conversion of St Paul
Saturday 25th January
Mk 16:15-18

And he said to them, "Go into all the world and preach the gospel to the whole creation. He who believes and is baptised will be saved; but he who does not believe will be condemned. And these signs will accompany those who believe: in my name they will cast out demons."

Dear St Paul: today we celebrate your Conversion. It all happened suddenly. It was unexpected for you but not for God. He had prepared the encounter from all eternity! And you, Saul of Tarsus, could never forget it. How many times you told the story! I can imagine you, Paul, old and tired in Rome, surrounded by young Christians hanging on your every word. I imagine your smile as you described the exact place, the day, the time...: "*As I made my journey and drew near to Damascus, about noon...*" (*Acts* 22:6)

I can imagine your grimace when they asked you about St Stephen. Maybe with red eyes you told them how he died, how he prayed for you, how you helped those who stoned him. '*How blind I was,*' you would say, '*How sure of myself I was! ... I just didn't know...*' But before you could continue someone would remind you of your Conversion, your fidelity, your apostolate, your missions here and there, your miracles, those thousands of Christians you brought to the Faith...

Yes, Saul of Tarsus, you weren't a saint before, but you were honest. You thought that was the right way to defend God's interests. When He came to change your mind you were honest enough to change your opinions, your 'convictions', your intentions, your words about Christians, about Christ, your friends, your work... EVERYTHING in an instant. How easy it would have been to say that it was a hallucination, that the heat and the sun played a trick on you...after all, no one else had heard the Voice. But you, St Paul, had heard the Voice. You never forgot that Voice. He asked you to change all your ways and you didn't make excuses. You did what He told you. That's why you are St Paul... despite having been Saul of Tarsus. I ask you today to intercede for me to be honest when God demands something from me - whatever it is. Mary, Queen of the Apostles, help me to hear the Voice of your Son and to follow it faithfully to the end.

Third Sunday in Ordinary Time
Sunday 26th January
Lk 1:1-4; 4:14-21

Inasmuch as many have undertaken to compile a narrative of the things which have been accomplished among us, just as they were delivered to us by those who from the beginning were eyewitnesses and ministers of the word, it seemed good to me also, having followed all things closely for some time past, to write an orderly account for you, most excellent Theophilus, that you may know the truth concerning the things of which you have been informed.

Thus begins the Gospel of St Luke. He explained to Theophilus (this name means '*God's Lover*') how he had researched the facts and then written them down. Theophilus (the name could refer to all the disciples who consider themselves God's Lovers) had 'heard' the preaching already. Now he was given an account (the Gospel) in order to "*know the truth concerning the things of which you have been informed.*"

When we are introduced to someone we first know what we are told about that person... but not the person. Once we start to converse with him or her, then we can get to know them. In order to foster a personal relationship with Jesus it's not enough to *hear* about Him; we need to get to know Him personally. And this happens through the reading of the Gospel, the letter that God has written to you and me.

A group of missionaries went to a country in Africa to preach the Gospel. Firstly, they distributed Bibles. Everyone took a Bible but no-one came back for more instruction. To the missionaries' surprise, the natives finally came back after a couple of weeks to ask for more Bibles. Then they found out that the indigenous people were using pages of the Bible to roll tobacco and smoke it! Needless to say, the missionaries were not at all impressed. After a long dispute, eventually they reached an agreement: they were allowed *to 'smoke' only the pages of the Bible that they had previously read*. After a while natives started coming to the church to ask questions about God and Jesus. In a few weeks many gave up smoking (at least the pages of the Bible), and had started to convert to Christianity. The turning point was the moment when they started reading Sacred Scripture.

Mary, my Mother, teach me to love the Holy Scripture, to read the Gospel every day, to help other people to do the same. That will be the turning point of their lives.

Monday 3rd week in ordinary time
Monday 27th January
Mk 3:22-30

Jesus said to the scribes, "Truly, I say to you, all sins will be forgiven the sons of men, and whatever blasphemies they utter; but whoever blasphemes against the Holy Spirit never has forgiveness, but is guilty of an eternal sin"- for they had said, "He has an unclean spirit."

How is it that blasphemy against the Holy Spirit can't be forgiven?' Christians have been told innumerable times that all sins can be forgiven. And now we read that, actually, there is one that can't be forgiven! In the past, some have even tried to use this passage to deny the existence of the Christian God: *'If God is Almighty He certainly can forgive all sins. If God can't forgive a sin... He is not Almighty.'* It is another formula of the classic argument: 'If God is Almighty... can He create a rock so heavy that He can't lift it?'

Leaving aside the fact that the sentence is a silly paradox, we could say that, in fact, God 'has actually created that rock'. It is called "freedom". God has made us free. He has paid for our freedom with all the Blood of Jesus. So, if a man decides to reject forgiveness, the Almighty God can't change the man's mind. That's the catch. An aspirin can relieve a headache, but only if you take it! Contemplating the box of aspirins, holding one in your hand or sticking one with adhesive tape to your forehead will not relieve the pain. That is not because the aspirin is faulty, but because your wit is faulty. It would be stupid to complain that a doctor is unable to cure your illness if you have never actually allowed him to touch you, talk to you or even if he has never seen you!

In the same way, God can forgive any sin... as long as we repent and ask for forgiveness. Blasphemy against the Holy Spirit has been called, ever since St Augustine's times, the *final impenitence*, the lack of repentance. They are like someone with a strong migraine who stubbornly refuses to take their medicine and prefers to live (and even die) in pain. That's the situation of a sinner who stubbornly rejects God's forgiveness and prefers to live (and even die) in the misery of their sins.

Let's pray, through the intercession of Our Lady, Mother of Mercy, for the conversion of those sinners who stubbornly reject God's Mercy.

Tuesday 3rd week in ordinary time
Tuesday 28th January
Mk 3:31-35

A crowd was sitting about him; and they said to him, "Your mother and your brethren are outside, asking for you." And he replied, "Who are my mother and my brethren?" And looking around on those who sat about him, he said, "Here are my mother and my brethren! Whoever does the will of God is my brother, and sister, and mother."

Doing the Will of God. That's how Mary became the Mother of God: by accepting and doing God's Will - "*Be it done unto me according to thy Word.*" If we want to be part of God's 'family' (brother, sister, mother...) that's all we have to do to take after Mary, our Mother and Jesus Himself in Gethsemane - "*not my will, but thine, be done.*"

Holiness comes down to one thing: *Doing God's Will.* "*Do you really want to be a saint?*" wrote St Josemaría, "*Carry out the little duty of each moment: do what you ought and concentrate on what you are doing.*" Some people think that holiness is about doing good things: praying, offering sacrifices, giving alms to the poor and saying the Rosary... But actually holiness is about doing the right thing at the right time. A saint is not the one who is praying all the time but the one who prays when it's time to pray, reads when it's time to read and eats when it's time to eat. A saint goes to bed when it's bedtime and gets up when it's time to wake up. A saint is, in this sense, 100% predictable. Saints are always doing what God wants them to do, whatever they should do at any time.

Any specific moment offers one right thing to do and an infinite number of wrong things to avoid. When it is time to study, studying is the right thing to do and all the rest is wrong. You might think that reading instead of studying is not 100% right but can be 50% right; at least, you can argue, 'it's better than being in my sister's room annoying her.' The truth is that studying is 100% right. Reading is 100% wrong. Annoying your sister would be 500% wrong. Do you understand? Those who do God's Will are doing the right thing at the right time. That is holiness. And that is why it is so difficult to do. Mary, my Mother, since holiness is for everyone, I believe that with your intercession and the help of God's grace, I can really achieve it!

Wednesday 3rd week in ordinary time
Wednesday 29th January
Mk 4:1-20

"A sower went out to sow. And as he sowed, some seed fell along the path, and the birds came and devoured it. Other seed fell on rocky ground, where it had not much soil, and immediately it sprang up, since it had no depth of soil; and when the sun rose it was scorched, and since it had no root it withered away. Other seed fell among thorns and the thorns grew up and choked it, and it yielded no grain. And other seeds fell into good soil and brought forth grain, growing up and increasing and yielding thirtyfold and sixtyfold and a hundredfold."

The sower was scattering seed everywhere. He wasn't analysing the quality of the soil or avoiding particular patches of land: he was sowing all over the place. Because he knew that some seed may not work but some other will yield a hundredfold. The sower knew that the seed is a small thing in comparison with the harvest. It is the same with our apostolate: a nice word, a reference to God in our conversation, giving good example, an act of kindness are also little things but they can have great consequences in souls. We should try never to miss an opportunity to help people. Whenever we meet people, even if it is for a short instant, we should try to leave in them a divine seed that God could use to bring them to Him.

On one occasion St Josemaría was inspecting the building works in a new house when an Italian builder yelled a blasphemy. The same builder explained years later, *"Suddenly I saw that priest looking at me. Silent. I can't describe his sorrowful glance. All I can say is that I wanted to cry there and then. I imagine that those were the same features that St Peter saw in Jesus' face when he denied Our Lord. That glance changed my life as words could never do."*

On another occasion St Josemaría went to buy new trousers with two other priests in Italy. As the other two were trying on the clothes he struck up a conversation with the shop assistant. When it was his turn to try on the trousers the shop assistant turned round and said to the others, *"Il vostro compagno non perde il tempo, eh!"* [Your friend wastes no time, eh!] Let us ask Our Lady, with the words of St Josemaría, to help us become *"burning embers that will set alight each heart they come into contact with"* and so 'that first spark' will turn one day *"into a burning fire."*

Thursday 3rd week in ordinary time
Thursday 30th January
Mk 4:21-25

And he said to them, "Is a lamp brought in to be put under a bushel, or under a bed, and not on a stand? For there is nothing hid, except to be made manifest; nor is anything secret, except to come to light."

Pedro shined with the light of Christ. At the age of 16 he accepted his vocation as a numerary in Opus Dei. When, two years later he was diagnosed with terminal cancer, he understood what God wanted him to do. For three years he underwent all sorts of sufferings and treatments, whilst trying to keep up with his university studies and lead a normal life. Like mosquitoes, people started being attracted by the light that Pedro spread around him. Many sought him out; in fact, when he was in hospital he was never alone. Young patients wanted to be with him, talk to him; so did nurses, doctors, relatives of other patients... When he was at home it was the same: bishops, priests, students, teachers - anyone who had met him even once felt the need to visit him again. And in the middle of all his suffering and pain, he always found time for everyone. He never allowed his parents to send anyone away, however bad the pain was; he wanted to talk with anyone who came to see him. During the last weeks of his life the influx only increased. He had words of encouragement for everyone, helping them to get closer to God.

Pedro Ballester died on January 13, 2018. At his funeral you could see part of the fruit of his short life: the bishop concelebrated with more than 30 priests and hundreds of people: relatives, friends, students, teachers, doctors, nurses, patients... A young lad asked him a few weeks before he died, "*Are you happy, Pedro?*" Pedro answered – after three years of suffering and aware of how close he was to death – "*I have never been happier.*" Lovers beam with happiness. Thousands of lives are touched by the light of Christ which shines in those who love Him. And that light can't be hidden.

Mary, Mother of the Light, help me to follow St Josemaría's advice: "*Don't let your life be barren. Be useful. Leave a mark. Shine forth, with the shining light of your faith and your love... and set aflame all the ways of the earth with the fire of Christ that you bear in your heart*" (St Josemaría).

More about Pedro on this site: https://www.pedroballester.org.uk

Friday 3rd week in ordinary time
Friday 31st January
Mk 4:26-34

"The kingdom of God is as if a man should scatter seed upon the ground, and should sleep and rise night and day, and the seed should sprout and grow, he knows not how. The earth produces of itself, first the blade, then the ear, then the full grain in the ear. But when the grain is ripe, at once he puts in the sickle, because the harvest has come."

Seeds take time to sprout and grow. The rain and the sun make them grow at the proper rate. Sometimes we might wish them to grow faster but we can't change nature. It would be of little help if the farmer went to a shoot of grain and started pulling at it to make it grow faster. It could actually kill the plant outright. A good gardener is patient. He knows when to plant, when to water, when to fertilise and when to reap. As the Gospel says, *"when the grain is ripe, at once he puts in the sickle, because the harvest has come."*

Souls take time to change. Bernard Nathanson was a medical doctor, director of the *"largest abortion clinic in the Western world,"* as he described it. For thirty years, he oversaw the destruction of about 75,000 foetuses. But God planted the seed in his heart. He was moved by hundreds of pro-lifers selflessly praying for the unborn (and for him) with constancy. He was changed definitively when he saw for the first time an ultrasound scan with a foetus moving inside its mother. He left the abortion clinic and little by little started to defend the life of the unborn. It took him more than 17 years to find God but he was eventually baptised in December of 1996. He spent the rest of his life *making up*, as he said, for his sins, defending life at all cost. He talked many times about the deep pain he felt for the lives he had taken. For years he fasted and travelled all around the world offering sacrifices in reparation for his past life. He entrusted himself to the Mercy of God to be able to go to Heaven, or at least to be allowed to visit all those babies he killed and say to them: *"I AM SORRY!"*

Overall, it was a long process. Forty years of misery. But through the persevering prayer of Bernard's friends and others, once the seed sprouted, he raised an amazing defence of life.

Mary, Refuge of Sinners, may I learn to be patient: If God has patience with souls... why shouldn't I?

February

Saturday 1st February
Mk 4:35-41

On that day, when evening had come, he said to them, "Let us go across to the other side." And leaving the crowd, they took him with them in the boat, just as he was. And other boats were with him. And a great storm of wind arose, and the waves beat into the boat, so that the boat was already filling. But he was in the stern, asleep on the cushion; and they woke him and said to him, "Teacher, do you not care if we perish?" And he awoke and rebuked the wind, and said to the sea, "Peace! Be still!" And the wind ceased, and there was a great calm.

We love to read the life of Our Lord and see that He is a perfect man: He gets tired, thirsty, hungry, and on a few occasions He also gets angry. We love to see that He is a man as we are, '*in all things but sin.*' So He can understand me perfectly when I am tired as well, or thirsty or hungry or angry, for He experienced it all centuries before I was born. 'OK', you say, 'He understands us. But then, why does He sometimes put us in such difficult situations and yet appear to be asleep in the middle of our ordeal?'

Good question! It was Jesus who said, "*Let us go across to the other side.*" Maybe St Peter saw the clouds and thought, '*Hmmm! It's going to be a rough one. But Jesus said 'let's go', so let's go.*' What Peter could foresee happened and the storm broke. Nevertheless, Jesus fell asleep. St Peter never forgot the lesson and many years afterwards he wrote in his first letter "*cast all your anxieties upon him, because he cares about you*" (5:7). He does care! Jesus might seem to be asleep but God keeps watching.

The last year of St Teresa of Calcutta's life on earth was a tough one. She had just turned 86, was very sick and was burdened by a difficult and painful surgery. However, she could send letters to her collaborators. To one of them she wrote: "*This year has been a gift from God to me, and I am happy that I have been able to offer something to Jesus. We should accept that all He wants from us is a smile... Let us always pray with great trust in God. He loves us and knows what is best for us. I do not know why all this has happened this very year, but I am sure about something: Jesus never makes mistakes.*" Mary, my Mother, never allow me to forget it: **Jesus NEVER makes mistakes!**

First Sunday of St Joseph
The Presentation of the Lord
Sunday 2nd February
Lk 2:22-40

Now there was a man in Jerusalem, whose name was Simeon, and this man was righteous and devout, looking for the consolation of Israel, and the Holy Spirit was upon him. And it had been revealed to him by the Holy Spirit that he should not see death before he had seen the Lord's Christ...he took him up in his arms and blessed God and said, "Lord, now lettest thou thy servant depart in peace".

He followed the inspiration of the Holy Spirit, and the promise was fulfilled. A long life was crowned with that encounter. You can imagine the old Simeon, so many years dreaming about it, wondering what the Child and His parents would look like... When he saw the Child coming into the temple in Mary's arms he asked if he could hold Him too. Joseph was a bit wary at the sight of that old weak man. But the man, full of faith and love, insisted. "*Now I can die*," he said (and at this point Joseph's wariness turned to real concern!) "*Now I can die*," he said, for he had finally seen and held Jesus! He spent his whole life getting ready for that moment...

Blessed Imelda Lambertini (1322 - 1333) is the patroness of First Holy Communicants. She had a special devotion to the Eucharist. From the age of five she insistently requested to receive Holy Communion but the custom of the time had fixed twelve as the earliest age for First Holy Communion. She would sometimes exclaim: "*Tell me, can anyone receive Jesus into his heart and not die?*" On May 12, 1333, when she was eleven years old she was attending Mass, as she did each day, watching in tears as others received Communion. But when the Mass finished and everyone was ready to leave, suddenly some of them were startled to see a Sacred Host hovering in the air above Imelda as she knelt before the closed tabernacle, absorbed in prayer. The priest understood that Our Lord wanted to be received by her and gave Imelda her first Holy Communion then and there. Immediately she was enraptured: she sank unconscious to the ground, and when they picked her up, they found that she was dead. "*Now I can die!*"

Mary, Mother of the Eucharist: teach me to attend Mass as if it were *my first Mass, my last Mass, my only Mass.*

Monday 4th week in ordinary time
Monday 3rd February
Mk 5:1-20

They came to the other side of the sea, to the country of the Gerasenes. And when he had come out of the boat, there met him out of the tombs a man with an unclean spirit, who lived among the tombs...And when he saw Jesus from afar, he ran and worshiped him; and crying out with a loud voice, he said, "What have you to do with me, Jesus, Son of the Most High God? I adjure you by God, do not torment me." For he had said to him, "Come out of the man, you unclean spirit!" And Jesus asked him, "What is your name?" He replied, "My name is Legion; for we are many."

A bit cowardly these unclean spirits, aren't they? Like bullies, they come in groups. Shame on them! A legion of bad angels against one single man. In this battle you can't expect nobleness and fair play. Fair play would be if the devil were to struggle against St Michael, but he doesn't dare. St Peter explains how "*the devil prowls around like a roaring lion, seeking someone to devour.*" Imagine yourself attacked not just by one lion but surrounded by a whole *legion* of them.

Yet God knows this. And He has kitted us out with appropriate means. Firstly, we have the Sacraments, especially the Holy Mass. Holy Communion is the most powerful weapon against the enemy. Then the Sacrament of Confession. The devil hates it! But apart from the Sacraments, the Church also counts on other effective weapons of 'devils destruction': the Sacramentals. They are consecrated objects like medals, scapulars, Holy Water, crucifixes... that indeed help when we use them with faith and when we are trying to live a virtuous life. But remember: they are not 'amulets'. They are spiritual weapons.

Have you ever used an insect repellent? We sometimes don't even smell it but insects can't stand being near it. Holy Water, a crucifix or your scapular have the same effect on the enemy. They don't work as if by magic. Their effect depends very much on your faith. Like any weapon, their effectiveness depends on the skills of the user. Little help is a machine gun against a *legion of roaring lions* if you don't know how to use it! Mary, most fearful antagonist of the devil, teach me to use these 'spiritual weapons'.

Tuesday 4th week in ordinary time
Tuesday 4th February
Mk 5:21-43

A great crowd gathered about Jesus...Then came one of the rulers of the synagogue, Jairus by name; and seeing him, he fell at his feet, and besought him, saying, "My little daughter is at the point of death. Come and lay your hands on her, so that she may be made well, and live." And he went with him...While he was still speaking, there came from the ruler's house some who said, "Your daughter is dead. Why trouble the Teacher any further?" But ignoring what they said, Jesus said to the ruler of the synagogue, "Do not fear, only believe."

We remember the story well. Jairus was a man of faith. He came to ask Jesus for a miracle. On the way there Jesus got delayed by a woman with a blood flow that Jesus healed as well. The miracle had happened in front of their faces when some servants of Jairus said to him, 'Too late. Your daughter is dead.' You may imagine the disappointment of the man who came to ask Jesus for help but a woman detained Jesus and got the miracle first. His daughter was now dead. Jesus couldn't heal her anymore.

But we know that Jesus is NEVER late. He had a plan and He didn't have to inform anyone about it. Jesus didn't want to heal Jairus' daughter... He had a better plan. And so when the 'wet blanket' servants came to discourage Jairus, the Gospel says that Jesus *ignored* what they said, He didn't listen to them. Instead He said to the grieving father, "*Do not fear, only believe.*" Only believe. You don't have to do anything else, Jairus - *only believe!*

The world is populated with 'wet blanket' people whose main argument is always: '*It's too late.*' You and I have to 'ignore' them and "*only believe.*" It's never too late for an 'eternal' God. When we pray we have to be convinced that it is never too late, that we don't need to know God's plans and timescales, that our only job is to believe. God does the rest in His own good time. It wasn't too late for Jairus' daughter, for the son of the widow of Naim, nor for Lazarus (four days dead), it wasn't too late for the woman with the haemorrhage, for the blind men, for the leper, for the paralytic... it wasn't too late for the prodigal son, for the Good Thief, for Saul of Tarsus or St Augustine... It's NEVER too late for God! Mary, Virgin Most Faithful, help me to '*only believe.*'

Wednesday 4th week in ordinary time
Wednesday 5th February
Mk 6:1-6

On the Sabbath he began to teach in the synagogue; and many who heard him were astonished, saying, "Where did this man get all this? What is the wisdom given to him? What mighty works are wrought by his hands! Is not this the carpenter, the son of Mary and brother of James and Joseph and Judas and Simon, and are not his sisters here with us?" And they took offence at him.

"*Where did this man get all this?*" they wondered. This happened in Nazareth, Jesus' hometown. It happened among His people, those who saw Him growing up. They couldn't make head nor tail of it. A carpenter is supposed to be a carpenter all his life, not a Rabbi. The Gospel says that "*they took offence at him.*" Why? There is no need to be offended just because they don't understand! But it happens sometimes. You find some 'learned' people who think that anyone who doesn't think as they do are not just wrong, but ignorant. Some think that religion is not just difficult to believe, but nonsense. Some are convinced that, just because they haven't found the truth, truth doesn't exist at all. They are like children who, just because a Maths problem is difficult to solve, claim that the formula is wrong and the problem *has no solution.*

A university student was seated on a train beside an old person praying the Rosary. "*Sir*", interrupted the student, "*do you still believe in gods and prayers?*" "*Yes, I do*" replied the man with a smile. "*Do you not?*" The student burst out laughing and said, "*I do not believe in such silly things. Take my advice: Learn what science has to say about religion.*" "*Science?*", asked the old man in distress, "*What Science?*" The student saw the man's grief and to avoid hurting his feelings further, said, "*Please give me your address and I will send you some literature to help you on the matter.*" The old fellow fumbled inside his coat pocket and gave the boy his visiting card. Glancing at the card, the student bowed his head in shame and became silent. On the card he read: '*Louis Pasteur, Director of the Institute of Scientific Research, Paris*' - the most famous French scientist of 19th century, discoverer of rabies and anthrax vaccines. He is popularly known as the *father of microbiology* so, not really ignorant, was he? Mary, Seat of Wisdom, may I grow in this gift of the Holy Spirit.

Thursday 6th February
Mk 6:7-13

And he called to him the twelve, and began to send them out two by two, and gave them authority over the unclean spirits. He charged them to take nothing for their journey except a staff; no bread, no bag, no money in their belts...And if any place will not receive you and they refuse to hear you, when you leave, shake off the dust that is on your feet for a testimony against them." So they went out and preached...

Jesus sent them to all those places instead of going Himself. Certainly He could have gone in Person and could have preached far more effectively than St Peter and the others. It seems better to receive Jesus in your village than to receive Philip or Andrew... But Jesus wanted to send His disciples instead. They didn't need anything else: "*no bread, no bag, no money...*" Because it wasn't about human means but supernatural ones. Just go! Just obey! But 'who am I', they could wonder, 'to preach in Jesus' Name?' You are an *apostle*, that's what you are! Apostle in Greek means envoy, ambassador or messenger. That's what every baptised person is.

The temptation comes when we compare ourselves with them and realise that we can't do what the Apostles did. We can't preach to multitudes, we can't go through the whole world and persuade crowds of unbelievers. You are right! But we don't have to. Our *apostolate* is personal. It's one-to-one; what Italians call '*a quattròcchi*' (with four eyes), just you and your friend. We can't help a hundred, but we can help one at a time.

A man was walking on the beach. The tide was out and had left thousands of starfish on the sand. There he came across a man bending down, picking up the starfish and throwing them back into the water. The first man smiled and said, "*Why do you bother? Don't you see that there are thousands of them and it won't make any difference?*" The other man reached down and picked up another starfish, threw it into the sea and replied, "*It has made a difference for **this one**. This one will live.*"

God wants "*all men to be saved and to come to the knowledge of the truth*" (1 Tim 2:4). All men; everyone! You can continue your prayer now thinking about those you can return to the sea of the Mercy of God.

Friday 4th week in ordinary time
Friday 7th February
Mk 6:14–29

When Herodias' daughter came in and danced, she pleased Herod and his guests; and the king said to the girl, "Ask me for whatever you wish, and I will grant it." And he vowed to her, "Whatever you ask me, I will give you, even half of my kingdom." And she went out, and said to her mother, "What shall I ask?" And she said, "The head of John the Baptist."

St John the Baptist and so many others were killed for being faithful to the truth. Thus they watered the seed of the Gospel with their blood. They never compromised the truth. That truth frustrated their enemies so much that they didn't discuss it or argue about it, nor even think about it. They killed Christians to stop the message from spreading… But it didn't work. St Maximus the Confessor (580 – 662), for instance, was a Christian monk, theologian and scholar. He fought against heresy with his teachings. He was condemned to exile but he kept preaching. Then they had his tongue cut out. But he kept writing. So they also had his right hand cut off. He died soon after but no one ever forgot what it really cost him to defend the truth.

We also have to *defend* the truth. And to achieve that it's not enough to pray and try to love God. We need to *know* the truth. And for that we need formation, study. We need both: learning and love. Because the more we learn about God the more we can love Him and defend the Truth. Theologian Frank Sheed explained how many times he had been told that some simple pious man, without much learning, could be holier than the theologian with all his knowledge. " *I daresay he is*," concluded Sheed, "*and for his own sake, I hope he is.*" But he continued saying that if the simple pious man is holier than the theologian, it is not because he knows no theology. "*Because while it is obvious that an ignorant man can be virtuous, it is equally obvious that ignorance is not a virtue.*" It is true that some martyrs had given their lives for the faith even when they didn't know the whole catechism. And martyrdom is the supreme proof of love. But, Sheed concluded, if those martyrs had known God more, "*they would have loved Him more still.*" Formation gives us more knowledge about God and therefore allows us to love Him more. Mary, Seat of Wisdom, help me to grow in the knowledge and defence of the Truth.

Saturday 8th February
Mk 6:30-34

The apostles returned to Jesus, and told him all that they had done and taught. And he said to them, "Come away by yourselves to a lonely place, and rest a while." For many were coming and going, and they had no leisure even to eat. And they went away in the boat to a lonely place by themselves.

The activity was intense; people were following them everywhere. But the Apostles needed to rest and spend time alone with God. And that was prayer time. They must have enjoyed those moments with the Lord, telling Him countless stories: what happened when they entered that town, what a woman told them after hearing His teachings, questions they asked them, comments, misunderstandings... Jesus already knew all that, but He must have enjoyed those stories and the enthusiasm with which the Apostles explained their experiences. Jesus loved those get-togethers. And now He also thirsts for a dialogue with you.

A woman asked a priest to visit her sick father. When the priest entered the sick man's room, he found a chair beside the bed and thought it was for him. But the sick man wasn't expecting him. *"I'm sorry,"* said the priest, *"When I saw the empty chair, I thought you were expecting me."* *"Oh, the chair,"* said the sick man. *"Would you mind closing the door?"* he asked from his bed. *"I have never told this to anyone. I didn't know how to pray. But one day a priest told me that prayer was simply a conversation with Jesus. He suggested that I place an empty chair in front of me and imagine that Jesus was sitting in it. Then, I should talk to Him as with a loving friend. So that was what I did. And it has helped me so much that I have been doing it ever since."* The priest urged the man to continue doing the same thing. Two days later, the daughter called the priest to tell him that her father had passed away. She explained how as she was about to leave the house, he called her and told her how much he loved her. An hour later, when she returned home, he had already passed away. *"But there is something strange,"* the woman explained. *"It seems that before he died, he got the chair that was beside his bed and placed his head upon the armrest. That was how I found him. What do you think this could mean?"* Mary, Master of Prayer, teach me to converse with God as friends do.

Second Sunday of St Joseph
Fifth Sunday in Ordinary Time
Sunday 9th February
Lk 5:1-11

Jesus said to Simon, "Put out into the deep and let down your nets for a catch." And Simon answered, "Master, we toiled all night and took nothing! But at your word I will let down the nets." And when they had done this, they enclosed a great shoal of fish; and as their nets were breaking... But when Simon Peter saw it, he fell down at Jesus' knees, saying, "Depart from me, for I am a sinful man, O Lord." And Jesus said to Simon, "Do not be afraid; henceforth you will be catching men."

The *Carpenter* gave instructions to the fisherman to go for a catch. Peter could have thought: 1) I'm the expert here, You are a carpenter! 2) we are tired; 3) we tried: we've spent the whole night fishing; 4) the fish may be on the other side of the lake today; 5) fishing during the night is better (fish don't see the nets), fishing during the day is nonsense; 6) the nets are a mess now, we are cleaning them; 7) You, Jesus, have been preaching from my boat for a while... I should've been back home by now! 8) You'll have to explain this to my wife! 9) You also may have to convince my companions; 10) What about trying tomorrow?

We don't know what came to Peter's mind but we do know what he did: he obeyed. The same happened at the wedding feast of Cana when Our Lady said to the servants, "*Do whatever he tells you.*" The servants obeyed and water was transformed into wine. By obeying you will have wine if you need wine, fish if you need fish, even bread for five thousand, if that's what you need.

But in today's Gospel the miracle wasn't only the amount of fish. The miracle was the change in Peter and his companions because from that day on, after having obeyed Him they stayed with Him for life, for death — and now, for eternity! Holy Mary, Virgin Most Obedient, St Peter, St Andrew, St John and St James, pray for me that I may become an obedient — and therefore effective — fisher of men and women.

"The power of obedience! The lake of Genesareth had denied its fishes to Peter's nets. A whole night in vain. Then, obedient, he lowered his net again to the water and they caught 'a huge number of fish.' Believe me: the miracle is repeated each day" (St Josemaría).

Monday 5th week in ordinary time
Monday 10th February
Mk 6:53-56

When they got out of the boat, immediately the people recognized him, and ran about the whole neighbourhood and began to bring sick people on their pallets to any place where they heard he was. And wherever he came, in villages, cities, or country, they laid the sick in the market places, and besought him that they might touch even the fringe of his garment; and as many as touched it were made well.

Wherever Jesus went, there was a procession of suffering people: lepers, blind and deaf people, paralytics, victims of evil spirits... Their only hope was to be able to touch the fringe of His garment, for they knew that Jesus is the only answer to suffering and the only effective relief. Just as they brought sick people to Him, so we have to do likewise: bring Him souls who suffer so they can touch Him, especially in the Eucharist.

In 1920 in Zaragoza St Josemaría saw a famous bullfighter in the street. Some children approached the celebrity and one of them exclaimed happily, "*I touched him! I touched him!*" The saint was moved and would often recall this memory to encourage us to stop and reflect on the real and extraordinary event of intimately approaching Jesus every day in the Eucharist.

On the 8th of October we celebrated the life of St Josephine Bakhita (1869 - 1947). Born in Sudan, when she was still a girl she was kidnapped and sold as a slave. She experienced the physical and moral sufferings of slavery. But one day she was 'bought' by an Italian consul and for the first time they didn't use the lash with her. From that family she was 'transferred' to a good Christian family where she was loved for the first time in her life. The 'touch' of Love healed her wounded heart. She was baptised and touched the Eucharist for the first time. She understood that it was Jesus who had released her, not from the slavery of men, but the slavery of sin. Then she fell in love with Him and became a Canosian Sister, spending 50 years in His service until she died. St Josephine reminds us how God is always close to those who suffer.

Mary, Mother of God, help me to remind people that only Jesus can settle wounded hearts with His healing 'touch'.

Tuesday 11th February
Mk 7:1-13

The Pharisees and the scribes asked him, "Why do your disciples not live according to the tradition of the elders, but eat with hands defiled?" And he said to them, "Well did Isaiah prophesy of you hypocrites, as it is written, 'This people honours me with their lips, but their heart is far from me; in vain do they worship me, teaching as doctrines the precepts of men'."

Poor Pharisees, they had lost the plot! You see? It's not that they didn't do anything; they usually did everything that God had asked them to do. Well... not everything. They omitted the first commandment: Love. They fulfilled their duties as good servants. But they forgot that God doesn't need servants. He wants children.

A priest explained his conversion like this: "*I wasn't a bad priest. I just wasn't a good one. I did all that I was supposed to do. I 'said' Mass every day; I 'said' the Breviary, the Rosary and my prayers every day. I did my prayer, half an hour in the morning and half an hour in the evening. I 'read' the Gospel and a spiritual book for 15 minutes every day. I did all that and thought that was fine. I wasn't unhappy but I wasn't happy either.*"

"*On the second day of my retreat I was reading the parable of the Prodigal Son. Suddenly the words of the older brother hit my soul: 'he answered his father, "Lo, these many years I have served you, and I never disobeyed your command"'. Here I had a son who was more like a butler. And I felt like that too: I was giving to God what 'I had to', but reluctantly. I was like the Pharisees. Then I looked at the Crucifix. I felt tears coming to my eyes. There, bleeding, was Him suffering for me to become a child... not a servant. I felt I was cheating Our Lord. From the Cross He seemed to be saying: 'This is not it! I didn't shed my Blood just to make you a butler! I died to make you a child! I don't want your 'things'. I want your love. I want your heart. I want you!*"

"*That day I asked Mary to help me to stop being a 'butler of God' and to become a child... to stop saying Mass and to start celebrating It; to stop doing my prayer and to PRAY instead. Since then, I don't feel like a servant who fears: I'm now a child who LOVES!*" Mary, my Mother, I ask the same for myself.

Wednesday 12th February
Mk 7:14-23

Jesus said, "What comes out of a man is what defiles a man. For from within, out of the heart of man, come evil thoughts, fornication, theft, murder, adultery, coveting, wickedness, deceit, licentiousness, envy, slander, pride, foolishness. All these evil things come from within, and they defile a man."

"For from within, out of the heart of man, come evil thoughts, theft, murder, covetousness…" But also from within, out of the heart come acts of love, of thankfulness and adoration. The world doesn't help much to be pure of heart. For that reason, St Josemaría wrote: *"There is need of a crusade of manliness and purity to counteract and undo the savage work of those who think that man is a beast. And that crusade is a matter for you."*

"I was born into a Christian family", wrote a young girl. *"My parents went to daily Mass and in school they taught me what was right and wrong in relation to the 6th and 9th commandments. As a child, I always wanted to be pure, but as an adolescent, my world changed. I fell in love with a boy. My friends encouraged me not to miss the opportunity: if I really loved him, they said, I should invite him to go a bit further and lose my purity with him. I allowed myself to be convinced that 'everyone did it', that it was 'normal'. So, one day when we were alone I suggested that we go a bit further… I thought he was going to accept. But to my dismay, he sprang up from the sofa, looked at me with the saddest face I had ever seen in my life and left without a word. I cried, I called him, texted him… But all to no avail. One day I went to see him. He opened the door – but he was still sad. Taking my hands in his, almost with tears in his eyes, he said,* **"You are worth much more than that."** *That day the penny dropped. I learned a lesson I never forgot. Still today I remember those sad eyes, like Christ's staring at me and reminding me:* ***I'm worth more…much more than that!"***

The world needs Christians like that boy. My Immaculate Mother, I ask you for Christians committed to this crusade of purity, able to remind everyone with their deeds and their words, boldly, that those who sell themselves to impurity are worth much more than that: they are worth all the Blood of your Son.

Thursday 5th week in ordinary time
Thursday 13th February
Mk 7:24-30

A woman, whose little daughter was possessed by an unclean spirit, heard of him, and came and fell down at his feet. Now the woman was a Greek, a Syrophoenician by birth. And she begged him to cast the demon out of her daughter…"you may go your way; the demon has left your daughter." And she went home, and found the child lying in bed, and the demon gone.

St Josemaria once said that the problem we face today is that "*few people pray, and those who pray… pray little.*" The world needs more and more Christians who 'believe' in the power of prayer. We could say that people don't know how to pray. The woman of the Gospel teaches us that prayer, to be effective, "*ought to be humble, fervent, resigned, persevering, and accompanied with great reverence. One should consider that he stands in the presence of a God, and speaks with a Lord before whom the angels tremble from awe and fear.*" (St Mary Magdalen de Pazzi)

Children can teach us. A parish priest decided to have a 24-hour vigil every Friday. To this purpose he left out a timetable for Adoration so that parishioners could sign up to take turns. When the timetable was complete, he discovered that a First Holy Communion boy had chosen the slot between 3 and 4am! He called the parents and found out that they had agreed to it. The boy told the priest that he wanted Jesus to 'heal his family'. His dad was an alcoholic, unemployed and violent at times. On the first Friday, his mum woke him up and brought him to the church and stayed with him. On the second Friday it was his dad's turn. He took the child to the church but waited for him outside. However, after a few weeks the dad started waiting 'inside'. Little by little the father started praying with the child during those vigils. In less than three months Jesus healed the family: dad stopped drinking, found a job and became a new man. When the priest saw what had happened he went to congratulate the boy for his perseverance. "*Congratulations,*" said the priest, "*Jesus has done it!*" The boy was surprised at the priest's words. "*Of course,*" he replied. "*Did you ever doubt it?*" The priest never forgot the lesson in faith given by an 8-year-old. How is my faith when I pray? Mary, Mother Most Faithful, teach me to pray.

Friday 5th week in ordinary time
Friday 14th February
Mk 7:31-37

They brought to him a man who was deaf and had an impediment in his speech; and they besought him to lay his hand upon him. And taking him aside from the multitude privately, he put his fingers into his ears, and he spat and touched his tongue; and looking up to heaven, he sighed, and said to him, "Ephphatha," that is, "Be opened." And his ears were opened, his tongue was released, and he spoke plainly.

Incommunicado, he could not hear or speak properly. He was unable to explain his problems. But when he put himself in Jesus' hands (*Ephphatha!*) "*his ears were opened, his tongue was released, and he spoke plainly.*" Many people have a '*speech impediment*'; they find it difficult to talk about their miseries. To recognise our sins and to talk about our mistakes can be embarrassing, but just like with a doctor, until we explain our problem and show our wound, Jesus can't help and heal us. That's the essence of Confession.

"*I was a good child,*" writes a young boy. "*I prayed, received the sacraments and went to Confession every other week. At the age of 14 I understood that God wanted something from me and started praying more intensely. But one day I made a mistake. I committed a sin against Holy Purity. I felt so embarrassed that I didn't dare go to Confession. After a while I stopped praying. I was grumpy, defiant and exploding for silly reasons. I was stuck. It wasn't my mind that was blocked, it was my soul. My mum suspected that something had happened; my sisters, my friends, my teachers too... But more than anyone else, I knew that something HAD happened. My silence was consuming me within. One day I couldn't take it anymore. I went to the priest and told him. I expected an angry reprimand. Instead, very kindly, he explained to me how silly it would be to keep a splinter in my finger hurting for weeks because I was afraid of the pain when it would be pulled out. In two minutes the priest solved all my problems. I went out in peace. I was again the same boy my mum, my sisters, my friends and teachers knew... but with more experience. How silly to keep silent, to feel embarrassed to go to Confession; what folly to carry my sins as splinters in my skin when the solution is so simple and easy to get.*" Mary, Mother of Good Counsel, may I never be embarrassed of being sincere, confessing my sins and starting again.

Sts Cyril and Methodius
Friday 14th February
Lk 10:1-9

After this the Lord appointed seventy others, and sent them on ahead of him, two by two, into every town and place where he himself was about to come. And he said to them, "The harvest is plentiful, but the labourers are few; pray therefore the Lord of the harvest to send out labourers into his harvest."

Jose Luis was twelve years old on December 27 1942. He was spending his Christmas holidays with his priest uncle in a country hamlet in the north of Spain. That night someone came from the neighbouring town to ask the priest to attend a dying old lady. It was dark and snowing. But nothing stopped the priest from taking his coat and setting off to walk the three-mile distance. His young nephew volunteered to accompany him. They had walked two miles when the snowfall became very heavy, covering their way. Their feet were freezing and, in few minutes, they got lost. Suddenly the old priest fell. In pain, he realised he couldn't walk anymore and sent the boy for help. Jose Luis ran and knocked at the first house he found. The word spread through the village. A party of young men came to rescue the priest. They found him unconscious, freezing. They took him to the house of the old lady and there, by the fire, the wounded man recovered a bit of strength. Then he asked to be placed close to the old dying lady to fulfil his duty. In the little room the priest comforted the old lady, heard her confession in whispers and gave her Holy Communion. The priest knew what was coming. He too received Communion. "*I sat next to the fire*", Jose Luis explained years later, "*hearing my uncle's heavy breath, like a broken machine; somehow I saw him being consumed like a log in the fire...fading away. His smile didn't fade, though. He was happy to die in the line of duty, warming up others like a log in the fireplace...Then it came clear to my mind: why couldn't I be the 'log' that had to replace him in the 'fire'?*" Both died the following day. Moved by the example of his uncle, Jose Luis became a priest years later, to '*keep the fire burning,*' to give light, warmth, comfort, to set others aflame.

Mary, my Mother, I pray for labourers, for generous souls – starting with myself – who would like to labour for your Son's harvest, to be consumed keeping the fire burning.

Saturday 5th week in ordinary time
Saturday 15th February
Mk 8:1-10

When again a great crowd had gathered, and they had nothing to eat, he called his disciples to him, and said to them, "I have compassion on the crowd, because they have been with me now three days, and have nothing to eat; and if I send them away hungry to their homes, they will faint on the way; and some of them have come a long way." And his disciples answered him, "How can one feed these men with bread here in the desert?...And they ate, and were satisfied; and they took up the broken pieces left over, seven baskets full. And there were about four thousand people."

"*How can **one** feed these men with bread here in the desert?*" the disciples asked Jesus. Yes. It was one against 4,000. Certainly not every*one* can... In fact, only *One*: Jesus is **the One**. '*How could it be possible?*' they were wondering. It was possible because Jesus is God and God is Almighty.

Four thousand people ate their fill of fish and bread and, at the end, the disciples collected seven baskets full of scraps. "*How can one feed these men...?*" they asked. God can feed all those - and many more. Jesus' power has no limits; that's the meaning of *Almighty*. If there were 7,000 or 100,000, it would be the same. It makes no difference for an *Almighty God* to perform a miracle multiplying a piece of bread by two... or by two million.

When we pray, when we offer the Mass for the conversion of a sinner or for a particular deceased, it is the same for God whether we pray for one or for 10,000. Some people may think that if you offer the Mass for two souls, each one gets '*half of a Mass*'. That's nonsense. If you offer a Mass for a million souls, they all get '*a Mass*'. Just as, when we bathe in the ocean we all get 100% wet regardless of how many are in the water. Let's not put limits when we ask, since God's power is limitless. They say of St Bernard that, when he was about to die, someone asked him if he regretted anything about his life. "*After all that God has given me,*" said the saint, "*I regret not having had more desires!*" He knew that, if he had asked for more, he would have received even more. Mary, Virgin Most Faithful, may I never set limits when I pray, may I never be mean in prayers or in demands.

Third Sunday of St Joseph
Sixth Sunday in Ordinary Time
Sunday 16th February
Lk 6:17, 20-26

"Blessed are you that weep now, for you shall laugh. Blessed are you when men hate you, and when they exclude you and revile you, and cast out your name as evil, on account of the Son of man! Rejoice in that day, and leap for joy, for behold, your reward is great in heaven; for so their fathers did to the prophets."

The message is clear: persecution on account of Jesus is a blessing. The history of the Church proves that it has always been a constant challenge. There are martyrs in every country, in every century. From the Apostles' times up until today, the enemy has been and still is furious, attacking the Church of Jesus Christ with all his might. But when Christians die, Christianity revives. And because of that, we feel blessed.

Fr Ragheed Ganni was an Iraqi priest born in 1972 in a town in the Plain of Ninevah. He studied theology in Rome between 1996 and 2003, after which he decided to return to Iraq, despite the war and persecution of Christians there. As soon as he arrived at his new parish in Mosul, he started receiving all sorts of threats. His church was blown up. His house was blown up. He had to say Mass in the basement. But he continued on. Attacks persisted until the day of his death, June 3, 2007, when a group of armed men confronted him after Mass. They asked him why he was still there and why he hadn't closed the church as they had demanded. *"How can I close the house of God?"* he responded, right before they shot and killed him. Ragheed was just 35 years old.

The Church grows with the blood of Martyrs and Martyrs bleed the Blood of Christ they receive in the Eucharist. Fr Ragheed once wrote, *"There are days when I feel frail and full of fear. But when, holding the Eucharist, I say, 'Behold the Lamb of God, who takes away the sin of the world,' I feel His strength in me. When I hold the Host in my hands, it is really He who is holding me and all of us, challenging the terrorists and keeping us all united in His boundless love."*

I pray today to you, Mary, Mother of the Persecuted Church, to help all those who suffer persecution for the sake of your Son, that they feel blessed, that they *'rejoice and leap for joy, for behold, their reward is great in heaven.'*

Monday 17th February
Mk 8:11-13

The Pharisees came and began to argue with him, seeking from him a sign from heaven, to test him. And he sighed deeply in his spirit, and said, "Why does this generation seek a sign? Truly, I say to you, no sign shall be given to this generation." And he left them, and getting into the boat again he departed to the other side.

The Gospel today comes after the multiplication of the loaves and fish for four thousand people. That miracle wasn't impressive enough for these Pharisees who came asking for another sign. There is no worse blind man than the one who doesn't want to see. There is no worse deaf man than the one who doesn't want to hear. For someone who doesn't want to believe no miracle is enough.

Those who don't believe in God do not look for proofs of His existence. They reject every argument before it is explained. They are like the lad who was taking driving lessons. His instructor was worried because every time a lorry was coming in the opposite direction the lad panicked and the instructor had to hold the steering wheel. But one day the instructor saw that the youngster had improved. *"You seem more confident now"*, he said. But then it was the teacher who panicked when he heard the reply: *"Yes. That's because now, every time I see a lorry coming, I just close my eyes."* That's what the Pharisees were doing with the Messiah.

But God still has a plan to meet those who don't want to believe. Giovanni Papini (1881-1956) was an Italian writer and famous atheist. No reason or argument was convincing enough for him. Until one day when he went for a walk with a friend – an atheist like him. They found a beggar, blue with cold, stretching out his hand for a coin. Papini produced a coin from his pocket and said with a big grin, *"This coin is yours if you utter two or three good blasphemies."* The beggar, astonished, hid his hand and walked away, saying *"Poor man! God have mercy on you."* To be called 'Poor man' by a beggar made Papini think and it changed his life. Keeping his eyes closed didn't take the truth away, like the lorries in the road. That day he 'crashed into' God and became a devout Catholic soon afterwards. Mary, Virgin Most Faithful, I pray through your intercession today for those who don't want to believe.

Tuesday 18th February
Mk 8:14-21

Jesus said to them, "Why do you discuss the fact that you have no bread? Do you not yet perceive or understand? Are your hearts hardened? Having eyes do you not see, and having ears do you not hear? And do you not remember? When I broke the five loaves for the five thousand, how many baskets full of broken pieces did you take up?" They said to him, "Twelve." "And the seven for the four thousand, how many baskets full of broken pieces did you take up?" And they said to him, "Seven." And he said to them, "Do you not yet understand?"

It looks like Jesus was losing His patience with His disciples. After all the time they had spent with Jesus, they were unable to understand Him. They were not in tune. They were focused on their own ideas and couldn't understand what Jesus was saying. Jesus often had to explain His parables to them. Many people have this same problem. From the same Bible, people can extract the most diverse and random conclusions. That is why God has given us the Holy Spirit and the Magisterium of the Church – to help us understand the Sacred Scriptures according to the mind of the Author Himself.

Imagine that, in an art gallery, you come across one of those modern paintings composed of a few warm colours mixed randomly and sold for £10,000. Perplexed, you ask some art enthusiasts what it represents and they all give you different opinions: that it represents internal suffering, a tornado, the Holocaust, violence, a tablecloth... one of them says that paint was probably spilt onto the canvas by a cat or the artist's baby... How can you tell who is right? Easy: you ask the artist!

In the same way, throughout history millions have read Sacred Scripture and concluded different things – even opposing things. That's why Our Lord sent the Holy Spirit. The Paraclete would explain everything to us (*Jn* 14:26) not just to everyone individually, but to the whole Christian Family through the Magisterium of the Church. Any individual interpretation of the Bible has to be compared and contrasted with two thousand years of meditation on Scripture by saints, condensed in that Magisterium. Mary, Mother of the Church, thank God with us for those *guidelines* that the Church offers us to understand the '*exact* meaning of your Son's Words.'

Wednesday 19th February
Mk 8:22-26

Some people brought to him a blind man, and begged him to touch him. And he took the blind man by the hand, and led him out of the village; and when he had spit on his eyes and laid his hands upon him, he asked him, "Do you see anything?" And he looked up and said, "I see men; but they look like trees, walking." Then again he laid his hands upon his eyes; and he looked intently and was restored, and saw everything clearly.

This miracle was not instantaneous, like some other miracles. This one was a 'process'. We know that Jesus could have said, 'You are healed' and it would have happened. He could also have touched him and that would have been enough. Instead, Jesus took him "*by the hand, and led him out of the village.*" The blind man – and probably those who brought him – didn't expect that. Where was Jesus taking him? What for? Jesus didn't say. But even more importantly: the blind man didn't ask.

The blind man abandoned himself, allowed himself to be led out because he trusted Jesus. Then Jesus put spittle on his eyes! Yes, you read it correctly: Jesus actually spat in his face! Did the blind man complain? No. Then Jesus laid His Hands on him. And something happened: the blind man could see... just a bit. Did the blind man complain? Did he feel disappointed that after the walk, the spit, the laying on of hands... he could only see a bit? No. He didn't understand what Jesus was doing, but he didn't care. Because he trusted. Then Jesus laid Hands a second time and the miracle happened. Was all that necessary? If Jesus thought it was, then... yes, it was.

When we pray for something, keep in mind that God has His own *modus operandi*. God does everything 'His Way'. When I ask for help on behalf of a friend or a relative, or to get rid of a particular defect or to achieve a particular virtue, can God grant me that? Yes. Does He want to grant it? Most surely, yes. So why doesn't it happen? Because God will do it 'His Way'. It may take time, it may be a long process, but remember this: **God's Way is 'way better' than 'my way'**. Mary, Virgin Most Prudent, teach me to trust God, to let myself be led by the hand, to be patient, because led by God's Hand, what can I fear, what can I lack?

Thursday 20th February
Mk 8:27-33

Jesus asked his disciples, "Who do men say that I am?" And they told him, "John the Baptist; and others say, Elijah; and others one of the prophets." And he asked them, "But who do you say that I am?" Peter answered him, "You are the Christ."

Jesus' Apostles had seen Him eating, sleeping, laughing, crying, healing, performing miracles... they had heard Him talking to peoples of all walks of life: shepherds, farmers, housewives, fishermen, centurions, tax collectors, outcasts, sick people, lepers and the possessed - and scribes, Pharisees... If Jesus had different sides, they had seen all of them. They knew Him well. What about me? How well do I know Him? How well do I know His Life, His Words, His Deeds, His Death? Meditating on the Gospel allows us to know God better and to start a personal relationship with Him.

Ernest Gordon wrote a book entitled 'Through the Valley of the Kwai' in which he describes his experience as a prisoner in Thailand during WWII. He worked on a railway which the Japanese were building. Over 12,000 allied prisoners died of starvation there. Gordon says an added enemy to the Japanese were some of the prisoners. Some got carried away by the law of the jungle. They stole from each other and informed on each other to win favours from the Japanese. Morale was at rock bottom. So two men whose faith kept them going decided to try and do something about it. They organized Bible reading and discussion groups. They met at night and at first the numbers were small but after a short while the numbers grew into the hundreds. When reading the Bible they noticed that Jesus faced the same problems as they did; he often had no place to lay His Head, no food, no friends in high places. He too had known weariness from too much toil; the suffering, rejection and disappointments that are part of life. Everything about Jesus began to make sense. The prisoners underwent a change of heart and stopped destroying one another as they had been doing. Reading Jesus' Life and Death, using it for prayer and discussion, transformed an entire prison camp. Mary, Mother of Christ, do not let one day go by without my reading your Son's life in the Gospel, without meditating on it, without getting to know Him better and learning from Him.

Friday 6th week in ordinary time
Friday 21st February
Mk 8:34-9:1

And he called to him the multitude with his disciples, and said to them, "If any man would come after me, let him deny himself and take up his cross and follow me. For whoever would save his life will lose it; and whoever loses his life for my sake and the gospel's will save it. For what does it profit a man, to gain the whole world and forfeit his life? For what can a man give in return for his life? For whoever is ashamed of me and of my words in this adulterous and sinful generation, of him will the Son of man also be ashamed, when he comes in the glory of his Father with the holy angels."

To follow Our Lord will always be to go against the grain. Those who are ready to save their lives (and many others' lives) have to be ready to lose it for Jesus' sake and for the Gospel. But it doesn't necessarily mean losing our lives as martyrs do. For many of us, to be ready to lose our lives means to be able to give up our comfort (good life), our good name, our prestige, our career, our projects, our plans... We have to be ready to stand for God and for Good.

'The Emperor's New Clothes' is a classic tale based on an old story written in Spain in 1335. It tells the story of a vain king fooled by two tailors. They promise him the finest, best suit made of a fabric invisible to anyone who is "hopelessly stupid". When the tailors report that the suit is finished, they mime dressing him and the king marches in procession before his subjects. No one can see the clothes but they don't dare to say it for fear that they will be seen as "hopelessly stupid". The tale finishes when a child in the crowd, too young to understand the pretence, blurts out *"But he hasn't got anything on!"* At that point everyone realises that no one dared to tell the truth for fear of being taken for fools.

Likewise, in today's society, standing up for God and for Truth often means challenging the views of the majority. We will probably be taken for fools, vilified or ridiculed; however, that's the only way we can open the eyes of many to recognise the Truth they feel but can't yet see. Mary, Mother of Confessors, may I never be ashamed to stand up for your Son, may I never keep silent, never be embarrassed to swim against the tide, to speak up, to help people see the Truth of Christ.

The Chair of St Peter
Saturday 22nd February
Mt 16:13-19

Now when Jesus came into the district of Caesarea Philippi, he asked his disciples, "Who do men say that the Son of man is?" And they said, "Some say John the Baptist, others say Elijah, and others Jeremiah or one of the prophets." He said to them, "But who do you say that I am?" Simon Peter replied, "You are the Christ, the Son of the living God." And Jesus answered him, "Blessed are you, Simon Bar-Jona! For flesh and blood has not revealed this to you, but my Father who is in heaven. And I tell you, you are Peter, and on this rock I will build my church, and the powers of death shall not prevail against it. I will give you the keys of the kingdom of heaven, and whatever you bind on earth shall be bound in heaven, and whatever you loose on earth shall be loosed in heaven."

Today we celebrate the feast of the Chair of St Peter which is not merely about a piece of furniture. The seat of the bishop is the Chair or 'cathedra' (origin of the word cathedral, a church that has the cathedra of the bishop). It signifies the authority of Peter. In the apse of the Basilica of St Peter you can see the chair, a bronze sculpture of Bernini (17th century). On top of it you see the Dove symbolizing the Holy Spirit who inspires the Pope.

Why did Jesus choose Peter? Only He knows. God didn't choose a wise man who knew the Scriptures and who could write, for Peter probably couldn't. He didn't choose a man of easy speech who could be persuasive when preaching the Gospel. He didn't choose a man with influence, a rich man, a politician...

Jesus needed a strong man, a rock on which to build His Church. A rock that serves as a foundation doesn't need to be beautiful; just strong. Peter wasn't perfect when Jesus chose him, but his faith and love would become strong enough to make the Church stand firm. Over the centuries many strong empires have fought against this Rock. They disappeared but the Church stands erect. Whoever fights against this Rock *"shall not prevail."*

Stronger than Superman, Iron Man, Spiderman or Batman... is our Fisherman!

Holy Mary, our Hope, Queen of the Apostles and Mother of the Church, pray for the Pope and for us!

Fourth Sunday of St Joseph
Seventh Sunday in Ordinary Time
Sunday 23rd February
Lk 6:27-38

But I say to you that hear, Love your enemies, do good to those who hate you, bless those who curse you, pray for those who abuse you...And as you wish that men would do to you, do so to them. "If you love those who love you, what credit is that to you? For even sinners love those who love them...But love your enemies, and do good, and lend, expecting nothing in return; and your reward will be great, and you will be sons of the Most High; for he is kind to the ungrateful and the selfish. Be merciful, even as your Father is merciful."

In other words, 'Don't let evil defeat you; defeat evil with good.' Joe Louis was a black world heavyweight champion. At age 23, he became the youngest man in history to win the heavyweight title, holding it for a record 12 years and retired in 1948, still undefeated. He invested some of his winnings in a 500-acre farm. One day he went out riding to visit his farm for the first time.

During his ride, he came upon a tiny whitewashed cabin in a secluded corner of his new farm. He got off his horse, walked over to it, and knocked on the door. An elderly white man opened it. *"What do you want?"* the man snarled. Joe tipped his hat and said, *"I was just riding by and..."* *"Well, keep riding!"* said the old man. *"Is there anything wrong?"* asked Joe, looking a bit sad. *"Wrong? Of course something's wrong,"* snapped the old man. *"Some nigger just bought this place."*

Joe looked down at his feet, paused a few seconds, and then said, *"Yes! That's why I'm here. I have a message for you from the new owner. He sent me to tell you that you're welcome to stay here for the rest of your life. He also said that you'll never be bothered, and that there won't be any rent."* Then Joe tipped his hat again, got back on his horse, and rode off, humming, leaving the man standing there speechless.

We love these kind of stories, don't we? But we are happier telling them than experiencing them in our own lives. Often we fail to recognise the many opportunities we have in our daily life to love those who are annoying, impertinent, rude, inconvenient, unpleasant, irritating, selfish, opportunist, insensitive... Take a few moments to identify your daily chances to love your 'enemies'. Mary, Mother of Mercy, help me to learn to be merciful like our Father in Heaven.

Monday 7th week in ordinary time
Monday 24th February
Mk 9:14-29

A man said to Jesus, "Teacher, I brought my son to you, for he has a dumb spirit...I asked your disciples to cast it out, and they were not able." And he answered them, "O faithless generation, how long am I to be with you? How long am I to bear with you? Bring him to me."...[The father] said, "if you can do anything, have pity on us and help us." And Jesus said to him, "If you can! All things are possible to him who believes." Immediately the father of the child cried out and said, "I believe; help my unbelief!"

This happened when Jesus was coming down from Mount Tabor with Peter, James and John after His Transfiguration. We can imagine what happened. This man brought his son to be healed but Jesus was up on the mountain. The Apostles waiting there thought, *'Well, maybe we can try. After all, we have done this before.'* One after another they did what they knew: imposition of hands, commanding the devil to leave, different prayers aloud, but all to no avail. The devil was still tormenting that boy and his father grew discouraged. The Apostles then told the man to have courage - Jesus wouldn't fail.

Maybe the father replied to them, *'Yes, He has done it before with others; but so have you, disciples of His, and today you couldn't! What if this case is different? What if this demon is more powerful? What if Jesus can't do anything either?!'* Then Jesus arrived. The father explained everything to Him and said that sad *tag line,* "*if you can do anything...*" Jesus didn't like that sentence. "*If you can!*" He repeated; it is not about what *I CAN*, but about what *YOU BELIEVE*, because "*all things are possible to him who believes.*" Then the man understood: his lack of faith could be responsible for his son not being healed. So he begged for faith: "*help my unbelief!*"

A doctor told a couple that, despite all their efforts, they would not be able to have children. The woman went to Mass and heard the priest proclaiming today's Gospel: "*all things are possible to him who believes.*" During Holy Communion she asked for 'the miracle' - and as soon as she arrived home, she took out her knitting needles and started making a baby outfit. The following year the same bewildered doctor was delivering the couple's baby. Holy Mary, Virgin Most Faithful, *increase my faith!*

Tuesday 7th week in ordinary time
Tuesday 25th February
Mk 9:30-37

Jesus was teaching his disciples, saying to them, "The Son of man will be delivered into the hands of men, and they will kill him; and when he is killed, after three days he will rise." But they did not understand the saying, and they were afraid to ask him.

The reaction of the Apostles is quite surprising: "*they were afraid to ask him.*" They knew Jesus well. They had heard Him preaching and teaching - and all of them had spent memorable times in conversation with Him. But now He was talking about suffering and death. They didn't like that. They preferred not to know. Later, on Good Friday, all of them (with the exception of John) ran away from the Cross.

In a primary school, the new RE teacher was asked by the headmistress what book she planned to use. She said that she only wanted to use the Bible. The headmistress pointed out, "*That's fine by me. But make sure that you leave aside **those nasty bits at the end**.*" By 'nasty bits' she was referring to the Passion and Death of Our Lord. For many Christians the Cross is just a *nasty bit* they prefer not to know about. Like an ostrich, some think that if they bury their head in the sand and don't see the Cross... It may disappear.

The Cross is necessary. It was necessary for Jesus to redeem us and it is necessary for us to follow Him: "*Whoever does not bear his own cross and come after me, cannot be my disciple.*" Those who prefer not to hear about sacrifice don't know anything about love, because *love suffers*. A mother suffers for her children. Husbands suffer for their wives. Friends suffer for their friends. God suffers for us. And we... we should be ready to suffer for Him.

St Josemaría wrote, "*Don't drag the Cross... Carry it squarely on your shoulder... Don't bear your Cross with resignation: resignation is not a generous word. Love the Cross. When you really love it, your Cross will be... a Cross, without a Cross*", a noble burden of love.

Mary, My Mother, with your help may I learn to take up my cross for Jesus with generosity, following Jesus' steps closely - because then (with Him) it won't be just 'my' cross, it will be 'ours', Jesus' and mine.

Wednesday 7th week in ordinary time
Wednesday 26th February
Mk 9:38-40

John said to him, "Teacher, we saw a man casting out demons in your name, and we forbade him, because he was not following us." But Jesus said, "Do not forbid him; for no one who does a mighty work in my name will be able soon after to speak evil of me. For he that is not against us is for us."

The Apostles saw someone preaching in Jesus' Name and, because he hadn't been 'officially appointed', they wanted to stop him. But to become an apostle we don't need a diploma. Jesus sent *everyone* to "*go into all the world and preach the gospel*" (Mk 16:15). There are many ways to proclaim the Gospel. God doesn't expect the same things of everyone. He has different missions, charisms and talents for different people. We don't need to approve or understand someone else's mission. We just need to fulfil ours.

The same Apostle, St John, became himself one day the object of suspicion. At the end of his Gospel he mentions how Our Lord called Peter to Him. '*Peter turned and saw following them the disciple whom Jesus loved [John himself]... When Peter saw him, he said to Jesus, "Lord, what about this man?" Jesus said to him, "If it is my will that he remain until I come, what is that to you? Follow me!"*' In other words: 'I don't have to explain to you the vocation of the others. You mind your own business!'

This is a very interesting lesson of Our Lord because often the sufferings of saints came, not from a lack of understanding from Jesus' enemies, but from His own disciples. Suspicions that arose from the fact that they are not like '*us*'. Fr Josef Kentenich was removed from Schoenstatt, the institution he had founded, due to slanders against his person and a misunderstanding about his institution. Previously he had spent 4 years in Dachau during WW2. But when he recalled those times, he confessed that the years he was removed from Schoenstatt were more painful than his experience in the concentration camp. In 1965 (after 15 years), everything was proved to be false and he could return to his rightful place. His 'detractors' were 'good Christians' who had their own opinion about his apostolate. Let us ask Our Lady for her to reassure those who suffer this kind of 'internal misunderstanding'.

Thursday 27th February
Mk 9:41-50

"For truly, I say to you, whoever gives you a cup of water to drink because you bear the name of Christ, will by no means lose his reward. Whoever causes one of these little ones who believe in me to sin, it would be better for him if a great millstone were hung round his neck and he were thrown into the sea ... For every one will be salted with fire. Salt is good; but if the salt has lost its saltness, how will you season it? Have salt in yourselves, and be at peace with one another."

It is a great consolation, Lord, that *everything* we do for You – no matter how little - will be rewarded. Something as small as a cup of water, My Jesus, will never be forgotten by You.

One cold winter's day, when St Martin was a young soldier, he met a shivering beggar in rags. As he had nothing to give him he took his sword and divided his cape in two, giving half to the beggar. That night in a dream he saw Jesus covered with half of his cape... It is not a valid excuse to say that we can only give a little. As St Teresa of Calcutta said, *"If you can't feed a hundred... then feed just one."*

In actual fact, what we can do for the others is usually very little. The great deeds of the saints were, very often, a large number of little deeds. Venerable Pope John Paul I taught: *"I have never had an opportunity to throw myself into the waters of a rushing stream to save someone whose life was in danger; very often I have been asked to lend something, to write letters, to give simple little directions. I have never run into a mad dog in the street; on the other hand, I have encountered any number of tiresome flies and mosquitoes; I have never had persecutors who beat me, but many people disturb me by speaking loudly in the street, by turning up the volume of their TV, or even by making certain noises while eating soup. To help others as best you can, to avoid losing your temper, to be understanding, to keep calm and smiling on these occasions (as much as possible!) is loving your neighbour, without fancy talk, but in a practical way."* And all that will never be forgotten by Our Lord who will reward us as if we did it to Him. That's the salt of Christians: when we can help, we do help. Even if it is a little thing. Because there is nothing little for God. Our Lady, how many times you helped your friends and neighbours! Mother, teach me to serve!

Friday 7th week in ordinary time
Friday 28th February
Mk 10:1-12

Pharisees came up and in order to test him asked, "Is it lawful for a man to divorce his wife?...Moses allowed a man to write a certificate of divorce, and to put her away." But Jesus said to them, "For your hardness of heart he wrote you this commandment. But from the beginning of creation, 'God made them male and female.' 'For this reason a man shall leave his father and mother and be joined to his wife, and the two shall become one.' So they are no longer two but one. What therefore God has joined together, let not man put asunder."

The plans and laws of God are meant to help us achieve happiness. But the fact that the plan comes from God's Love doesn't mean that it isn't demanding. A man was extremely overweight. He was double the weight he used to be. He went to the doctor because he had constant headaches, sleep problems, difficulties in concentrating and being productive at work. His family life was also difficult. He was grumpy all the time and found it hard to make time for his wife and children. The doctor gave him the solution to all his problems: a diet.

After a few months he went back to his normal weight and found himself better than ever. He could now sleep well, his headaches disappeared, he felt cheerful again and was more productive than ever at work. Everything was great except at meal times. His diet was demanding. On his next visit to the doctor he relayed the good news of his new condition but asked if certain allowances could be made: could he eat *pasta*, or a *cake* every now and then? Could he have a *snack* before going to bed? Was alcohol really prohibited? Couldn't he go to the gym only once a week instead of four times? The doctor had to say, "*It is your headache, not mine, your mood, your work, your sleep and your family... Do what you want but remember how it was before!*"

We find happiness when we make the effort to fulfil the Loving Plan of God. It is always demanding, but God doesn't just give us a set of rules, a 'diet'. He gives us the Grace we need and He also follows the diet with us.

My Mother, Virgin Most Faithful, may I learn not just to fulfil God's Loving Law as an obligation, but to cherish it every day of my life.

March

Saturday 1st March
Mk 10:13-16

And they were bringing children to him, that he might touch them; and the disciples rebuked them. But when Jesus saw it he was indignant, and said to them, "Let the children come to me, do not hinder them; for to such belongs the kingdom of God. Truly, I say to you, whoever does not receive the kingdom of God like a child shall not enter it." And he took them in his arms and blessed them, laying his hands upon them.

We don't find in the Gospels a detailed description of Jesus. In the old days people wrote about the deeds and words of ancient figures and left aside physical and psychological details about the person. Nevertheless, we find interesting words in the Gospels that give us a glimpse of how He was. Jesus loved children, their games and songs, their running around, their chatter and constant enjoyment. Children can be a nuisance sometimes. For Jesus, though, it was a joy to be surrounded by children, to kiss them and hug them. But it is also a fact that children loved Jesus. Little kids are not easily attracted by grown-ups. But they felt confident with Jesus because He was a lovable Man.

A five-minute documentary about *St John Paul II and children* (http://ow.ly/10pnC6), explains his relationship with the little ones. It opens with the statement: "*Six years have passed. And we are still wondering, why did we love him so much?*" As images pass through the screen we are reminded of his 'popularity' among children, his affection, his smile, his warmth. At the end children give the answer to the opening question: "*We loved him because he was like us. But especially because... he was like Christ.*"

Children loved Jesus because He was like them. He was cheerful. He told funny stories (like the guy with the plank in his eye...) He didn't hesitate to play their games, sing their songs or tell them stories. And He asked His disciples to be like them. We need to learn a lot from children: their cheerfulness, their trust, their lack of personal concerns. They easily forget their wounds and offences and can laugh ten seconds after crying. They don't need much; they can enjoy themselves with a twig. Mary, my Mother, help us to be like children, to be like your Son.

Fifth Sunday of St Joseph
Eight Sunday in Ordinary Time
Sunday 2nd March
Lk 6:39-45

"Why do you see the speck that is in your brother's eye, but do not notice the log that is in your own eye? Or how can you say to your brother, 'Brother, let me take out the speck that is in your eye,' when you yourself do not see the log that is in your own eye? You hypocrite, first take the log out of your own eye, and then you will see clearly to take out the speck that is in your brother's eye."

A newly married couple went to live in a new flat. On their first morning, during breakfast, the wife looked through the window and saw her neighbour hanging out the laundry on the clothes line. "*Look!*" she said sarcastically to her husband. "*She is hanging dirty clothes to dry! Someone should teach her to wash clothes...*" The following morning the criticism was repeated; and the same the next day. But on Sunday, she noticed a change and commented, "*Look! Seems that she found the soap. Now her clothes are clean!*" To which the husband replied, "*I woke up early this morning... and cleaned our windows.*"

Remember the song written by Garrett and Ballard: if I want to make a change in the world, then "*I'm starting with the man in the mirror. I'm asking him to change his ways. And no message could have been any clearer. If you want to make the world a better place, take a look at yourself, and then make a change.*"

The Pharisees were unable to see themselves in the mirror. That's why the nightly examination of conscience is so important, a short break before going to bed when we reflect on our behaviour during the day. St Josemaría recommended that we ask ourselves what we did right (to give thanks to God for it), what we did wrong (and ask for forgiveness) and what we can improve tomorrow (and ask God for help to implement our resolution.) That's how we can start with the man in the mirror, to change our mistakes instead of complaining about other people's failures. It will keep you on your toes in your struggle for holiness, it will bring you close to God with lovely acts of contrition and it will also bring you close to others because, having seen the beam in your own eye, you will understand those who have specks or even beams in theirs. Mary, Refuge of Sinners, help me to see myself as God sees me and to start changing the man in the mirror.

Monday 8th week in ordinary time
Monday 3rd March
Mk 10:17-27

A man ran up and knelt before him, and asked him, "Good Teacher, what must I do to inherit eternal life?" And Jesus said to him, "You know the commandments: 'Do not kill, Do not commit adultery...'" And he said to him, "Teacher, all these I have observed from my youth." And Jesus looking upon him loved him, and said to him, "You lack one thing; go, sell what you have, and give to the poor, and you will have treasure in heaven; and come, follow me." At that saying his countenance fell, and he went away sorrowful; for he had great possessions.

We can't help feeling sorry for this young man who had been chosen personally by Jesus to follow Him and become an Apostle. The Gospel says that Jesus, "*looking upon him, loved him,*" but he didn't want to follow Jesus.

Perhaps afterwards he tried to convince himself that he was right: that selling all his sheep, cattle and fields and giving the money to the poor would have been crazy; that leaving everything to follow that man without knowing where they were going would be nonsense. Maybe a couple of years later someone came to the village with the news that Jesus had been crucified - and he thought, '*You see? I was right!*'; perhaps a few months later he heard that some said He had risen from the dead and was alive... And he hesitated. But a few years afterwards he heard about the persecutions and Christians running away and probably thought again that he'd made the right decision. At the end of his life he contemplated his possessions and achievements but could not forget that one day, many years before, Jesus wanted to change his life, to make him an Apostle, but he said no...

But the story could have a different ending. Perhaps, after a few weeks hesitating he thought, '*I don't want to spend the rest of my life worried about my cattle and fields and money! Jesus needs me; there are people waiting for me... I can change the course of history with Him!*' And he left everything and went after Jesus, became an Apostle and is now in Heaven helping souls to be generous with God to become the Apostles of the 21st century...

Holy Mary, Queen of the Apostles, help me to be generous, to forget about my things and my comfort - and to follow your Son.

Tuesday 4th March
Mk 10:28-31

Peter began to say to him, "Lo, we have left everything and followed you." Jesus said, "Truly, I say to you, there is no one who has left house or brothers or sisters or mother or father or children or lands, for my sake and for the gospel, who will not receive a hundredfold now in this time, houses and brothers and sisters and mothers and children and lands, with persecutions, and in the age to come eternal life."

Jesus asked the young man to leave everything and follow Him. Peter and the others were there, maybe smiling at the idea of that youth joining the group but he went away sad. Then Peter broke the tense silence to comfort Jesus: *'Don't worry, Jesus'* he would say, *'we are with You; we know what is important; see, we have left everything and followed You.'* And we can imagine Jesus looking back at His disciples, touched and reassured by their generosity, His kind Voice persuading them that it was worthwhile: *"there is no one who has left house or brothers or sisters or mother or father or children or lands, for my sake and for the gospel..."*

St Philip Neri was a priest gifted with good wit. One day, when he was old, a young man came to see him. The saint sat in his chair, listening attentively to the kneeling boy's plans. *"And, after the exam, what then?"* asked the saint. *"Then I shall try for a degree in law"*. *"And then?"*, insisted the wise old priest. *"I want to be a barrister: everyone tells me I'm cut out for it."* *"And then?"* *"Well, as a barrister, I could marry and settle down and be a rich man."* *"And then?"* *"Oh, well, I might end up as a judge, and obtain some high office in the court of Rome."* *"And then?"* *"Some day I should retire with a big pension and be able to enjoy an honourable old age."* *"And then?"* *"Then? Well father, some day I suppose I should have to die."* St Philip drew the boy's head closer and whispered in his ear: *"And what then?"* The lad, Francesco Zazzara, never forgot that conversation, and later threw away all his worldly ambitions to join St Philip Neri's Congregation of the Oratory.

Our Lady, my Mother, help me to understand that it is worthwhile to leave everything and follow your Son, that there is a real hundredfold in this life and real happiness in the Eternal one.

Ash Wednesday
Wednesday 5th March
Mt 6:1-6, 16-18

Jesus said to his disciples: "Beware of practising your piety before men in order to be seen by them; for then you will have no reward from your Father who is in heaven. Thus...when you pray, you must not be like the hypocrites; for they love to stand and pray in the synagogues and at the street corners, that they may be seen by men. Truly, I say to you, they have received their reward. But when you pray, go into your room and shut the door and pray to your Father who is in secret; and your Father who sees in secret will reward you".

Today we start Lent, a time of preparation for Easter. The word "Lent" comes from an old English word which means "springtime". It reminds us of 'spring cleaning' and the new life evident in nature at this time of year. Lent is a time of special grace for us when we can do some spring cleaning in our lives and enjoy new life as a result. Sometimes people ask, *'What are you doing for Lent?'* And they expect an answer like: *'I'm giving up chocolate!'* Jokingly, someone would say that he is giving up 'homework' or a particular chore... But there is only one thing that we should all strive to give up during Lent – sin!

To encourage people to try to do their best, you often hear motivational slogans like 'You can do anything if you really believe', or 'You are powerful' or 'You have no limits'… Instead, if you attend Mass today you will receive the ashes on your forehead. Then you will be reminded that you are 'dust and unto dust you shall return'. That's the way the Church explains to us the purpose of Lent: an exercise in holy desire. Lent is like a stool which has three legs: prayer, sacrifice and charity. Lent cannot stand if a leg is missing. So our Lenten resolutions should be in these three areas. Maybe we do not need to pray more but to pray better, to offer our usual mortifications but with a firmer intention; to be more generous when we give, and always give with a smile... Think carefully: What can I do during Lent that will make a big difference to my prayer life?

Mary, my Mother, help me to be generous this Lent, to make a real change in my life of prayer, in my sacrifice and in charity with those around me.

Thursday after Ash Wednesday
Thursday 6th March
Lk 9:22-25

"The Son of man must suffer many things, and be rejected by the elders and chief priests and scribes, and be killed, and on the third day be raised...If any man would come after me, let him deny himself and take up his cross daily and follow me. For whoever would save his life will lose it; and whoever loses his life for my sake, he will save it. For what does it profit a man if he gains the whole world and loses or forfeits himself?"

There is just one way to follow Jesus: *with the Cross*. Trying to follow You, Lord, while avoiding sacrifice would be like a bird trying to fly without wings. It's not that Christians *like* pain or suffering in itself; but that they recognise it as a means to improve.

Bosco Gutierrez was an architect who was kidnapped for 257 days. He underwent all kinds of suffering locked in a tiny room without windows and with no verbal contact with anyone for months. One day his captors saw that he had given up on himself and offered him a whiskey. He loved whiskey! Slowly, in order to enjoy it to the full, he smelt it and ran the glass along his unshaven dirty face. Then he heard an internal prompt: "*Give up the whiskey! Give me something that is under your control.*" He hesitated for a moment. That was his only pleasure for months. He told himself: "*I have offered enough already...*" But then he understood the difference. All the hardships and sufferings he had offered before had been 'inflicted' on him. This was the first time 'he' could choose to offer up something. And so, he poured it on the floor. That day everything changed for him: "*That day I won my first battle.*"

We have many battles to win this Lent. Let's be practical and choose *useful* mortifications: let's wake up straightaway, eat more of what we do not like, and less of what we like; do the dishes, smile at someone we may find annoying, avoid complaining (about anything, to anyone); tidy our room, do the jobs we don't like before the ones we find easier, rather than putting them off; accept what we have been told without answering back, and many others... Mary, Mother of God and my Mother, help me to take up my cross to the bitter end, no matter how bitter it is. I will try to make a list of sacrifices that I intend to fulfil so as to be close to your Son throughout Lent.

Friday after Ash Wednesday
Friday 7th March
Mt 9:14-15

Then the disciples of John came to him, saying, "Why do we and the Pharisees fast, but your disciples do not fast?" And Jesus said to them, "Can the wedding guests mourn as long as the bridegroom is with them? The days will come, when the bridegroom is taken away from them, and then they will fast."

There is a time for celebration – such as a wedding – and a time for mortification – such as Lent. Today is the third day of Lent; let's check how my mortification is going so far. Do I have a list of sacrifices? Am I following it? Can I improve or be more consistent in my sacrifice? *Let's be really generous!*

In terms of generosity in sacrifice, let's look at Jesus on the Cross. He didn't accept the Cross half-heartedly and nor should we. Besides, mortification doesn't harm your health; if anything it makes you stronger. Carthusian monks offer many sacrifices each day; among them, not eating meat on any day of the year. When Pope Urban V (1310-1370) was told about this harsh diet, he decided it must stop because it would give the monks *health* problems. Ten Carthusians were sent to visit the Pope and explain their sacrifices; the youngest of them was already over 90 years old. Another approached the Pope, walking without any support, and said, "*I'm over 100 years old... What do you mean by health?*" The Pope then understood, and the monks were allowed to continue with their diet which has remained unchanged for 1000 years!

There is no holiness without mortification. Jesus was very clear: "*If any man would come after me, let him deny himself and take up his cross and follow me.*" It is necessary for personal holiness and for the salvation of others. As Jesus said to St Faustina: "**You will save more souls through prayer and suffering than will a missionary through his teachings and sermons alone.**" St Philip Neri summarised it well when he taught "*without mortification nothing can be done.*"

My Mother, I learn to be generous in sacrifice when I contemplate you at the foot of the Cross, accompanying your Son throughout His ordeal. With my daily sacrifices, may I come close to Jesus on Mount Calvary, so that, with you, Mother, I can help Jesus to save the world.

Saturday after Ash Wednesday
Saturday 8th March
Lk 5:27-32

Levi made him a great feast in his house; and there was a large company of tax collectors and others sitting at table with them. And the Pharisees and their scribes murmured against his disciples, saying, "Why do you eat and drink with tax collectors and sinners?" And Jesus answered them, "Those who are well have no need of a physician, but those who are sick; I have not come to call the righteous, but sinners to repentance."

Jesus came to seek those who need conversion and He wants your help and mine to reach out to them. With our apostolate, we can help others to realise that Jesus has given His Life for each one of them. No one can be left behind. We are apostles and there are many souls to save. One of the reasons why we offer more sacrifices during Lent is precisely to pray that many sinners receive the grace of conversion.

In the apparitions at Fatima in 1917, Our Lady insisted, "*Men must amend their lives, and ask pardon for their sins... They must no longer offend Our Lord, Who is already so much offended.*" Lucia wrote: "*What has remained most deeply imprinted on my heart is the prayer of our heavenly Mother begging us not to offend Almighty God any more, Who is already so much offended.*" But for people to amend their lives, Our Lady asked the three children, "*Pray, pray very much and make a sacrifice for sinners, because many souls are going to hell because no one offers sacrifices for them.*" The three children started to look for ways to mortify themselves. One day Lucia found a rough rope that irritated her skin and suggested it be cut into three pieces so each of them could wear it continuously around their waists. Pleasing as it was to God, Our Lady had to ask them not to use the rope at night, for they couldn't sleep. They also gave their lunches to poor children they met along the way, or would spend all the daylight hours without drinking a single drop of water. The three children were aged 10, 9 and 7!

If those little children could please God with their sacrifices, what about me? Mary, my Mother, would you help me this Lent to be generous in my sacrifices? In that way, like the children of Fatima, I can have a big impact on the conversion of souls.

Sixth Sunday of St Joseph
First Sunday of Lent
Sunday 9th March
Lk 4:1-13

Jesus, full of the Holy Spirit, returned from the Jordan, and was led by the Spirit for forty days in the wilderness, tempted by the devil. And he ate nothing in those days; and when they were ended, he was hungry. The devil said to him, "If you are the Son of God, command this stone to become bread." And Jesus answered him, "It is written, 'Man shall not live by bread alone.'"...And when the devil had ended every temptation, he departed from him until an opportune time.

The Spirit drove Jesus out into the wilderness. That doesn't mean that Jesus was 'forced'. The Holy Spirit 'drives' us in the right direction, always counting on our freedom. The Holy Spirit is like a Satellite Navigation System giving directions to reach our destination. It doesn't 'drive' the car for you. That's the way the 'promptings' of the Holy Spirit work. Instead of clashing with our will, they strengthen it - reinforcing our freedom.

Did Jesus choose to be tempted by Satan in the desert? In a way, we could say that the Holy Spirit suggested the idea and Jesus liked it and implemented it. His freedom was necessary. And the same applies to us: our freedom is a very expensive gift (it cost Jesus all His Blood) and we have no right to neglect its use. Without freedom nothing that we do has any value. Indeed, even *love* is impossible if it is not *free*. We can only love God because we want to.

A mother was having problems during the pregnancy of her eighth child. Every day the whole family would pray and offer sacrifices for mum and the baby. The eldest boy was in charge of bathing his younger siblings and putting them to bed. Each night mum was surprised to hear the laughter and shouting in the bathroom. One day, on kissing her three-year-old son before he went to bed, she noticed he was freezing and asked what was going on. He explained that, each night, like soldiers in formation, they all stood up in the bathtub; then the eldest brother shouted, "*Shower WITH or WITHOUT sacrifice?*" They all replied in unison: "*With sacrifice!*" And then he proceeded to drench them all with cold water. Mum ended the ritual that very day. This is certainly not the way the Holy Spirit 'drives' us to offer up sacrifices. He has more respect for our freedom. Mary, Spouse of the Holy Spirit, help me to be generous in my response to the promptings of the Paraclete.

Monday 10th March
Mt 25:31-46

"Before the Son of man will be gathered all the nations, and he will separate them one from another as a shepherd separates the sheep from the goats, and he will place the sheep at his right hand, but the goats at the left. Then the King will say to those at his right hand, 'Come, O blessed of my Father, inherit the kingdom prepared for you from the foundation of the world; for I was hungry and you gave me food, I was thirsty and you gave me drink, I was a stranger and you welcomed me, I was naked and you clothed me, I was sick and you visited me, I was in prison and you came to me...Truly, I say to you, as you did it to one of the least of these my brethren, you did it to me.'"

Lent is a time for charity. And charity is something we should pray about. When you talk to Jesus about your family members, your friends... you discover things that you can do for them. If we don't pray for them, we spend our lives missing opportunities to practise charity with people that need us. I can imagine You, Lord, smiling when You told your followers about the Last Day, thinking of the millions of billions of acts of charity that people would do for Your sake until the end of time.

One day St Teresa of Calcutta was interviewed for a TV programme. Before the interview, as an introduction, they recorded her performing various tasks; among others, caring for some lepers. The wounds left by leprosy can be very repulsive in the final stages. But St Teresa was washing each leper with the same affection that a mother uses with her baby. The reporter, unable to restrain her repugnance, said aloud, "*I wouldn't do that for a million dollars!*" St Teresa looked at her peacefully and answered, "*Neither would I!*"

Because she didn't do that for any other reason than for Christ. She knew that every time she did something for a sick person, she was doing it *to* Christ because she was doing it *for* Christ.

Jesus: I imagine Your look and the expression on Your face when I meet You at the end of my life and You see all that I did for others. Then You will smile at me and Your lovely Voice will say, in front of all the Angels and my Mother, "**Come, O blessed of my Father...**"

Holy Mary, our Hope, Help of Christians, pray for us that we may grow in charity during this Lent.

Tuesday 11th March
Mt 6:7-15

"And in praying do not heap up empty phrases as the Gentiles do; for they think that they will be heard for their many words. Do not be like them, for your Father knows what you need before you ask him. Pray then like this: Our Father who art in heaven, Hallowed be thy name. Thy kingdom come. Thy will be done, On earth as it is in heaven. Give us this day our daily bread; And forgive us our debts, As we also have forgiven our debtors; And lead us not into temptation, But deliver us from evil. For if you forgive men their trespasses, your heavenly Father also will forgive you; but if you do not forgive men their trespasses, neither will your Father forgive your trespasses."

Today's Gospel reminds us that prayer is one of the legs of Lent, along with sacrifice and charity. During Lent we are offering sacrifices for the conversion of sinners. We are charitable towards others as we considered yesterday, because everything that we do for them we do for Our Lord. Now we do the same when we pray. Jesus told us to say, *Our* Father, and not simply *Father*; and in the four last petitions we say, "give *us*" ... "forgive *us*" ... "lead *us* not" ... "deliver *us*". For God loves it when we are united in prayer, when we pray together and we pray for each other as a family.

During Lent you can go slowly over the Lord's Prayer, the Our Father. In her autobiography, St Thérèse of Lisieux says "*Sometimes when I am in such a state of spiritual dryness that not a single good thought occurs to me, I say very slowly the 'Our Father,' or the 'Hail Mary,' and these prayers suffice to take me out of myself, and wonderfully refresh me.*" Let's ask ourselves: how many times do I pray these prayers every day, and how many times do I not pay attention to what I am saying? Pray the Lord's Prayer today with St Thérèse, slowly, to get the most out of it, rather than rattling it off on auto-pilot, as we all do sometimes!

"*Slowly,*" St Josemaría wrote, "*Consider what you are saying, who is saying it and to whom. For that hurried talk, without time for reflection, is just noise, the clatter of tin cans. And with Saint Teresa, I will tell you that, however much you work your lips, I do not call it prayer.*"

Mary, my Mother, help me to be focused in my prayers so that I can follow St Josemaría's advice.

Wednesday 12th March
Lk 11:29-32

When the crowds were increasing, he began to say, "This generation is an evil generation; it seeks a sign, but no sign shall be given to it except the sign of Jonah. For as Jonah became a sign to the men of Nineveh, so will the Son of man be to this generation...The men of Nineveh will arise at the judgment with this generation and condemn it; for they repented at the preaching of Jonah, and behold, something greater than Jonah is here."

God needed someone to preach in Nineveh, and decided that Jonah was 'the man for the job'. But you know the story, don't you? The instructions were simple: *set out for the great city of Nineveh and preach against it.* As a matter of fact, the Ninevites were an idolatrous, proud, and ruthless people who had long been a threat to Israel. So Jonah, being an Israelite, decided to put as much distance as he could between himself and them. Whatever happened to Nineveh, Jonah would not be there to see it. So he *fled in the opposite direction*; he got on a boat to go to Tarshish. 'God has His plans,' Jonah may have thought: *'but I have mine!'*

God loves us; He created us and knows what we can do. We can be certain that He will never ask you for 'more' than you can give... But He will never ask you for 'less'. Because it is not just about you. It's about the many souls who depend on you. Nineveh could have been condemned if God had not gone after Jonah to '*convince*' him (in a very persuasive way) that the people of Nineveh needed him. When Jonah eventually complied and did what God had asked for, the result was impressive: the people of Nineveh converted and turned to God.

What would have become of those thousands of people if Jonah had not gone back? What will become of your relatives and friends who may be far from God if you do not do anything to help them?

There are many souls who depend on my generosity in following my vocation; souls who will not hear about God's Love for them if I don't tell them; souls whose salvation depends greatly on me. Mary, Refuge of sinners, I beg your assistance to help those souls and, if ever I run away from those who need me, please come and *fetch me!*

Thursday 1st week of Lent
Thursday 13th March
Mt 7:7-12

"Ask, and it will be given you; seek, and you will find; knock, and it will be opened to you. For every one who asks receives, and he who seeks finds, and to him who knocks it will be opened. Or what man of you, if his son asks him for bread, will give him a stone? Or if he asks for a fish, will give him a serpent? If you then, who are evil, know how to give good gifts to your children, how much more will your Father who is in heaven give good things to those who ask him!"

Everyone who asks receives. Everyone means *everyone*. And in order to explain it, Our Lord cites the example of a good father who gives his children what they need. If fathers do that on earth, Jesus teaches, **how much more** *will your Father God give good things to those who ask Him*! Have you ever prayed slowly about those words: "*how much more*"?

But sometimes we ask God for things and either nothing changes or the situation gets worse! True. What happens to us sometimes is what *Coldplay* explain in the song 'Fix You': "*When you try your best but you don't succeed. When you get what you want but not what you need.*" Sometimes people get what they want... but not what they need. God, as the best of fathers, gives His children what they need; not what they want. That's His way of 'fixing you' from the effects of original sin and when everything goes wrong.

Remember when your mum wouldn't give you fizzy drinks before bed or sweets before lunch? Because she loved you, she didn't give you what you wanted, but rather what was best for you. God is not a 'vending machine' in which you *insert* prayers to get what you fancy. God is not even a 'grandad' who could be easily convinced to give you what you wanted. He's a Father Who loves, and therefore He only gives the best. So, our best prayer is to ask: *Your Will be done*, for that is the best for me, always.

That's what we need to keep asking for: '*Lord, I want the best. I want what you want.*' Holy Mary, my good Mother, help me to have always on my lips your words to St Gabriel: "*Be it done unto me according to thy word*", because asking for what God has in store for me is asking for the best!

Friday 1st week of Lent
Friday 14th March
Mt 5:20-26

"You have heard that it was said to the men of old, 'You shall not kill; and whoever kills shall be liable to judgment.' Everyone who is angry with his brother shall be liable to judgment; whoever insults his brother shall be liable to the council, and whoever says, 'You fool!' shall be liable to the hell of fire. So if you are offering your gift at the altar, and there remember that your brother has something against you, leave your gift there before the altar and go; first be reconciled to your brother, and then come and offer your gift."

Few things wound the heart of a father more than seeing that his children don't love one another. And few sins wound the Divine Heart of our Father God more than bitterness between His children. During Lent we try to grow in charity, which is always the most important virtue. So much so, that Jesus warns us, '*if ever you come to offer anything to Me,*' make sure that you are at peace with my other children first. If you aren't, then "*leave your gift there before the altar and go*", for I will not accept your offering until you are "*reconciled to your brother.*"

Some people think that only Cain, with his blood-stained hands, would be forbidden to offer up other sacrifices. But there are so many ways to harm others! Indifference, scorn, insensitivity, laughing at others' mistakes, indiscretion, rudeness, ingratitude, sarcasm, irony, gossip, bearing grudges, impatience, and so many other names for selfishness...

During Lent there are lots of suitable sacrifices to offer up, but remember: over and above any sacrifice… Charity! It would be useless to give up chocolate and be angry all the time, talking back to everyone. 'Keep eating chocolate, please', your friends will advise you, 'and leave us alone!' What's the point of fasting in Lent if you become insufferable at home? 'Stop fasting, please', your family will tell you, 'we can't cope with *your* fasting!' So first of all, choose sacrifices that those around you would like.

Ask Our Lord for help to always be charitable towards everyone, so that, at any time of our life, we're ready to stand before His altar.

Holy Mary, Mother of Mercy, help me grow in the virtue of charity!

Saturday 1st week of Lent
Saturday 15th March
Mt 5:43-48

"I say to you, Love your enemies and pray for those who persecute you, so that you may be sons of your Father who is in heaven; for he makes his sun rise on the evil and on the good, and sends rain on the just and on the unjust. For if you love those who love you, what reward have you? Do not even the tax collectors do the same?...You, therefore, must be perfect, as your heavenly Father is perfect"

To hold a grudge is like building a prison and locking oneself inside. We have to ask Jesus for the gift of being able to love everyone, no matter what they do or think or say. That is to be like our *heavenly Father*: Perfect in Love. St John of the Cross has given us a great piece of advice: *"Where there is no love, put love - and you will draw out love."*

"If you love those who love you, what reward have you?" That is very *easy*! But to love those who despise you, who scorn you, who insult you... That is very *'virtuous'*! In 1993 Cardinal Joseph Bernardin was falsely accused by a young fellow of improper conduct. The story was spun by the media and a big campaign flared up against him. He confessed later that his internal suffering during that time would hardly be endurable were it not for his faith and knowledge of his innocence. After three months of ordeal and media persecution, his accuser admitted that the accusation was false. Soon after, Stephen (the accuser) was dying from AIDS in a hospital bed. Cardinal Bernardin went to visit him. The poor man apologised for the wrongs he had committed against the Cardinal. Bernardin forgave him immediately and with affection, becoming concerned only with Stephen's spiritual health and making sure that he could prepare himself properly for his death.

This has been the example of the saints. As soon as he managed, St John Paul II went to visit Ali Agca, the man who shot him. There, in his prison, Ali Agca was forgiven and ended up kissing the hand of the Pope he had tried to kill just a few weeks before.

Mary, Mother of Mercy, help me to forgive *everyone... everything... always...* and to bring to your Son in my prayer those who offend me in any way.

Seventh Sunday of St Joseph
Second Sunday of Lent
Sunday 16th March
Lk 9:28b-36

Jesus took with him Peter and John and James, and went up on the mountain to pray. And as he was praying, the appearance of his countenance was altered, and his raiment became dazzling white. And behold, two men talked with him, Moses and Elijah... Peter said to Jesus, "Master, it is well that we are here; let us make three booths, one for you and one for Moses and one for Elijah"—not knowing what he said. As he said this, a cloud came and overshadowed them; and they were afraid as they entered the cloud. And a voice came out of the cloud, saying, "This is my Son, my Chosen; listen to him!" And when the voice had spoken, Jesus was found alone. And they kept silence and told no one in those days anything of what they had seen.

How good it is to be with You, Lord; and to be able to talk to You as Elijah and Moses did, face-to-face! And we still listen to the echoes of the Voice of the Father giving us a commandment: **listen to him!** How I would love to listen to You, Lord, as Moses did, as Elijah, and Peter and James and John...! And to Peter, who *did not know what to say* we can reply, "*Say nothing! It is time to keep silent and contemplate.*" Silence is an important part of our prayer. Because if we talk, we don't listen. And prayer is a dialogue, not a speech.

Some people panic when there is silence. Like the boy who reluctantly accompanied his parents to a concert of classical music. In the middle of a symphony there were three (just three!) seconds of silence broken by the voice of the boy shouting, "*Now... what?! I can't hear anything!*" No one had explained to him that silence is an important part of music.

In the presence of Our Lord in the Eucharist, silence is necessary. To contemplate Him, silent and remain silent ourselves, looking at Him as Peter did on that day. Don't panic if you spend a few minutes in silence. "*We need to find God, and God cannot be found in noise and restlessness. God is the friend of silence*" taught St Teresa of Calcutta. Mary, my Mother, teach me to keep silent in the presence of your Son, Jesus, in the Tabernacle, as you did in Bethlehem, in Nazareth many times, and specially beside the Cross.

Monday 2nd week of Lent
Monday 17th March
Lk 6:36-38

Be merciful, even as your Father is merciful. "Judge not, and you will not be judged; condemn not, and you will not be condemned; forgive, and you will be forgiven; give, and it will be given to you; good measure, pressed down, shaken together, running over, will be put into your lap. For the measure you give will be the measure you get back."

Have you heard the story of the teacher in the college for 'Older Students'? This man loved asking questions about the things he had explained before in order to keep his students attentive in his lessons. "*Let's see, you...the fellow in the corner,*" the teacher said. "*When was Rome destroyed by fire?*" "*To be honest...*" the unfortunate 'student' replied, taken by surprise, "*I...don't remember.*" "*Very well, then,*" the teacher insisted, "*do you remember when Vesuvius wiped Pompeii off the map?*" The man, visibly embarrassed, answered, "*No idea, really.*" "*This is quite disappointing,*" the annoyed teacher complained. "*What about the destruction of Jerusalem?*" "*My mind is a blank right now,*" the poor man said. "*May I know,*" the teacher asked in anger, "*why did you come to my class?*" The man produced a bulb from his pocket and replied shyly, "*To change this bulb...I'm the caretaker.*"

"*Judge not, and you will not be judged*"; since we never know everything about others, we are not in a position to judge anyone. You know the saying, 'Before you judge a man, walk a mile in his shoes.' The truth is that walking a mile in someone else's shoes can give you an idea of what they feel. But even after a mile, you don't know anyone well enough to judge them. You should walk more than a mile, in his shoes, along the paths he walks, in the same weather, at the same time, in same company, stepping on the same footprints... yet still that wouldn't be enough; you should walk not just in his shoes but in his feet. Of course, that is impossible. That is why it is unwise to judge anyone, since our judgements are always flawed, unless you are either him - or God. God has given us a conscience to judge ourselves. No one can know better than myself when I haven't been generous with God (except God).

Mary, my Mother, if you teach me to love everyone, I will always understand and help them to be holy, instead of wasting time and humility trying to judge them.

St Patrick, bishop
Monday 17th March
Mt 13:24-32

Another parable Jesus put before them, saying, "The kingdom of heaven is like a grain of mustard seed which a man took and sowed in his field; it is the smallest of all seeds, but when it has grown it is the greatest of shrubs and becomes a tree, so that the birds of the air come and make nests in its branches."

After the Ascension of Our Lord, the Apostles went all over the world sowing the seed of faith. And when the Apostles had gone to Heaven, God appointed new apostles who would go and propagate the seed. Using them as faithful instruments, God could reach "*the ends of the world*," just as He promised.

St Patrick was one of those apostles. Born in Roman Britain, when he was about fourteen he was captured by Irish pirates and taken to Ireland as a slave to herd and tend sheep. There, in captivity, God started training his apostle. "*The love of God and his fear grew in me more and more, as did the faith,*" he wrote in his memoirs. "*My soul was rosed, so that, in a single day, I have said as many as a hundred prayers and in the night, nearly the same. I prayed in the woods and on the mountain.*" His captivity lasted until he was twenty, when he escaped back to Britain.

Patrick had a vision a few years after returning home: a man bringing him a letter headed 'The Voice of the Irish.' "*I imagined in that moment that I heard the voice of those very people,*" he wrote years later. "*They cried out, as with one voice: 'We appeal to you...to come and walk among us.'*" And so he did. He was ordained bishop and sent to spread the Gospel's seed to Ireland.

Patrick preached in Ireland for 40 years, living in poverty, travelling and enduring much suffering until he died on March 17, 461. "The Breastplate," St Patrick's poem, can help us pray today: "*Christ be within me, Christ behind me, Christ before me, Christ beside me, Christ to win me, Christ to comfort and restore me, Christ beneath me, Christ above me, Christ inquired, Christ in danger, Christ in hearts of all that love me, Christ in mouth of friend and stranger.*" Mary, Queen of the Apostles, may we never lack sowers of the Gospel.

Tuesday 2nd week of Lent
Tuesday 18th March
Mt 23:1-12

Then Jesus said to the crowds and to his disciples, "The scribes and the Pharisees sit on Moses' seat; so practice and observe whatever they tell you, but not what they do; for they preach, but do not practice...They do all their deeds to be seen by men...He who is greatest among you shall be your servant; whoever exalts himself will be humbled, and whoever humbles himself will be exalted."

Humility is indispensable for following Christ. The best example of humility is Jesus Himself: being God, He became Man for us; and later, He became a Host of Bread. Who could ever humble himself so much? The second best example of humility is His Mother: being the most perfect creature, she recognised that all the good in her was a gift from God. The third example of humility is St Joseph: being a man gifted beyond comparison, he never let himself become the centre of attention. Saints are humble souls who know how to remain in the background and let people see God instead.

The problem with the scribes and Pharisees was that they loved to be seen, recognised and praised for all their deeds and talents. They wanted to be the centre of attention. A Spanish saying describes this kind of person well: '*They want to be the bride at all the weddings, the baby at all the baptisms and the dead at all the funerals.*'

Holiness is just the opposite: you see? *Holiness and humility are proportionate.* In the words of St Josemaría, the passion of the saints is "*to hide and disappear. That only Jesus could be seen.*" In the lifetime of the Holy Curé of Ars, St John Mary Vianney, people came from distant places to listen to his homilies. He did everything in his parish (Ars had about 350 inhabitants), which he very seldom left.. He could be found in the confessional most of the time (16 hours a day!) Elsewhere in France at the same time there was another famous preacher who attracted many people with his brilliant sermons. One day someone asked this preacher which of them was the *better preacher*. "*Most certainly he is,*" answered the man, "*for when people listen to my homilies they say: 'How good this preacher is!', but when they listen to Vianney they say: 'How good God is!'.*"

Mary, my Mother, help me to learn from you the virtue of humility, "*to hide and disappear, so that only Jesus might shine*" (St Josemaría).

St Joseph, Spouse of Mary
Wednesday 19th March
Lk 2:41-51

After three days they found him in the temple, sitting among the teachers, listening to them and asking them questions...and his mother said to him, "Son, why have you treated us so? Behold, your father and I have been looking for you anxiously." And he said to them, "How is it that you sought me? Did you not know that I must be in my Father's house?" And they did not understand the saying which he spoke to them. And he went down with them and came to Nazareth, and was obedient to them.

The most wonderful Treasures of God (Jesus and Mary) could not be entrusted to anyone other than St Joseph. No one, ever, has been trusted more and so, no one ever has been given more. St Joseph is compared to the other Patriarch, Joseph, the son of Jacob. Sold by his brothers, he ended up a slave in Egypt. But God was with him and eventually he was entrusted with all of Pharaoh's fortune. So when the famine came and people started asking Pharaoh for help, he just told them: *Ite ad Joseph!* (Go to Joseph!)

If you want to find Jesus, go to Joseph – he found Him after three sorrowful days; if you want to love Jesus, go to Joseph – he loves Him madly; if you want to love Mary, go to Joseph – no man has ever loved his wife like him; if you want to be always close to Jesus and Mary, go to Joseph – no one has ever been closer to them; if you want to pray, go to Joseph – he spent his life in dialogue with God; if you go through difficulties, go to Joseph – he knows all about suffering. If you want to be strong, he is the saint to go to; if you want to be obedient, chaste, generous, humble, joyful, sincere... if you want to be holy: *Ite ad Joseph!* Go to Joseph.

If you want to be in love with God, to work with God, to live with God, to stay always with God, to dream God's dreams, to serve God and spend your eternity with Him... *Ite ad Joseph!*... Go to Joseph. God entrusted him with His Family, he is in charge of the house of God; he will open for us the door of Bethlehem, of Nazareth and of Heaven if we go to him. He protected God and His Immaculate Mother... he can protect you as well if you want. Holy Mary, Spouse of Joseph, remind me to go to him, for it would be foolish of me not to count on him in my struggle!

Thursday 2nd week of Lent
Thursday 20th March
Lk 16:19-31

"There was a rich man, who was clothed in purple and fine linen and who feasted sumptuously every day. And at his gate lay a poor man named Lazarus, full of sores, who desired to be fed with what fell from the rich man's table; moreover the dogs came and licked his sores. The poor man died and was carried by the angels to Abraham's bosom. The rich man also died and was buried; and in Hades, being in torment, he lifted up his eyes, and saw Abraham far off and Lazarus in his bosom. And he called out, 'Father Abraham, have mercy upon me, and send Lazarus to dip the end of his finger in water and cool my tongue; for I am in anguish in this flame.' But Abraham said, 'Son, remember that you in your lifetime received your good things, and Lazarus in like manner evil things; but now he is comforted here, and you are in anguish...And he said, 'Then I beg you, father, to send him to my father's house, for I have five brothers, so that he may warn them, lest they also come into this place of torment.' But Abraham said, 'They have Moses and the prophets; let them hear them.' And he said, 'No, father Abraham; but if someone goes to them from the dead, they will repent.' He said to him, 'If they do not hear Moses and the prophets, neither will they be convinced if someone should rise from the dead'."

This well-known parable of Our Lord brings to our prayer today the importance of omissions. This rich man didn't fall into Hades (Hell) because he used to scorn Lazarus or because he became rich taking advantage of the poor or because he kicked the poor out of his property. We can imagine the rich man at the Last Judgment, being told that he can't enter Heaven. He would protest, saying *'But why? What did I do? I didn't do anything!'* And we imagine God's devastating answer: *'Precisely!'*

St Josemaría used to say that Hell is paved with sins of omission. Often we don't commit these sins because *we decide not to help*. Usually it is because we *didn't notice* that they needed our help, material or otherwise: time, encouragement, comfort, appreciation, understanding, a smile... Every day people need our help. How many times we can miss opportunities to help others if we are not attentive! We then become like the rich man in the parable: he never saw the needs of Lazarus at his door – he was too busy thinking about himself. Holy Mary, our Hope, Handmaid of the Lord, pray for us that we may learn to see the needs of others and help them.

Friday 2nd week of Lent
Friday 21st March
Mt 21:33-43, 45-46

"There was a householder who planted a vineyard, and set a hedge around it, and dug a wine press in it, and built a tower, and let it out to tenants, and went into another country. When the season of fruit drew near, he sent his servants to the tenants, to get his fruit; and the tenants took his servants and beat one, killed another, and stoned another. Again he sent other servants, more than the first; and they did the same to them. Afterward he sent his son to them, saying, 'They will respect my son.' But when the tenants saw the son, they said to themselves, 'This is the heir; come, let us kill him and have his inheritance.' And they took him and cast him out of the vineyard, and killed him."

This is called '*breach of contract*'. When God gave them the vineyard, He gave them a mission: to produce grapes. Vineyard and mission came together. The tenants liked the vineyard; it was kitted out with everything they needed to produce fruit. But they rejected their mission. So they decided to keep the vineyard and its fruit for themselves. They didn't want to obey. They preferred to be their own masters, 'appropriating' something that wasn't theirs. The same can happen in our lives. God has given us everything we need to bear fruit. He has given us our lives, our family, our talents, our formation... and our mission. But some love all that so much that instead of being grateful for it, they decide to keep it for themselves: '*It's my life!*', they say, '*I do with it what I like.*' And they guard it jealously, taking hold of it as a child grasps his ice cream and licks it slowly with a look that says, '*It's mine; only mine!*'

But we know that it is not. Life, and all it brings with it, is given by God. We are tenants and have to render fruit. We have been given life, family, friends, talents, formation... but also a mission! That was the problem of the rich young man (Mk 10:17-31), do you remember him? "*He went away sorrowful*" (v. 22) says the Gospel. He kept his possessions - but lost his joy, his enthusiasm, his mission, his Lord...

"Cast yourself with confidence into the arms of God," recommends St Phillip Neri, *"and be very sure of this, that if he wants anything of you he will fit you for your work and give you strength to do it."*

Saturday 2nd week of Lent
Saturday 22nd March
Lk 15:1-3, 11-32

"There was a man who had two sons; and the younger of them said to his father, 'Father, give me the share of property that falls to me.' And he divided his living between them. Not many days later, the younger son gathered all he had and took his journey into a far country, and there he squandered his property in loose living. And when he had spent everything, a great famine arose in that country, and he began to be in want. So he went and joined himself to one of the citizens of that country, who sent him into his fields to feed swine ... But when he came to himself he said, 'How many of my father's hired servants have bread enough and to spare, but I perish here with hunger! I will arise and go to my father, and I will say to him, "Father, I have sinned against heaven and before you; I am no longer worthy to be called your son; treat me as one of your hired servants."' And he arose and came to his father. But while he was yet at a distance, his father saw him and had compassion, and ran and embraced him and kissed him..."

There is common agreement that this is one of the most beautiful parables told by Our Lord. Because not all of us are always moved by seed, darnel, fish, leaven, fig trees, good soil or lost sheep... But all of us are moved by this father, all of us have been at times - and still are - prodigal sons. Are you not moved by the last line of today's Gospel quote?

Jacques Fesch (1930 – 1957) was a young French lad who gave up a position at his father's bank and left his wife and their daughter to live the life of a playboy. Disillusioned with his life, he decided to rob a money changer of his gold coins. During the escape he killed a police officer; he was arrested and condemned to death by guillotine. At first Fesch was indifferent and mocked his lawyer's Catholic faith. However, after a year in prison he experienced a profound conversion and bitterly regretted his crime. He asked for forgiveness and started to pray, attend Mass and go regularly to Confession as well as help his mates get close to God. He kept a spiritual journal. His last journal entry was *"In five hours, I will see Jesus!"* When his journal was published after his death he became an inspiration to many. His process of beatification is now open. He was an example of repentance and redemption. It's never too late to come back to God! Holy Mary, our Hope, Refuge of sinners, pray for us who are so much in need of conversion.

Third Sunday of Lent
Sunday 23rd March
Lk 13:1-9

There were some present at that very time who told him of the Galileans whose blood Pilate had mingled with their sacrifices. And he answered them, "Do you think that these Galileans were worse sinners than all the other Galileans, because they suffered thus? I tell you, No; but unless you repent you will all likewise perish."

When a priest suggested that a certain man go to confession, he replied that he had no sins because "*he hadn't killed anyone.*" "*My friend,*" answered the priest, "*it is not only murderers who should go to confession. There are also those who are liars and gossipers, people who are lustful, lazy, vain, proud, ill-tempered, gluttonous, imprudent, dishonest, uncharitable...*" "*Stop it! Father, stop it!,*" interrupted the man: "*Bless me father for I have sinned...*"

Everyone has sins and so everyone needs repentance. Another priest came across a parishioner in the street and reminded him that he should go to confession 'from time to time.' The man answered, "*But I don't have any sins, father.*" "*There are two kinds of people who have no sins,*" answered the priest, "*Children and madmen. Which one are you?*" The first step to conversion is recognising our own sins. God, in His Mercy, is always ready to forgive our sins, but He needs to find in us a repentant heart. As St Augustine put it, "*You accuse yourself: God excuses you. You excuse yourself: God accuses you.*" But it is hard to admit our mistakes in front of another person, even if that person is a priest behind a grille.

Prussian king Frederick the Great was once touring a Berlin prison. One after another, when he asked inmates the reason for their imprisonment, they fell on their knees proclaiming their innocence: 'There is a mistake', 'I am innocent', 'I didn't do what they said...' Suddenly, at the question of the king, "*Why are you here?*", a prisoner replied, "*Armed robbery.*" Surprised, the king asked, "*Are you guilty?*" "*Yes indeed, I deserve my punishment,*" said the man. The king then summoned the jailer and ordered him, "*Release this guilty wretch at once. Otherwise he will corrupt all the fine innocent people who live in this prison.*" Holy Mary, Refuge of Sinners, intercede for me so that I find the courage to recognise my guilt.

Monday 3rd week of Lent
Monday 24th March
Lk 4:24-30

Jesus said to them, "Truly, I say to you, no prophet is acceptable in his own country...there were many lepers in Israel in the time of the prophet Elisha; and none of them was cleansed, but only Naaman the Syrian." When they heard this, all in the synagogue were filled with wrath. And they rose up and put him out of the city, and led him to the brow of the hill on which their city was built, that they might throw him down headlong. But passing through the midst of them he went away.

Many fellow Nazarenes didn't believe Jesus to be a prophet. 'Because if You *were* a prophet', they might say, 'we would know'. In other words these people were saying something like: 'We decide who is and who isn't a prophet here'.

Imagine the '*Poets' Society of Stratford-upon-Avon*' suing Shakespeare for publishing his work without their approval: it would have been ridiculous! The people of Nazareth were about to throw Jesus off the cliff just because He was chosen by God without *their* permission. Perhaps they told Jesus: 'Listen, it is fine if You perform miracles here... we love that stuff... but do not try to lecture us, because we know You are the Son of Joseph, the artisan'.

But Jesus' attitude here is remarkable. He didn't waste a second trying to argue or convince them. Their problem wasn't a lack of faith but an excess of pride. There is a classic Greek saying that reads: "*The worst deaf person is the one who doesn't want to hear.*" Until they get rid of their pride they will never receive the supernatural virtue of Faith.

Charles de Foucauld was a young rich playboy who had done whatever he wanted throughout his whole life. He even had a lover he didn't intend to marry. One day he met a priest, Fr. Huvelin, and asked him to explain the Catholic Faith to him. The priest, instead of explaining anything, "*made me kneel down,*" wrote Foucauld, "*made me go to Confession, and sent me to Communion right away.*" St Charles de Foucauld, as he is known now, could then understand the Faith. Without grace, how difficult it is to be humble; without humility, how difficult it is to know the truth! Let's ask Our Lady for the grace that many may come to the Truth in this Season of Lent.

The Annunciation of Our Lord
Tuesday 25th March
Lk 1:26-38

The angel said, "Hail, full of grace, the Lord is with you!" But she was greatly troubled at the saying, and considered in her mind what sort of greeting this might be. And the angel said to her, "Do not be afraid, Mary, for you have found favour with God. And behold, you will conceive in your womb and bear a son, and you shall call his name Jesus".

Today we celebrate the Annunciation, which is also the Incarnation: God becoming a human being, like you and me. He was already in the world nine months before Christmas but only Mary and St Joseph knew it. Jesus was not in a hurry, you see? He didn't have to spend all those months in Mary's womb but He wanted to. Jesus didn't want to be an exception. Today is a good day to pray for all those children who are still in their mothers' wombs, called to be the saints of the 21st century with you and me.

St Gabriel announced to Mary the Name of her Son, **Jesus**; that Name which was going to be pronounced billions of times and which we try to keep on our lips frequently every day. A Name that is often associated with that other name, 'Mary', in the lovely prayer that the Angel taught us. Every time we say the *Hail Mary* we remind Our Lady of the happiest moments of her existence. She always listens to her children through this prayer.

A priest was asked by a hospital sister to visit a patient in Ward 3. On entering he found the man dying, surprised to see the priest since he hadn't received the Sacraments for many years. "*Nevertheless,*" he explained to the priest, "*I have always kept up a promise I made to my mum on her deathbed: to pray three Hail Marys every night.*" After a long conversation, the man made his Confession and received the Eucharist with great devotion. Leaving the Ward, the priest met the sister and found that he had been in Ward 4, and patient number 7 in Ward 3 was still waiting for him! This was soon put right, but the priest felt thankful for the mistake. He felt still more thankful when the following day he found out that the man in Ward 4 had died suddenly that night. The man had kept his promise... and Our Lady kept hers! *Holy Mary, Mother of God, pray for us, sinners, now and at the hour of our death.*

Wednesday 26th March
Mt 5:17-19

"Think not that I have come to abolish the law and the prophets; I have come not to abolish them but to fulfil them. For truly, I say to you, till heaven and earth pass away, not an iota, not a dot, will pass from the law until all is accomplished. Whoever then relaxes one of the least of these commandments and teaches men so, shall be called least in the kingdom of heaven; but he who does them and teaches them shall be called great in the kingdom of heaven."

How easy it is to water down the Gospel and make it a bit *less demanding*! How easy it would be to get disciples if you only taught the nice bits of the Gospel and took out any reference to the Cross or the demands of becoming a real disciple of Jesus! But the Gospel is the Word of God: the *whole* Gospel, and no one has the right to change so much as one letter of it.

An African bishop returned to his home town – which was mostly non-Christian – soon after ordination. In the welcome speech, the people expressed how happy they were that *one of them* now had 'direct access' to God. Then they promised him they would all embrace Christianity if he would use his episcopal power to suppress one of the Ten Commandments for them. Before they could say which of the Commandments they had in mind, the young bishop shocked them by explaining that the Commandments are from God and, therefore, unchangeable. The celebratory mood turned into disappointment and the bishop had to make a hasty departure from his own people.

People may ask for a reduction of their moral responsibilities as they ask for a reduction of taxes. It would be like someone who wants to change doctor because the physician has put him on a diet. He could think that tablets would certainly be easier to take... Taking medicine can be less demanding than following a diet, but tablets aren't what that patient needs.

Imagine that a government wanted to change the law of gravity for its country because the one 'still in use' is old fashioned or doesn't take into account our 'national identity'. Well, he can try, but he definitely cannot change the Law of God. Mary, Mother of Justice, help me to love God's Law and fulfil His Commandments to the full.

Thursday 27th March
Lk 11:14-23

Some people said, "He casts out demons by Beelzebul, the prince of demons"... But Jesus said to them, "Every kingdom divided against itself is laid waste, and a divided household falls. And if Satan also is divided against himself, how will his kingdom stand?...When a strong man, fully armed, guards his own palace, his goods are in peace; but when one stronger than he assails him and overcomes him, he takes away his armour in which he trusted, and divides his spoil."

Evil is not an impersonal force that just happens. It has a name (actually it has many: 'Satan', 'Beelzebul, the prince of demons', 'the deceiver', 'the father of lies', 'Lucifer', 'the fallen angel') and it seeks to master every heart and soul through sin.

He who habitually gives in to temptation leaves the door of his soul unlocked and allows the devil to come in and 'make himself at home'. It is easy then for the enemy to defend himself from the inside; especially if he is fully armed as the devil always is. But we live with the conviction that Jesus is stronger: stronger than doors, locks, walls and windows, and stronger than the devil and his weapons. Let's repeat it often: *the devil has no chance against me if Jesus is with me!*

We need to go to Him in time of temptation and ask for help; otherwise we will have no chance. A Christian facing temptation who doesn't ask Jesus for help is like a gladiator in the arena, surrounded by ten hungry and angry lions, and armed... with a tea spoon! He has no chance. However, with the help of Jesus we are like the same gladiator but armed with a *tank*: the lions have no chance. Jesus, do not leave me alone when the enemy comes; and if I ever forget to ask you to help me, help me anyway!

Once St Faustina was suffering some dreadful temptations. She went to the Tabernacle and said: "*Do what You will with me, O Jesus.*" Suddenly she saw Our Lord saying to her: "***Fear nothing: I am always in your heart.***" If Jesus is there... the devil can't get in! Furthermore, beside Jesus we always find Our Mother, and she is the spouse of St Joseph, who will certainly be with her; she is also the Queen of Angels, so Angels are also there; and Queen of Martyrs, Patriarchs, Saints... the whole of Heaven is in your heart in Grace!

Friday 3rd week of Lent
Friday 28th March
Mk 12:28-34

One of the scribes asked him, "Which commandment is the first of all?" Jesus answered, "The first is, 'Hear, O Israel: The Lord our God, the Lord is one; and you shall love the Lord your God with all your heart, and with all your soul, and with all your mind, and with all your strength.' The second is this, 'You shall love your neighbour as yourself.' There is no other commandment greater than these."

The man asked for "the first" commandment, but Jesus answered quoting 'the first and the second'. There is a poem written by Leigh Hunt about a man called Abou Ben Adhem who woke from his sleep one night and saw an Angel writing the names of those who love God in a book. "*And is mine there?*" inquired Abou. "*Nay, not so,*" replied the Angel. "*I pray thee, then,*" said Abou, "*write me as one who loves his fellow men.*" The following night the Angel came again and displayed the names of those who love God and Abou's name topped the list, making the point that true love of God and true love of our neighbour are like two sides of the same coin.

But this charity has to be lived in practical ways. We need to take to our prayer the people who are around us and think of particular acts of charity that they would appreciate. Some are things that you 'can do'. Some are things that you 'shouldn't do'. It can help to write down a list of things that we can do for others and check it in our examination of conscience to see if we have loved our 'neighbour' with deeds.

In 1940 a train was taking some Jews to a concentration camp. A 15-year-old girl was travelling with her little brother who was 8. Separated from their parents, they were scared. Suddenly the girl realised that her brother had lost his shoes and burst out in anger, "*For goodness' sake! Couldn't you be responsible for once in your life and take care of your shoes?!*" Almost 80 years later she was telling the story in tears. She never saw her little brother again. Those were the last words she said to him. She made the resolution to never say anything that she would regret if they were to be the last words that someone would ever hear from her.

Mary, my Mother, help me to always be charitable in my words, to take care of *what* I say and *how* I say it...

Saturday 29th March
Lk 18:9-14

"Two men went up into the temple to pray, one a Pharisee and the other a tax collector. The Pharisee stood and prayed thus with himself, 'God, I thank thee that I am not like other men, extortioners, unjust, adulterers, or even like this tax collector. I fast twice a week, I give tithes of all that I get.' But the tax collector, standing far off, would not even lift up his eyes to heaven, but beat his breast, saying, 'God, be merciful to me a sinner!' I tell you, this man went down to his house justified rather than the other."

How ridiculous the prayer of the Pharisee is! He likes to compare himself with others to prove that he is good! How ridiculous it would be if we ever had the temptation to pray like this: *'Thank you, Lord, that I'm not like the others: I use the iPray every day, I go to Mass during the week, say my three Hail Marys and do the dishes on Tuesdays... but other people in my class, well, they lie, they cheat with their homework..., some of them do not even go to Mass on Sundays!'* We cannot compare because we are all different and only God fully knows the different circumstances of each person. Lent is a time for penance and atonement, a time to ask for forgiveness for our sins because we are all sinners.

The power of contrition... This Pharisee was doing lots of good things. He only quotes a few but there were many more. The tax collector did just one: repent. If we weigh up the hundreds of things that the Pharisee did on one side and the contrition of the sinner on the other, contrition wins. Because it's not about how much we do, but about how much we love. And contrition is real love!

A man went to Confession after a long life full of sins. With great contrition he said to the priest at the end: *"You see, father, how much filth and refuse in my life."* *"Indeed,"* replied the priest, *"but your filth and refuse makes a great manure to grow love!"*

We live in the recycling era. Lent is a good time to 'recycle' our sins and miseries with good acts of contrition.

Mother of God and my Mother, as I make many mistakes during the day, help me to make many acts of contrition, for they are real acts of love!

Fourth Sunday of Lent, Laetare Sunday
Sunday 30th March
Lk 15:1-3, 11-32

"His elder son was in the field; and as he came and drew near to the house, he heard music and dancing....But he was angry and refused to go in. His father came out and entreated him, but he answered his father, 'Lo, these many years I have served you, and I never disobeyed your command; yet you never gave me a kid, that I might make merry with my friends. But when this son of yours came, who has devoured your living with harlots, you killed for him the fatted calf!' And he said to him, 'Son, you are always with me, and all that is mine is yours.'"

We are familiar with parable of the 'Prodigal Sons'; yes, the two brothers. Sometimes we don't pay much attention to the bitter elder brother. He was living in his father's house, working, obeying, serving his father without 'ever disobeying his commands'... but he wasn't free. He was like a *slave* in his father's home. He was physically close to his father, living in the same home, but his heart was miles away.

This can remind us of Christians who comply with the commandments, but do not love God, their Father. Christians who have forgotten that we are God's children and not His slaves. Jesus shed all His Blood to pay our ransom and set us free. It was an expensive price and we have no right to be slaves anymore. God doesn't want us to comply; He wants us to love Him.

Social Services were short of staff in a particular city and they ran a campaign to attract volunteers. On a particular occasion a Social Service worker went accompanied by a young Christian volunteer to put an old woman to bed. *"You are too young for Social Services,"* the old lady said to the lad. *"I am a volunteer, madam,"* replied the boy. The granny was moved and, with tears in her eyes, she said, *"You do this because you want to?"* "No, madam," said the boy with a big smile, *"I do this because I love!"*

God needs good and loving children who fulfil His Will because they love Him. Then, only then, when there is freedom and love, we will be happy. *"Rejoice, Jerusalem! Be glad"* (Entrance Antiphon, *Laetare Sunday*.) Holy Mary, Cause of our Joy, teach me to be a loving child, to keep my Father God happy and to be, therefore, full of joy myself.

Monday 4th week of Lent
Monday 31st March
Jn 4:43-54

An official whose son was ill...went and begged him to come down and heal his son, for he was at the point of death. Jesus therefore said to him, "Unless you see signs and wonders you will not believe." The official said to him, "Sir, come down before my child dies." Jesus said to him, "Go; your son will live." The man believed the word that Jesus spoke to him and went his way. As he was going down, his servants met him and told him that his son was living.

It is true that many people loved to see Your signs, Lord: they were spectacular! Blind people started to see, deaf people recovered their hearing, paralytics could walk again, loaves and fish were multiplied... But these signs always happened in front of You. The miracle in today's Gospel is different.

It is as if You, Jesus, are telling the crowd: 'Those of you who came looking for miracles are going to be disappointed. However, this man has faith and is not seeking any display of power; just the healing of his child'. You, Lord, said: "*your son will live*" and he believed You, even if he didn't see it. That is the faith that I'm asking for, Lord.

Have you watched *Indiana Jones* in '*The Last Crusade*'? Indiana has to get across a seemingly bottomless chasm. All he sees is an insurmountable gap separating him from the other side with no logical way to get across. The 'historical guidebook', which he refers to, says crossing over will be 'a leap of faith' and his dying father (Sean Connery) whispers "*You must believe, boy, you must believe.*" And so Indiana Jones does: he courageously extends his foot and then, thud, his foot lands on solid ground. The camera pans around to show a bridge that had been invisible to him before. You see? He summoned up enough faith to take a first step and *then* he could *see* the bridge. Our trust in God is always expressed in that first faithful step that we take. Although it's only a film, it provides an example of how we should trust in God, especially when we don't see what God sees.

Our Lady is a great example of Faith. She said '*Yes*' to her vocation without knowing what was coming, with absolute trust in God. May we take after Our Mother in trust.

April

Tuesday 4th week of Lent
Tuesday 1st April
Jn 5:1-16

One man was there, who had been ill for thirty-eight years. When Jesus saw him and knew that he had been lying there a long time, he said to him, "Do you want to be healed?" The sick man answered him, "Sir, I have no man to put me into the pool when the water is troubled, and while I am going another steps down before me." Jesus said to him, "Rise, take up your pallet, and walk." And at once the man was healed, and he took up his pallet and walked.

Thirty-eight years persistently trying to get into that pool but ***no one helped him***. We understand the man's complaint: "*Sir, I have no man.*" No one ever told him '*Listen, forget the pool. I know a better solution: go to Jesus. He can and would love to help you...*' We have friends to help, people who need our assistance to go to God. Lent is a time to bring people to God. It doesn't matter how bad they are or how long they have been in that state. They need a push.

During a retreat, a man heard this piece of advice: "*Never let a day pass without talking to someone about God*," and he decided to put it into practice. One night, arriving home, he remembered that he hadn't talked to anyone about God that day. At that moment he met a neighbour in the elevator. He hesitated for a moment because he wasn't very familiar with that man, but then he thought, 'This is going to be my last chance.' He turned to him and said: "*Good night! I am going to say the rosary with my family in a few minutes; do you want me to pray for anything in particular?*" The neighbour was shocked for an instant; then he said, "*Please pray for my fiancée.*" He explained that they were going through a difficult patch in their relationship. They chatted a bit more and agreed to meet again. That was the beginning of a long friendship. Ten months later, in a ceremony in the parish, that neighbour – by now a close friend – and his fiancée became Catholic, received their first Holy Communion and Confirmation and got married all in one go! What would have happened if he hadn't decided to talk to that unknown person that God had placed in front of him in the elevator that night? The neighbour could have complained, '*No one has ever talked to me about God!*' Holy Mary, Queen of Apostles, may I never miss any opportunities to bring people to your Son.

Wednesday 4th week of Lent
Wednesday 2nd April
Jn 5:17-30

Jesus said, "My Father is working still, and I am working...Truly, truly, I say to you, the Son can do nothing of his own accord, but only what he sees the Father doing; for whatever he does, that the Son does likewise...I can do nothing on my own authority; as I hear, I judge; and my judgement is just, because I seek not my own will but the will of him who sent me."

Today's Gospel follows immediately on from yesterday's account of the healing of the crippled man by the pool. Apparently some Jews thought that healing on the Sabbath was a bad idea. But Jesus answered them that His Father was working on the Sabbath and so was Jesus, because He does what the Father does.

Jesus is a Good Son, always doing what His Father wants, in perfect unity with Him. Like Father like Son. That's what good children do: they learn everything from their parents. They take after their father and mother in the way they move, speak, or act... It may have happened to you sometimes that someone recognises in you some features or gestures of your mother or father and says: '*you remind me a lot of your mother*' or '*your father does the same thing*'. Do I remind people of my Father God with my bearing?

Jesus' mission was "*to remind us of His Father*" so that we become good children of God, because we learn from Jesus, our Brother, to take after Our Father: '*birds of a feather*'... If we are like Jesus Christ, we will be like the Father. And that's what He commanded us: "*be perfect, as your heavenly Father is perfect*" (Mt 5:48).

A protestant man was asking a priest about some points of our Faith that he didn't understand: the devotion to Mary, priestly celibacy, the practice of mortification, obedience... The prudent priest said: "*I love Mary because Jesus loves Mary; I'm celibate because Jesus is celibate; I mortify myself because Jesus mortified Himself, I obey because Jesus obeyed... I want to be like Him, I want to say what He says, I want to do what He does, I want to love what He loves, I want to be where He is, I want to go where He went... so I do what He did: **I follow in His footsteps**.*" Mary, my Mother, help me to do the same.

Thursday 3rd April
Jn 5:31-47

Jesus said to the Jews: "You sent to John, and he has borne witness to the truth. Not that the testimony which I receive is from man; but I say this that you may be saved. He was a burning and shining lamp, and you were willing to rejoice for a while in his light. But the testimony which I have is greater than that of John; for the works which the Father has granted me to accomplish, these very works which I am doing, bear me witness that the Father has sent me."

St John the Baptist had told his disciples who Jesus was, calling Him 'the Lamb of God'. Many followed Jesus because of John the Baptist, but when they got to know Him, they didn't need testimony from anyone else: they saw with their own eyes what Jesus did. And it was His works which explained Who He was.

Do you remember the encounter of Jesus with the Samaritan woman? She discovered who Jesus was, went back to her village and brought everyone to see Him. When they had met Our Lord they said to her, "*It is no longer because of your words that we believe, for we have heard for ourselves, and we know that this is indeed the Saviour of the world.*" When they saw Him they understood.

We Christians have been given the same task – to give witness to Him with our works. Jesus urged us: "*Let your light so shine before men, that they may see your good works and give glory to your Father who is in heaven*" (*Mt* 5:16). People follow 'examples' more than 'words'. With our Christian works we give witness to Him. People know that you are Christian not because of what you say or because you wear an 'I-love-Jesus' T-shirt, but because of how you behave.

One day an artist was trying to enter an art gallery. All the artists from his academy had been given a free ticket but he had forgotten his. The booking clerk thought he was lying and asked him to pay for a ticket. Instead, the painter took a piece of paper and started drawing a marvellous portrait of him – to the admiration of the people in the queue and the embarrassment of the clerk. The conclusion was evident: he was an artist. By his works they knew him. In the same way, by our Christian works we will help others to know Jesus. Holy Mary, help me to be recognised as a Christian by my good works!

Friday 4th week of Lent
Friday 4th April
Jn 7:1-2, 10, 25-30

Some of the people of Jerusalem said, "Is not this the man whom they seek to kill? And here he is, speaking openly, and they say nothing to him! Can it be that the authorities really know that this is the Christ? Yet we know where this man comes from; and when the Christ appears, no one will know where he comes from." So Jesus proclaimed, as he taught in the temple, "You know me, and you know where I come from. But I have not come of my own accord; he who sent me is true, and him you do not know. I know him, for I come from him, and he sent me."

"*We know where this man comes from...*" They are perplexed: they are waiting for the Messiah; they think that Jesus might even be He, in view of the miracles He works and the doctrine He teaches; but they are not sure... because it doesn't match with what they '*know*'. Oh, no! You can't fool them... because '*they know everything*'!

The truth is that they didn't *know* Him. They *thought* they did. This kind of prejudice has always been an obstacle to knowing the truth. Many people are not interested in looking for the truth because they 'think' they know it. Lent is a good time to pray for those who suffer from prejudices. Throughout history thousands of converts have had to undergo that process to get rid of their prejudices and open the door to the truth.

We would need a Wiki-converts to write all their names and stories. The story of Saul of Tarsus is one of them. Do you remember? He was convinced that he had to crush Christianity and put all his effort, time and money into fighting against it. But when Jesus left him blind for three days, the 'scales fell from his eyes'. If Jesus could change that heart... why should He not change those you have in mind right now?

"*Many people do not know or do not want to know who Jesus Christ is, and they remain perplexed and disconcerted... The great tragedy of history is that Jesus is not known, and therefore is not loved, not followed. You know Christ! You know who He is! Yours is a great privilege! Always be worthy and aware of it!*" (St John Paul II)

Mary, my Mother, help me to keep this reality always fresh in my mind.

Saturday 4th week of Lent
Saturday 5th April
Jn 7:40-53

The officers then went back to the chief priests and Pharisees, who said to them, "Why did you not bring him?" The officers answered, "No man ever spoke like this man!" The Pharisees answered them, "Are you led astray, you also? Have any of the authorities or of the Pharisees believed in him? But this crowd, who do not know the law, are accursed."

There is a joke about an optician testing a lady's eyesight. He asks, *"Madam, which letter do you see on the screen?"* "A", answers the lady. *"Please, concentrate"*, insists the optician. *"Which letter do you see there, madam?"* "A", replies the lady again. *'Come on, Madam!'* the exasperated optician asks once more, *"Try again!"* "A", she insists. The optician, totally frustrated, turns around to the screen to point at the letter with his finger and, looking at it, he exclaims, *"Gosh! You were right! It's 'A'."*

Pharisees, like the optician, didn't check before jumping to conclusions. They 'knew better'. Why didn't the Pharisees believe in Jesus? Because they didn't listen to Him. They never bothered to find out about His message. But those officers did listen to Him; and their lives would never be the same. What good was all their 'knowledge' if they couldn't recognise the Truth?

Good reading leads to the truth: the life of Jesus and the lives of the saints transform people. Edith Stein was a German philosopher. By her teenage years, she no longer practiced her Jewish faith and considered herself an atheist. She was reading all sorts of books by philosophers and psychologists. In the summer of 1921 she spent several weeks with some friends. One evening, a bit bored, Edith picked up an autobiography of St. Teresa of Avila and couldn't put it down, reading for the whole night. *"When I had finished the book,"* she wrote years later, *"I said to myself: This is the truth."* St Edith Stein became a Catholic and a Carmelite nun. On 7 August 1942, she was deported to Auschwitz where she died in a gas chamber two days later. It all started with good reading!

Holy Mary, our Hope, Seat of Wisdom, pray for me to be always consistent in my spiritual reading.

Fifth Sunday of Lent
Sunday 6th April
Jn 8:1-11

The scribes and the Pharisees said to him, "Teacher, this woman has been caught in the act of adultery. Now in the law Moses commanded us to stone such. What do you say about her?" ...Jesus bent down and wrote with his finger on the ground. And as they continued to ask him, he stood up and said to them, "Let him who is without sin among you be the first to throw a stone at her." And once more he bent down and wrote with his finger on the ground. But when they heard it, they went away, one by one, beginning with the eldest, and Jesus was left alone with the woman standing before him. Jesus looked up and said to her, "Woman, where are they? Has no one condemned you?" She said, "No one, Lord." And Jesus said, "Neither do I condemn you; go, and do not sin again."

Our Lord doesn't want to stone sinners but to forgive them. He has died for them. He loves sinners! Nevertheless, He didn't just say, *'No, don't kill her.'* He wanted the Pharisees to recognise that they were also sinners so they could also be forgiven. His words sounded like: *'No problem, you can stone her, – let's start with the one of you who has never sinned.'* He knew them well. Jesus could write their sins in the sand, one after another, if He wanted. You can imagine them restless, anxious, wary... Because there is no peace without forgiveness.

In order to be forgiven, we need to acknowledge our sins. Once we have repented and go to confess our sins, those miseries exist no more. Then, we can be at peace: The Mercy of Our Lord burns our sins up and leaves no ashes, no trace of them.

Mother Angelica was walking by the sea when a huge wave crashed at her feet. A small drop of seawater fell on her hand and she returned it to the sea. Then she heard Jesus' Voice inside her say: *"Angelica, have you seen that drop of water?"* "Yes, Lord," she answered. *"Those drops are like your sins, your weaknesses, your feebleness and your imperfections. And the ocean is like my Mercy. If you search for that drop, will you be able to find it?"* She said, "No, Lord." *"If you looked and looked, could you find it?"* Our Lord repeated. She said, "No, Lord." "So," Jesus concluded, *"why do you keep looking?"*

After confession our sins exist no more, there is no more guilt, just joy and peace. Holy Mary, Mother of Mercy, help me to adore God's Mercy.

Monday 5th week of Lent
Monday 7th April
Jn 8:1-11

The scribes and the Pharisees brought a woman who had been caught in adultery, and placing her in the midst they said to him, "Teacher, this woman has been caught in the act of adultery. Now in the law Moses commanded us to stone such. What do you say about her?"...And as they continued to ask him, he stood up and said to them, "Let him who is without sin among you be the first to throw a stone at her." And once more he bent down and wrote with his finger on the ground. But when they heard it, they went away, one by one, beginning with the eldest, and Jesus was left alone with the woman standing before him. Jesus looked up and said to her, "Woman, where are they? Has no one condemned you?" She said, "No one, Lord." And Jesus said, "Neither do I condemn you; go, and do not sin again."

We are sinful. God is Merciful. Everyone has sins. Everyone needs Mercy. The issue wasn't that the woman was a sinner but that the scribes and Pharisees thought they were sinless. It took a moment for Jesus to remind them that they were not. The real problem is not sin, but the lack of repentance. How could they repent if they didn't admit their sins?

Jesus said it many times: He came looking for sinners. He didn't have any problem giving the keys of His Kingdom to Peter, who denied Him; or choosing the greedy Matthew, or appointing Paul as Apostle after having persecuted Christians, or making Augustine Bishop of Hippo. History is full of examples of sinners who became saints. When we accept our sins and ask for forgiveness, we use them to grow in holiness.

One day, Simon Wright found out about a load of apples that were going to be thrown out. Then he came up with the idea of using those apples to make cider. Hawkes Cider is sold now all over the UK. This is one example of a business based on the principle *'From Trash to Cash'*, or how to make a profit from waste. That is what we do, supernaturally speaking, when we go to Confession. God takes those sins that we confess, He puts them on the Cross during the Holy Mass and transforms them into grace. Mary, Mother of Mercy, may I always go to Confession with contrition, allowing Jesus to turn the enemy's weapons against him and transform my sins into grace to overcome sin.

Tuesday 8th April
Jn 8:21-30

Again he said to them, "I go away, and you will seek me and die in your sin; where I am going, you cannot come...You are from below, I am from above; you are of this world, I am not of this world. I told you that you would die in your sins, for you will die in your sins unless you believe that I am he." They said to him, "Who are you?" Jesus said to them, "Even what I have told you from the beginning".

Jesus' disciples had been with Him a long time by then. They have heard His Words and seen His miracles. And after all that they are still asking, *"Who are You?"* We have the special task of praying for those who still don't know Who He is. Many souls are looking for the answer that can give meaning to their lives.

All the saints have had that passion (some call it 'zeal') to reach out to everyone and explain to them who Jesus Christ is, and where He is to be found so that they can go to Him. We also have that apostolic mission, to tell them that Jesus has died for them and that it is, in actual fact, He who is looking for each one of them.

On September 10, 1946, St Teresa of Calcutta felt that Jesus was asking her to take His Love to all the abandoned, the sick and the poor. In order to do that, she had to overcome many difficulties and had to take the final step of leaving her convent walls; but Jesus was in a hurry to reach many souls, and was spurring her on to reach out to those who weren't finding Jesus and didn't know Him yet. Then she heard these words from Him: **"You have come to India for me. Are you now afraid to take one more step for me? Has your generosity cooled down? Am I only secondary for you? You did not die for souls; that's why you don't care what happens to them. Your heart was never drowned in sorrow as was my Mother's heart. We both gave ourselves up totally for souls. What about you? ... Will you refuse?"**

St Teresa of Calcutta didn't refuse, as you know, and brought Jesus to thousands of those souls. Now, what about you and me? We have a similar mission... will we refuse? Mary, Handmaid of the Lord, you didn't refuse your mission either; help me to be faithful to mine and never *refuse it.*

Wednesday 9th April
Jn 8:31-42

Jesus then said to the Jews who had believed in him, "If you continue in my word, you are truly my disciples, and you will know the truth, and the truth will make you free." They answered him, "We are descendants of Abraham, and have never been in bondage to any one. How is it that you say, 'You will be made free'?" Jesus answered them, "Truly, truly, I say to you, every one who commits sin is a slave to sin".

There is the story of a farmer who found an egg in an eagle's nest. He took it and put it with his chickens. In time an eagle-chick hatched together with the other younglings. This eagle learned the chicken customs: walking through the yard, eating worms... Sometimes he would climb up on to a fence and crash to the ground, crying out, just as chickens do. That yard was his world and he was happy in there.

Sinners are like that eagle. They are locked in their vices but they don't know they are imprisoned. They don't know there is a whole world behind the fence and they can pass over that fence because they are meant to fly. But one day, the story goes, the eagle-chick saw a bird soaring through the skies. *"Who is that?"* he asked. And one of the chickens beside him answered, *"It is an eagle that flies majestically, without any effort. But don't look at it any more! Do not look at it, because our life is not like hers; our life is here, in the barnyard."*

The story can finish in two ways: 1) the eagle spent the rest of his life in the barn learning to cluck and flutter; or else 2) after trying many, many times, one day - a day he would never forget - he managed to fly, soaring up to the skies. Every sinner has those two options: to remain in their sins and defects without trying to overcome them, as if that were their only reality - or to try to fly. There is a truth that they need to know, a *truth* that will set them free: *They are created to soar to the heights!*

Mary, my Mother, help me to encourage people never to settle for living a mediocre life, to remind them that (with the grace of the Sacraments) they will never "*flutter about like a hen, when they can soar to the heights of an eagle*" (St Josemaría).

Thursday 5th week of Lent
Thursday 10th April
Jn 8:51-59

Jesus said to the Jews: Truly, truly, I say to you, if any one keeps my word, he will never see death." The Jews said to him, "Now we know that you have a demon. Abraham died, as did the prophets; and you say, 'If any one keeps my word, he will never taste death.' Are you greater than our father Abraham, who died? And the prophets died! Who do you claim to be?"...Jesus said to them, "Truly, truly, I say to you, before Abraham was, I am." So they took up stones to throw at him; but Jesus hid himself, and went out of the temple.

Jesus didn't say, 'before Abraham was, I was', but "**I AM**". Moses had heard God refer to Himself as '**I AM**' – and Jews, out of reverence, would thereafter never pronounce that Name. But Jesus not only said it, He said it of Himself! They had heard Him say, "*I am the Bread of Life, the Light of the world, the Door, the Good Shepherd, the Resurrection and the Life, the Way, the Truth and the Life, the true Vine...*" but never before had they heard anyone say 'I AM' except God Himself. No wonder they took up stones!

Some people think that Jesus was a good man, a teacher, a prophet, but that He never said He was God. However, it is clear that the Jews understood He did claim to be God. Next Sunday we will revisit His trial before the Sanhedrin. When the High Priest asked Jesus if He was indeed the Son of the Living God, Jesus answered again, "*I AM*". That was the end of the dialogue. Jesus was sentenced to death for blasphemy, for claiming to be God.

The first Christians understood well that Jesus was God and faced martyrdom for it. St Justin (A.D. 100-165) was a pagan philosopher who converted to Christianity. After his conversion he wrote several books arguing for the divinity of Christ. He was arrested along with four others during the persecution under Marcus Aurelius. When Rusticus - prefect of Rome - asked them to sacrifice to idols, they refused. "*If you do not obey,*" the Prefect said, "*you will be tortured without mercy.*" Justin replied, "*That is our desire, to be tortured for Our Lord, Jesus Christ.*" When asked about his beliefs, Justin proclaimed that Jesus was *God* and the *Son of God*. They were all beheaded for their fidelity to these beliefs. Mary, Queen of Martyrs, may I be a true witness to the divinity of your Son.

Friday 5th week of Lent
Friday 11th April
Jn 10:31-42

The Jews took up stones again to stone him. Jesus answered them, "I have shown you many good works from the Father; for which of these do you stone me?" The Jews answered him, "It is not for a good work that we stone you but for blasphemy; because you, being a man, make yourself God." Jesus answered them... "do you say of him whom the Father consecrated and sent into the world, 'You are blaspheming,' because I said, 'I am the Son of God? If I am not doing the works of my Father, then do not believe me; but if I do them, even though you do not believe me, believe the works, that you may know and understand that the Father is in me and I am in the Father."

No matter what miracle or even how many miracles they saw, they would not believe. They were blind because they didn't want to see. They wanted to stone Jesus because *being a man, He made himself God*, when it was exactly the opposite: *being God, He made Himself a man!* The truth is that these Pharisees didn't want to believe in Him. Believing in Jesus would entail changing their way of life.

This happens sometimes with those who don't want to accept the moral law because it is not 'convenient' for them. They don't want to know the truth – so they can carry on doing what they want. If a driver is stopped by the police for speeding, it is no use him saying, '*sorry officer, I didn't know there was a speed limit*'. Like it or not, and whether you know it or not... there *is* a speed limit. It isn't there to take the fun out of driving; it's there so that everyone can get to their destination safely.

An old man thought that his wife was losing her hearing. To check it out he approached her from behind while she was sitting in her lounge chair, and whispered, "*Honey, can you hear me?*" He got no response. He moved a little closer and repeated softly, "*Honey, do you hear me?*" No response. Finally he moved right next to her and said, "*Honey, can you hear me now?*" This time she looked up with surprise in her eyes and replied, "*For the third time, Henry, yes, I can hear you!*" It was Henry, then, who really had the hearing problem. It was the Pharisees who were deaf, not Jesus who wasn't 'sound'.

My Mother, intercede for me so that I may never become blind or deaf to the Will of God.

Saturday 12th April
Jn 11:45-56

Many of the Jews therefore, who had come with Mary and had seen what he did, believed in him; but some of them went to the Pharisees and told them what Jesus had done. So the chief priests and the Pharisees gathered the council, and said, "What are we to do? For this man performs many signs. If we let him go on thus, everyone will believe in him."

When someone doesn't want to believe, he won't believe, in spite of all the miracles he might see. The previous verses of St John explain the resurrection of Lazarus from the dead after being buried for four days in his tomb. Many Jews were there and saw the miracle. As a matter of fact, the miracle couldn't be denied. Therefore, the Gospel says, many people *"believed in him."* However, some of those who saw the miracle went to inform the Pharisees, who decided to kill Jesus for performing miracles!!! Can you believe it?

This explains the Gospel a few verses later, *"the chief priests planned to put Lazarus also to death, because on account of him many of the Jews were going away and believing in Jesus."* So that was it: they were losing people who were following Jesus now. They were ready to kill Jesus, Lazarus and anyone else they needed to kill in order to stop people from believing in Jesus. They did kill Jesus - and after Him they killed many of His followers, beginning with St Stephen. But the more people they killed, the more Christians converted. The truth can't be killed. Like a grain of wheat, it grows and gives fruit when it is dead and buried.

Tomorrow we start Holy Week, a week of intense prayer to be spent with Him. Jesus won't die on the Cross alone this time; you and I will be there. *"My Lord and my God, under the loving eyes of our Mother, we are making ready to accompany you along this path of sorrow, which was the price for our redemption. We wish to suffer all that You suffered, to offer you our poor, contrite hearts, because you are innocent, and yet you are going to die for us, who are the only really guilty ones. My Mother, Virgin of sorrows, help me to relive those bitter hours which your Son wished to spend on earth"* (St Josemaría.)

Palm Sunday
Sunday 13th April
Lk 22:14-23:56

Jesus went to the Mount of Olives; and the disciples followed him. And when he came to the place he said to them, "Pray that you may not enter into temptation." And he withdrew from them about a stone's throw, and knelt down and prayed, "Father, if thou art willing, remove this cup from me; nevertheless not my will, but thine, be done." Then an angel from heaven appeared to him and gave him strength. In his anguish he prayed more earnestly, and his sweat became like great drops of blood falling down on the ground. And when he rose from prayer, he came to the disciples and found them sleeping for sorrow, and he said to them, "Why do you sleep? Rise and pray that you may not enter into temptation." While he was still speaking, there came a crowd, and the man called Judas, one of the twelve, was leading them. He drew near to Jesus to kiss him; but Jesus said to him, "Judas, would you betray the Son of man with a kiss?"

Today we read the whole account of the Passion of Our Lord as an introduction to Holy Week. We see Our Lord in agony in Gethsemane. As He is God, He could see in great detail what was coming. He could see the blows and shoves of the soldiers. He could feel the shackles and chains clamping His Sacred Limbs. He could count the whippings one after another. He could number the thorns in His Crown, the blows of the reed on His Sacred Head. He could hear the mockery and insults, all the blasphemies that would come out of those shouting mouths. He could perceive the weight of the Cross on His Shoulders tearing His already wounded Skin. He could feel the nails piercing His Hands and Feet, the spear breaking His Sacred Heart...

These left scars on His Body but there were also wounds in His Soul: desertion, rejection, abandonment, the betrayal of those He loved. They fell asleep with indifference, ran away in fear, hid out of cowardice... And one of them 'sold' Him out of greed.

A priest once had a dream. He met the Angel who comforted Our Lord during His Agony. Out of curiosity, he asked the Angel, *"What did you say to Jesus to console Him that night?"* The Angel replied, *"I talked to Him about you..."* Dear Lord, I love You. I don't want to fall asleep. I don't want to run away. I want to comfort You, staying close to Your Mother during this Holy Week.

Monday of Holy Week
Monday 14th April
Jn 12:1-11

Mary took a pound of costly ointment of pure nard and anointed the feet of Jesus and wiped his feet with her hair; and the house was filled with the fragrance of the ointment. But Judas Iscariot, one of his disciples (he who was to betray him), said, "Why was this ointment not sold for three hundred denarii and given to the poor?" This he said, not that he cared for the poor but because he was a thief, and as he had the money box he used to take what was put into it. Jesus said, "Let her alone, let her keep it for the day of my burial. The poor you always have with you, but you do not always have me."

Thank you, Mary of Bethany, for your generosity! Thank you for your example, for loving Jesus so much. Thank you for giving Him joy before His Passion, for pouring on Him all of the perfume and not just a few drops. Thank you for filling the atmosphere with the fragrance of your generosity, the scent of your love.

How happy Jesus was in your home, Mary, where He knew you would do anything and give anything to keep Him happy! Thank you for your generosity - for the more you gave, the more you were given. That jar was like your heart: you poured out not just a bit of love but your whole heart. That fragrance was the perfume of your love. Thank you, Mary of Bethany, for teaching me to love Jesus Christ!

Thank you, Mary, for not being intimidated by Judas, by anyone, nor even by what others might think of you. Thank you for comforting Jesus, Who would carry the fragrance of that love in His Heart during His last sorrowful week. Thank you for your courage. For there will always be people who think, like Judas, that there is too much wealth in our churches. They forget that these riches are for God. And certainly, they forget the words of Jesus praising Mary. There is not enough gold and silver in the world to hold the Body of Christ as He deserves. And whilst some spend their money on expensive holidays or possessions, we try to dignify the places where Jesus lays.

Forget Judas' comment, Mary, for he has vanished; but the aroma of your love will never vanish. Oh, Mary of Bethany, I am a sinner, as you were... will you teach me to be a generous lover of Jesus, as you are? Mary, Mother of Christ, help me to grow in love for your Son.

Tuesday of Holy Week
Tuesday 15th April
Jn 13:21-33, 36-38

Simon Peter said to Jesus, "Lord, where are you going?" Jesus answered, "Where I am going you cannot follow me now; but you shall follow afterward." Peter said to him, "Lord, why cannot I follow you now? I will lay down my life for you." Jesus answered, "Will you lay down your life for me? Truly, truly, I say to you, the cock will not crow, till you have denied me three times.

Oh, Peter! You loved but you were weak. You trusted too much in yourself. You used the sword against the High Priest's guard but trembled before a little servant. Peter, the Rock, Prince of the Apostles, to save your own skin you swore and denied Jesus three times. You could say, '*I was not the only coward that night!*' Certainly. Matthew and Mark's Gospels explain that the other disciples also said they would die with Jesus, but all except John took to their heels and abandoned Him.

Your conversion, Peter, comforts me. Because I have also said to Jesus many times that I love Him and I have later turned my back on Him too. At times I thought that I could overcome a vice or would never commit a particular sin again. I have told Jesus often, '*I'll never do that again!*' and a little bit later I did it once more. But you, Peter, giving witness to Jesus in front of three thousand, standing before of the Sanhedrin defending Jesus, locked in prison many times, persecuted... you comfort me. For you are the same Peter who had denied Jesus three times and had been afraid of a little servant - yet you became the stronghold of Christianity, the Rock!

Your conversion happened at a Look of Our Lord. You, Peter, never forgot those beautiful Eyes of Jesus looking at you with sorrow and disappointment. That Look remained with you for the rest of your life. Those Eyes which saw your own eyes weep with sorrow. Those Eyes which saw you giving witness to Jesus Crucified. Those Eyes saw you hanging on a cross upside down, faithful, firm, strong like a Rock! Those Eyes received you in Heaven with a satisfied and loving smile. Yes, Peter, you failed but your contrition made you greater than ever! Peter, going to Our Lady for consolation as you surely did, help me to learn the lesson: "*Lord, You know everything,*" you know my miseries... but "*You know that I love You!*"

Wednesday 16th April
Mt 26:14-25

Judas Iscariot went to the chief priests and said, "What will you give me if I deliver him to you?" And they paid him thirty pieces of silver...When it was evening, he sat at table with the twelve disciples; and as they were eating, he said, "Truly, I say to you, one of you will betray me...The Son of man goes as it is written of him, but woe to that man by whom the Son of man is betrayed! It would have been better for that man if he had not been born." Judas, who betrayed him, said, "Is it I, Master?" He said to him, "You have said so."

Oh dear! Judas! Judas!! What had happened to him? Where is the Judas who was a chosen *Apostle*? Where is the man whom Jesus met and told, "*Come, follow me*"? Judas did follow Our Lord, he heard Him, he saw His miracles, and surely, he loved Jesus for a while. Had he forgotten the days on which he saw wonders and went to sleep smiling, regardless of being exhausted and having to sleep in the open? Judas, someone so privileged! "*Many prophets and righteous men longed to see what you* saw, *and did not see it, and to hear what you* heard, *and did not hear it*".

When did Judas start feeling disappointed? When did he start taking for granted those times he spent with Jesus? When did he become inattentive or insensitive to His Words? When did he start thinking about himself and his future, his plans, instead of thinking about what Jesus was telling him? When did he stop praying? When did he stop telling Jesus what was going on in his soul? It was then that Judas started rating Jesus in coins; it was then that his betrayal began. Because that betrayal didn't happen overnight. It was a slow distancing, a slippery slope from which Jesus could have saved him if he had only asked for help...

But why didn't he come back to Jesus afterwards? It didn't matter what he had done; Jesus would have forgiven him everything. Why? Why didn't he go to Him - repentant - and kiss Him again but this time out of love and not fear? Judas did know how much Jesus loved him. He could have imagined how much Jesus cried for him! Judas! Why didn't he come back, like Peter and Mary Magdalene and Dimas (the Good Thief) and Paul... and me? If it was too difficult, he could always have asked for Our Lady's help!

Maundy Thursday
Thursday 17th April
Jn 13:1-15

Now before the feast of the Passover, when Jesus knew that his hour had come to depart out of this world to the Father, having loved his own who were in the world, he loved them to the end... He rose from supper, laid aside his garments, and girded himself with a towel. Then he poured water into a basin, and began to wash the disciples' feet, and to wipe them with the towel with which he was girded.

My Dear Jesus, when I see You washing the feet of the Apostles I understand what Love is. When I see You – Son of God – on Your Knees, washing with Your Divine Hands some of the dirtiest feet in Judea at the time, including the two feet of the disciple who had already betrayed You... I see how much You love! The Master at the feet of His servants, God kneeling before His creatures, the Superior serving the inferior... But don't mums do the same when they tie their children's laces or feed them or help them get dressed?

Love engenders humility. We could say that humility is the daughter of charity and always goes with her mother. The more we live charity, the more humble we become. I know how much You love me, Lord, when I see You as a poor Child in Bethlehem for me; or when I contemplate You Crucified for my sins... But I understand it plainly when I see You in a Piece of Bread.

When St John Paul II was elected Pope, he began his papal ministry at an intense pace. A young priest who started working with him for the first time complained to the Pope's secretary, "*I am exhausted! I can't follow him! What does he have for breakfast? Where does he get the energy?!*" The secretary smiled and said nothing at the time, but after lunch he asked the young priest to follow him. He led him to the Pope's chapel and explained, "*What he eats in the mornings is the Body of Christ... and where he gets the energy is from here!*" On entering the Oratory they found St John Paul II prostrated on the floor in front of the Tabernacle, absorbed in prayer.

Ask Our Lady to teach you to love Our Lord. You can pray often the spiritual communion St Josemaría learnt as a child: "*I wish, Lord, to receive You with the purity, humility and devotion with which Your most holy Mother received You, with the spirit and fervour of the saints.*"

Good Friday
Friday 18th April
Jn 18:1-19:42

So they took Jesus, and he went out, bearing his own cross, to the place called the place of a skull, which is called in Hebrew Golgotha. There they crucified him, and with him two others, one on either side, and Jesus between them. Pilate also wrote a title and put it on the cross; it read, "Jesus of Nazareth, the King of the Jews"...When the soldiers had crucified Jesus they took his garments and made four parts, one for each soldier; also his tunic. But the tunic was without seam, woven from top to bottom; so they said to one another, "Let us not tear it, but cast lots for it to see whose it shall be"...But standing by the cross of Jesus were his mother, and his mother's sister, Mary the wife of Clopas, and Mary Magdalene. When Jesus saw his mother, and the disciple whom he loved standing near, he said to his mother, "Woman, behold, your son!" Then he said to the disciple, "Behold, your mother!" And from that hour the disciple took her to his own home. After this Jesus, knowing that all was now finished, said (to fulfil the scripture), "I thirst." A bowl full of vinegar stood there; so they put a sponge full of the vinegar on hyssop and held it to his mouth. When Jesus had received the vinegar, he said, "It is finished"; and he bowed his head and gave up his spirit.

St Thomas Aquinas said his manual was the Crucifix. Certainly in the Cross we find the answer to all questions, the example of all virtue, the solution to every problem. Today I want to contemplate Your Passion slowly, thoroughly, in detail. Your Head bleeding with thorns. Your Eyes swollen. Your Cheeks bruised with blows. Your Lips broken and dry. Your Beard yanked. Your Face covered with Blood, sweat and spit. Your Torso torn up. Your Arms stretched open, dislocated and ripped. Your Hands pierced. Your Lungs waterlogged. Your gasping Breath, Your pierced Feet, Your bruised Knees... And on top of that physical suffering I consider the moral one: Judas, Your friend, hanged. Your disciples hidden. People insulting You, laughing and jeering at You.

*"The Blessed Eucharist is the perfect Sacrament of the Lord's Passion, since It contains Christ Himself **and** His Passion"* (St Thomas Aquinas). My Lord, I can't take Your sufferings away from You but I can comfort You with my own sufferings and during the Holy Mass. That's what Your Mother - my Mother - does; and John, and Mary Magdalene and Mary the wife of Clopas... and I.

Holy Saturday
Saturday 19th April
There's no Mass today

Today the altar is left bare and no Mass is celebrated. Holy Saturday is a silent day. Creation is in silence. Heaven is in silence too; the angels haven't forgotten what men - you and I - did to Jesus yesterday. Christ's Body lies in the grave and you and I sit by the Corpse in grief. His cold, dead Body still bears the scars of the intense suffering, those mortal wounds that will remain visible on His Body for all eternity. They remind humanity of the *price of our sins*. See on His serene Face the injuries received to erase our sins. See there the marks of the blows received in order to refashion our warped nature in His Image. On His Back see the impression of the scourging endured to remove the burden of sin that weighs upon our shoulders. See those Hands, nailed firmly to a tree, for us; the holes in those Feet that walked the earth, giving hope.

His disciples are weeping in a dark corner of Jerusalem, not daring to hope. Their Master is dead. Their hopes are dead. Their dreams are over. The Body that they followed, the One they loved, is now cold and stiff. Jesus is dead. We would love to remind them that Holy Saturday is past. Holy Saturday was only 'once' and is now over. Easter Sunday has come and the Dead is now *alive*. He will never die again! To all those Christians who today still live in a perpetual 'Holy Saturday', discouraged and without hope, we can proclaim that Jesus *died* but is not *dead* anymore. And the Tabernacle is not a tomb. Jesus is alive!

But today let's stay with Our Mother. Still in sorrow as she recalls her Son's Passion, Our Mother is serene; she has hope. She remembers the promise of the Resurrection. She teaches us to trust. With her, we hold her divine Son's Body. "*I will press my arms tightly round the cold Body, the corpse of Christ, with the fire of my love... I will unnail it, with my reparation and mortifications... I will wrap it in the new winding-sheet of my clean life, and I will bury it in the living rock of my breast, where no one can tear it away from me, and there, Lord, take your rest! Were the whole world to abandon you and to scorn you... serviam!, I will serve you, Lord*" (St Josemaría).

Easter Sunday
Sunday 20th April
Jn 20:1-9

Now on the first day of the week Mary Magdalene came to the tomb early, while it was still dark, and saw that the stone had been taken away from the tomb. So she ran, and went to Simon Peter and the other disciple, the one whom Jesus loved, and said to them, "They have taken the Lord out of the tomb, and we do not know where they have laid him." Peter then came out with the other disciple, and they went toward the tomb. They both ran, but the other disciple outran Peter and reached the tomb first; and stooping to look in, he saw the linen cloths lying there, but he did not go in. Then Simon Peter came, following him, and went into the tomb; he saw the linen cloths lying, and the napkin, which had been on his head, not lying with the linen cloths but rolled up in a place by itself. Then the other disciple, who reached the tomb first, also went in, and he saw and believed.

Apparently everyone is rushing around today, from the tomb to Jerusalem and back. After the three saddest days of their lives, Jesus' disciples are now all over the place. '*Could it be possible?*' the disciples were wondering. '*They saw the empty tomb! They say that Jesus is alive! But how?*' Now there is hope and two of the Apostles who had been still and motionless for hours begin to run. A new hope urges them to search for Him: 'What if the women are right?!'... 'What if Jesus was right?!!!'

According to Christian tradition, while everyone else was scurrying around, Our Lady waited expectantly in prayer. During those three days Mary had been counting the hours until she would see her Son alive. She was the first to see the Risen Body of her Son, to kiss His pierced Hands, to caress His open Side, to rest her head on the Sacred Shoulders marked by the Cross, and to embrace the Glorious Body of her Son, to mix her tears with His and to converse with Him... forever. My Mother, Our Lady, help me remain very close to you today so that I can see Our Risen Lord and spend my prayer contemplating the Wounds that He received for my sins. Holy Mother, Our Hope, may I always be at your side, next to your Son. May I never lose hope!

[Remember that today, and during the whole season of Easter, we pray the *Regina Coeli*.]

Easter Monday
Monday 21st April
Mt 28:8-15

So the women departed quickly from the tomb with fear and great joy, and ran to tell his disciples. And behold, Jesus met them and said, "Hail!" And they came up and took hold of his feet and worshipped him. Then Jesus said to them, "Do not be afraid; go and tell my brethren to go to Galilee, and there they will see me."

They say that the sentence: "*Do not be afraid!*" can be found in the Bible more than 300 times. Good teachers always repeat the message that they want to get across. And You, Lord, said it many times to Your disciples. So many times that they never forgot the tone of Your voice saying, "*Do not be afraid!*"

But what could Mary Magdalene be afraid of now?! Probably she had one single fear: the fear of losing Jesus again. Have you ever found a little child in a crowd, crying because he or she couldn't find Mum? You saw the mother looking for the child nearby and said to the child, "*Look, there she is!*" and the tearful child rushed off towards her. Children of God should never be afraid of anything. The disciples were afraid because they had lost Jesus on Good Friday. Their hopes were over, their discouragement stopped them moving forward; fear paralyses. It happens to Christians when, like the little child, they don't feel Jesus' close presence, when they move away from Him by sinning.

My God, may I never be afraid of anything except losing You through sin. And if that happens again - for I know very well how weak I am - I beg You to come and search me out as You did these holy women and Your frightened Apostles. O my Jesus, if ever You see me in distress or on the verge of temptation, come and let me hear Your voice again: "*Do not be afraid.*"

"I plead with you - never, ever give up on hope, never doubt, never tire, and never become discouraged. Do not be afraid... Do not be afraid to become the saints of the new millennium!" (St John Paul II). *"Today I say to you, dear young people: Do not be afraid of Christ! He takes nothing away, and he gives you everything"* (Pope Benedict XVI). My Mother, stay close to this little child of yours that I am. Then I will fear nothing.

Easter Tuesday
Tuesday 22nd April
Jn 20:11-18

Mary stood weeping outside the tomb...she turned round and saw Jesus standing, but she did not know that it was Jesus. Jesus said to her, "Woman, why are you weeping? Whom do you seek?" Supposing him to be the gardener, she said to him, "Sir, if you have carried him away, tell me where you have laid him, and I will take him away." Jesus said to her, "Mary." She turned and said to him in Hebrew, "Rab-boni!" (which means Teacher). Jesus said to her, "Do not hold me, for I have not yet ascended to the Father; but go to my brethren and say to them, I am ascending to my Father and your Father."

Mary loved Jesus but something prevented her from recognising Him. When she heard her name, spoken by *that Voice*, with that '*tone*', we can imagine how she shuddered with delight. That name she had heard so many times coming from Jesus' Lips, "*Mary!*"

There are many ways to pronounce a name. Think about the many people who have said your name, always differently: your parents, grandparents, siblings, friends... you could recognise each one of them on the phone just by hearing them say your name. But even the same person (your mother, for instance) could say your name in different tones and modes. You could tell what was coming just by listening to her say your name in the distance.

Jesus didn't need to say anything else to Mary; just her name. Jesus called everyone by their name. All of them remembered well how Jesus pronounced their names: Peter, John, Andrew, James, Nicodemus, Martha... and Our Lady, "*Mother*", and St Joseph, "*father*". And you... Can you imagine the sound of Jesus' voice speaking your name? Because He uses it every day to talk to you in your prayer.

"Just like our mother, he calls us by our name, by the name we're fondly called at home, by our nickname. There, in the depths of our soul, he calls us and we just have to answer: Ecce ego quia vocasti me - here I am, for you have called me" (St Josemaría).

My Mother, Handmaid of the Lord, you also use my name when you talk to your Son about me. Help me to always have that answer on my lips: "*Here I am, Lord, for you have called me by my name.*"

Easter Wednesday
Wednesday 23rd April
Lk 24:13-35

That very day two of them were going to a village named Emmaus, about seven miles from Jerusalem, and talking with each other about all these things that had happened. While they were talking and discussing together, Jesus himself drew near and went with them. But their eyes were kept from recognizing him. And he said to them, "What is this conversation which you are holding with each other as you walk?" And they stood still, looking sad. Then one of them, named Cleopas, answered him, "Are you the only visitor to Jerusalem who does not know the things that have happened there in these days?" Jesus said to them, "O foolish men, and slow of heart to believe..." And beginning with Moses and all the prophets, he interpreted to them in all the scriptures the things concerning himself. So they drew near to the village to which they were going. He appeared to be going further, but they constrained him, saying, "Stay with us, for it is toward evening and the day is now far spent." So he went in to stay with them. When he was at table with them, he took the bread and blessed, and broke it, and gave it to them. And their eyes were opened and they recognised him; and he vanished out of their sight. They said to each other, "Did not our hearts burn within us while he talked to us on the road, while he opened to us the scriptures?"

How naïve you are, Cleopas, you and your friend, trying to explain to Jesus His own story! Walking side-by-side with Jesus... and you couldn't recognise Him. He explained to you the Scriptures that you knew so well but had never fully understood. After that, you had the "breaking of the bread", as they called the Eucharist at the beginning. And then your *"eyes were opened."* I see the picture now: first, Scripture and homily; secondly, Eucharist and Holy Communion: that was the first Holy Mass after His Death and Resurrection.

Today, Lord, you walk at my side, ready to talk to me even if I don't see or recognise You. Today my heart burns when You explain the Scripture to me in my prayer. I listen to You and I receive You in Mass as well. May I always recognise You at my side; may I always see You, in Mass, as we break the Bread; may You explain to me what I can't understand and may my heart burn also when I talk to You and beg You, *Stay with me, Lord!*

My Mother, Mary, help me to always *stay with Him!*

Easter Thursday
Thursday 24th April
Lk 24:35-48

As they were saying this, Jesus himself stood among them, and said to them, "Peace to you"...And when he had said this, he showed them his hands and his feet...Then he opened their minds to understand the scriptures, and said to them, "Thus it is written, that the Christ should suffer and on the third day rise from the dead, and that repentance and forgiveness of sins should be preached in his name to all nations, beginning from Jerusalem. You are witnesses of these things."

First He showed His Wounds; through those Wounds our sins can be forgiven. But those Wounds can't heal the wounds of your sins if there is no repentance; that is why *"repentance and forgiveness of sins should be preached in his name to all nations."*

You and I have that mission now: to remind everyone, no matter what sins they have committed, that through His Sacrifice, through those Wounds, Jesus can forgive any sin in Confession; to remind people that there is no sin, no misery that can't be wiped away by His infinite Mercy. In Confession the Wounds of Jesus erase forever the sins that we confess with contrition. But there has to be real contrition, real sorrow for our sins.

A boy went to confess: *"Father, forgive me for I have stolen £7 to buy chocolates... but for the penance let's say £10."* "So, which one is it?" asked the priest, puzzled, *"did you take £7 or £10?"* "It was £7, father," answered the boy, *"but it wasn't enough; I need £3 more!"* Obviously he wasn't very sorry for his sin. Remember: if there is no contrition, there is no forgiveness.

St John Vianney would hear up to 300 Confessions per day! One day, he started weeping on hearing the Confession of a man who spoke without any sign of sorrow; hearing his sobbing, the penitent asked why he was weeping. The holy Curé of Ars replied, *"My friend, I weep because you do not weep."*

"Turn to Our Lady and ask her - as a token of her love for you - for the gift of contrition. Ask that you may be sorry, with the sorrow of Love, for all your sins and for the sins of all men and women throughout the ages... 'Acts of contrition, the more the better!'" (St Josemaría).

Easter Friday
Friday 25th April
Jn 21:1-14

Simon Peter said to them, "I am going fishing." They said to him, "We will go with you." They went out and got into the boat; but that night they caught nothing. Just as day was breaking, Jesus stood on the beach; yet the disciples did not know that it was Jesus. Jesus said to them, "Children, have you any fish?" They answered him, "No." He said to them, "Cast the net on the right side of the boat, and you will find some." So they cast it, and now they were not able to haul it in, for the quantity of fish. That disciple whom Jesus loved said to Peter, "It is the Lord!"

There were at least seven of Jesus' disciples in the boat. But only one recognises Him from a distance: *the Beloved one*. Imagine St John squinting, shielding his eyes from the sun and looking at the Man on the shore when he heard those words, "*Cast the net on the right side of the boat.*" Maybe he thought, 'I have heard that phrase before. That voice reminds me of...' He was still hesitant, but when he saw the amount of fish they caught, the penny dropped. He smiled first, then laughed to himself, like someone who has been tricked for a while, and, full of joy, like a madman - madly in love - he shouted, "*It is the Lord!*"

"*He was more beloved than all the other Apostles,*" writes St. Thomas Aquinas, "*on account of his purity.*" And St. Anselm wrote, "*God revealed more mysteries to him than to the other Apostles, because he surpassed all in virginal purity.*" Let's keep our eyes today on that teenager, his look clean, his heart in love: his purity allowed him to recognise Jesus from a distance. Our Lord Himself taught, "*Blessed are the pure in heart, for they shall see God.*" Many people are unable to see Jesus, not because He is hidden but because their glasses are dirty; sins blind men, purity gives light.

St John was also pure because he was close to Our Lady. Mary, Mother most pure, Mother most chaste, intercede for me to resemble the young St John, to be pure like him and always close to you. "*How I would like - you told me - the young apostle, John, to take me into his confidence and give me advice: and encourage me to acquire purity of heart. If you really would like it, tell him so: and you will feel encouraged, and you will receive advice*" (St Josemaría).

Easter Saturday
Saturday 26th April
Mk 16:9-15

Now when he rose early on the first day of the week, he appeared first to Mary Magdalene...they would not believe it. After this he appeared in another form to two of them, as they were walking into the country...but they did not believe them. Afterward he appeared to the eleven themselves as they sat at table; and he upbraided them for their unbelief and hardness of heart, because they had not believed those who saw him after he had risen. And he said to them, "Go into all the world and preach the gospel to the whole creation".

First there is a reproach; then there is a command. The reproach is that they didn't believe those whom Jesus sent to them. The command is to go and preach the Gospel to the whole creation. First, we need faith; then we can bring that faith to others; and this is what Jesus has commanded us to do.

The French Cardinal Roger Etchegaray once told a story which he had heard from an Orthodox priest. After the Passover, as Jesus ascended into Heaven, He gazed down on earth and saw it in darkness, except for a few tiny lights in Jerusalem. On His way to Heaven He met the Angel Gabriel, who was accustomed to undertaking earthly missions. The Angel asked Him, *"What are those little lights?"* *"They are the Apostles that surround my Mother,"* Jesus answered him. *"This is my plan: once I return to Heaven, I will send them the Holy Spirit so that these small lights can turn into a great bonfire that will ignite the world with charity."* The Angel dared to ask, *"And if this plan does not work?"* After a moment's silence, Jesus answered, *"I do not have any other plan!"*

God has no other plans! If the Apostles had failed, many souls would have remained oblivious of the Gospel message. We are the Apostles now. What a great responsibility! How many souls may depend on whether you and I become real apostles! What we don't do... remains undone, because God has no other plans. *"Many great things depend - don't forget it - on whether you and I live our lives as God wants"* (St Josemaría).

My Mother, Queen of the Apostles, pray for me that I may never forget it: many souls depend on me.

Divine Mercy Sunday
Sunday 27th April
Jn 20:19-31

Jesus came and stood among them and said to them, "Peace be with you." When he had said this, he showed them his hands and his side. Then the disciples were glad when they saw the Lord. Jesus said to them again, "Peace be with you. As the Father has sent me, even so I send you." And when he had said this, he breathed on them, and said to them, "Receive the Holy Spirit. If you forgive the sins of any, they are forgiven; if you retain the sins of any, they are retained." Now Thomas, one of the twelve, called the Twin, was not with them when Jesus came. So the other disciples told him, "We have seen the Lord." But he said to them, "Unless I see in his hands the print of the nails, and place my finger in the mark of the nails, and place my hand in his side, I will not believe."

Today is the Second Sunday of Easter, known as Divine Mercy Sunday, when we commemorate the day on which Jesus gave his Apostles authority to forgive sins in His Name. The text is very clear: "*If you forgive the sins of any, they are forgiven.*" It couldn't be easier! Some, like the Apostle St Thomas, would only believe if Jesus Himself appeared to them and gave them absolution.

Saints went to Confession very often; many of them even went every week. They went to Confession because they were sinners and needed forgiveness as well. They loved Our Lord and wanted to erase their sins, including venial ones. When G. K. Chesterton was asked why he became a Catholic, his short answer was: "*To get rid of my sins.*"

Once Jesus told St Faustina, **"Tell souls to look for relief in the Tribunal of Mercy [Confession]. To benefit from this miracle, it is enough to come with faith to the feet of My representative [the priest] and to reveal to him one's misery. Were a soul like a putrefying corpse so that from a human standpoint, there would be no [hope of] restoration and everything would already be lost, it is not so with God. The miracle of Divine Mercy restores that soul in full. Oh, how miserable are those who do not take advantage of the miracle of God's Mercy!"**

Mary, Mother of Mercy, help me to become 'an Apostle of Mercy' so that I can bring many to the Sacrament of Reconciliation.

Monday 2nd week of Easter
Monday 28th April
Jn 3:1-8

Jesus answered to Nicodemus, "Truly, truly, I say to you, unless one is born anew, he cannot see the kingdom of God." Nicodemus said to him, "How can a man be born when he is old? Can he enter a second time into his mother's womb and be born?" Jesus answered, "Truly, truly, I say to you, unless one is born of water and the Spirit, he cannot enter the kingdom of God. That which is born of the flesh is flesh, and that which is born of the Spirit is spirit."

The reference to water and the spirit here becomes the official presentation of the Sacrament of Baptism. St John the Baptist declared, '*I baptise with water*,' and the Messiah will baptise '*with the Holy Spirit*.' Water, then, is now no longer enough.

The Holy Spirit is brought to our attention in a special way during Eastertide. The Risen Jesus is preparing everything to entrust His Church to the care of the Holy Spirit. And now, the Holy Spirit is at work. You don't see Him, as you don't see the wind, but you see His effects. St John XXIII said: "*The saints are the masterpieces of the Holy Spirit.*" Those who have been baptised with water have the Holy Spirit at work inside them.

On Tuesday November 8 1932, St Josemaría's spiritual director told him: "*Make friends with the Holy Spirit. Don't speak: listen to him.*" That was a new discovery. "*Until now I knew that the Holy Spirit was dwelling in my soul to sanctify it,*" St Josemaría wrote later that day, "*but I hadn't really grasped this truth about his presence. I feel the Holy Spirit's Love within me, and I want to talk to him, to be his friend, to confide in him. I want to facilitate his work of polishing, uprooting, and enkindling. I wouldn't know how to set about it. He will give me strength. He will do everything, if I so want. And I do want! Divine Guest, Master, Light, Guide, Love, may I make you truly welcome inside me and listen to the lessons you teach me. Make me burn with eagerness for you, make me follow you and love you. Resolution: to 'keep up', without interruption as far as I can, a loving and docile friendship and conversation with the Holy Spirit. Veni Sancte Spiritus!... Come, Holy Spirit!*" (St Josemaría).

Mary, Spouse of the Holy Spirit, help me to remain faithful to my resolution.

Tuesday 2nd week of Easter
Tuesday 29th April
Jn 3:7b-15

Jesus said to Nicodemus: 'You must be born anew'...Nicodemus said to him, "How can this be?" Jesus answered him, "Are you a teacher of Israel, and yet you do not understand this? Truly, truly, I say to you, we speak of what we know, and bear witness to what we have seen...No one has ascended into heaven but he who descended from heaven, the Son of man. And as Moses lifted up the serpent in the wilderness, so must the Son of man be lifted up, that whoever believes in him may have eternal life."

Nicodemus - a doctor of the Law and learned in the Scriptures - was confused. Therefore, he did what we should do in our mental prayer: ask You, Jesus, because You are the only One Who has all the answers. You, Lord, are the only One Who can reveal the Truth that we need to believe because You are the **Truth**. But You can't get all these things across in just one conversation! You need us to foster a habit of chatting with You. Nicodemus probably met and talked with You on many more occasions because eventually, as we read in the Gospel, when all the others left You during Your Agony and Death on that Good Friday, he was there to stand up for You, to take Your Body and bury It.

That is the effect of regular and frequent prayer. And that is also why I need to foster that daily conversation with Jesus. It's like eating healthily: you don't notice striking changes after one meal or one week; but after a time you can tell something has changed, even though you don't remember your meals. Only over time do we come to see its good effect. Likewise, to pray every day can be demanding and many times you will not remember what you chatted with God about the day before... but only by that daily contact with Jesus can He get across what you need to believe and transform you into another Nicodemus: a faithful friend who stands with Him when others have deserted!

Let's give Our Lord the great comfort of our daily conversation with Him. *"Mental prayer in my opinion is nothing else than a close sharing between friends; it means taking time frequently to be alone with Him who we know loves us"* (St Teresa of Avila). My Mother Immaculate, teach me to talk to Him as you did then, as you do now.

St Catherine of Siena, virgin, Doctor of the Church
Tuesday 29th April
Mt 11:25-30

At that time Jesus declared, "Come to me, all who labour and are heavy laden, and I will give you rest. Take my yoke upon you, and learn from me; for I am gentle and lowly in heart, and you will find rest for your souls. For my yoke is easy, and my burden is light."

St. Catherine of Siena was the 25th child born to her mother. At the age of 16, Catherine's sister died leaving her husband as a widower. Her parents proposed Catherine to marry the widower but she opposed. She began fasting and cut her hair short to mar her appearance. While living at home, she confirmed her vow of virginity made privately when she was still an adolescent and dedicated herself to prayer, penance and works of charity, especially for the benefit of the sick. She learned to read with difficulty and dictated letters, prayers and her mystical work, *'The Dialogue'*. For those works she was named *'Doctor of the Church'*.

Those were difficult times for the Church. She faced opposition and slander for speaking with the confidence of one completely committed to Christ. Pope Gregory XI had left Rome to live in Avignon. Out of love for the Church and the Pope, she went to mediate to Avignon but she was virtually ignored by the pope. After the death of the pope in 1378, the Great Schism began, confusing Christians with the presence of three popes. Catherine spent the last two years of her life in Rome, in prayer and pleading on behalf of the unity of the Church. She offered herself as a victim for the Church and died on 29 April 1380 at the age of 33.

St Josemaria had great admiration for her *"because of her courage to speak the truth for the love of Christ, of the Church and of the Pope,"* he said. Next to her relic, he wrote: *"Dilexit opere et veritate Ecclesiam Dei ac Romanum Pontificem"* (She loved the Church and the Pope truly and with deeds).

My Mother Immaculate, help us to have the courage of St Catherine to stand for the truth. St Catherine, Patron saint of Europe, teach me to love the Church and the pope!

Wednesday 30th April
Jn 3:16-21

For God so loved the world that he gave his only Son, that whoever believes in him should not perish but have eternal life. For God sent the Son into the world, not to condemn the world, but that the world might be saved through him...This is the judgment, that the light has come into the world, and men loved darkness rather than light, because their deeds were evil.

For God so loved the world... did you get that?! God loves the world. He always has and always will, for He is its 'Craftsman' (or *Crafts-God*). As a good artist loves his paintings, God loves His creation. Some people think that the world is bad and takes us away from God. How come, if it's God's gift to us? Genesis states clearly that *"God saw everything that he had made, and indeed, it was very good."* If He Himself said that *it's good*, who am I to disagree?

Men have sometimes masked the beauty of creation with their sins, but that doesn't diminish its value. You can crumple a £20 note and step on it with your dirty shoes; it doesn't lose a penny of its worth. Every artist leaves some trace of himself in his work. Experts can recognise an artist's work without looking at the signature. Have you ever found yourself astounded looking at a beautiful sunrise, a sunset of fire, a magnificent rainbow, gentle waves lapping the seashore, a thin crescent moon hung in a crystal-clear sky, a spectacular waterfall...? God made it for you and He loves it because of you. As a Good Father, He loves to see that you delight in His gifts to you, not for the gift itself, but because He gave it to you; just like a child keeps a pen or a watch for years and cherishes it, because '*my dad gave it to me.*'

God loves His creation so much *that he gave his only Son*, to be part of it. Think about it: this world has been walked upon by God. He has worked in it. He has rested His Head on its grass, had His Face stroked by the wind, heard its birds singing... He has looked up to the sky and loved it. He has drunk from its brooks and swum in its lakes. And now He has entrusted this world to me as a stage for my happiness, and I love our world passionately, as a gift from my loving Father. My Mother, Queen of the Universe, help me to give thanks to God for His wonderful creation.

May

Thursday 2nd week of Easter
Thursday 1st May
Jn 3:31-36

John the Baptist said to his disciples: "He who comes from above is above all; he who is of the earth belongs to the earth, and of the earth he speaks; he who comes from heaven is above all. He bears witness to what he has seen and heard, yet no one receives his testimony; he who receives his testimony sets his seal to this, that God is true."

Some people only seem able to view things negatively. One such cynic was walking by the pier watching a man trying to start a boat's engine. Feeling 'obliged' to give his opinion on everything, he commented, *"That engine will never start."* Immediately the engine made a big noise and started. Not wishing to be proven wrong, he held his ground, *"Anyway... it'll probably never stop."* All those who belong to the earth are like this fellow. They only see shadows, never lights.

He who is *"of the earth belongs to the earth, and of the earth he speaks,"* says Our Lord. That person only knows how to utter calamities, complaints, criticism and sarcasm. They see everything dimly, as through very dark shades. But we belong to Heaven, don't we? We were made for happiness, for love, for paradise. And we must bear witness to it. That's what a Christian should be. Wherever a Christian walks by, Jesus is passing by with him and, therefore, there is light.

Our conversation and our attitude in life should reflect our supernatural faith. That behaviour will bring others to the realisation that there is more to life than meets the eye; there is a God who loves us so much that He made the world as the anteroom of Heaven. Real Christians overflow with joy. People want to be with them, to stay with them, to converse with them. St Josemaría taught that *"happiness in Heaven is for those who know how to be happy on earth."* Like Jesus Himself: do you remember how people were looking for Him? Even children loved to be with Him. And children aren't fools: they don't like to be with gloomy people. Let's show the world, with our lives, that we have many reasons to be happy. *"How I wish your bearing and conversation [your smile!] were such that, on seeing or hearing you, people would say: This man reads the life of Jesus Christ"* (St Josemaría). Holy Mary, Cause of our Joy, pray for us.

St Joseph the Worker
Thursday 1st May
Mt 13:54-58

Coming to his own country Jesus taught them in their synagogue, so that they were astonished, and said, "Where did this man get this wisdom and these mighty works? Is not this the carpenter's son? Is not his mother called Mary? And are not his brethren James and Joseph and Simon and Judas? And are not all his sisters with us? Where then did this man get all this?" And they took offense at him.

A powerful person is the one who has been entrusted with great responsibilities. A king is powerful, not because he can rule over millions, but because millions of people depend on him. The same applies to a Prime Minister, a President or the CEO of a company. Think about the talents and skills that a person has to have in order to be entrusted with such responsibilities.

In the history of mankind God has given great responsibilities to many people. But no one has ever been entrusted with more than St Joseph. God could commend His most precious treasures (His Only Begotten Son and His Mother) only to one man. What was it that Joseph could do better than any other man in history? For Joseph didn't appear to be a great speaker, a popular rabbi, a famous politician or a gifted writer or philosopher. God didn't want to entrust His Only Begotten Son to Alexander the Great, Socrates, Dante or Michelangelo but to an artisan in Nazareth. This is a mystery for many but not for a Christian. Because Jesus Christ, the Son of God Himself was... an artisan in Nazareth!

How much God loved Joseph! How much He loved everything that Joseph did! Because it was done with love, for love and to love. How much time Jesus spent looking in silence at His father Joseph, working, sweating, his muscles tense, the veins of his forehead pulsating. How much God loved those tables, those boards, those doors his father made under his watchful gaze. How proudly Jesus would walk through the streets, reminding His young friends, '*My dad made that door*', '*my dad made that fence...*' Now God is contemplating my work with the same look. Does it please Him? St Joseph, my father and lord, teach me to work like you so that God can be proud of my work. Mary, my Mother, help me to work like your husband.

Friday 2nd May
Jn 6:1-15

Seeing that a multitude was coming to him, Jesus said to Philip, "How are we to buy bread, so that these people may eat?" This he said to test him, for he himself knew what he would do. Philip answered him, "Two hundred denarii would not buy enough bread for each of them to get a little." One of his disciples, Andrew, Simon Peter's brother, said to him, "There is a lad here who has five barley loaves and two fish; but what are they among so many?"

"*There is a lad here...*" We don't know the name of the *lad*. We only know that he had five loaves and two fish and that he gave them all. This anonymous lad gave them (and us) a lesson in how to be generous. What we can give to God is always little, but He multiplies the effect of it. Jesus doesn't '*need*' our help, but He *wants to need* our generosity.

It is like a mother who lets a 3-year-old child help her bake a cake: beating the eggs, for instance. She could do it herself, of course (probably quicker and better) but she is teaching and having a great time with her child. And she loves it when Dad comes and the little one says, "*We made your favourite cake!*" Dad surely knows the child did very little, but he likes the cake all the more for it.

When St Josemaría was a young priest and still no one had joined his Work (Opus Dei), he used to meet a beggar-woman next to the church. In those days he was extremely poor. One day he approached her and said, "*My daughter, I have no money to give you. All I have, I give it to you,*" and making the sign of the Cross, he gave her a blessing. Finally he added, "*I beg you to offer up what you can for an intention of mine.*" The intention was his 'Work'. A couple of months later St Josemaría found the woman dying from tuberculosis in a hospital he used to visit. "*But how come... what happened to you?*" he asked on seeing her. She replied, "*Don't you understand, father? You told me: "Offer up what you can". I didn't have anything to offer up... So I offered up my life!*" St Josemaría was deeply moved and never forgot the generosity of that woman whom he called '*the first vocation of his future daughters.*' Mother, what I can give to Our Lord is very little, but help me to give it all.

Sts Philip and James, Apostles
Saturday 3rd May
Jn 14:6-14

Jesus said to Thomas, "I am the way, and the truth, and the life; no one comes to the Father, but by me."...Philip said to him, "Lord, show us the Father, and we shall be satisfied." Jesus said to him, "Have I been with you so long, and yet you do not know me, Philip? He who has seen me has seen the Father; how can you say, 'Show us the Father? Do you not believe that I am in the Father and the Father in me?...he who believes in me will also do the works that I do...Whatever you ask in my name, I will do it, that the Father may be glorified in the Son; if you ask anything in my name, I will do it."

First Thomas asked a question and Jesus answered. Then Philip asked another question and Jesus replied. How vivid and pleasant must have been those dialogues with Jesus where they could talk about whatever they wanted! In those conversations the Apostles learned from Jesus, solved their dilemmas, grew in faith, had the best times of their lives and gave Jesus the comfort of their friendship. Surely there were nice comments, encouraging anecdotes from one, jokes from another, songs from their various hometowns... How much Jesus loved those get-togethers!

That's what prayer is: a vivid and pleasant dialogue with God. Those dialogues transformed them into the Apostles that Jesus needed, able to *do the works that Jesus did* with the power to ask **anything** in the Name of Jesus and obtain it. Because for those who pray, who are friends with Jesus, He does **anything**.

Philip took a long time to realise who Jesus was. When Jesus asked him to feed the multitude, Philip replied, "*Two hundred denarii would not buy enough bread for each of them to get a little*". Actually five loaves and two fish did the job. James (The Lesser) was a relative of Jesus (probably son of Jesus' aunt Mary of Cleopas). He knew Jesus before He became a public figure. It took him a while to understand who He really was. But those long conversations with Our Lord opened his mind. He eventually became bishop of Jerusalem and was stoned to death for his faith in Jesus. Our daily dialogue with Jesus will also transform us into modern apostles; we will grow in faith and do the works that He does. Holy Mary, Queen of the Apostles, pray for us.

Third Sunday of Easter
Sunday 4th May
Jn 21:1-19

Simon Peter, Thomas called the Twin, Nathanael of Cana in Galilee, the sons of Zebedee, and two others of his disciples were together. Simon Peter said to them, "I am going fishing." They said to him, "We will go with you." They went out and got into the boat; but that night they caught nothing. Just as day was breaking, Jesus stood on the beach; yet the disciples did not know that it was Jesus. Jesus said to them, "Children, have you any fish?" They answered him, "No." He said to them, "Cast the net on the right side of the boat, and you will find some." So they cast it, and now they were not able to haul it in, for the quantity of fish.

St Josemaría always had great devotion to those "*two others of his disciples,*" two anonymous disciples of Jesus whose names we don't know. We don't know where the other disciples were, but they weren't with Peter that day. Those who went fishing with Peter saw Jesus. Before one of his audiences, St John Paul II was greeting some people among the crowd. He was talking with a group of young ladies when the MC suggested that he keep moving because it was getting late and he had to give a speech. Amused, he looked at the youth and said in Latin, "*Vado piscari*" ('*I am going fishing*'.) To his amazement some of them answered also in Latin, "*Venimus et nos tecum!*" ('*We will go with you!*') The holy Pope smiled, turned to them, and said, '*Please, do!*'

That's what Christians are called to do. We always go with the 'Fisher of men', whoever the Pope is at the time, to catch souls for God. Those who didn't fish with Peter that day didn't see the miraculous catch. Unity with the Pope is a sign of efficiency in the apostolate.

But Peter was well aware that all was Jesus' doing. They had caught nothing by themselves a few minutes before. Peter followed Jesus' instructions and fished. Peter obeyed Jesus, the disciples followed Peter and fished. And for centuries Christians who have followed St Peter have never run out of fish. Nowadays, even in our current 'stormy weather', we are heirs of these anonymous disciples who went fishing with Peter.

Let's pray often the aspiration that St Josemaría recommended: "*Omnes cum Petro, ad Iesum, per Mariam*" ('All with Peter to Jesus through Mary.')

Monday 3rd week of Easter
Monday 5th May
Jn 6:22-29

When the people saw that Jesus was not there, nor his disciples, they themselves got into the boats and went to Caperna-um, seeking Jesus. When they found him on the other side of the sea, they said to him, "Rabbi, when did you come here?" Jesus answered them, "Truly, truly, I say to you, you seek me, not because you saw signs, but because you ate your fill of the loaves. Do not labour for the food which perishes, but for the food which endures to eternal life."

This happened right after the multiplication of the loaves and fish. These people came after Jesus again but maybe not for the right reason. They ate delicious loaves and fish for free and, perhaps, just wanted some more! So Jesus invited them not to look for ordinary bread, but for the Bread of Heaven: the Eucharist. That is the content of the whole sixth chapter of St John.

At the end of this chapter we read that "*many of his disciples drew back and no longer went about with him.*" We can recognise people like that today: they follow Him when it is easy, when it isn't demanding, when they need something, but not when Jesus is crucified, not when He asks for help, for their time, for their presence in the Holy Mass or before the Tabernacle, for their time of prayer... Those are not 'real' friends of Jesus. They are like 'friends' who turn up to a birthday party without a present and disappear before it is time to clear up. It's like a *one-way* friendship: there is no 'give and take'. They take but don't give.

In the summer of 1921 three boys discovered Red Army soldiers breaking into the church of Petrograd, near Finland. They resolved to "*shield the dear, loving Jesus*" and entered the church, greeting the soldiers. When the soldiers threatened to shoot they replied that they "*would not suffer their dear Jesus to be insulted.*" Two boys were killed. The third boy blocked the altar steps with his body and was brutally beaten. Before he died, though, he managed to tell the people of the village what had happened: Jesus had appeared on the altar steps and blessed the two dead boys. The soldiers screamed that the church was haunted and fled. The third boy died radiant, saying, "*We have shielded Jesus.*" My Mother, may I learn from you to shield Jesus in the Eucharist with my prayer and love.

Tuesday 3rd week of Easter
Tuesday 6th May
Jn 6:30-35

So they said to him, "Then what sign do you do, that we may see, and believe you?...Our fathers ate the manna in the wilderness..." Jesus then said to them, "Truly, truly, I say to you, it was not Moses who gave you the bread from heaven; my Father gives you the true bread from heaven. For the bread of God is that which comes down from heaven, and gives life to the world." They said to him, "Lord, give us this bread always." Jesus said to them, "I am the bread of life; he who comes to me shall not hunger, and he who believes in me shall never thirst."

This whole Chapter 6 of St John focuses on the Eucharist. Saints have always been in love with the Eucharist. They could endure anything except to be deprived of the Mass. Bishop Van Thuan was imprisoned in Vietnam for more than 9 years in solitary confinement. Years later he wrote: "*The day I was arrested I had to leave everything behind. The following day I was allowed to write and ask my friends to bring my clothes, toothpaste, etc. I also asked them to include some wine 'as medicine'. They sent me a little bottle of Mass-wine labelled 'Medicine for Stomach Aches'. Every night I kept a tiny piece of bread for the following day's Eucharist.*"

He explained how every day he would ask the guards for a bit of 'medicine', and they would hand him the bottle of wine. "*I never will be able to express my great joy,*" he said later. "*Every day for many years I had the joy of celebrating Mass with three drops of wine and one of water in my palm. This was my altar, my cathedral. For me it was the true medicine of body and soul...Each day in reciting the words of Consecration, I confirmed with all my heart and soul a new pact, an eternal pact between Jesus and me through His Blood mixed with mine. Those were the most beautiful Masses of my life!*"

St Josemaría taught: "*When you approach the Tabernacle remember that he has been awaiting you for twenty centuries.*" My Immaculate Mother, help me to convince Our Lord with deeds that His '20-century wait' for me has been worthwhile. Help me, Mother, to become a Eucharistic soul, because a Eucharistic soul is a powerful soul. Teach me to fall in love with Jesus in the Eucharist, and to receive Him with the purity, humility and devotion with which you, Mary, received Him.

Wednesday 7th May
Jn 6:35-40

Jesus said to them, "All that the Father gives me will come to me; and him who comes to me I will not cast out. For I have come down from heaven, not to do my own will, but the will of him who sent me; and this is the will of him who sent me, that I should lose nothing of all that he has given me, but raise it up at the last day. For this is the will of my Father, that every one who sees the Son and believes in him should have eternal life; and I will raise him up at the last day."

The Father has entrusted Jesus with a mission: that He "*should lose nothing of all that the Father has given Him*". Not a single soul should be lost. All are destined to rise with Him at the end of time. Jesus Himself says, "*him who comes to me I will not cast out*"; no one who *comes* to Him... but they need to *come*. Yet, some don't come to Him; some even run away from Him when He wants to bring them close to Him. They want to be saved, but not *badly*. They want to go to Heaven, but '*kind of*' or '*more-or-less*'. They lack determination.

They pray as St Augustine did when he was young. Although he had no desire to renounce his life of misery and sin, he knew that he had to change. He explains in his *Confessions* how he would pray: "*Lord, give me chastity and continence, but not yet.*" Our Lord needed him for an important mission. Many souls depended on Augustine and his fulfilling the Will of the Father, so God granted him the grace of conversion when he was 31 years old.

After his conversion he worked hard to serve God. He made up for his delay in bringing himself to do the Will of God. Nevertheless, when he looked back at his early life and thought about how much he made Jesus wait until he followed Him, he wrote this lovely prayer: "*Late have I loved you, O Beauty ever ancient, ever new, late have I loved you! You were within me, but I was outside. You were with me, but I was not with you. You called, you shouted, and you broke through my deafness. You flashed, you shone, and you dispelled my blindness. You breathed your fragrance on me; I drew in breath and now I pant for you. I have tasted you, now I hunger and thirst for more. You touched me, and I burned for your peace.*"

Holy Mary, our Hope, may I never make God wait for me to fulfil His Will.

Thursday 3rd week of Easter
Thursday 8th May
Jn 6:44-51

Jesus said to them, "I am the bread of life. Your fathers ate the manna in the wilderness, and they died. This is the bread which comes down from heaven, that a man may eat of it and not die. I am the living bread which came down from heaven; if any one eats of this bread, he will live for ever; and the bread which I shall give for the life of the world is my flesh."

"*I am the bread of life.*" We never have enough of the Eucharist for we can't ever have enough of God. He is that Bread that we ask for many times a day, "*Give us this day our daily bread.*" This is the fuel of the saints. To go up to Heaven we need the Bread that came down from Heaven. Remember *E.T. the Extra-Terrestrial* pointing to the sky and saying "*Home*"? Well, he was right. Our home is up there, and to climb up there our 'rocket' runs on the Eucharist.

In the same way that E.T. managed to get a device to "phone home", persecuted Christians have found the most amazing resources to be able to receive the Eucharist. In nearly two thousand years the Sacramental Jesus has been in all kinds of places: cathedrals and dungeons, basilicas and caves... The daily Bread can reach everywhere when needed. A Latvian Bishop, Boleslas Sloskans (1893-1981), was arrested soon after his episcopal ordination, jailed in seventeen Soviet prisons, deported to Siberia and exiled for over thirty years. With other priests, prisoners also in the Solovki Archipelago, they used a glass for a chalice and the lid of a tin can for a paten. The bread was provided by the jailers. The wine was made from raisins soaked in water. They celebrated Mass at night, in secret. In the morning, in the convoy going to work, Bishop Sloskans distributed the consecrated Hosts to the Catholics, under the utmost secrecy. He hid the remaining Hosts under the roots of a tree, wrapped in a piece of cloth so that those who had not received Communion could do so during the day.

Living in such difficult conditions (hard labour, insufficient food and all sorts of inhuman deprivations and treatment) they survived - as the bishop pointed out - thanks to that "*daily Bread.*"

Mary, Mother of the Eucharist, may I never get used to receiving Jesus in this *daily Bread*.

Friday 3rd week of Easter
Friday 9th May
Jn 6:52-59

The Jews then disputed among themselves, saying, "How can this man give us his flesh to eat?" So Jesus said to them, "Truly, truly, I say to you, unless you eat the flesh of the Son of man and drink his blood, you have no life in you; he who eats my flesh and drinks my blood has eternal life, and I will raise him up at the last day. For my flesh is food indeed, and my blood is drink indeed. He who eats my flesh and drinks my blood abides in me, and I in him."

Jesus couldn't be clearer: "*my flesh is food indeed, and my blood is drink indeed*" and "*he who eats me will live because of me.*" He didn't say 'my flesh is *like* food' or 'kind of food' or 'reminds you of food' or 'if you *sort of* eat my *kind of* flesh...' The meaning was so obvious that the Jews were scandalised, saying, "*How can this man give us his flesh to eat?*" But Jesus repeated the same message again with different words.

In October 1995 St John Paul II was to greet the seminarians at St. Mary's Seminary in Baltimore (USA). On arriving, he expressed his desire to first visit the Blessed Sacrament in the oratory. The security personnel quickly flew into action, doing a sweep of the building and especially the chapel. They brought highly trained dogs used to locate survivors trapped in collapsed buildings after earthquakes and other disasters. The dogs went through the halls, offices and classrooms quickly, and then ran through the chapel and into the side chapel where the Blessed Sacrament was reserved. Upon reaching the Tabernacle, the dogs sniffed and whined and pointed it out, refusing to leave (as if they had discovered '*Someone trapped*' there) and firmly remained, their attention riveted on the Tabernacle. Their handlers asked in amazement what was in that box. And they were told that the right question wasn't '*what*' but '*Who*' was there.

The bishop of that diocese commented, "*It's funny that even dogs can recognise what some Catholics can't: that there is a real living Person in the Tabernacle and that He has been there for 20 centuries waiting for each one of us.*"

Holy Mary, Mother, your Son has been 'trapped' in the Tabernacle for twenty centuries out of love for me; help me to be grateful with deeds of love.

Saturday 3rd week of Easter
Saturday 10th May
Jn 6:60-69

Many of his disciples, when they heard it, said, "This is a hard saying; who can listen to it?"...After this many of his disciples drew back and no longer went about with him. Jesus said to the twelve, "Do you also wish to go away?" Simon Peter answered him, "Lord, to whom shall we go? You have the words of eternal life; and we have believed, and have come to know, that you are the Holy One of God."

The sixth chapter of St John's Gospel ends like this. It could have ended: "*many of his disciples drew back and no longer went about with him.*" But that is not the end. No. It finishes on a high note: '*Jesus said to the twelve, "Do you also wish to go away?"*' And Peter gave the answer for all those Christians who, throughout history, have decided to stay with Jesus no matter what. We could translate his answer from ancient Aramaic into modern English: '*No, no way! Absolutely not!*'

Perseverance is the virtue that allows us to be steady, persistent and loyal in spite of difficulties, obstacles, or discouragement. Where there are obstacles, perseverance is needed. And saints have had tons of both. Of course there have been people who haven't been faithful and have left Our Lord. But that has only been a stimulus for saints to be holier. When St Peter saw that multitude leaving Jesus, he decided to stay. And sure enough, he did. He made mistakes, like on Good Friday, but he died crucified upside down, faithful, loyal. St Maximillian Kolbe had decided to leave the seminary when his mum visited him to explain that his brother wanted to join the seminary too. As you may know, he persevered and became a martyr.

A young priest was moved when chatting with a sixteen-year-old lad. He had decided at a very young age to follow God in a life of celibacy. Many of his best friends also joined him in his vocation. But over time all his friends left that vocation to live mundane lives. "*They have gone! All of them!*" said the boy, weeping, "*they have left me alone.*" Then he took the crucifix that was in front of him in his hands, and looked the priest in the eyes. The priest was speechless when he saw tears streaming down the lad's cheeks and heard him say, "*But I will NOT leave Him alone. I will NOT! I'd rather die.*" Mother most Faithful, pray for us!

Fourth Sunday of Easter
Sunday 11th May
Jn 10:27-30

Jesus said: "My sheep hear my voice, and I know them, and they follow me; and I give them eternal life, and they shall never perish, and no one shall snatch them out of my hand. My Father, who has given them to me, is greater than all, and no one is able to snatch them out of the Father's hand. I and the Father are one."

Those who pray hear the voice of Jesus. They will not hear a 'voice' as such, but will be able to recognise what He says. Like a mother can 'understand' her child even if the baby doesn't pronounce words but just makes random noises. That familiarity with the baby allows the mother to understand. The same happens in our life of prayer. The more we talk to God the more we communicate; the more we communicate, the more we understand His Will for us.

The shepherd's voice gives peace and confidence to the sheep. They trust the shepherd; they know his voice and so follow him. Therefore, no-one shall snatch them out of his hand: they are safe. It's the same with us: there is no safer place than God's Hand.

A man was taking care of his blind daughter when he left her for a moment to go to the grocery store and back. Shortly after, a fire broke out in the building. The fire brigade blocked the street and evacuated the neighbours from the building. With a megaphone, the fire chief was encouraging the people still trapped in the building to jump onto the safety net. They all jumped except the blind girl. She was petrified, frozen to the spot at the window, where her father had left her. At that moment the father arrived and was horrified to discover what was happening. He grabbed the megaphone and said, '*Honey! It's daddy down here. Jump on the count of three!*' Instantly, without a moment's hesitation she jumped. That voice was well known to her!

This Sunday was designated by St John Paul II World Day of Prayer for Vocations. We ask through the intercession of Our Lady that many will hear the voice of God and know the Will of God for them. May they learn to trust in Him and jump into His Hands, for there is no safer place than the Hands of Our Father God.

Monday 4th week of Easter
Monday 12th May
Jn 10:1-10

Jesus again said to them, "Truly, truly, I say to you, I am the door of the sheep. All who came before me are thieves and robbers; but the sheep did not heed them. I am the door; if any one enters by me, he will be saved, and will go in and out and find pasture. The thief comes only to steal and kill and destroy; I came that they may have life, and have it abundantly.

Jesus warned His disciples that not everything that sounded like the voice of God was actually God's voice. Jesus is 'the only door' that leads to God. There was a clever philosopher who was also a bit absent-minded. He had moved with his family to a different area of London were all the Victorian houses looked the same. On one of the first days returning home from work he confused the different streets, since many houses were identical. He found a girl playing in the street and asked her, "*Sorry, little girl. I got confused and I am not sure which of these is my house.*" The girl took pity on the 'lost man', held his hand and replied, "*Don't worry… DADDY. I'll take you home.*" He was really confused!

Many doors may look the same but not all open to the same home. Jesus is the only door to happiness, to eternal life, to peace and hope. He is the only door to the House of God. There is no back door. Many other doors will offer happiness, but they lead to emptiness. That's why it's important for us to get to know Jesus well, to read the Gospels and talk to Him.

Jesus warned against many thieves and robbers who would try to mislead the sheep. But we can't be fooled. No-one who may try to 'impersonate' His voice would deceive a soul of prayer because it knows Jesus' Voice. Like the man, recently converted to Catholicism, who decided to buy a book on the life of Jesus. In the bookshop they told him, "We only have *'The Imitation of Christ'*" (a spiritual classic by Thomas à Kempis). But the man got upset: "*'Imitation'? I don't want an 'imitation'… I want the Real One!*" That's what we need: the Real Jesus, the real Door to happiness. My Mother, you are by the gate, holding the door wide open and calling us, as mothers do when it's time to go indoors for dinner, or because it has started raining or it is getting cold outside. Help me to respond to your call.

Tuesday 4th week of Easter
Tuesday 13th May
Jn 10:22-30

The Jews gathered round him and said to him, "How long will you keep us in suspense? If you are the Christ, tell us plainly." Jesus answered them, "I told you, and you do not believe. The works that I do in my Father's name, they bear witness to me; but you do not believe, because you do not belong to my sheep."

The problem wasn't that Jesus didn't speak plainly enough. The problem was that the Pharisees weren't ready to listen. Some people ask Jesus questions but don't want to hear His reply. They may say, *'If God wants me to do this or that... He can tell me plainly!'* He does; but they don't get it because they are not ready to listen. A radio station can emit music, but if you don't tune in to the station you won't be able to hear it.

It was winter, 1917. A 15-year-old boy was walking through the little town of Logroño (Spain), early in the morning. He stared at the spectacle of the snow-covered town. Then something caught his attention that changed his whole life: some footprints of bare feet in the snow. He followed their trail until he caught up with the Carmelite friar whose feet had made the prints. The boy was dumbfounded. He couldn't stop considering those people in the world, like that man, who are able to make great sacrifices for God and for others. *'What about me?'* he thought, *'Am I not going to be able to offer him anything?'* That was the beginning of his vocation... and a life of sanctity which led this young lad to become St Josemaría, as he is known today.

How many other people saw those same footprints that morning? Did they react as Josemaría did? He was ready to listen to the voice of God, because he was tuned in; he was starting to be a soul of prayer. And he continued to listen to God's voice throughout his life until the end of his days, trying to do the Will of God in everything. *"Blessed are those who hear the word of God,"* said Our Lord, *"and obey it!"* (Lk 11:28)

Those were the words of Jesus when someone mentioned His Mother, for that is precisely what she did. She was always in tune with God. She listened to Him... and obeyed. Mother, teach me to listen and obey always, just as you did.

St Matthias, Apostle
Wednesday 14th May
Jn 15:9-17

"Greater love has no man than this, that a man lay down his life for his friends. You are my friends...No longer do I call you servants...but I have called you friends, for all that I have heard from my Father I have made known to you. You did not choose me, but I chose you and appointed you that you should go and bear fruit and that your fruit should abide."

Matthias was chosen to replace Judas. For a while, Judas was Jesus' friend, but eventually he betrayed Our Lord. "*A faithful friend is a sturdy shelter,*" says Sacred Scripture, "*he that has found one has found a treasure*" (*Sirach* 6:14). We need friends and so does God; loyal friends, strong friends, who are ready to do anything for their friends; just as Jesus did: "*Greater love has no man than this, that a man lay down his life for his friends*". He then concluded, "*You are my friends.*" Judas didn't accept the 'friend request'. Matthias did.

A little girl named Liza was suffering from a rare disease. Her only chance of recovery was a blood transfusion from her five-year-old brother, who had the antibodies needed to combat the illness. The doctor explained the situation to the little boy, and asked him if he would be willing to give his blood to his sister. They saw him hesitate for only a moment before taking a deep breath and saying, "*Yes, I'll do it if it will save Liza.*" As the transfusion progressed, he lay in bed next to his sister and smiled seeing the colour returning to her cheeks. Then his face grew pale and his smile faded. He looked up at the doctor and asked with a trembling voice, "*When will I start to die?*" Being so young, the boy had misunderstood the doctor; he thought he was going to give her *all his blood*. And he was ready to do it because he loved!

"*You are my friend,*" Jesus says. And He could add '*I have* **poured out all my Blood** *for you. And now, what kind of friend of mine are you?*' Maybe I am not as good a friend as I should be. Am I there when *You* need *me*, Lord, at Mass, in my prayer...? Maybe, sometimes, I'm not the most faithful friend, certainly not the most grateful... Mary, my Mother, help me to be a true friend of your Son, through thick and thin, even ready to die for Him if necessary, just as He did for me.

Thursday 4th week of Easter
Thursday 15th May
Jn 13:16-20

After he had washed the feet of his disciples, Jesus said to them: "Truly, truly, I say to you, a servant is not greater than his master; nor is he who is sent greater than he who sent him. If you know these things, blessed are you if you do them. I am not speaking of you all; I know whom I have chosen; it is that the scripture may be fulfilled."

"*I know whom I have chosen.*" You, Lord, knew those you had chosen. You knew them better than they knew themselves. You taught Your Apostles and gave them example, and they learned from You, the Master. You have chosen me as well, for some definite mission in life. And it reassures me to remember that You know me very well, and You know what You made me for.

You, Lord, are like a film director who is trying to find the perfect actor for a perfect role in a particular screenplay. Film directors have to go through catalogues of actors until they find someone who fits the description of the character they need. In the end they find someone who *may be*, more or less, *suitable* for the job, though he or she is rarely perfect.

The difference between the film director looking for actors and You, Lord, is that You don't look for them - You make them! And therefore, You make each one perfect for the role that they have to do: 'You know *whom* You have chosen' and '*what* You have chosen them *for*'. St John Henry Newman expressed it in his prayer: "*God knows me and calls me by my name. God has created me to do Him some definite service; He has committed some work to me which He has not committed to another. He has not created me for naught.*"

I too am made perfect for my role, my mission in life. And I want to do with my life exactly what You, Lord, think is best, for You know me better than I know myself. You know what I can do, Lord, and also what I can't. You, my God, will never ask me for *more* than I can give... but You will never ask me for *less* either.

My Mother, Handmaid of the Lord, intercede for me before your Son for the grace I need to fulfil my mission; to be able to say with you all the days of my life, "*Behold, I am the handmaid of the Lord; let it be done unto me according to your word.*"

Friday 4th week of Easter
Friday 16th May
Jn 14:1-6

Let not your hearts be troubled; believe in God, believe also in me. In my Father's house are many rooms; if it were not so, would I have told you that I go to prepare a place for you? And when I go and prepare a place for you, I will come again and will take you to myself, that where I am you may be also. And you know the way where I am going. Thomas said to him, "Lord, we do not know where you are going; how can we know the way?" Jesus said to him, "I am the way, and the truth, and the life; no one comes to the Father, but by me."

"*Let not your hearts be troubled*" doesn't mean that there won't be troubles. Our Lord also warned about them a couple of chapters later in the same Gospel: "*In the world you have tribulation; but be of good cheer, I have overcome the world*" (*Jn* 16:33). Leave your troubles aside. Don't let them touch your heart. '*Sounds nice*', someone might think, '*but how do I do that?*' The answer is given by Jesus: "*Believe in God.*" Faith!

You see? *Gaudium cum pace* [joy and peace], are fruits of the Holy Spirit. You don't get fruits directly from nothing. They come from trees or plants. From the tree of the virtue of Faith we get the 'fruits' of peace and joy. If we believe in God, we trust Him. If we trust, then we have peace and joy. You find these virtues together in the lives of the saints. They were in love and, therefore, happy. "*May God protect me from gloomy saints,*" prayed St Teresa of Avila.

A four-year-old girl had a new baby brother. On the day he was born she was told that he was a "Gift from Heaven". But the sister found it a bit annoying that the baby was crying all the time. A few days later, seeing the baby crying again, she asked her mum, "*Mum, is it true that the baby came from Heaven?*" "*Of course, sweetheart,*" replied her mother. "*No wonder Jesus threw him out!*" Even if it wasn't the true reason, it fits with the definition of Heaven that gloomy people aren't found there. Saints had many troubles and tribulations, but they never allowed these to affect them. It doesn't mean that they went around with a '*selfie grin*' all the time. They just "*believed in God*", trusted Him.

Holy Mary, Cause of our Joy, pray for me that I may never lose my peace and cheerfulness.

Saturday 4th week of Easter
Saturday 17th May
Jn 14:7-14

"If you had known me, you would have known my Father also; henceforth you know him and have seen him. Philip said to him, "Lord, show us the Father, and we shall be satisfied." Jesus said to him, "Have I been with you so long, and yet you do not know me, Philip?"

It sounds like a reproach, doesn't it? I have been with you all this time, "*and yet you do not know me*". How often this happens with Our Lord! St John Mary Vianney told the story of St Alexis, the only son of a rich Roman senator, who left everything to follow God and, in disguise, he travelled to Syria in the East and lived in great poverty near a Church of Our Lady. After seventeen years, he became a famous holy man there, which was the last thing he wanted, so he ran away and ended up, one day, begging at his parents' home. His parents used to do great works of mercy for the poor. Whilst helping hundreds of other poor people, they assisted him as well; but they did not recognise him. They let him stay in a corner under the stairs, where Alexis lived for seventeen more years, until he died. On the day he died, his own mother was taking care of his dead body when she recognised that it was her son who had lived for years under the stairs in her own palace. Tradition says that she exclaimed in tears, "*O my son! Too late have I known thee!*"

Commenting on the story, St John Mary Vianney said, "*The soul leaving this life will at last see Him, whom she possessed in the Eucharist so many times, and at the sight of the consolations, beauties and riches that she had ignored, she will likewise cry out: "O Jesus! O my Life! O my Treasure! O my Love! Too late have I known Thee!*"

Saints could recognise Jesus in the Eucharist from the very beginning of the history of Christianity: "*I hunger for the bread of God, the flesh of Jesus Christ...I long to drink of his blood, the gift of unending love,*" said St Ignatius of Antioch in the first century. Let's adore Him with the Angels who stand in His presence, constantly glorifying Him: before the *Divine Host* there is always an *angelic host* in adoration. Mary, my Mother, Jesus received His Body from you. Help me to recognise Him in every Tabernacle of the world.

Fifth Sunday of Easter
Sunday 18th May
Jn 13:31-33a, 34-35

When Judas had gone out, Jesus said, "You will seek me; and as I said to the Jews so now I say to you, 'Where I am going you cannot come.' A new commandment I give to you, that you love one another; even as I have loved you, that you also love one another. By this all men will know that you are my disciples, if you have love for one another."

The composition of Jesus' speech is important. The New Commandment was introduced by two facts: One is the departure of Judas; the other is Jesus' statement: *"You will seek me."* This is significant - Jesus said that they will know we are His disciples by the virtue of Love. Judas wasn't a true disciple. He wasn't interested in this New Commandment. He loved money, not Jesus or his neighbour.

The second fact is also important: Jesus was announcing His departure as well: *"You will seek me,"* He said, but *"where I am going you cannot come."* 'Nevertheless,' He could add, 'there is something that you can do: *love one another.*' As if saying: Seek me and you will find Me… in your neighbour. Jesus is in Heaven. We will find ourselves in Heaven with Him if we love one another.

The measure of that love is also given: *"as I have loved you,"* said Jesus. When we love others as Jesus loves them, then we are 'another Jesus' to them and they are 'a Jesus' to us: *"as you did it to one of the least of these my brethren, you did it to me."* Like that young girl, who was thinking about her vocation. She went to visit an old people's home. She was providing all kinds of service: cleaning, feeding, tidying… When she popped into one room to ask if anything was needed, she discovered an old lady crying alone. She came in, held her hands and asked again: *"What do you need?"* *"Just that,"* the old lady answered, *"affection!"* The girl spent the rest of the evening there. When she finished, she went to meet with the priest and told him that she wanted to give her life to God. The priest asked her, *"How did you find out your vocation?"* *"I held Jesus' Hands today,"* she answered, *"and I was so happy that I thought, 'this is what I want to do for the rest of my life: to lend a hand to others… to hold Jesus' hand!'"* Mother of Fair Love, teach me to love everyone as Jesus loves them.

Monday 5th week of Easter
Monday 19th May
Jn 14:21-26

"He who has my commandments and keeps them, he it is who loves me; and he who loves me will be loved by my Father, and I will love him and manifest myself to him." Judas (not Iscariot) said to him, "Lord, how is it that you will manifest yourself to us, and not to the world?"

This same question has been asked many times in history: Why does Jesus reveal Himself to only some people? Why am I a Christian and my neighbour is not? Why doesn't God manifest Himself to everyone? The Apostles had been chosen by Jesus to spend more time with Him. He taught them all they had to know and then, sent them to preach to the 'whole world'. And so, like the links of a chain, all the others depended on them.

God has created every human being to love Him and be happy. Everyone in the depths of their heart longs for happiness, goodness and beauty. They long for God. And God plans to meet everyone. However, why don't they find Him? Maybe because they are not in the habit of listening to their hearts for that longing. That's where you and I have work to do.

Have you ever swum in cold water and accidentally cut or bruised your skin without noticing it? Eventually, someone may have drawn your attention to it or you went out of the water and saw the blood but felt no pain. The reason is that cold numbs your skin's sensitivity. In the same way, the absence of God in the world, the coldness of the spiritual life, can have this effect in people's souls. They feel no longing for God because they feel nothing at all. The continuous rumble and racket, the ceaseless rush and activity, numbs their souls and makes them oblivious to the fact that their souls are bleeding for God, for true happiness.

When those people get out of the water, out of themselves, they get a bit warmer and gradually begin to feel the wound. Then they will want to go to the Doctor. The mission of Christians is, in the words of St Josemaría, to strive to *'raise the spiritual temperature'* so that people will feel the loss of God and will want to search Him out. Mary, my Mother, may I raise the spiritual temperature around me, with my Christian life, to help everyone feel their need of God.

Tuesday 5th week of Easter
Tuesday 20th May
Jn 14:27-31a

Jesus said to his disciples: "Peace I leave with you; my peace I give to you; not as the world gives do I give to you. Let not your hearts be troubled, neither let them be afraid. You heard me say to you, 'I go away, and I will come to you.' If you loved me, you would have rejoiced, because I go to the Father."

Jesus prepared His disciples for His Ascension: He will go to Heaven, but they shouldn't be afraid. Christians have no reason whatsoever to be anxious, because He didn't leave us by ourselves. The Holy Spirit, the Paraclete, is in charge now. And when you work for God and with God, there is nothing that can shake your 'spirit'.

One day a journalist asked Pope St John XXIII if he could sleep well at night with all the worries and anxieties of having to lead the Church. He explained that he had problems at the beginning, until one night he told himself, "*John, why don't you sleep? Is it you or the Holy Spirit who governs the Church? The Holy Spirit, right? Well then, what are you worried about? Go to sleep, John!*" Since then, he said, "*I've been able to sleep like a log.*"

When Bl Alvaro del Portillo was dying, the doctor who was assisting him was very upset. Bl Alvaro took his hand and calmed him down. Many remember how his face and his look always filled those around him with peace. On one occasion someone who worked with him was very anxious about the economic situation they were in. He thought that Bl Alvaro didn't understand it well and said to him, "*Don Alvaro, if this continues you could end up in prison.*" Bl Alvaro replied with serenity, "*If that ever happens, remember to bring me plenty of paper and the type-writer. I can work from there... no problem.*"

Peace is a common feature of all saints; when you are with them you feel at peace. Their own peace 'infects' everyone around them. Our worries and anxieties have to be seen in perspective. When you have a speck of dust on your glasses you see it as a huge stain obstructing your vision. But in reality it is a tiny speck. Mother, Our Lady of Peace, bring peace to the world; bring this fruit of the Holy Spirit into my soul so that I can become, wherever I am, a source of peace for everyone.

Wednesday 5th week of Easter
Wednesday 21st May
Jn 15:1-8

I am the true vine, and my Father is the vinedresser...If a man does not abide in me, he is cast forth as a branch and withers; and the branches are gathered, thrown into the fire and burned. If you abide in me, and my words abide in you, ask whatever you will, and it shall be done for you.

If you remain in Him and His words abide in you then you can "*ask whatever you will, and it shall be done for you.*" This sounds like a great promise, doesn't it? "*Whatever*" shall be "*done for you.*" And because we have a vested interest in this promise, we should remain in Him. To abide in Him is to be always united, as a branch to the trunk. We also need to make sure that His words abide in us; the Word of the Gospel that we meditate on every day. Ask Him now to help you keep His Word in you.

But the promise "*it shall be done for you*" obviously doesn't mean that God is like a shop assistant who has to give us 'anything' we fancy; for you know that we can ask for things that would do us no good. It can also happen that God may delay granting your wish. St Augustine explains that He sometimes delays answering our prayers to increase our '*desire*' for what we pray for and so that we really value what he has given us when it finally comes. Therefore we need to insist when we ask and be appreciative when we receive.

And then, of course, some things are more important to pray for than others. Joyce Kilmer, a soldier in WWII, wrote from the battle fields to a priest asking for prayers. That is nothing new. The amazing thing is what he asked for. He didn't ask that his life might be spared, that he might soon get back safely to his loved ones or that his family would be fine... no. He said in his letter, "*Pray for me, Father, that I may love God more and that I may be unceasingly conscious of Him. That is the greatest wish I have.*" This is one of the best things to ask for; you can do it now.

We can pray today for that same love for God: Holy Mary, My Mother, intercede for me so that "*I may love God more and that I may be unceasingly conscious of Him*". May that always be my "*greatest wish.*"

Thursday 22nd May
Jn 15:9-11

Jesus said to his disciples: "abide in my love. If you keep my commandments, you will abide in my love, just as I have kept my Father's commandments and abide in his love. These things I have spoken to you, that my joy may be in you, and that your joy may be full."

Have you ever felt happy... very, very happy? Can you imagine what it means for our joy to be *"full"*? No, you can't. Because human beings still don't know how *'full'* the human heart can be. If we 'abide' in the Love of God, we will be filled with His joy. He will 'share' His joy with us. If we are united with Him, like branches to the vine, we will absorb His sap and receive the 'fruit of joy' - the joy that all saints had. Could you ever imagine a sad saint? No. It would be like a square circle... Nonsense!

Charles IX, King of France, once asked the poet Torquato Tasso, *"Who do you think is the happiest person?" "God, most certainly,"* said Tasso. *"Bah! I know that; I mean among men"* replied the king. *"The happiest man?,"* replied Tasso, *"he who is closer to God."* Like the vine and the branches: Jesus can share His joy if we are united to Him, if we *'abide in His Love'*.

When she was a child, St Thérèse of Lisieux was upset to learn that not all souls enjoy the same joy in heaven. Her sister Pauline told her to get her thimble and her father's water tumbler and fill them with water. She asked Thérèse which was fuller. But neither was fuller than the other; one simply contained more because it was bigger. That was it! Each soul is filled to its brim and can hold no more; each, being full of God, is completely happy. But saints had bigger hearts, and so, more of Jesus' joy.

"Let anyone who comes to you go away feeling better and happier. Everyone should see goodness in your face, in your eyes, in your smile. Joy shows from the eyes. It appears when we speak and walk. It cannot be kept closed inside us. It reacts outside. Joy is very infectious" (St Teresa of Calcutta).

Holy Mary, Cause of our Joy, intercede for me to enlarge my heart, so that it can be filled with your Son's joy which I can then spread to those around me.

Friday 5th week of Easter
Friday 23rd May
Jn 15:12-17

Greater love has no man than this, that a man lay down his life for his friends. You are my friends...No longer do I call you servants, for the servant does not know what his master is doing; but I have called you friends, for all that I have heard from my Father I have made known to you. You did not choose me, but I chose you and appointed you that you should go and bear fruit and that your fruit should abide; so that whatever you ask the Father in my name, he may give it to you. This I command you, to love one another.

Freedom is a really important part of friendship. You aren't given your friends, you choose them. Jesus chooses His friends as well. And your name is written on the list of His friends. But friendship is like a delicate plant, a bonsai, for instance. You need to take care of it every day; you need at least to put it in the light and water it; in particular seasons plants require more attention (pruning, feeding...) and friends also demand more dedication.

Friends sometimes argue; they may fall out, but they always make up, with humility, after asking for forgiveness and recognising their mistake. That's what we do in Confession when we fail our Friend Jesus Christ. Disagreement isn't the main enemy of friendship; the main enemy of friendship is forgetfulness. If you forget your plant and neglect it... the plant dies. The same could happen to our friendship with Jesus. Let us put a special effort into checking that relationship: Am I being the friend that He wants? Can He find me when He needs me? Do I talk to Him, listen to Him? Do I give Him my time?

"This very moment I may, if I desire, become the friend of God," taught St Augustine. I do desire! You chose me, Lord, to be Your friend, and You made it possible by giving Your Life for me on the Cross. For that reason, I choose You as my best Friend; I want to grow in friendship with You every day, to be with You. Help me not to forget You ever.

Holy Mary, my Mother, ask your Son to treat our friendship like a delicate plant: that He may water it with our daily conversation, feed it with Holy Communion, repair it with Confession. May I abide in His Love to keep our friendship exposed to the rays of the Divine Sun.

Saturday 5th week of Easter
Saturday 24th May
Jn 15:18-21

"If the world hates you, know that it has hated me before it hated you...Remember the word that I said to you, 'A servant is not greater than his master.' If they persecuted me, they will persecute you; if they kept my word, they will keep yours also. But all this they will do to you on my account, because they do not know him who sent me."

Ignorance is the great enemy of God. Those who hate Christians or Jesus Christ do so *"because they do not know him who sent me"*; they just don't know! Do you remember the words of Jesus on the Cross? *"Father, forgive them; **for they know not what they are doing**."* St Stephen, too, as he was stoned by a mob, said a similar prayer (*Acts* 7:60).

Consider the humble reaction of the centurion when Jesus died. He said, *"Truly this man was the Son of God!"* And among the people stoning St Stephen to death was the young Saul of Tarsus, who eventually became St Paul. Some people who don't understand our faith may feel attracted by our 'deeds'. They may think '*Let me see what you believe*' or '*Do you believe in God? Show me!*'

The 40 Martyrs of Sebaste were a group of Christian soldiers condemned in 320AD to freeze to death in an icy pond. The executioners set a warm bath in front of the pond to tempt them to give up. Anyone who wanted to renounce his faith would be invited into the warm bath. One of them yielded, leaving his companions; coming out of the waters, he accepted the offer to renounce his faith. But at that, one of the guards watching over the martyrs (who had seen their example and faithfulness) proclaimed himself a Christian, threw off his garments and joined the other martyrs to complete the number of 40. In the icy waters of the pond he was baptised and in those waters he died with the other martyrs. You see? The centurion, Saul or the guard in the story weren't evil people; they were just ignorant. To convert they didn't need any speech, just the example of Jesus (Master) and the saints (disciples).

My Mother, may I learn to prove my faith with deeds: *"There is a story of a soul who, on saying to our Lord in prayer, 'Jesus, I love you', heard this reply from heaven: 'Love means deeds, not sweet words'"* (St Josemaría).

Sixth Sunday of Easter
Sunday 25th May
Jn 14:23-29

Jesus said, "If a man loves me, he will keep my word, and my Father will love him, and we will come to him and make our home with him. He who does not love me does not keep my words; and the word which you hear is not mine but the Father's who sent me ... Peace I leave with you; my peace I give to you; not as the world gives do I give to you. Let not your hearts be troubled, neither let them be afraid."

If we love Jesus, He and the Father will come and make their home in us. Think about it. It doesn't say a house, but a home. A house is not always a home. We know that God is in every soul in a state of grace. St John of the Cross explains that in some souls God is as if in a foreign place whilst in others God is in His own Home; we could express it as 'in His slippers'. What kind of home do you offer to Him?

Because we can give Him a house but still leave Him 'homeless'. To feel 'at home', God needs to be allowed to enter every room, to have every key of every cupboard and chest. '*If a man loves me*' Jesus seems to be saying, '*he will give me the keys of his home.*' Then He is no longer a guest but the householder. And a householder has permission to arrange his home as he likes.

C. S. Lewis explains: "*Imagine yourself as a living house. God comes in to rebuild that house. At first, perhaps, you can understand what He is doing. He is getting the drains right and stopping the leaks in the roof and so on; you knew that those jobs needed doing and so you are not surprised. But presently He starts knocking the house about in a way that hurts abominably and does not seem to make any sense. What on earth is He up to? The explanation is that He is building quite a different house from the one you thought of - throwing out a new wing here, putting on an extra floor there, running up towers, making courtyards. You thought you were being made into a decent little cottage: but He is building a palace. He intends to come and live in it Himself.*" Yes, you are a living house, a home for God. But you should allow Him to do what He pleases to shape you into the person you need to be. Holy Mary, House of God, you were a perfect dwelling place for Jesus: help me to become a good home for God myself.

Monday 6th week of Easter
Monday 26th May
Jn 15:26-16:4a

"But when the Counsellor comes, whom I shall send to you...he will bear witness to me; and you also are witnesses, because you have been with me from the beginning. I have said all this to you to keep you from falling away...the hour is coming when whoever kills you will think he is offering service to God. And they will do this because they have not known the Father, nor me. But I have said these things to you, that when their hour comes you may remember that I told you of them."

The Holy Spirit, the Paraclete (which means the Advocate or Counsellor) makes us witnesses of Jesus. We become witnesses because we have been '*with Him*'. And in our lives we have to bear witness to our Faith. That's what '*martyr*' means: witness. But don't get it wrong - martyrs didn't become saints only because they 'died' for Jesus, but because first of all, they 'lived' for Jesus. Martyrs could give witness with their 'deaths' because they had already given witness with their 'lives'. They were ready 'to die' for Christ because first they were ready 'to live' for Christ.

On 20th July 1936 in Barbastro (Spain), 49 Claretian Missionaries, most of them young seminarians, were arrested by the militia to be killed for their (our) Faith. They were kept in a hall with small windows through which people in the street could shout and ridicule them. But two of the seminarians were Argentinian and the authorities didn't want to kill foreigners since this course of action would have created diplomatic conflicts. They asked their superiors what to do. On the one hand, they would have liked to die as martyrs and give their lives for Christ. On the other hand, they didn't have to. The superiors agreed that they should ask to be released. '*Your martyrdom,*' they were told, '*will be a long life of service to Our Lord.*' And so it was.

We too can be 'witnesses' (martyrs) of Jesus Christ with our lives: when we work as we should, pray on time, speak confidently about our faith, when we stop a bad conversation, some gossip, a blasphemy, or we stand up for the lives of the innocent... That's how we bear witness to Jesus. That's our martyrdom. And that's what we ask through the intercession of Our Lady: the Holy Spirit's gift of fortitude.

Tuesday 27th May
Jn 16:5-11

"But now I am going to him who sent me; yet none of you asks me, 'Where are you going?' But because I have said these things to you, sorrow has filled your hearts. Nevertheless I tell you the truth: it is to your advantage that I go away, for if I do not go away, the Counsellor will not come to you; but if I go, I will send him to you. And when he comes, he will convince the world concerning sin and righteousness and judgment."

It's to our advantage that You, Lord, have to go, because then we can receive the Holy Spirit. Nevertheless, sorrow fills the hearts of the Apostles when they realise that they won't be able to see You until the end of their lives, because they love You. I can well understand it. You are the Light. And our lives with You are like hiking in beautiful snow-capped mountains reflecting the brilliance of the sun. But when You aren't with us night falls: the same landscape is dark, solitary and devoid of all warmth.

One day in Rome, during an audience with Pope St John Paul II, a lady was greeting the Pontiff with her husband. After a brief introduction she took the hand of her husband, put it in the hands of the Pope and said, "*Holy Father, could you say something to my husband?*" And, to the poor man's embarrassment, she added, "*He hasn't gone to Confession for a very long time.*" St John Paul II smiled at him, pressed that man's hand and, gazing affectionately into his eyes answered, "*Go to Confession. It's so sad to be away from God!*"

It is sad to live without God, especially when we have been created, not just to live with God but to be, in actual fact, his dwelling. That is the point: God isn't content by just being 'with us'; He wants to be 'in us'. When St Paul wanted to remind the Corinthians that they should strive to live according to moral law, he asked them, "*Do you not know that your body is a temple of the Holy Spirit within you, which you have from God?*" (6:19) As if saying, 'Are you unaware of the most important truth about yourselves? Then, why don't you behave accordingly?'

Mary, my Mother, I am aware of it. The Holy Spirit wants to dwell in me and with your help, Spouse of the Holy Spirit, I will give Him a good 'accommodation'.

Wednesday 6th week of Easter
Wednesday 28th May
Jn 16:12-15

"I have yet many things to say to you, but you cannot bear them now. When the Spirit of truth comes, he will guide you into all the truth; for he will not speak on his own authority, but whatever he hears he will speak, and he will declare to you the things that are to come. He will glorify me, for he will take what is mine and declare it to you. All that the Father has is mine; therefore I said that he will take what is mine and declare it to you."

"*I have yet many things to say to you...*" Jesus had revealed part of the truth to His disciples but not everything. Who would reveal the rest? The Holy Spirit, the Paraclete, the Counsellor. He would guide them "*into all the truth*". As Jesus promised, the Holy Spirit assists the Church now and gently guides her into *all* the truth".

"*Without the Holy Spirit everything is cold,*" said St John Vianney. "*The Sacraments instituted by Our Lord wouldn't have saved us without the Holy Spirit. Even the very Death of Our Lord would have been useless without Him. It's like being given a treasure; it would be necessary for someone to distribute it: the Father gave His Son, the Son gave Himself and the Holy Spirit came to distribute all His graces.*" Our Lord said it: "*It is to your advantage that I go away.*" We need the Holy Spirit to complete what Jesus had started. Otherwise His Work would be incomplete, wasted, like a race that is not finished.

The Counsellor comes clarifying everything. He is the Teacher. You can have the manual, but you need someone to explain the difficult parts. That's one of the gifts of the *Counsellor*: the gift of counsel. One day a priest from the diocese of Autun had a very difficult moral case that he couldn't solve. After consulting many other priests and finding no solution, he decided to go to Ars and ask St John Vianney. The Curé had had a hard time in the seminary trying to study theology and pass his exams. Nevertheless, he gave a quick and simple answer: three words were enough. "*How could you possibly know?! Where did you learn that?*" asked the surprised priest. In answer, St John Vianney just smiled and pointed at the kneeler. It's to 'our advantage' that we ask the *Counsellor* for advice. Holy Mary, Spouse of the Holy Spirit, teach me to listen to the Paraclete.

Day 1 of the Ten-Day Devotion to the Holy Spirit
The Ascension of Our Lord
Thursday 29th May
Lk 24:46-53

Jesus said to his disciples "Thus it is written, that the Christ should suffer and on the third day rise from the dead, and that repentance and forgiveness of sins should be preached in his name to all nations... You are witnesses of these things..." Then...while he blessed them, he parted from them, and was carried up into heaven.

He told them to "*go*" and they went: "*they went forth and preached everywhere.*" They split and went to different cities, different countries, different continents... they learned different languages, travelled by land, on horseback, on foot or by sea to reach as many destinations as they could. In some places they were listened to; in others they were laughed at, taken for fools, insulted or stoned; when they were cast out of one city they went forth to the next. Jesus told them to "*go*" and so off they went.

Jesus had sent His disciples in pairs to many places previously, to tell everyone that the Kingdom of God was near. But they couldn't say much more. When they were asked if Jesus was the Messiah, they probably said "*We think so.*" The news was still incomplete. But now they could go and spread the Good News. Good News? What 'Good News'? That Jesus had died for them on the Cross, that He died but wasn't dead anymore, that He rose from the dead, that their sins had been washed away with His Precious Blood, that Heaven was open now, that God loved them so much that He gave up His Son for them; that He promised His grace to anyone who asked for it. That God was in Heaven but also here, in the shape of Bread to meet them; that He wanted to talk to them, to converse with them, to live with them... in them! That they were free now; that God wasn't just their Creator... He was their Father! And to tell them that He was waiting for their reply.

They went forth and never stopped until they were killed. But many others followed them; and the more they killed, the more people '*went forth*' to preach in other places that God is madly in love with them and He is still there... waiting for each of them to give an answer. Lord, I have given You my answer. Now I need Your grace and the intercession of my Mother, Queen of Apostles, to go to those I can reach out to and tell them the 'Good News'.

Day 1 of the Ten-Day Devotion to the Holy Spirit
Thursday 6th week of Easter
Thursday 29th May
Jn 16:16-20

"A little while, and you will see me no more; again a little while, and you will see me." Some of his disciples said to one another, "What is this that he says to us ... Jesus said to them, "Truly, truly, I say to you, you will weep and lament, but the world will rejoice; you will be sorrowful, but your sorrow will turn into joy."

Sometimes we don't see Our Lord, but that is only for "*a little while*"; moments in which we "*weep and lament*". During these moments God's enemies will rejoice, thinking that they have won; but not for long, because we have been promised by Him that we are on the winning side – and God always fulfils His promises.

Do you remember the story of the Trojan horse? The city of Troy was protected by a wall, 20 feet high. The Greek warriors had been trying to breach the wall around Troy for about ten years. Finally, Odysseus, a Greek general, had an idea. They built a huge, beautiful wooden horse and left it outside the gate. The Greek army pretended to leave, as if they had finally admitted defeat. But the horse was hollow and 30 men were hiding inside. The following morning the Trojans thought they had defeated the Greeks and rushed outside, cheering. They found the horse and dragged it inside the city as a '*trophy of victory*'. That night, while the Trojan people were sleeping, the men hiding inside the wooden horse climbed out and opened the gates. The waiting Greek army entered the city. That was the end of Troy.

Likewise, when the devil saw the dead Body of Our Lord hanging on the Cross, he was convinced he had overcome Him and thought that the Cross had become his '*trophy*'. Like the Trojan people, he was confident and at peace. But at dawn on the third day the Risen Body of Jesus Christ came out of the Tomb and shone, living and radiant. Then the enemy saw his mistake; he understood *he* had been overcome on the Cross and defeated for all eternity! Altogether it was just one day - Good Friday - on which Jesus' Body was beaten and abased. But the enemy has been beaten and abased forever. Mary, my Mother, always be close to me when it is time to "*weep and lament*"; remind me then that it'll be just for a "*little while*"... because in the end your Son wins!

Day 2 of the Ten-Day Devotion to the Holy Spirit
Friday 6th week of Easter
Friday 30th May
Jn 16:20-23

"Truly, truly, I say to you, you will weep and lament, but the world will rejoice; you will be sorrowful, but your sorrow will turn into joy. When a woman is in travail she has sorrow, because her hour has come; but when she is delivered of the child, she no longer remembers the anguish, for joy that a child is born into the world. So you have sorrow now, but I will see you again and your hearts will rejoice, and no one will take your joy from you."

He never promised it was going to be 'easy'; He said it was going to be 'worthwhile'. Jesus makes several promises here. The first one is rather negative: "*You will weep and lament*". But then the positive ones come: "*Your sorrow will turn into joy*" and "*no one will take your joy from you.*" No one; ever! Know it well: gloominess is the mark of the enemy; it is the ally of the devil. But the joy of the children of God is like rubbing salt in the enemy's wound. St Paul said it: "*Rejoice in the Lord always; again I will say, Rejoice.*"

Billy Joel says in one of his songs, "*I'd rather laugh with the sinners than cry with the saints. The sinners are much more fun.*" We are really certain (and sad) that he never met a saint. Saints have never lost their joy and good humour in the middle of their distress. "*Laugh and grow strong,*" St. Ignatius said; and to one of his novices, "*I see you are always laughing, and I am glad of it.*" St Josemaría said that he founded Opus Dei just with "*the grace of God, twenty six years of age and good humour.*" St Francis de Sales comforted a hunchback with these words: "*The works of God are perfect.*" "*What!*" replied the man. "*Perfect, and yet deformed?*" "*Well...*" answered the saint, "*a perfect hunchback!*" St Philip Neri, St John Vianney, St Teresa, St Francis of Assisi... There are thousands of stories in any saint's life.

In 1534 two martyrs were on trial for refusing to swear a solemn oath acknowledging Henry VIII as head of the church in England. The judge said plainly, "*If you don't swear you'll be tied up and thrown into the Thames*". They replied with a big smile, "*We just want to go to Heaven. We don't really mind if it is by water or by land!*" That is it: good-humoured and cheerful until the end. My Mother, Cause of our Joy, when things become difficult for me, please make me consider slowly: ***no one, ever*** *'will take my joy away from me.'*

Day 3 of the Ten-Day Devotion to the Holy Spirit
Visitation of Our Lady
Saturday 31st May
Lk 1:39-56

In those days Mary arose and went with haste into the hill country, to a city of Judah, and she entered the house of Zechariah and greeted Elizabeth. And when Elizabeth heard the greeting of Mary, the babe leaped in her womb; and Elizabeth was filled with the Holy Spirit and she exclaimed with a loud cry, "Blessed are you among women, and blessed is the fruit of your womb! And why is this granted me, that the mother of my Lord should come to me?" And Mary remained with her about three months, and returned to her home.

We imagine Our Lady sometimes as a calm and contemplative woman who never did anything in a hurry. Just like one of those statues of saints that adorn our churches: motionless, hands joined in prayer and looking at the skies... But the Gospel teaches something very different: Our Lady went "*with haste.*" Although she certainly was a contemplative woman who was never anxious or impulsive, she was also a woman of action.

The Angel told her that she was to be the Mother of God. She didn't have to do anything special. The Holy Spirit performed the miracle. But there were lots of things to think about... what about Joseph? What about her family? She could be stoned to death if people found out that Joseph wasn't the father of that Child. What about preparing for the Child's Birth? But over and above all those 'personal' problems, she had been told of Elizabeth's situation: old and pregnant. Nothing else was needed for Our Mother to set out "*with haste*" to help her cousin. No one had asked her to help. She had many worries to think about, certainly. But someone needed her. And she stayed there for three long months, for as long as she was needed.

We need to stop thinking about Our Mother as a pious and still statue absorbed in prayer and imagine her more like a superhero, a woman of action. Someone is in need of help and she flies there instantly. And if she *went with haste* to help her cousin... will she not come even faster to assist her children? For that's what we are: her children.

How comforting it is to know, Mother, that you fly promptly to my side when I need you. Thank you, Mary, for being such a Mother!

June

Day 4 of the Ten-Day Devotion to the Holy Spirit
Seventh Sunday of Easter
Sunday 1st June
Jn 17:20-26

"I do not pray for these only, but also for those who believe in me through their word, that they may all be one; even as thou, Father, art in me, and I in thee, that they also may be in us, so that the world may believe that thou hast sent me...Father, I desire that they also, whom thou hast given me, may be with me where I am."

See how Jesus prays, how He talks to His Father-God. He prayed for His disciples... and for you and me, *"those who believe in Him through their word."* In a few words, Jesus prayed for billions of people. This is a good lesson on how we should pray.

Some may think that, when they ask God for particular graces, their prayers could be more effective if they focused on a few rather than on many; they may think that, if you pray for one friend instead of praying for ten, your 'one friend' gets a greater 'dose of prayer'. That is not how it works with God. The Mercy of God and His Love are infinite. It's nonsense to think that if you swim in the sea alone you get wetter than if you swim with a hundred more people. Well, we could run out of waters in the ocean, but God's Love for us will never wear out.

God loves it when His children ask Him for whatever they need. It is a token of trust. He loves to be told, *"Jesus, I leave this in Your Hands"* or *"Lord, I entrust to You this and that."* Saints are the ones who asked God for more. They never tired of asking, they never stopped pestering, they never had too many intentions or too many people to pray for or too little time to pray... They never said to anyone, *'Sorry, I am currently engaged, praying for something or someone else...'*

St Josemaría explained that for a time he stopped asking God to allow Him to give according to His Will. But later on he started praying *"without ceasing"* with a *"continuous clamour, day and night."*

Saints are 'addicted' to asking for God's intercession and loved to be entrusted with more intentions to pray for. Mary, Help of Christians, teach me to pray for more, without ceasing.

Day 4 of the Ten-Day Devotion to the Holy Spirit
The Ascension of Our Lord
Sunday 1st June
Lk 24:46-53

Jesus said to his disciples "Thus it is written, that the Christ should suffer and on the third day rise from the dead, and that repentance and forgiveness of sins should be preached in his name to all nations... You are witnesses of these things..." Then...while he blessed them, he parted from them, and was carried up into heaven.

He told them to "*go*" and they went: "*they went forth and preached everywhere.*" They split and went to different cities, different countries, different continents... they learned different languages, travelled by land, on horseback, on foot or by sea to reach as many destinations as they could. In some places they were listened to; in others they were laughed at, taken for fools, insulted or stoned; when they were cast out of one city they went forth to the next. Jesus told them to "*go*" and so off they went.

Jesus had sent His disciples in pairs to many places previously, to tell everyone that the Kingdom of God was near. But they couldn't say much more. When they were asked if Jesus was the Messiah, they probably said "*We think so.*" The news was still incomplete. But now they could go and spread the Good News. Good News? What 'Good News'? That Jesus had died for them on the Cross, that He died but wasn't dead anymore, that He rose from the dead, that their sins had been washed away with His Precious Blood, that Heaven was open now, that God loved them so much that He gave up His Son for them; that He promised His grace to anyone who asked for it. That God was in Heaven but also here, in the shape of Bread to meet them; that He wanted to talk to them, to converse with them, to live with them... in them! That they were free now; that God wasn't just their Creator... He was their Father! And to tell them that He was waiting for their reply.

They went forth and never stopped until they were killed. But many others followed them; and the more they killed, the more people '*went forth*' to preach in other places that God is madly in love with them and He is still there... waiting for each of them to give an answer. Lord, I have given You my answer. Now I need Your grace and the intercession of my Mother, Queen of Apostles, to go to those I can reach out to and tell them the 'Good News'.

Day 5 of the Ten-Day Devotion to the Holy Spirit
Monday 7th week of Easter
Monday 2nd June
Jn 16:29-33

Jesus said to his disciples, "The hour is coming, indeed it has come, when you will be scattered, every man to his home, and will leave me alone; yet I am not alone, for the Father is with me. I have said this to you, that in me you may have peace. In the world you have tribulation; but be of good cheer, I have overcome the world."

Jesus knew that His disciples were going to be scattered. He knew that over the years many Christians would have to leave their homes and run away with their families as St Joseph had to do. Knowing this, He wanted to record in the memory of His disciples the fact that they would never be alone: God would be with them.

Despite having been brought up a Christian, Roman Emperor Julian the Apostate (331 – 363) decided to persecute the Church with all his might. He was determined to wipe out the religion of 'the Galilean', Jesus Christ, and restore the pagan religion. Old temples were renovated and new ones built, and the pagan priesthood was reinstated. On June 26th 363, in the battle against the Sassanid army, he was wounded with a spear and died at the age of 32. As he lay dying, he realised that all his efforts to stamp out the message of Christ had failed. "*You have won, O Galilean!*"

Now, 2,000 years on, there are over 1,000,000,000 Catholics in the world. The Church survived and even flourished despite times of terrible persecution by Romans, barbarians and Saracens; and more recently from communism, fascism and Nazism. Those 'kingdoms' have come and gone, while the spiritual kingdom of Christ continues in the hearts of those who love Him. We, therefore, can never be surprised or afraid of the difficulties that Christians may find in their lives, including our interior lives: temptations, dryness, misunderstandings, loneliness. We need to be aware that we usually go against the grain. We will always "*have tribulation*", said Jesus. But let's not stop there. Let's read the rest of the sentence and keep it fresh in our hearts: *be of good cheer, I have overcome the world.*"

My Mother, Help of Christians, intercede for those who suffer persecution of any kind, for those who undergo any tribulation, and especially for those who need my prayer most today.

Day 9 of the Ten-Day Devotion to the Holy Spirit
Tuesday 7th week of Easter
Tuesday 3rd June
Jn 17:1-11a

Jesus said, "I glorified thee on earth, having accomplished the work which thou gave me to do...I have manifested thy name to the men whom thou gave me out of the world; thine they were, and thou gave them to me, and they have kept thy word ... and I am glorified in them. And now I am no more in the world, but they are in the world."

Men are obliged to glorify God, to worship Him. And the best worship that men can give is when we glorify God with Jesus Christ. The summit of Christian worship is the Holy Mass; in it Jesus *'glorifies the Father on earth'* and we (who are still 'in the world') unite ourselves to Him. For that reason there is nothing more important in the world than the Mass; each and every single Mass, because it is the Sacrifice of Jesus on Calvary.

During World War II Nazis forced many priests into concentration camps and many of these were sent to Dachau. At least 2,720 priests were together in a single area, the *'Priesterblock'*, and they were permitted to have a single altar on which to celebrate one Mass a day. One priest said the Mass and others attended it. Bl Karl Leisner was then a deacon. His ordination to the priesthood was delayed because he was suffering from tuberculosis. But before he could be ordained the war broke out and he was arrested. He had already spent 5 years in concentration camps. On December 17, 1944, knowing that his health was getting worse, he was secretly ordained by a fellow prisoner, a French bishop. He said he wanted to die as a priest and he especially wanted to say the Mass before he died. Already very ill with tuberculosis, Leisner's first Mass on December 30 was in fact his last, because he died soon after. Many priests who attended it said that they could never forget his love and devotion for the Mass. They could see in his face that he had prepared that Mass and longed for it his entire life.

To help the priest prepare himself for the Mass, in some sacristies you can find the following text: "*O Priest of God, say this Mass as though it were your first Mass, your last Mass, your only Mass.*" Mary, Mother of the Eucharist, help me to attend the Mass as if it were my first Mass, my last Mass ... the only Mass of my life.

Day 7 of the Ten-Day Devotion to the Holy Spirit
Wednesday 7th week of Easter
Wednesday 4th June
Jn 17:11b-19

"Holy Father...I have given them thy word; and the world has hated them because they are not of the world, even as I am not of the world. I do not pray that thou should take them out of the world, but that thou should keep them from the evil one."

Have you ever been on one of those boats which are so comfortable that once you are on board you forget you are travelling? But every now and then you pop your head out and are reminded that we didn't get on the vessel to stay on it: we are on our way to somewhere else. The same happens with the world. We are not 'of' the world, but we are 'in the world'. Remember the quote of St Thérèse of Lisieux, "*The world's thy ship and not thy home.*"

A priest was one day telling a story in his homily. A young student went sailing for the weekend with a friend and his dad. But when they were out to sea, a storm broke out; the boat capsized and started sinking. The father saw with horror that the waves had separated the two boys. Grabbing a rescue line, he had to make the most excruciating decision of his life: which boy he would save with the other end of the line. His son saw him hesitating and shouted, "*Save him, Dad, he is not Christian. I am in the state of grace!*" The father then threw the line to his son's friend whilst his own child drowned. After Mass someone approached the priest and said, "*Nice story, father, but I don't think it was very realistic for a father to give up his son's life in the hope that the other boy would become a Christian*". The priest smiled and replied, "*Well, that is what God did: He sacrificed His Son so that you and I can be saved. And apart from that, you see? I was the son's friend.*"

Life is just a ship and we are on a voyage to Heaven. We are not of this world (this ship) but on it. On this trip there are dangers (the devil), but ever since Jesus died for us, we are safe. There will be storms but Our Father will protect us. He will not take us "*out of the world*" (we need the ship to reach Heaven) but, if we ask Him, He will "*keep us from the evil one.*"

My Mother, Star of the Sea, please guide my journey and always be close to me when the storm breaks out.

Day 8 of the Ten-Day Devotion to the Holy Spirit
Thursday 7th week of Easter
Thursday 5th June
Jn 17:20-26

"I do not pray for these only, but also for those who believe in me through their word, that they may all be one; even as thou, Father, art in me, and I in thee, that they also may be in us, so that the world may believe that thou hast sent me...Father, I desire that they also, whom thou hast given me, may be with me where I am."

It fills me with confidence to know that You, Lord, prayed for me to the Father. Because I'm one of those who believed in You "*through their word.*" Over the years, in the Church, the faith has been transmitted by witnesses who received it and passed on faithfully what they were given. As Easter comes to an end, we commemorate the moment in which You, Lord, gave the last push to Your Church to keep moving steadily forward: we hear Your prayer for unity in Your Church, '*that we may be one.*'

The Church will be effective as long as it is united, as happens with a football team. We have one Manager (the Father), one Founder (Christ), one Coach (the Holy Spirit), one Captain (the Pope), one goal (the salvation of everyone). If we are united there is no enemy that could be a threat. Nothing is impossible if we are really 'united'.

The rock band U2's hit single 'One' had the following lyrics: "*We're one, but we're not the same.*" In the Church we are also many and all of us are different from each other, just as in the football team all the players have different positions, different skills and different roles. It would be ridiculous to have 11 goalkeepers on the field!

An old man gave his grandson a tiny stick and asked him to break it. He broke it easily. Next he gave him ten sticks all stuck together; the boy couldn't break the bundle. Then he explained, "*This is like the family: you can't break it if we are together.*" And that's what the Church is - our big family. You, Mary, Mother of the Church, are the Mother of this family of ours. I pray today with your Son for the unity of the Church. That we may learn to play together as a team, all in different positions, following the instructions of the Coach (Paraclete) and playing together with the Captain (Pope).

Holy Mary, Mother of the Church, pray for us... and actually, also '*play*' for us!

Day 9 of the Ten-Day Devotion to the Holy Spirit
Friday 7th week of Easter
Friday 6th June
Jn 21:15-19

Jesus said to Simon Peter, "Simon, son of John, do you love me more than these?" He said to him, "Yes, Lord; you know that I love you." He said to him, "Feed my lambs." A second time he said to him, "Simon, son of John, do you love me?" He said to him, "Yes, Lord; you know that I love you." He said to him, "Tend my sheep." He said to him the third time, "Simon, son of John, do you love me?" Peter was grieved because he said to him the third time, "Do you love me?" And he said to him, "Lord, you know everything; you know that I love you."

Before His Ascension, Jesus had to prepare St Peter for the task that God had prepared for him. Peter denied Jesus three times on Good Friday so Jesus asked him three times if he loved Him. Peter wasn't perfect. It is clear when we read the Gospels. But his love for Jesus was sincere and intense. "*All you need is love,*" says the famous Beatles' song. That's all Peter needed to start again and change the course of history.

God doesn't need perfect instruments. He needs people who know how to love and follow Him, who begin and begin again, without giving up, for love. A saint is a sinner who keeps trying. Saints are in Heaven not because they didn't fall, but because they always picked themselves up. Michael Jordan, probably the best basketball player of all times, said once, "*I've missed more than 9000 shots in my career. I've lost almost 300 games. 26 times, I've been trusted to take the game-winning shot and missed. I've failed over and over and over again in my life. And that is why I succeed...*" - because he didn't give up. St Peter fell but didn't remain down. He loved Jesus, trusted Him, and empowered by God's strength, Peter began again.

"*When Christ at a symbolic moment was establishing His great society, He chose for its cornerstone neither the brilliant Paul nor the mystic John, but a shuffler, a snob, a coward – in a word, a man. All the empires and the kingdoms have failed because they were founded by strong men and upon strong men. But the historic Christian Church was founded on a weak man, and for that reason it is indestructible*" (G K Chesterton).

Holy Mary, Mother of the Church, pray for the Pope and for all Christians.

Day 10 of the Ten-Day Devotion to the Holy Spirit
Saturday 7th week of Easter
Saturday 7th June
Jn 21:20-25

This is the disciple who is bearing witness to these things, and who has written these things; and we know that his testimony is true. But there are also many other things which Jesus did; were every one of them to be written, I suppose that the world itself could not contain the books that would be written.

This is the end of the Gospel of St John, who saw all these things and many more. This witness couldn't write everything. So Jesus sent the Holy Spirit and founded the Church. The meaning is clear: Sacred Scripture isn't everything; we need also what the Spirit has said through the apostles (Tradition) and their successors (the Church's teaching, that we call '*Magisterium*'). In this way, the Holy Spirit can still reveal the meaning of Scripture to us.

Sacred Scripture is like a letter from Jesus to everyone, and He made sure that everyone could receive it and understand it: *Everyone!* from any race, language or background. That's the mission of the Church, governed by the Holy Spirit watching over Scripture, Tradition, and the Magisterium. How beautiful Our Mother the Church is, and how much we should love her and behave as her good children! Love her for being the immaculate Bride of Christ, for having been born from His opened Side, for having begotten us as children, nourished us, brought us forgiveness and for teaching us to love God.

But not everyone can see her beauty. It is like the stained glass windows of an old cathedral. Seen from the outside, you just perceive strips of dark dusty glass joined with black lead. However, seen from the inside, with the sun's rays passing through them, you contemplate a spectacle of colours and figures that fill you with awe. The same happens with the Church: seen from the outside, with a worldly vision, as an 'institution' or an 'organization', you don't see anything but darkness and miseries. But from the inside, with the eyes of faith and the light of grace, you see a wondrous edifice, a perfectly assembled body, the beautiful Spouse that Jesus Christ loves.

"What joy to be able to say with all the fervour of my soul: I love my Mother the holy Church!" (St Josemaría). Mary, Mother of the Church, teach me to love her as the Bride of Christ.

Pentecost
Sunday 8th June
Jn 20:19-23

Jesus came and stood among them and said to them, "Peace be with you." When he had said this, he showed them his hands and his side. Then the disciples were glad when they saw the Lord. Jesus said to them again, "Peace be with you. As the Father has sent me, even so I send you." And when he had said this, he breathed on them, and said to them, "Receive the Holy Spirit. If you forgive the sins of any, they are forgiven; if you retain the sins of any, they are retained."

"*Receive the Holy Spirit.*" In the first reading of today's Mass we hear the account of Pentecost, the day on which the growth rate of the Church exploded; when three thousand people from all walks of life listened to a 'fisherman' speak about Jesus Christ, whose death they had asked for a few weeks before, and they asked to be baptised. This is the power of the Holy Spirit that Jesus breathed on His disciples. The Holy Spirit transformed all those, but no transformation was more astonishing than the conversion of Peter. Oh Peter! Who can recognise you now? You don't run away today, and don't hide for fear of the Jews; you now deploy more energy in preaching than you did before in hiding. A few days ago you, Peter, were frightened by the voice of a servant, and very soon you will stand unshakable under the blows of the chief priests.

Who could now doubt the transforming power of the Holy Spirit, when we can see this transformation in St Peter? Who wouldn't pray to that same Spirit: '*Come, O Holy Spirit, do the same with me*'? If He did that in Peter, what couldn't He do in your soul and mine who also need conversion in so many things? If I let the Holy Spirit work in me, if I'm docile to Him, I will get rid of that defect, acquire that virtue...

Holy Mary, Spouse of the Holy Spirit, you were there on that day too. I can imagine your eyes glowing with love and joy as you saw that transformation in Peter, whom you loved. And you are now with me every day, helping me to be docile to the Holy Spirit. I can imagine your smile when you see me transformed by the Holy Spirit into another Peter, a daring apostle of your Son, telling everyone about how much God loves them, and all that He has in store for them if they too become temples of the Holy Spirit!

The Blessed Virgin Mary, Mother of the Church
Monday 9th June
Jn 19:25-34

Standing near the cross of Jesus were his mother, and his mother's sister, Mary the wife of Clopas, and Mary Magdalene. When Jesus saw his mother and the disciple whom he loved standing beside her, he said to his mother, 'Woman, here is your son.' Then he said to the disciple, 'Here is your mother.' And from that hour the disciple took her into his own home.

Mary, my Mother, you are not only the Queen of the Church, you are also her Mother. And the Church needs a Mother now more than ever. We are safe on your lap. The enemy attacks the Church but we are not afraid. The world howls against Christians but we fear nothing. Christians are persecuted, vilified, scorned, but we are shielded under your mantle, Tower of Ivory, and do not dismay.

She is not Queen only because she is the Mother of the King. She is Queen also by 'conquest', since she has beaten the enemy who now dares not approach her or any of those who are close to her. Where she reigns there is no room for the dragon.

Do you remember the battle of 'The Lord of the Rings', after the unexpected advance of the Rohirrim? The witch-king Nazgûl attacks Théoden, who had outrun his own riders. The king's horse, struck by a dart, falls upon Théoden. As the witch-king approaches him to kill him, Éowyn, the king's niece, bars his way. She decapitates his mount and the Witch-king sends a powerful blow from his mace, breaking her arm and her shield. As he prepares to finish her off, he says, "*You, fool, no man can kill me!*" [Merry stabs the back of the witch-king's knee with a Dúnedain dagger which bears enchantments deadly to the witch-king.] Then Éowyn says, "*I am no man!*" and then thrusts her sword into the witch-king's face and he vanishes with a wailing cry.

Don't think about our Queen as one of those delicate, timid and weak little photoshopped models in fashion magazines. She is the Queen of a warrior people and knows how to defend her children. Remind the enemies of the Church when they surround you: '*We've got a Mother and a Powerful Queen, and we're not afraid to use her!*'

Tuesday 10th June
Mt 5:13-16

Jesus said: "You are the light of the world. A city set on a hill cannot be hid. Nor do men light a lamp and put it under a bushel, but on a stand, and it gives light to all in the house. Let your light so shine before men, that they may see your good works and give glory to your Father."

Christians are called to shine, not like the sun, but like the moon. The sun produces light, the moon only reflects it. God produces light and saints reflect the light of God. When a house has no lights on we think it is empty. When we enter the house and turn lights on, the 'dark' atmosphere changes into a living home. In the same way, we Christians carry our own bright atmosphere wherever we go.

An atmosphere such as that of the concentration camps can make a profound impression on the inmates. In those situations, previously good, well-tempered people started to fall into arguments, fights and even criminal behaviour. In all, 2,579 Catholic priests were sent to Dachau concentration camp. But the atmosphere in the 'Priest Block' was quite different and puzzling for the SS guards. They could hear them sometimes singing, and often see them smiling. Not a few of the guards were bowled over by the priests' example: they served each other, they helped each other. They never fought for food unless to save it for the sick or weak ones. The oppressive atmosphere of the camp was challenged by the bright Christian atmosphere that the 'Priest Block' irradiated over the camp. This 'challenge' infuriated the Nazi guard, who tortured them with even more cruelty, ignorant of the source of their joy. '*But the more hatred they received*' said one of the survivors from another barrack, '*the more love they spread. The Priest Block was a beacon of light that prevented us getting lost in the darkness of despair. They sowed peace and joy all over the camp. They taught us to counteract an environment of hatred and brutality with love and forgiveness. They filled us with hope and so, saved our lives.*'

That's the light that Christ places in our hearts. My Mother, help me to maintain a bright Christian atmosphere wherever I am, following the advice of St Josemaría: "*Don't let your life be barren. Be useful. Make yourself felt. Shine forth with the torch of your faith and your love.*"

St Barnabas, Apostle
Wednesday 11th June
Mt 10:7-13

Jesus said to his apostles, "preach as you go, saying, 'The kingdom of heaven is at hand.' Heal the sick, raise the dead, cleanse lepers, cast out demons. You received without paying, give without pay. Take no gold, nor silver, nor copper in your belts, no bag for your journey, nor two tunics, nor sandals, nor a staff; for the labourer deserves his food. And whatever town or village you enter, find out who is worthy in it, and stay with him until you depart. As you enter the house, salute it. And if the house is worthy, let your peace come upon it; but if it is not worthy, let your peace return to you."

This is the commandment for all Christians: "*Preach as you go.*" Wherever you go, whatever you do, whomever you are with, whoever you are... preach as you go! Today we celebrate the feast of St Barnabas, the apostle. He wasn't one of the Twelve but probably was among the 72 disciples who Jesus sent to preach ahead of Him. In today's Gospel we read the instructions that Jesus gave to them, and that we can summarise as: '*preach as you go, and don't worry about anything else; just rely on God.*' And that is exactly what St Barnabas did.

We know two important things about Barnabas. 1) He was generous: he "*sold a field which belonged to him, and brought the money and laid it at the apostles' feet*" to be distributed among the needy. 2) He was a '*good scout*' a great '*talent-spotter*'. After the martyrdom of St Stephen many Christians ran away from Jerusalem. Many went to Antioch and spread their faith there. The Apostles heard of it and sent St Barnabas there. In Antioch he found that Christians had multiplied by the thousands. He realised he couldn't cope with all that apostolic work by himself, and so he did something that changed the history of the world: "*Barnabas went to Tarsus to look for Saul; and when he had found him, he brought him to Antioch.*" He searched for St Paul and set him to work. God called St Paul with the help of St Barnabas. You see? Saul became St Paul because Barnabas went for him! You and I are apostles who have to look for more apostles, find them, bring them to Jesus and, together with them, change the course of history. Holy Mary, Queen of the Apostles, help me to be generous, to be an apostle and to set out to find others whom God wants to make into apostles too.

Thursday 10th week in ordinary time
Thursday 12th June
Mt 5:20-26

"I tell you, unless your righteousness exceeds that of the scribes and Pharisees, you will never enter the kingdom of heaven...if you are offering your gift at the altar, and there remember that your brother has something against you, leave your gift there before the altar and go; first be reconciled to your brother, and then come and offer your gift."

We can't approach the Altar of Sacrifice in any old way. To be ready to participate in the Sacrifice of the Altar we need first to be *'reconciled'*. St Paul was very clear when he explained to the first Christians that *"whoever eats the Bread or drinks the Cup of the Lord in an unworthy manner will be guilty of profaning the Body and Blood of the Lord"* and so he invited them to *"examine"* themselves first, because *"any one who eats and drinks without discerning the Body eats and drinks judgement upon himself."* (1Co 11:27-29)

In April 390 Emperor Theodosius sent his army to Thessalonica to crush a revolt. The Roman soldiers slayed seven thousand people without trial, innocent and guilty alike. According to historian Theodoret, when the emperor, accompanied by his court, tried to enter the Milanese cathedral to attend Mass, the bishop St Ambrose rebuked the emperor and forbade him to attend the Holy Mass until he repented and did penance. Theodoret explains that Theodosius *"had been brought up according to divine words and understood well"*: he could do nothing but return *"weeping and sighing"* to the palace.

Receiving Holy Communion in a state of mortal sin is a sacrilege that demands reparation. The Angel of Fatima asked the three children to say this prayer in reparation: *"Most Holy Trinity, Father, Son and Holy Spirit, I adore You profoundly, and I offer You the Most Precious Body, Blood, Soul and Divinity of Jesus Christ, present in all the tabernacles of the world, in reparation for the outrages, sacrileges and indifferences by which He is offended. And by the infinite merits of His most Sacred Heart and the Immaculate Heart of Mary, I beg the conversion of poor sinners."*

Holy Mary, Mother of the Eucharist, increase my love for Our Lord really present in Holy Communion and teach me to make reparation for sacrileges against the Eucharist.

Friday 10th week in ordinary time
Friday 13th June
Mt 5:27-32

"You have heard that it was said, 'You shall not commit adultery.' But I say to you that every one who looks at a woman lustfully has already committed adultery with her in his heart. If your right eye causes you to sin, pluck it out and throw it away; it is better that you lose one of your members than that your whole body be thrown into hell."

Our Lord loves Holy Purity. He said of the pure of heart that they would see God. The virtue of Holy Purity is a gift we need to ask God for every day. Some people think of chastity as a continuous negation: 'you can't do that', 'you can't look at that', 'you can't think about that', 'you can't... you can't... you can't...' But it is quite the opposite. Holy purity is a joyful *affirmation* of love. A good husband, out of love for his wife and family, is able to struggle against any temptation. Love gives strength.

Jesus used some 'exaggerated' examples (such as pluck out your eye) to make the point that, to stay pure, sometimes we will have to be 'heroic'. At times, temptation can be particularly strong. One day, for instance, St Francis of Assisi found himself attacked by a strong temptation. To get rid of it he took off his habit and rolled in the snow until it was over (it did work!) In a similar situation, St Benedict threw himself into a thorn bush and St Bernard plunged into an icy pond. If saints had to do that, and you and I want to be saints too, then sometimes we may have to be 'radical' as well.

During the Spanish civil war priests were being killed. St Josemaría had to be hidden, moving from house to house to avoid being arrested. On one occasion when he had no house to hide in, a friend offered him the key of an apartment. St Josemaría took the key and asked if there was anyone else in the apartment. He was told that only a young woman was there. Immediately he threw the key into the sewer and said that he preferred to die than to be exposed to temptation by staying in the same house alone with a young woman at a time of civil war, when fear and danger made people vulnerable. We may have to take 'radical measures' as well sometimes to keep our Purity. My Immaculate Mother, stay with me in time of temptation, for I know well that the enemy is never anywhere near you.

Saturday 10th week in ordinary time
Saturday 14th June
Mt 5:33-37

"Again you have heard that it was said to the men of old, 'You shall not swear falsely, but shall perform to the Lord what you have sworn.' But I say to you, do not swear at all, either by heaven, for it is the throne of God, or by the earth, for it is his footstool, or by Jerusalem, for it is the city of the great King. And do not swear by your head, for you cannot make one hair white or black. Let what you say be simply 'Yes' or 'No'; anything more than this comes from evil."

Our Lord was very clear about the danger of not keeping our tongue tamed. It is not about finding the line between vulgarity, rude words and blasphemy. A few chapters later St Matthew refers to other powerful words of Jesus, *"I tell you, on the day of judgment men will render account for every careless word they utter"* (12:36). The teaching is simple: 'what you wouldn't say in front of the throne of God, don't say it'. For you are in fact before God all the time.

The Apostle St James explained in his letter the importance of taming the tongue with an example: *"Look at the ships also: though they are so large and are driven by strong winds, they are guided by a very small rudder wherever the will of the pilot directs. So also the tongue is a small member, yet it boasts of great things. How great a forest is set ablaze by such a small fire!"* That is the first teaching of today's Gospel – to think carefully what we say before we say it.

But there is a second point. What about 'those' who swear and even blaspheme, in front of us? They should be helped with charity. When St John Bosco was about 9 years old he had a dream. He was in a yard full of poverty-stricken boys who were blaspheming and swearing. Wanting to stop them mouthing *"these evil words"*, John ran at them and started striking them with his fists. But he was prevented from throwing punches by a man in a white cloak whose face shone so brightly that young John could hardly look at him. The man said: *"You will have to win over these friends of yours not by blows but by gentleness and love… I want you to teach them the ugliness of sin."*

When people utter bad words we can't just remain silent. Mary, Virgin Most Prudent, help me to tame my tongue and teach me to find the way to help others do the same.

The Most Holy Trinity
Sunday 15th June
Jn 16:12-15

"I have yet many things to say to you, but you cannot bear them now. When the Spirit of truth comes, he will guide you into all the truth; for he will not speak on his own authority, but whatever he hears he will speak, and he will declare to you the things that are to come. He will glorify me, for he will take what is mine and declare it to you. All that the Father has is mine; therefore I said that he will take what is mine and declare it to you."

Here we have an explanation of the Trinity. The Most Holy Trinity, Father, Son and Holy Spirit: three divine Persons in One God. St John Paul II said that God is a very happy Family. So happy that God decided to share the happiness of that Family with us. God invites us to belong to it and we enter God's family when we are baptised. That is why we are baptized "*in the name of the Father, and of the Son, and of the Holy Spirit.*" Jesus didn't say '*in the **Names** of the Father...*' Just one 'Name', the "Name" of God. Let's repeat it often: "*In the Name of the Father, the Son and the Holy Spirit*"; "*Glory be to the Father, and to the Son and to the Holy Spirit!*"

Yet no matter how much you think about the Trinity, it will remain a Mystery. One day, as St. Augustine was walking on the beach considering the Mystery of the Trinity, he saw a boy who had dug a hole in the sand and was going back and forth to the sea, filling his bucket with water to pour into the hole. St. Augustine asked him, "*What are you doing?*" "*I'm going to pour the entire ocean into this hole.*" "*That is impossible, the whole ocean will not fit in the hole you have made*" said St. Augustine. The boy replied, "*I will finish before you fit the Mystery of the Trinity into your tiny little brain.*"

It is a Mystery. And yet, the soul needs to spend time with each of the Three Persons separately. Sometimes talking to the Father, as good children do; talking to Jesus, as faithful friends do, talking to the Holy Spirit, as loving spouses do. "*Talk to the Three Persons, to God the Father, to God the Son, to God the Holy Spirit. And so as to reach the Blessed Trinity, go through Mary*" (St Josemaría).

Monday 11th week in ordinary time
Monday 16th June
Mt 5:38-42

"You have heard that it was said, 'An eye for an eye and a tooth for a tooth.' But I say to you, Do not resist one who is evil. But if any one strikes you on the right cheek, turn to him the other also; and if any one would sue you and take your coat, let him have your cloak as well; and if any one forces you to go one mile, go with him two miles. Give to him who begs from you, and do not refuse him who would borrow from you."

In the old days, if someone struck you and you lost one of your teeth, you had the right to strike back. But you needed to calculate the strike well, for if two teeth fell, he may have had to strike you again to get even. You can guess how this could end: both toothless. To answer one injustice with another injustice only makes things worse. Children say sometimes: *'He started it!'* Or even: *'It all started when he punched me back!'*

But Our Lord's lesson is infallible. We Christians have to be ready to receive injustice and never hit back. That's the end of the argument. Have you ever thought what would happen if, when they call you 'ugly' you smile and keep doing what you were doing? *'Nothing'*. Exactly! And if, on the contrary, you find another name to call that person back...? This is the lesson, the infallible way to stop all arguments, discussions and fights: don't answer back.

We can ask Jesus for the humility we need to be able to receive injustice and remain always calm and cheerful. Follow the example of the saints. One day a group of envious priests wrote a letter to the bishop asking for St John Mary Vianney, Curé of Ars, to be removed from the parish of Ars because he was ignorant and useless. The letter was sent round the parishes to be signed by all other priests who might want to sign it. By accident, the letter ended up on St John Mary's desk as well. He read it and saw the names and denunciations. What was his reaction? He signed his own name on it, stamped it and sent it off to the bishop! You can imagine how funny the bishop thought it was. Of course, he was never removed. He was humble enough to react to injustice calmly and cheerfully.

Holy Mary, Mother of Good Counsel, teach me to always react meekly to any injustice I may suffer.

Tuesday 11th week in ordinary time
Tuesday 17th June
Mt 5:43-48

"Love your enemies and pray for those who persecute you, so that you may be sons of your Father who is in heaven; for he makes his sun rise on the evil and on the good, and sends rain on the just and on the unjust. For if you love those who love you, what reward have you?...You, therefore, must be perfect, as your heavenly Father is perfect."

Loving our enemies is a sign of taking after our *'Father who is in heaven'*. To be like our heavenly Father implies also that we *'must be perfect'*. When Jesus says *"be perfect"*, He's not asking us to be obsessive perfectionists, but rather to strive for perfection; not to settle for mediocrity but to want to improve always. He didn't say 'don't fight back against your enemies', He said, *"love your enemies and pray for them"*. That's perfection. Because *'loving those who love us'* is very easy! Of all of Jesus' teachings, loving our enemies is one of the most difficult to live.

In 2002, 24-year-old Eric Smallridge was drink-driving. He hit and killed two young girls: Meagan Napier and Lisa Dickson. He was sentenced to prison for 22 years. Distraught, he had even thought about ending his life when, at the end of the trial, Renee Napier, Meagan's mum and a good Christian, approached him, forgave him and hugged him. Eric broke into tears. Eventually all the members of the two families forgave him. He changed his ways and came close to God. Later both the Napier and Dickson families approached the legal system to ask for Eric's sentence to be reduced and it was granted. Since then, Eric has spent his life fighting against drink-driving. Because he was forgiven, he in turn was able to change many lives. That's the power of forgiveness.

One day Jesus said to St Faustina: *"Have great love for those who cause you suffering. Do good to those who hate you. Be always merciful as I am merciful. Love everyone out of love for Me, even your greatest enemies"*.

Our Lady, Refuge of Christians, intercede for persecuted Christians and for those who persecute them, the enemies of humanity, those who enslave others, who loot, who murder, who sell their fellow human beings, terrorist organisations, and regimes that imprison Christians or forbid religion...

Wednesday 11th week in ordinary time
Wednesday 18th June
Mt 6:1-6, 16-18

"Beware of practicing your piety before men in order to be seen by them...Thus, when you give alms, sound no trumpet before you, as the hypocrites do in the synagogues and in the streets, that they may be praised by men. Truly, I say to you, they have received their reward. But when you give alms, do not let your left hand know what your right hand is doing, so that your alms may be in secret; and your Father who sees in secret will reward you."

You, Lord, are 'my audience'. Help me to do everything only for You, always. May I never be worried by what others think about me... only about what You think. Considering what others think of me, of my work, my deeds or my appearance is a waste of time, of peace, of humility and of every virtue. Not worrying about any opinion of me except God's one sounds good - but it's not easy.

Pope John Paul I wrote the following story about a cook called John: He slaughtered a calf and threw the entrails into the yard where some dogs ate them, and said: *'He's a good cook; he cooks well.'* Some time after that, John was shelling peas, peeling onions; he threw the husks into the yard and the dogs rushed over again, but, sniffing scornfully, they said: *'The cook is spoiled; he's worthless now.'* John, however, was not upset by this opinion; he said, *'It is the master who must eat and enjoy my meals, not the dogs. The master's appreciation is enough for me'.*"

Narciso Yepes, a concert guitarist, said once in an interview: "*almost always, the one I really play for is God ... I said 'almost always' because there are times when, through my fault, I can get distracted in the middle of the concert. The public does not notice. But God and I do*". Then the interviewer asked him: 'Does God like your music?' "*He loves it!*" exclaimed the guitarist "*More than my music, what He likes is that I give Him my attention, my sensitivity, my effort, my art ... my job. And besides, to play an instrument the best you can and to be aware of the presence of God is a wonderful way to pray, to worship. I have experienced it so many times!*" It raises the question: What about me? Does God like my works? If I do them for Him, He certainly does. Mary, my Mother, help me to do everything for God's glory, so that He may love my work!

The Most Holy Body and Blood of Christ
Thursday 19th June
Lk 9:11b-17

Jesus said to his disciples, "You give them something to eat." They said, "We have no more than five loaves and two fish - unless we are to go and buy food for all these people." For there were about five thousand men...And taking the five loaves and the two fish he looked up to heaven, and blessed and broke them, and gave them to the disciples to set before the crowd. And all ate and were satisfied. And they took up what was left over, twelve baskets of broken pieces.

Leftovers? Did Jesus miscalculate? Unlikely. Most probably some people were missing. The same could be said today about the Eucharistic Bread. So many people are hungry for God and starving! How is my hunger for Divine Bread, Lord?

Venerable Teresa Maria de Jesus Ortega explained her experience during the religious persecution of the Spanish Civil War. She was in Teruel, sieged by the enemy. They lacked everything except "*hunger and thirst for God*" as she explained. "*We had to receive Holy Communion, we had to do the impossible. It was the cry of our soul, it was the need of our life. Communion, Communion! Above all, receive Holy Communion. What would life be without Communion? I looked for two coal plates and heated them in a fire that was there, I looked for flour and a little water. With that I made some dough and put it between the two plates. Dusty, deformed breads came out, but God came down to them all the same. A Franciscan father consecrated them daily...We lacked everything: bread, water, rest, but God, we didn't miss Him, because He was thirstier for us than we were for Him... The siege was over and they put me in jail... O, a month went by without Communion! After leaving prison, someone gave me a very small box, full of Consecrated Hosts. I took Him everywhere. How many hidden Communions! How many daily secret 'deliveries'! Communions in catacombs! I was walking around Valencia with the Mystery... What procession of Corpus Christi among those revolutionary militiamen! He went hidden through the streets, anonymously. Invisible Mysteries! How good You are, Lord!*" **Mary, Mother of the Eucharist, help me to receive your Son '*with the purity, humility and devotion with which you received Him, with the spirit and fervour of the saints.*'

Thursday 11th week in ordinary time
Thursday 19th June
Mt 6:7-15

"And in praying do not heap up empty phrases as the Gentiles do; for they think that they will be heard for their many words. Do not be like them, for your Father knows what you need before you ask him. Pray then like this: Our Father who art in heaven, Hallowed be thy name..."

When you pray, don't be like those who "*think that they will be heard for their many words.*" Prayer isn't about beautiful and creative speeches. In fact, every prayer is *creative* no matter what you say, providing you say something. To create means to produce something new that didn't exist before, and none of your words existed before you said them. So then... what should I say? *Anything*. God loves your prayer so much that anything you say is good enough. "*Prayer*" teaches St Josemaría "*is not a question of what you say or feel, but of love. And you love when you try hard to say something to the Lord, even though you might not actually say anything*". You see? "*you love when you **try hard***", that's it!

Certainly some things are better than others. Can I speak about a film? Well, do you speak about films with your friends? And... is Jesus your friend? Then... if it helps you... go ahead! But as you do when you have a guest, try to talk about what 'He' likes, more than about what 'you' like. You shouldn't pray for your sake, but for His sake: '*I pray because You love it, Lord*'. St Josemaría used to be in the confessional first thing in the morning. Every morning he would hear the door of the church being opened, and then a clatter of metal, followed by the slamming of the door. Curious to know what was going on, one day he stationed himself at the entrance to the church. When the door flew open he found himself face to face with a milkman, carrying the cans for his milk-round. He asked him what he was doing. '*Father*,' the man replied, '*every morning I come up here, open the door ... and say to him, Jesus, here's John the milkman.*' St Josemaría was left speechless. He spent the rest of the day repeating the aspiration: '*Lord, here is this wretch, who doesn't know how to love you like John the milkman*'. God loved the milkman's prayer. *Does Jesus like my prayer?* Be sure: **He LOVES it!** My Mother Immaculate, St Joseph my father and lord, my Guardian Angel... teach me to pray.

Friday 11th week in ordinary time
Friday 20th June
Mt 6:19-23

"Where your treasure is, there will your heart be also. The eye is the lamp of the body. So, if your eye is sound, your whole body will be full of light; but if your eye is not sound, your whole body will be full of darkness. If then the light in you is darkness, how great is the darkness!"

Watch what you watch! Because through the eyes you feed your soul. Someone has compared the human heart to a food processor. It has many functions (steaming, emulsifying, blending, mixing, milling, whipping, kneading, chopping, grinding, stirring...) If you put in lemon and ice, you get lemon slush; if you put in good fruits you get good juice; with vegetables you can do creams and soups. But if you put in soil and dirt and sticks... that's disgusting, unhealthy and inedible.

Protect your heart by guarding your sight: "*Blessed are the pure in heart, for they shall see God.*" Those who don't guard their sight may see many things... but not God. To see God you need to *watch what you watch*! This may be demanding at times. We have to be prudent, because, as St Peter explains, "*the devil prowls around like a roaring lion, seeking some one to devour.*"

We have to be on the watch to be prudent and determined not to *play* with temptations. If we know that there are thieves in a dark alley, we won't go that way... If we know that the devil will make trouble when we use the internet in this place, or watch TV at that time or talk with friends about that topic... we don't go there.

A young lad was always trying to change the topic of his friend's conversations. Every time one of them started talking about *girls* without respect, he would ask, "*Did you watch the football match at the weekend?*" If they said 'No', he would start explaining it; if they said 'Yes', he would ask them to explain it to him. One day a friend confronted him: "*Why do you always change the topic when we talk about girls?*" Can you imagine the answer? He quickly replied, "*Did you watch the football match on Sunday?!*"

Mary, Virgin most Pure, help me to be pure and determined to avoid any situation that can lead me into temptation.

Saturday 11th week in ordinary time
Saturday 21st June
Mt 6:24-34

Jesus said to his disciples "do not be anxious about your life, what you shall eat or what you shall drink, nor about your body, what you shall put on...Consider the lilies of the field, how they grow; they neither toil nor spin; yet I tell you, even Solomon in all his glory was not arrayed like one of these. But if God so clothes the grass of the field, which today is alive and tomorrow is thrown into the oven, will he not much more clothe you, O men of little faith?"

The command is clear: "*Don't be anxious*"; God is in command. We should always trust God who, as the best of Fathers, knows what He is doing. So, when we pray, we should remember that the best words for praying are: "*Your Will be done,*" because that's always the best.

Do you remember the end of the film *Ratatouille*? Linguini asks Anton Ego to choose a dessert; he hesitates for a moment and then, looking at the rat Remy through the kitchen window, says, "*Surprise me!*" That's a confident way to address God in our prayer. Sometimes we may not understand what He does or why He doesn't do something, but we shouldn't be anxious - He knows best.

We shouldn't be anxious if God makes us wait, because prayers are ALWAYS heard. But God isn't like a vending machine. He is a Father, and fathers give what their children *need*, not always what their children *want*. Our trust fills God's Heart with joy. Let's allow Him to decide and surprise us. Let's never be anxious.

The sole survivor of a shipwreck arrived on a desert island. After great sufferings he managed to fish and find water to drink. For weeks he saw no sign of rescue of any kind. With great effort he built a hut and spent hours praying for his rescue. One night there was a storm, not torrents of rain but lots of lightning and thunder. To his dismay he saw a lightning bolt strike his hut and set it on fire. He was indignant with God and shouted at Him, "*Why?! Why do you treat me like this?!*" The following morning a ship came to rescue him. When he met his rescuers he asked them, "*How did you find me?* They replied, "*It was very easy; we saw your fire!*"

Mary, Mother most Faithful, teach me to trust in God like you.

Twelfth Sunday in Ordinary Time
Sunday 22nd June
Lk 9:18-24

Jesus asked his disciples, "Who do the people say that I am?" And they answered, "John the Baptist; but others say, Elijah; and others, that one of the old prophets has risen." And he said to them, "But who do you say that I am?" And Peter answered, "The Christ of God." But he charged and commanded them to tell this to no one, saying, "The Son of man must suffer many things, and be rejected by the elders and chief priests and scribes, and be killed, and on the third day be raised."

There were many different opinions about Jesus. He was famous and people talked about Him everywhere. 'A holy man? A wise rabbi? A prophet, even?' 'Could be', people argued among themselves. None of these answers could have had Him arrested and killed. But He wasn't just that... He was "*the Christ of God*"; and that could certainly sign His death warrant as well as that of His followers.

Even today, Jesus is referred to as a prophet, a 'spiritual leader', a 'wise philosopher', a 'social reformer', or something of that sort. Those titles have 'public acceptance'. But declaring that *He is God* can certainly get us into trouble. Our Lord knew that. He warned His disciples that they should be ready to lose their lives for His sake. We will probably never be asked to give our lives, but we can be asked to endure hard times for confessing our faith in Him. *What are we ready to lose for Him?*

During the persecution of Christians in Mexico it was difficult to attend Mass. Priests went into hiding and Masses were said in a different house every day. One day the Mass was going to be celebrated in a barn in the countryside. Right before it started a squad of soldiers stormed in, catching everyone by surprise. The officer addressed the people saying: '*Those who are ready to die can stay.*' People started leaving the barn, one by one, until in the end just the priest and half a dozen people were left. Then, the officer said to the priest: '*Now, father, that all those who are ready to die for Jesus are here, we can start the Mass.*'

Mary, my Mother, Help of Christians, be at my side that I may not fail to defend boldly my faith in your Son.

The Most Holy Body and Blood of Christ
Sunday 22nd June
Lk 9:11b-17

Jesus said to his disciples, "You give them something to eat." They said, "We have no more than five loaves and two fish - unless we are to go and buy food for all these people." For there were about five thousand men...And taking the five loaves and the two fish he looked up to heaven, and blessed and broke them, and gave them to the disciples to set before the crowd. And all ate and were satisfied. And they took up what was left over, twelve baskets of broken pieces.

Leftovers? Did Jesus miscalculate? Unlikely. Most probably some people were missing. The same could be said today about the Eucharistic Bread. So many people are hungry for God and starving! How is my hunger for Divine Bread, Lord?

Venerable Teresa Maria de Jesus Ortega explained her experience during the religious persecution of the Spanish Civil War. She was in Teruel, sieged by the enemy. They lacked everything except *"hunger and thirst for God"* as she explained. *"We had to receive Holy Communion, we had to do the impossible. It was the cry of our soul, it was the need of our life. Communion, Communion! Above all, receive Holy Communion. What would life be without Communion? I looked for two coal plates and heated them in a fire that was there, I looked for flour and a little water. With that I made some dough and put it between the two plates. Dusty, deformed breads came out, but God came down to them all the same. A Franciscan father consecrated them daily...We lacked everything: bread, water, rest, but God, we didn't miss Him, because He was thirstier for us than we were for Him... The siege was over and they put me in jail... O, a month went by without Communion! After leaving prison, someone gave me a very small box, full of Consecrated Hosts. I took Him everywhere. How many hidden Communions! How many daily secret 'deliveries'! Communions in catacombs! I was walking around Valencia with the Mystery... What procession of Corpus Christi among those revolutionary militiamen! He went hidden through the streets, anonymously. Invisible Mysteries! How good You are, Lord!"* Mary, Mother of the Eucharist, help me to receive your Son *'with the purity, humility and devotion with which you received Him, with the spirit and fervour of the saints.'*

Monday 12th week in ordinary time
Monday 23rd June
Mt 7:1-5

"Judge not, that you be not judged. For with the judgment you pronounce you will be judged, and the measure you give will be the measure you get. Why do you see the speck that is in your brother's eye, but do not notice the log that is in your own eye? Or how can you say to your brother, 'Let me take the speck out of your eye,' when there is the log in your own eye? You hypocrite, first take the log out of your own eye, and then you will see clearly to take the speck out of your brother's eye".

This teaching of Our Lord is repeated in the Gospels several times. The doctrine is clear: the one who judges is God. We are not judges but brothers and sisters. We can easily see the defects of others and be blind to our own defects. St Augustine wrote: *"Try to acquire the virtues you believe lacking in your brothers, then you will no longer see their defects, for you will no longer have them yourself."* In other words: we see in the others the projection of our own imperfections. There is a story of two people drinking in the pub. After a few beers one of them says to the other, *'Mate! You have to stop drinking now… you are becoming blurry...'*

But even worse than judging others is talking about them behind their backs. Gossiping is an injustice that is difficult to restore. St Philip Neri once heard the confession of a man who had been gossiping. *"For your penance,"* said St Philip, *"kill one of your chickens and bring it to us tonight for supper. Pluck its feathers on your way here."* The man accepted his penance and on his way back, he gleefully tossed chicken feathers all about, presenting the naked bird to his confessor. Then St Philip said quietly to him, *"Now go, if you please, and collect all the feathers, and bring them to me, as well."* "But Father," the man objected, *"the feathers are strewn all about Rome by now, and beyond! Who knows where the wind has blown them; I could never recapture every feather."* "Yes," replied the saint, *"just so with gossip."*

We can follow the advice of St Josemaría: 'When you talk about someone, do it as if he could be hearing you and be always grateful for your words.'

Mary, my Mother, help me to love others instead of judging them.

The Nativity of St John the Baptist
Tuesday 24th June
Lk 1:57-66, 80

Elizabeth gave birth to a son...And on the eighth day they came to circumcise the child; and they would have named him Zechariah after his father, but his mother said, "Not so; he shall be called John"...they all marvelled...And all these things were talked about through all the hill country of Judea; and all who heard them laid them up in their hearts, saying, "What then will this child be?"

"What then will this child be?" That question could be asked about every baby in the world, because God has made everyone for something. This isn't the first time that we hear about St John. Three months before, Our Lady came to visit her cousin and *"when Elizabeth heard the greeting of Mary, the babe leaped in her womb"*. St John felt the presence of Jesus in Mary's womb and leaped for joy.

When babies are little, all their features are tiny, like the eyes or the nose. Little by little they develop and we can start recognising more and more the features of their parents. We know that, from the beginning, they have everything; but it takes time to mature. They - like St John – also have a mission from the moment of their conception. That vocation is there from the beginning, but it takes time to recognise and carry it out.

My Lord, help me to remind people that all human beings have a purpose; all babies have a mission; to remind them also that You, Lord, are a Father, Who loves them so much that You sent Your Only Son to die for them. *"What then will this child be?"* said my parents when I was born. You, Lord, knew well what I was going to be. I don't know yet many of the things that I should be, but there is one I do know, Lord: *'I'm meant to be a saint!'*

Holy Mary, Mother of the children of God, I pray today for all those who are facing difficult decisions about the life of their children. I pray especially for all those babies that aren't allowed to live and to become what God wanted them to be. What would have happened if St John had never been allowed to be born? We can't know for certain; all we know is that, as with any other baby, there would have been a hole in the heart of his parents and in history; and tears in the eyes of God.

Wednesday 25th June
Mt 7:15-20

"Beware of false prophets, who come to you in sheep's clothing but inwardly are ravenous wolves. You will know them by their fruits. Are grapes gathered from thorns, or figs from thistles? So, every sound tree bears good fruit, but the bad tree bears evil fruit. A sound tree cannot bear evil fruit, nor can a bad tree bear good fruit…Thus you will know them by their fruits."

Today's Gospel is a warning. Our Lord's warning against false prophets. The difficulty is that sometimes they are not easily recognisable. They are wolves that look like sheep or, as the Lord puts it, they *"come to you in sheep's clothing."* And because it's hard to distinguish, Jesus gives us a clue: their fruits. By the fruit you get to know not just the kind of tree, but also the quality of it. A good apple can only come from a good apple tree.

Nevertheless, we need to be aware that fruits are not easily seen. Only God knows the exact fruit of the saints. There is a fable of a man who used to carry water from the well in two jars. The jars were tied to a stick that the man carried on his shoulders, one jar on each end. One of the jars was old and although its cracks had been repaired, it was leaking water all the way. Every day, when the man arrived home, this jar was empty. And the old jar felt useless and was sad (jars can have feelings in fables…) and told the man (they also can speak!) *"Leave it! I'm useless. Why do you insist on taking me all the way to the well and back if I can't retain the water?"* The man took the old crock back to the well and said, *"Look at the path. Do you see? There are plenty of flowers on one side but none on the other. Those flowers exist because of you. That's why I take you with me every day."*

The fruits that Our Lord is talking about are not the fruits that people can easily measure. God knows the fruit that we can give and that's the fruit which He expects from us. The real fruits of holiness are the 12 fruits of the Holy Spirit: charity, joy, peace, patience, kindness, goodness, generosity, gentleness, faithfulness, modesty, self-control, chastity. Those are the fruits that you can see in the saints. By those fruits you will know them! Holy Mary, Spouse of the Holy Spirit, help me to give the fruits that God expects from me.

Thursday 12th week in ordinary time
Thursday 26th June
Mt 7:21-29

"Not every one who says to me, 'Lord, Lord,' shall enter the kingdom of heaven, but he who does the will of my Father who is in heaven ... Every one then who hears these words of mine and does them will be like a wise man who built his house upon the rock; and the rain fell, and the floods came, and the winds blew and beat upon that house, but it did not fall, because it had been founded on the rock."

Not everyone who prays 'Lord, Lord...', not everyone who does some good things or says some prayers will enter the kingdom of Heaven. You can do lots of things, like build a ten-story building, but if you don't do the Will of God... it has no foundation, and it collapses. Some may think that Christian life is about accumulating prayers: if you pray ten Hail Marys instead of one, they think, you are ten times holier. But it's not so. Only if you 'do the Will of God' will you become a saint.

Praying the rosary during your maths lesson is praying, but not doing what God wants you to do (pay attention and offer it to God). If you read the Gospel whilst riding your bicycle you risk your life. Holiness is about doing what we ought to do at a particular moment; that is the Will of God and the foundation of your holiness. When it's time to pray, we pray; when it's time to study, we study; when it's time to sleep... we sleep.

Have you ever read the story of Sisyphus? In Greek mythology, Sisyphus was a king of Ephyra. He was punished for chronic deceitfulness by being compelled to roll an immense boulder up a hill, only to watch it roll back down, repeating this action forever. Some may think that Christian life is like that: just doing good things over and over, like Sisyphus rolling his boulder. Doing many things but not sincerely trying to do what God wants, is building without foundation - like sewing without thread - and like Sisyphus, all he does comes to nothing.

"Do you really want to be a saint? Carry out the little duty of each moment: do what you ought and concentrate on what you are doing" (St Josemaría). Mary, my Mother, teach me to do always, and in everything, only the Will of God.

St Josemaría, priest
Thursday 26th June
Lk 5:1-11

Jesus was standing by the lake of Gennesaret. And he saw two boats by the lake; but the fishermen had gone out of them and were washing their nets. Getting into one of the boats, which was Simons, he asked him to put out a little from the land. And he sat down and taught the people from the boat. And when he had ceased speaking, he said to Simon, "Put out into the deep and let down your nets for a catch."...And when they had done this, they enclosed a great shoal of fish...when Simon Peter saw it, he fell down at Jesus' knees, saying, "Depart from me, for I am a sinful man, O Lord."...And Jesus said to Simon, "Do not be afraid; henceforth you will be catching men."

Peter and Andrew spent the whole night fishing and caught nothing. They were exhausted and probably upset. They had called it a day and were washing their nets, thinking about their breakfast and their rest... when You, Lord, showed up. Peter saw You getting into his boat, without asking for permission or saying anything! That is the way You get into the lives of your disciples. But You, Lord, can do that, can't You? When you want, as You want, where You want, You meet Your disciples and get into their lives. That's what You did with Peter, without asking his permission, because You had plans for him. And from then on Peter followed You everywhere. Later, when You ascended into Heaven, he continued following the Holy Spirit until he died in Rome.

As a young boy St Josemaría had decided to study architecture. But one snowy day in 1917, without warning, You, Lord, entered his life using those footprints in the snow. You changed his plans and young Josemaría went to the seminary to become a priest. And on October 28 1928, You gave another direction to his life and showed him a new vocation: the founder of Opus Dei. From then on, St Josemaría followed You saying 'Yes', through wars, persecutions, misunderstandings, illness, moving to Rome (as Peter did to die there) and travelling around the world to take the seed of the Work to many different countries. He died at the age of 73, almost blind, very weak, weighing less than 60 kilograms, as he put it '*squeezed like a lemon*', giving everything, like Peter, to do God's Will. Mary, my Mother, help me to be generous to do always, and in everything, only what God wants.

The Most Sacred Heart
Friday 27th June
Lk 15:3-7

Jesus told them this parable: "What man of you, having a hundred sheep, if he has lost one of them, does not leave the ninety-nine in the wilderness, and go after the one which is lost, until he finds it? And when he has found it, he lays it on his shoulders, rejoicing...Just so, I tell you, there will be more joy in heaven over one sinner who repents than over ninety-nine righteous persons who need no repentance.

This is a good description of the feelings in God's Heart. The Good Shepherd treats each sheep as if it were the only sheep of the flock. The whole month of June is devoted to the Most Sacred Heart of Jesus because of today's Solemnity. We could say that this feast has two aspects: on the one hand *gratefulness* for the wonders of God's Love for us, and on the other, *reparation*, because our response to that Love is often so poor.

Our Lord appeared to St Margaret Mary Alacoque, showing her His Most Sacred Heart and saying, "**See this Heart that has loved men so much and has spared itself nothing until it has exhausted itself and consumed itself in order to show them its love. I receive in return scarcely anything but ingratitude because of their irreverence and sacrileges, and because of the coldness and disdain they show towards Me in this sacrament of love**."

One day in the 8th century A.D. as a Basilian monk was saying Mass, he doubted Jesus' Real Presence in the Eucharist. Suddenly the Host changed into live Flesh and the Wine changed into live Blood. The miracle has been kept in the town of Lanciano ever since. In 1981 Professor Linoli and his team conducted a scientific investigation. Many astonishing facts came out of those tests. One of the most remarkable ones was that the Flesh, that had been preserved without any human procedures or chemical products for more than 12 centuries, proved to be a part of a *human Heart*.

In Holy Communion we touch the Sacred Heart and we can comfort Jesus and so, in some way, return His love for us. Today is a day of reparation. Let's turn to Mary for help: Mary, my Mother, today I also want to console Jesus with you; help me to make up, with my love, for the lack of gratitude of men and women and help others to "*look on him whom they have pierced*" with their sins.

The Immaculate Heart of Mary
Saturday 28th June
Lk 2:41-51

His parents went to Jerusalem every year at the feast of the Passover. And when he was twelve years old, they went up according to custom; and when the feast was ended, as they were returning, the boy Jesus stayed behind in Jerusalem...After three days they found him in the temple...And when they saw him they were astonished; and his mother said to him, "Son, why have you treated us so? Behold, your father and I have been looking for you anxiously."

Imagine how Mary must have felt searching for Jesus for those three long days: her anxiety... Her Immaculate Heart was full of love for Jesus and suffered at His absence. But her Heart is also full of love for us and she suffers when we are far away from God. As St Louis de Montfort explains, "*If you put all the love of all the mothers into one heart it still would not equal the love of the Heart of Mary for her children.*" You have a place in her Immaculate Heart and so now, if you are lost, she is in distress until she gets you back.

Mary's Immaculate Heart is the Refuge of Sinners. They say of the whale, that when she sees her young in peril she opens her mouth and receives it into her to protect it. That's what Mary does. She revealed to St. Bridget, "*As a mother who sees her son exposed to the sword of the enemy makes every effort to save him, thus do I, and will I ever do, for my children, sinful though they be, if they come to me for help.*"

"*If the winds of temptations arise, if you run into the rocks of tribulations, look at the star, invoke Mary. If you are tossed about by the waves of pride, look at the star, invoke Mary. If anger or avarice or the seductions of the flesh shake the little boat of your soul, look at Mary. If, troubled by the enormity of your crimes, confounded by the uncleanliness of your conscience, frozen with fright at the thought of judgement, you start to be swallowed up by the gulf of sadness and the abyss of despair, think about Mary. In perils, in anguish, in doubt, think about Mary, invoke Mary. If you follow her, you do not go astray. If you pray to her, you do not despair. If you consult her, you are not wrong. If she supports you, you do not fall. If she protects you, you fear nothing. If she leads you, you do not tire. If she is favourable to you, you reach your aim*" (St Bernard).

Saturday 12th week in ordinary time
Saturday 28th June
Mt 8:5-17

As he entered Capernaum, a centurion came forward to him, beseeching him and saying, "Lord, my servant is lying paralysed at home, in terrible distress." And he said to him, "I will come and heal him." But the centurion answered him, "Lord, I am not worthy to have you come under my roof; but only say the word, and my servant will be healed".

We use the words of this man before Holy Communion: "*Lord, I am not worthy that you should enter under my roof.*" We aren't worthy - that's a fact! Jesus didn't say to the man, '*Oh, come on! Don't say that!*' because it was true. We are not worthy to have Our Lord with us, but Jesus doesn't come to us because *we* are good, but because *He* is Good. You can deserve a prize or a salary, but not a gift. We receive the gift because the giver wants to give it to us.

Listen to what St John Mary Vianney says about the Eucharist: "*Don't say that you're not worthy. It's true: you're not worthy, but you have need of Holy Communion. If Our Lord had in view our dignity, he would never have instituted his beautiful sacrament of love, because no one in the world is worthy of it. But he had in mind our needs and we have need of it.*"

Anyone who receives Our Lord should have this conviction. An old priest was one day preaching about this, saying, "*No priest is worthy to hold Jesus in his hands.*" He looked at his hands and said, "*We all wonder many times 'why me?'*" Then he looked at the Tabernacle and repeated "*Why me?*" After a moment's silence, glancing down, he said again, "*Why me, Lord? ... I'm nothing, I'm worth nothing... Why me?*" His voice faded, moved, as he understood Our Lord's reply inside him saying, "*Why you? Because I love you!*"

We aren't worthy, but God can change that with just one word. His Love makes us worthy. What makes the Vatican, Buckingham Palace or the White House so special? The ones who live there. What makes you and me so special? God, Who lives in us.

My Mother, House of Gold, mums always insist on having our room tidy and the house in order; help me to tidy this dwelling of God that I am, to make it '*worthy*'.

St Peter and St Paul, Apostles
Sunday 29th June
Mt 16:13-19

Jesus asked his disciples, "Who do you say that I am?" Simon Peter replied, "You are the Christ, the Son of the living God." And Jesus answered him, "Blessed are you, Simon Bar-Jona! For flesh and blood has not revealed this to you, but my Father who is in heaven. And I tell you, you are Peter, and on this rock I will build my church, and the powers of death shall not prevail against it. I will give you the keys of the kingdom of heaven, and whatever you bind on earth shall be bound in heaven, and whatever you loose on earth shall be loosed in heaven."

"*You are Peter, and on this rock I will build my church*"; 'I know you well, Peter', Our Lord could say, 'I know you are weak, but you are Peter! I know that you will fail me in the moment when I will need you most; I know that you still argue with the others about who is to be the first and the greatest, but I know as well that you love Me, and I know what you will be able to do for love of Me. I know you well, Peter, but feeble and vain, denying Me and running away, I will still build my Church on you; and I tell you here, in front of all the other Apostles and the entire world so that it may never be forgotten until the end of time, that you are MY ROCK, and the gates of hell and the powers of death and the enemies of the Church and the persecutors of My disciples SHALL NOT PREVAIL!'

One day St Paul saw Peter misbehaving with some gentiles (*Gal* 2:11-14). He had to correct St Peter and he did so. St Peter didn't need correction for his teachings (he was the Pope), but he was a man and made mistakes. Nevertheless, St Paul never hesitated to follow the Rock and to go to Jerusalem to see St Peter (*Gal* 1:18).

That's the power of the Church: she's built on Rock. "*There is nothing more powerful than the Church; give up fighting her, lest she overpower your strength. Wage not war against heaven. If you fight a man, you conquer or are conquered. But if you fight the Church, you cannot conquer. For God is stronger than all... Heaven and earth shall pass away, but My words shall not pass away. What words? You are Peter, and upon this rock I will build My Church, and the gates of hell shall not prevail against it*" (St John Chrysostom). Holy Mary, Mother of the Church, St Peter and St Paul, pray for us!

Thirteenth Sunday in Ordinary Time
Sunday 29th June
Lk 9:51-62

Jesus said to a man "Follow me." But he said, "Lord, let me first go and bury my father." But he said to him, "Leave the dead to bury their own dead; but as for you, go and proclaim the kingdom of God." Another said, "I will follow you, Lord; but let me first say farewell to those at my home." Jesus said to him, "No one who puts his hand to the plough and looks back is fit for the kingdom of God."

Many people want to follow Jesus but they have second thoughts when meeting difficulties. They 'plan' to follow Him but not now... maybe later... tomorrow perhaps. They have other priorities now. Eventually it happens to them as to that old British man who was working in a garage in Spain for nearly 40 years. When they asked him why he was living there he would say, '*I came for a gap year when I was 18.*' Some people start a 'gap year' before committing themselves to follow Jesus and spend their lives in a spiritual 'gap-year'.

St Augustine was leading a life of sin and striving for a career as an orator. Listening to St Ambrose, a great speaker, he realised that God could change him but... he wasn't interested yet. He knew what to do but was too lazy to change. Looking for the truth, he kept repeating to himself, "*Tomorrow I shall find it; it will appear manifestly and I shall grasp it.*" When he asked God for help he was praying, "*Give me chastity and continence, only not yet*" because he feared to be heard and healed too early. What a battle inside his heart! He would say to his heart: 'Come on! Now, now!' But when he was close he'd stop at the edge - until one day when he couldn't put it off anymore: "*I cast myself down I know not how, under a certain fig-tree, giving full vent to my tears...I sent up these sorrowful words: How long, how long, 'tomorrow, and tomorrow?' Why not now?*" And that was the day he changed. He was 33 years old. He would regret his wasted time: "*Too late I loved Thee, O Thou Beauty of ancient days, yet ever new! Too late I loved Thee!*"

Next time the enemy whispers in your ear 'later... tomorrow', you can use the aspiration that St Josemaría prayed many times: "*Nunc coepi!* (Latin for 'Now I begin!') My Mother, if ever the enemy tempts me into procrastinating in my response to God, help me to pray with determination: *Nunc Coepi!*

Monday 13th week in ordinary time
Monday 30th June
Mt 8:18-22

A scribe said to Jesus, "Teacher, I will follow you wherever you go." And Jesus said to him, "Foxes have holes, and birds of the air have nests; but the Son of man has nowhere to lay his head." Another of the disciples said to him, "Lord, let me first go and bury my father." But Jesus said to him, "Follow me, and leave the dead to bury their own dead."

The first man offers himself to Our Lord and Jesus warns him to be ready to do without even the most basic needs at times. The other one promises to follow Jesus, but only 'after' he had cared for his father until the old man died. Then, he argued, he would have no further commitments and he could follow Jesus.

However, Jesus doesn't agree with the plan. He is not happy having to wait for us to do what we want to do; He is not a God who waits until we have no further commitment, so that we can give Him the 'leftovers'. To follow God means to let Him decide our agenda. We may find ourselves without some comforts, the possibility to do what we fancy at any time, because now God 'leads' and we 'follow'.

In September 1991, Cardinal Ratzinger suffered a haemorrhagic stroke that impaired his eyesight temporarily. He was fitted with a pacemaker. From 1997, when he turned 70, he asked St John Paul II for permission to retire on several occasions but each time the Pope asked him to carry on. Joseph Ratzinger was 78 years old when he was elected Pope. He explained his thoughts when he realised he was going to be elected: "*I started to feel quite dizzy. I thought that I had done my life's work and could now hope to live out my days in peace. I told the Lord with deep conviction, 'Don't do this to me. You have younger and better candidates who could take up this great task with a totally different energy and strength.' Evidently, this time He didn't listen to me...The ways of the Lord are not comfortable, but we were not created for comfort, but for greatness.*" God had different plans. Many years before, as a young lad, Pope Benedict XVI had said to Our Lord that he would follow Him. He obviously kept his word. Mother most Faithful, help me to say to your Son "*I will follow you wherever you go.*" With your help I'll keep my word.

July

Tuesday 13th week in ordinary time
Tuesday 1st July
Mt 8:23-27

And when he got into the boat, his disciples followed him. And behold, there arose a great storm on the sea, so that the boat was being swamped by the waves; but he was asleep. And they went and woke him, saying, "Save, Lord; we are perishing." And he said to them, "Why are you afraid, O men of little faith?" Then he rose and rebuked the winds and the sea; and there was a great calm.

Jesus knew the storm was coming, and yet wanted His disciples to go through it. Yes, Jesus wants us to fight. Temptations are allowed by God because they are good for us. As St Augustine teaches: if there is no temptation there is no fight; if there is no fight there is no victory; if there is no victory there is no prize, no Heaven. Jesus wouldn't stop the storm straightaway, but He wouldn't leave His disciples alone either. He doesn't take the temptations and difficulties from us, nevertheless He helps us to overcome them, to never give up: He is with us in the same boat.

Richard was 17 years old. He wanted to become a priest but his exams didn't go well. The rector of the seminary called Richard's father, a humble blacksmith, for a chat. Richard came into the rector's office with his dad. The rector, with affection, said to his dad, "*Listen, your son is a very good lad; but maybe God is not calling him to be a priest. You have to study hard and pass difficult exams for this. Don't worry; your son can give glory to God in a different way.*" In silence they left the rector's office. Richard writes: '*As if it was yesterday, I remember that cold, dark, wet night. We went home in silence, each of us thinking our own thoughts. Mine were sad. Finally, showing indifference as boys sometimes do, I said, "They can keep their title! I'll get a job and help you, dad." My father put his hand on my shoulder and said: "Don't give up"; then he said 'three words' that I would never forget: "Go ahead, son." These three words were echoing in my ears for hours, days... years:* **Go ahead, son.**" *And I went ahead...*' He certainly did. He was ordained priest, bishop and, eventually, Richard Cushing became Cardinal of Boston.

Holy Mary, Help of Christians, be with me in times of temptation, and if I get tired of the struggle, help me to feel God at my side, with His Hand on my shoulder repeating: "*Don't give up; Go ahead, son.*"

Wednesday 13th week in ordinary time
Wednesday 2nd July
Mt 8:28-34

When he came to the other side, to the country of the Gadarenes, two demoniacs met him, coming out of the tombs, so fierce that no one could pass that way. And behold, they cried out... "If you cast us out, send us away into the herd of swine." And he said to them, "Go." So they came out and went into the swine; and behold, the whole herd rushed down the steep bank into the sea, and perished in the waters. The herdsmen fled, and going into the city they told everything, and what had happened to the demoniacs. And behold, all the city came out to meet Jesus; and when they saw him, they begged him to leave their neighbourhood.

It's a very sad ending, isn't it? We read that the whole city came out to find You. That's not new. We are used to that (people coming to see You); however, this time when they saw You, they begged You "*to leave their neighbourhood.*" I can't believe it! These people saw the miracle: You, Lord, had healed two men who were "infested" with devils and were now safe and sound; but these people just didn't care. They were more concerned about their swine than the two healed men.

They have put all their heart into their pigs and forgotten to put it into their God. Of course, today not many people have swine, but they have other things to set their hearts on. When they go on holiday they may be more worried about finding a WiFi signal than about finding a church and checking out local Mass times.

In 1852 St John Mary Vianney met François Dorel walking his beautiful dog in the streets of Ars. He was a plasterer who found it 'hard' to go to Mass because of frequent duck-hunting trips. The holy priest spotted him and told him, "*It is greatly to be wished that your soul was as beautiful as your dog.*" The hunter got hunted: The following year that man became a monk! You see? Some people care more about their DOG than about their GOD. Some care more about their tablet, or phone or computer... And God is asking for our attention. Sometimes we ask Him to leave, like a beggar, like a street dog... *But God always comes back!* Mary, my Mother, if a friend or family member seems to be putting 'things' before God, help me to do them a big favour by pointing it out, gently, like St John Mary Vianney.

St Thomas, Apostle
Thursday 3rd July
Jn 20:24-29

Now Thomas, one of the twelve, called the Twin, was not with them when Jesus came. So the other disciples told him, "We have seen the Lord." But he said to them, "Unless I see in his hands the print of the nails, and place my finger in the mark of the nails, and place my hand in his side, I will not believe." Eight days later, his disciples were again in the house, and Thomas was with them. The doors were shut, but Jesus came and stood among them, and said, "Peace be with you." Then he said to Thomas, "Put your finger here, and see my hands; and put out your hand, and place it in my side; do not be faithless, but believing." Thomas answered him, "My Lord and my God!" Jesus said to him, "Have you believed because you have seen me? Blessed are those who have not seen and yet believe."

Thomas, Thomas... where were you? A few days before then, when Jesus was going up to Jerusalem to die, Thomas, you weren't afraid to go with Him and say, "*Let us also go, that we may die with him*" (Jn 11:16). But you didn't die with Him... you ran away from Him in Gethsemane. I can imagine your suffering, Thomas, during those days after Jesus died, your discouragement, your disappointment... because I know you loved Him.

But I give you thanks, Thomas, because you didn't go away; you stayed in Jerusalem, even if everything was over for you, because you were loyal! I give you thanks, because when the others told you they had seen the Lord, even if you didn't believe them (and that wasn't right) you didn't think they were crazy, or liars. What more could you wish for than seeing Jesus, conversing with Him, touching Him again as in the old days?! I thank you, Thomas, for waiting with the Apostles until Jesus came to cure your disbelief. I thank you for your beautiful act of faith: "*My Lord and my God!*"

Thanks to you, Thomas, I believe in Him all the more; thanks to you I long to touch Him in Holy Communion even more; thank you, Thomas, for not going away when your faith was weak, for your loyalty to Him and His Apostles; thank you for touching His wounds for me and teaching me to come to touch Him as well when my faith is weak. Thank you for staying with Him until your death, martyred for love of the One I want to love like you did: "*My Lord and my God!*" Mary, Virgin Most Faithful, intercede for me to increase my faith.

Friday 13th week in ordinary time
Friday 4th July
Mt 9:9-13

As Jesus passed on from there, he saw a man called Matthew sitting at the tax office; and he said to him, "Follow me." And he rose and followed him. And as he sat at table in the house, behold, many tax collectors and sinners came and sat down with Jesus and his disciples. And when the Pharisees saw this, they said to his disciples, "Why does your teacher eat with tax collectors and sinners?" But when he heard it, he said, "Those who are well have no need of a physician, but those who are sick. Go and learn what this means, 'I desire mercy, and not sacrifice.' For I came not to call the righteous, but sinners."

The Gospel today describes St Matthew's conversion. What did he do after joining Our Lord? He brought his friends (sinners like him) to Jesus. That was the first mission of St Matthew, do you see? Before he set out to find souls for God, he addressed those who were close to him: relatives and friends. Then he became an instrument in God's Hands for the conversion of many others.

That's our mission too. Before we set out to meet souls who can come to Christ, we should look around and go first to those who are closer to us. Our family, our friends... That's what the first Christians did. The Church was expanded not only by preachers who proclaimed the Word, but especially by Christians who brought their family members and friends to Christ. God can likewise bring others to Him using us as His instruments.

There was a beggar playing the violin in front of a train station when a renowned violinist passed by. The artist couldn't help asking the beggar, *"Would you mind if I tuned the violin for you?"* As he plucked the strings with his fingers, people started to gather around. Then the master started playing a classic and more and more people stopped. The beggar couldn't believe it! He started passing the hat round, saying to everyone, *"It's my violin! It's my violin!"*

That's what we are, instruments in God's Hands. It wasn't the violin's merit, but the musician's. If the violin is in tune, the violinist can play wonderfully. Mary, Queen of the Apostles, help me to be in tune, to become a good, docile instrument in the Hands of your Son so that He can bring many souls to Him through this poor instrument that I am.

Saturday 13th week in ordinary time
Saturday 5th July
Mt 9:14-17

Then the disciples of John came to him, saying, "Why do we and the Pharisees fast, but your disciples do not fast?" And Jesus said to them, "Can the wedding guests mourn as long as the bridegroom is with them? The days will come, when the bridegroom is taken away from them, and then they will fast."

The Pharisees and the disciples of John had compared themselves to Jesus' disciples, coming to the inescapable conclusion that Jesus' disciples were just not measuring up to the high standards of their religion. Their complaint sounds something like '*we keep the rules and are therefore righteous, so why don't You and Your disciples keep the rules?*' They couldn't imagine that God can ask different things of different people.

Just because an act of piety is good for you, it doesn't mean that it's good for everyone. The Church has given some commandments that apply to everyone; but even those sometimes shouldn't be applied to some (like sick people or children, or pregnant women...) The children of God form a family and in this family we are all different and all free. To compare what I do with what others do only generates distress. Moreover, what would happen if in your home everyone did the same task, if everyone loaded the dishwasher for example?

Let's not waste our time comparing our acts of piety with others. We have to become like Jesus, not like the others; we have to be saints, not clones. Jesus asks different things from different people, and we have to do what God asks us to do, not what other people do. Once St Teresa of Avila was thinking of the severe penance that another nun was performing and she wanted to do the same. But when she asked her confessor, he told her to do something else. She was complaining during her prayer to Our Lord that she couldn't perform that sacrifice to show her love for Him. In that moment she heard the voice of Jesus saying, "*Do you see all the penance she does? I value your obedience much more.*" So let's not try to imitate anyone; let's just do the Will of God for us.

Holy Mary, if ever I start worrying about what others do and expect me to do, help me, only and in everything, to fulfil the Will of God like you - "*be it done unto me according to thy word.*"

Fourteenth Sunday in Ordinary Time
Sunday 6th July
Lk 10:1-12,17-20

The Lord appointed seventy others, and sent them on ahead of him, two by two, into every town and place where he himself was about to come ... The seventy returned with joy, saying, "Lord, even the demons are subject to us in your name!" And he said to them, "I saw Satan fall like lightning from heaven. Behold, I have given you authority to tread upon serpents and scorpions, and over all the power of the enemy; and nothing shall hurt you."

Our Lord sent His disciples to preach. They went around teaching what Jesus was teaching, explaining what Jesus was doing and how the victory of God was near. We don't know what they did or where they went. We just know what they reported to Jesus upon their return. To summarise all that they were able to do they said to Jesus that not just men, but "*even the demons are subject to us in your name!*" Jesus rejoiced with them as He saw the enemy falling like lightning from heaven.

Jesus had given His disciples authority "*to tread upon serpents and scorpions*", meaning all beasts and dangers of the earth, but especially, He had given them authority "*over **all** the power of the enemy.*" And He concludes with a promise: "***nothing** shall hurt you.*" There are two highlighted words: 'all' and 'nothing'. They do not allow *any* exception.

We, Jesus' disciples, have authority over the devil and all his power, so we have nothing to fear. The enemy is like a shark in an aquarium. As long as we don't try to put our hand in the water, he is powerless. Many saints have had experience in these battles. The devil can do nothing but be angry at those who try to bring souls to Christ. On one occasion St John Vianney was hearing confessions when someone reported to him that his bedroom was in flames. He smiled, unconcerned, and said, "*The grappin ['pitchfork' was his nickname for the devil] is very angry. He couldn't catch the bird so he has burned the cage. It is a good sign. We will have many sinners this day.*" He was only trying to avert the attention of the saint from the confessional. From there he falls, powerless, like lightning.

Holy Mary and St Joseph, terror of the devil, help me to go in search of souls.

Monday 14th week in ordinary time
Monday 7th July
Mt 9:18-26

A ruler came in and knelt before him, saying, "My daughter has just died; but come and lay your hand on her, and she will live" ...And when Jesus came to the ruler's house, and saw the flute players, and the crowd making a tumult, he said, "Depart; for the girl is not dead but sleeping." And they laughed at him. But when the crowd had been put outside, he went in and took her by the hand, and the girl arose.

They laughed at Jesus; they actually *laughed*! They thought they knew better than anyone else. They 'thought' they knew better. But *thank God*, they were wrong. We can imagine their jaws dropping when Jesus led the girl out by the hand, alive and well. It's not unusual that they laughed at Jesus. As with the saints, if you are His disciple you should expect some to laugh at you. But you know the saying: 'He who laughs last, laughs best'. They will laugh at us, but we will keep laughing for all eternity.

There was at university a group of bullies who used to make fun of a good Christian in their class, named Bill. They would make sarcastic comments about him: that he was a 'sacristan' or 'seminarian in disguise', and comments of that sort. Bill never answered back; he always smiled and never lost his cool. They were 'good' people but without respect for God or religion. As Bill was coming into class one day, one of the bullies said in a loud voice, "*We've got a party on Friday, you know: girls, alcohol...*" then he turned to the other students and added, "*but of course, you CAN'T come! It is a sin... isn't it?*" The whole class had their eyes fixed on Bill to see his reaction. After an awkward moment of silence, he answered, "*I won't be able to join you... not because it's a sin, but because I'm planning to go to an old people's home with some friends to cheer up a few of the elderly who are lonely.*" Then, turning to the rest of the spectators, added, "*Everyone's welcome if you want to join us!*"

The party was a flop. More than twenty mates helped Bill to organise a better 'party' for the elderly that Friday. There was such laughter there that some elderly people even lost their false teeth! Holy Mary, Cause of our Joy, may we never be concerned about the laughter of those who don't understand us; may it never prevent us from being true to your Son and laughing ourselves, with *real* joy.

Tuesday 8th July
Mt 9:32-38

Jesus went about all the cities and villages, teaching in their synagogues and preaching the gospel of the kingdom, and healing every disease and every infirmity. When he saw the crowds, he had compassion for them, because they were harassed and helpless, like sheep without a shepherd. Then he said to his disciples, "The harvest is plentiful, but the labourers are few; pray therefore the Lord of the harvest to send out labourers into his harvest."

Jesus' compassionate Heart, full of love for His people - for each one of them - made Him go around teaching, preaching and healing "*every disease and every infirmity.*" One of the things that makes Him so compellingly attractive is His compassion for people and their problems, His willingness to be at their side and feel what they are feeling, to *reach out* to them, to do something for them or say something they need to hear... to die for them.

We learn how to be compassionate from Our Lord Himself. And with our acts of compassion we bring souls to Him; souls who become compassionate themselves and bring other souls to Him. How many lives have been transformed by an act of compassion! Bishop Myriel is a fictional character in Victor Hugo's 'Les Misérables': "*There are men who toil at extracting gold*", writes Hugo; "*he toiled at the extraction of pity. Universal misery was his mine. The sadness which reigned everywhere was but an excuse for unfailing kindness. Love each other; he declared this to be complete, desired nothing further, and that was the whole of his doctrine.*" One night Jean Valjean, a convict, shows up at his door asking for a place to stay the night. The bishop graciously accepts him, feeds him, and gives him a bed. Valjean takes most of Myriel's silver and runs off into the night but the police capture him. When the gendarmes inform the bishop, he tells them that he had 'given' it to Valjean as a gift. After the police leave, Myriel tells Valjean, "*[with that silver] is your soul that I buy from you; I withdraw it from black thoughts and the spirit of perdition, and I give it to God.*" From that moment Valjean becomes an honest man.

Mary, Mother of Mercy, help me to grow in compassion for those whom I can serve in any way.

Wednesday 14th week in ordinary time
Wednesday 9th July
Mt 10:1-7

The names of the twelve apostles are these: first, Simon, who is called Peter, and Andrew his brother; James the son of Zebedee, and John his brother; Philip and Bartholomew; Thomas and Matthew the tax collector; James the son of Alphaeus, and Thaddaeus; Simon the Cananaean, and Judas Iscariot, who betrayed him.

St Matthew gives us the list of the twelve Apostles (including himself). If you give a list of people in your class, for instance, you don't have to say *'first'*, because it's not a classification. You write them in random order or just in alphabetical order. St Matthew starts the list saying: "*first, Simon, who is called Peter.*" St Mark (3:13-19) and St Luke (6:12-16) also give us a list of the Apostles. In actual fact, St Luke does it twice, because in the Acts of the Apostles (1:13-14) he mentions them again. In all these lists the Apostles' names are mentioned in a different order, except for Peter: in the four lists he is *always* mentioned first.

Another interesting point is that if you say: 'this is the list: first, Peter', then you expect the text to continue with the word... *'second...'* But in St Matthew's list there is no 'second'. There is only one 'first' and then eleven more. Since the Apostles at times had been discussing who was the first among them, Jesus solved the riddle before He ascended into Heaven: Peter was.

First things first: "*First, Simon, who is called Peter.*" St Peter gave unity to the twelve. We find him solving the problems that arose after Jesus' Ascension. Today our Peter is called Francis and he needs our prayers. Mons. Chichester, bishop of Salisbury (Zimbabwe) once surprised Pope Pius XII with this question: "*Your Holiness, do you sleep well at night?*" The Pope, amazed, replied, "*Yes, I do ... but why do you ask me that?*" "*When I was little,*" the African bishop replied, "*a lady used to take care of us. Every night, when she got us into bed she prayed with us one Hail Mary 'for the Pope of Rome, so that he can sleep peacefully despite his many concerns.' I have always been praying it, and, to be honest, I was curious to know if it works.*" It certainly does! Holy Mary, Queen of the Apostles, Mother of the Church, pray for Pope Francis!

Thursday 10th July
Mt 10:7-15

Heal the sick, raise the dead, cleanse lepers, cast out demons. You received without paying, give without pay. Take no gold, nor silver, nor copper in your belts, no bag for your journey, nor two tunics, nor sandals, nor a staff; for the labourer deserves his food. And whatever town or village you enter, find out who is worthy in it, and stay with him until you depart.

This is an interesting lesson for us, apostles of the New Evangelization. It worked. You see? The early Christians turned the world upside down *without* the Internet, Facebook and smartphones! Saints didn't waste a second of their lives complaining about what they didn't have, but used what they *did* have. We certainly need means; but we don't need to be worried about them. We are only worried about souls, and God does the rest. Think about this: in the end, the success of the Apostles didn't depend on what they '*had*', but on what they '*were*': saints!

Bl. Dominic Barberi was an Italian priest who came to England so as to preach and convert many souls. He wasn't very welcome; an eyewitness explains how, on entering a town, "*the crowds rushed out to gape at and insult him, as if he were a savage beast... the more respectable citizens joined in the hideous outcry against the 'Demon, the Papist, the Devil!', as they called him.*" His English was very poor. The 'th' in words was always an insuperable obstacle. Thus, he warned them that to meditate well they had to be good 'tinkers'; or to make the point that without faith we can't be saved, his actual words were: "*Without face it is impossible to be shaved*" (which is also true, anyway.) But with all his difficulties, he eventually received hundreds of people into the Catholic faith, including St John Henry Newman. A book on the second spring of Catholicism in England (also called the reconversion of England) explains how it "*did not begin when Newman was converted nor when the hierarchy was restored. It began on a bleak October day of 1841, when a little Italian priest in comical attire shuffled down a ship's gangway at Folkstone*" (J. Brodrick). Bl. Dominic Barberi arrived with no other means than love for God and zeal for souls. Holy Mary, Queen of the Apostles, help me to become an apostle for the New Evangelization.

Friday 14th week in ordinary time
Friday 11th July
Mt 10:16-23

Behold, I send you out as sheep in the midst of wolves; so be wise as serpents and innocent as doves. Beware of men; for they will deliver you up to councils, and flog you in their synagogues, and you will be dragged before governors and kings for my sake, to bear testimony before them and the Gentiles. When they deliver you up, do not be anxious how you are to speak or what you are to say; for what you are to say will be given to you in that hour; for it is not you who speak, but the Spirit of your Father speaking through you.

Following yesterday's Gospel, Our Lord offers today another interesting lesson about how to do apostolate and evangelize: "*do not be anxious how you are to speak or what you are to say*," just go and look for souls and talk to them. The Holy Spirit will give you the words you need to say. He knows what each human heart needs. Sometimes we are worried about trying to find the perfect argument that could convince our friends and we forget that they are not moved by arguments, but by the grace of God.

A good Christian boy was coming back from school with a friend. He wanted to help him to go to Confession again after a long time, but couldn't think of anything to say. Eventually, as they drew near the parish church, he told his friend that he wanted to pay a visit to the Blessed Sacrament and invited him to come along. His friend mocked him and said scornfully, "*You go, and give my kind regards to Him.*" He went in and prayed, asking the Holy Spirit to suggest 'something' he could say. But after a while, nothing came to his mind and he went out.

When he was coming out, his friend asked him sarcastically, "*Did He give you any message for me?*" Without a second's hesitation he answered, "*Sure! He said that He's still waiting for you.*" There was an uneasy moment of silence; his friend grew serious. They kept walking for a while until the friend broke the silence, asking, "*Are you kidding me?*" "*No,*" he replied. "*In that case,*" said his friend, a bit disconcerted, "*I'd better go back inside. I think I have to speak with Him.*" That day his friend went back to Confession for the first time in years... Holy Mary, Spouse of the Holy Spirit, teach me to rely on the Paraclete and remind me to go to Him when there are souls in need of help.

St Benedict, abbot
Friday 11th July
Mt 19:27-29

Then Peter said in reply, "Lo, we have left everything and followed you. What then shall we have?" Jesus said to them, "Truly, I say to you, in the new world, when the Son of man shall sit on his glorious throne, you who have followed me will also sit on twelve thrones, judging the twelve tribes of Israel. And every one who has left houses or brothers or sisters or father or mother or children or lands, for my name's sake, will receive a hundredfold, and inherit eternal life.

"*What then shall we have?*" We have read the promise of our Lord many times: "*a hundredfold*" and "*eternal life.*" Some think that, if we give ourselves completely to God here on earth, we may be miserable in this present life, although we will be rewarded in Heaven. But that's not what Jesus said: a hundredfold is to be given now, on earth... and eternal life, as well, in Heaven. Happiness in Heaven is for those who know how to be really happy here, in this life.

Do you see the point? To give oneself to God is a win-win situation: you win here on earth, and you win there in Heaven; because being with God is being happy (here or there, anywhere). That's the promise we read today in the Gospel, "*What then shall we have?*" 'Everything!' God blesses those who blessed Him; not necessarily in material things, but in happiness. Saints have been the happiest people in history.

When St Benedict was a boy he was sent to Rome to study rhetoric – the art of persuasive speaking. There he learned not to convey the truth but to use eloquence to convince. He had everything - education, wealth, youth, but he wasn't happy. Afraid for his soul, Benedict gave up his inheritance and founded the first monastery in history. His monasteries - and before Henry VIII England had hundreds of Benedictine monasteries - were devoted to providing the local community with employment for local people, help for the poor, free education and health care, as well as free hospitality to travellers. St Benedict's monks and nuns got '*the hundredfold*' and brought it to everyone by their service and self-giving.

Mary, my Mother, you are another good example of self-giving; help me to be generous as well, to give God 'everything' He asks for, to get 'everything' He wants to give me.

Saturday 14th week in ordinary time
Saturday 12th July
Mt 10:24-33

A disciple is not above his teacher, nor a servant above his master; it is enough for the disciple to be like his teacher, and the servant like his master. If they have called the master of the house Be-elzebul, how much more will they malign those of his household...Do not fear those who kill the body but cannot kill the soul; rather fear him who can destroy both soul and body in hell...So every one who acknowledges me before men, I also will acknowledge before my Father who is in heaven; but whoever denies me before men, I also will deny before my Father who is in heaven.

If they have called God Beelzebub... what will not be said about His disciples? But Our Lord says, "*do not fear them.*" All the saints have had to defend our Faith against persecutions of different kinds. We should also be ready to do whatever it takes to defend God and our Faith. It may take effort sometimes; it may take courage at times; it may require lots of things but we should be ready to give whatever is necessary in order to make the Name of Our Lord known everywhere.

During the beginnings of Opus Dei St Josemaría suffered the misunderstandings of certain people. It didn't take long for a full-blown campaign of rumours and even calumnies to start. Those were days of great suffering. All these slanders took their toll on him: he found it difficult to forget about them and to fall asleep at night. In a letter to his bishop, he had written, "*I don't have any tears left for crying.*" One night, exasperated with a heavy workload and wagging gossiping tongues, he couldn't take it anymore. He went to the oratory in the middle of the night, knelt before the Tabernacle and said, "*Lord, if you don't need my good name, what should I want it for?*" Then, leaving things in God's hands, he peacefully went back to bed. After having given up everything else, he also gave up his good name.

Let's be ready to offer even our good name to acknowledge His Good Name. Let's be bold like so many saints and martyrs who went throughout the world preaching the Gospel. Holy Mary, Queen of Martyrs, intercede for us so that we are ready to acknowledge your Son today in any circumstance of the environment where God wants us to be.

Fifteenth Sunday in Ordinary Time
Sunday 13th July
Lk 10:25-37

Jesus said, "A man was going down from Jerusalem to Jericho, and he fell among robbers, who stripped him and beat him, and departed, leaving him half dead. Now by chance a priest was going down that road; and when he saw him he passed by on the other side. So likewise a Levite, when he came to the place and saw him, passed by on the other side. But a Samaritan, as he journeyed, came to where he was; and when he saw him, he had compassion, and went to him and bound up his wounds, pouring on oil and wine; then he set him on his own beast and brought him to an inn, and took care of him. And the next day he took out two denarii and gave them to the innkeeper, saying, 'Take care of him; and whatever more you spend, I will repay you when I come back.' Which of these three, do you think, proved neighbour to the man who fell among the robbers?" He said, "The one who showed mercy on him." And Jesus said to him, "Go and do likewise."

Our Lord wasn't just telling a nice story. He was giving a command: "*Go and do likewise.*" The Good Samaritan saw the man in need, he bound up his wounds, carried him on his own horse, brought him to the inn, took care of him there and, when he had to go, he paid for someone to look after him. Jesus says that he "*had compassion.*" The teaching is clear: '*real compassion drives action*'.

The text started with the commandment of Our Lord to love God and neighbour. They didn't have any doubt about Who God is, but they did want to know who exactly *my neighbour* is. 'Your neighbour', says Our Lord, 'is the one you *see* in need.' The three characters in the parable *saw* the man. The three of them were *close* (*neighbours*) to him. But two of them decided to '*move away*'. Only one *saw* him and *had compassion*.

It is always easier to feel compassion for people we don't see (hungry children in Africa, families devastated by earthquakes or floods in the news) but not to feel compassion for those we see (my sister, my brother, my teacher, my classmate, the shop assistant, the postman, the policeman, the cyclist in the street…). There is always a good number of people we can help every day. We can't sit on the fence when we *see* people in need. Mary, Help of Christians, help me to *see* those who need me and to have '*compassion*' on them; 'compassion that will drive action.'

Monday 15th week in ordinary time
Monday 14th July
Mt 10:34-11:1

He who receives you receives me, and he who receives me receives him who sent me. He who receives a prophet because he is a prophet shall receive a prophet's reward, and he who receives a righteous man because he is a righteous man shall receive a righteous man's reward. And whoever gives to one of these little ones even a cup of cold water because he is a disciple, truly, I say to you, he shall not lose his reward.

Nothing is small in terms of charity, especially when it comes to helping a good person to do good. Imagine the best football players in the world, all gathered in the same team. That team would be terrific! But now imagine that they don't have boots, sports gear or money for public transport to get to their matches... However good they are, in those situations, they are useless. Or imagine a man in the best physical condition for cycling never discovering his talent because he never had a bicycle or money to get one. What a loss it would be for the cycling world!

Many people around us, our parish, our school, a youth club, some charities or small groups of good people want to help and plan to do great things for many others, but usually they need help themselves. When we help them we multiply and participate in the good they do; we also become 'good people doing good things'.

Do you know what 'crowdfunding' is? It's a way of raising money by asking a large number of people for a small amount of money each. We can promote 'Spiritual Crowdfunding', raising supernatural means for the success of many good projects. Because sometimes we can't give money, but we can give time, advice, prayer, sacrifice, encouragement... Anything! Anything that we give to them is always important, "*even a cup of cold water*". Like the old widow who decided to spend her time helping in a centre for disabled children. When they asked her what she was willing to do, she said, "*Anything! I don't have much money or strength, but I still have a **heart**... I can give that to these children.*" And that really was a great deal; wasn't it?!

Mary, my Mother, make me generous and help me to see where, who and how I can help. Help me to help others!

Tuesday 15th week in ordinary time
Tuesday 15th July
Mt 11:20-24

Then he began to upbraid the cities where most of his mighty works had been done, because they did not repent. "Woe to you, Chorazin! Woe to you, Bethsaida! For if the mighty works done in you had been done in Tyre and Sidon, they would have repented long ago in sackcloth and ashes. But I tell you, it shall be more tolerable on the day of judgment for Tyre and Sidon than for you."

Jesus had been preaching and performing miracles in those cities, but they would not repent. He had gone all the way to Chorazin and Bethsaida to teach them about the Mercy of God and the possibility of helping them to repent and restart a new life, but not many were willing to change. Their problem wasn't that they had done bad things (we all have). They probably had grown used to their sins and didn't have any interest in changing.

A family went to the circus. As they arrived early at the show they went to see the animals that were due to perform. Among them was a massive elephant. The boy was surprised that the elephant was tied to a small pole with a thin rope. He asked the handler why the elephant never escaped. "*Oh boy, it did try!*" answered the man. "*When elephants are little they are tied to the pole. They try for a long time to escape with all their might but, since they are still babies, they can't. Eventually they give up. Elephants have a good memory. They never forget that it was impossible. So they never try again!*"

It happens sometimes with sinners. They get used to their sins and eventually consider it impossible to change. In a way, it is true that it is 'impossible' for them to change... but "*with God nothing will be impossible*" (*Lk* 1:37). Chorazin, Bethsaida, Sodom, Gomorra, Tyre or Sidon, or Judas or Peter or Saul or Augustine or you or me... all of us can change for the better. We are all sinners called to be saints. We all have sins to regret and grace to accept. We can all stay, like the elephant, tied to our miseries and sins, wallowing in the mud of our temptations, or else we can cut off our ties with the help of God and break free to fly high, to Heaven! Just as Jesus went to those places, so He always comes to help sinners to repent. Quite rightly, St Augustine wrote, "*there is no saint without a past, no sinner without a future.*" Mary, Refuge of Sinners, pray for us!

Wednesday 16th July
Mt 11:25-27

Jesus declared, "I thank thee, Father, Lord of heaven and earth, that thou hast hidden these things from the wise and understanding and revealed them to babes; yea, Father, for such was thy gracious will. All things have been delivered to me by my Father; and no one knows the Son except the Father, and no one knows the Father except the Son and any one to whom the Son chooses to reveal him.

St Therese of Lisieux explained: "*Our Lord needs from us neither great deeds nor profound thoughts. Neither intelligence nor talents. He cherishes simplicity.*" Sometimes people with great intellectual talents are unable to understand You, Lord. Many people attended Your sermons. Some, like Scribes and Pharisees, were wise; they had studied the Scriptures and knew by heart many of the prophecies. They "understood" all Your words. But they didn't get it. The great and the powerful of Your time, Jesus, didn't follow You, but some fishermen, publicans and a few illiterate men and women did.

Simple saints have turned the world upside down; their memory is alive still, while powerful men, kings, emperors and thinkers have been buried and long forgotten. The virtue of simplicity allows God to do His part. Simplicity prevents saints from pretending that they are someone they are not; it allows them to be seen by men as they are seen by God. They listen to God, and God listens to them.

St Josemaría met a holy woman called Enriqueta, who was mentally ill. The only thing she could do was pray. There was at the time a very anti-Catholic newspaper; so St Josemaría asked Enriqueta to pray for that newspaper to close down. In a few months, without any explanation, the newspaper went bankrupt and closed forever. St Josemaría was sure that the simplicity of Enriqueta was more powerful than the newspaper's editors.

Simplicity and humility attract Our Lord's gaze. The most simple and humble of all was a Woman of Nazareth. She had all the talents that anyone could think of. Yet, she caught the attention of God when she considered herself the "*handmaid of the Lord.*" To her everything was *revealed*. God liked her simplicity so much that He made her His Mother... and yours and mine. May she help us to take after her in this virtue as well.

Our Lady of Mount Carmel
Wednesday 16th July
Mt 12:46-50

While he was still speaking to the people, behold, his mother and his brethren stood outside, asking to speak to him. But he replied to the man who told him, "Who is my mother, and who are my brethren?" And stretching out his hand toward his disciples, he said, "Here are my mother and my brethren! For whoever does the will of my Father in heaven is my brother, and sister, and mother."

We all have fond memories of our own mother: her expressions, the tone of her voice, her gestures, her favourite song... Every time Mary is mentioned, Jesus has this one thought: She is the woman who "*does the will of my Father.*" And if we are to be good sisters and brothers of Jesus, we should take after our Mother in this attribute.

If we ask her to teach us to be like her, she will come to our aid straight away, as good mothers do. God has given her that mission. But she doesn't just teach by giving lectures like a normal teacher, she actually helps us make it happen. In 1254 St Simon Stock was elected Superior-General of the Carmelites during difficult times. He prayed intensely to Our Lady for help and then had the vision of her bringing the Brown Scapular with the promise that "*whosoever dies clothed in this shall never suffer eternal fire...It shall be a sign of salvation, a protection in danger, and a pledge of peace.*" Also Pope John XXII stated that Our Lady had told him in a vision, concerning those who wear the Scapular: "*I, the Mother of Grace, shall descend on the Saturday after their death and whomsoever I shall find in Purgatory, I shall free.*"

Bl Gregory X was buried with his scapular. When his grave was opened 600 years later, there were only bones, dust... and his fabric scapular intact! The same thing happened to St Alphonsus whose scapular is today on display at his monastery in Rome. He wrote: "*Just as men take pride in having others wear their livery, so the Most Holy Mary is pleased when Her servants wear Her Scapular as a mark that they have dedicated themselves to Her service, and are members of the Family of the Mother of God.*" Holy Mother, thank you for your Scapular, for your protection, for your help. May I imitate you in doing always and in everything only the Will of my Father.

Thursday 15th week in ordinary time
Thursday 17th July
Mt 11:28-30

Jesus said: "Come to me, all who labour and are heavy laden, and I will give you rest. Take my yoke upon you, and learn from me; for I am gentle and lowly in heart, and you will find rest for your souls. For my yoke is easy, and my burden is light."

You, Lord, know about burdens. You probably also had some clients asking for 'urgent' jobs; You may have seen St Joseph being mistreated by some unreasonable client who didn't want to pay what he had agreed; maybe You saw him in distress when he had to pay taxes to the tax-collector who was demanding too much; perhaps You also saw Your Mother counting pennies to calculate whether she could buy some special food for Your Birthday; You probably suffered because of friends who started leading a bad life or neighbours who were suffering the loss of children.

You, Lord, know human burdens. You didn't just give us a tip to cope with them or a pat on the back to encourage us to carry them. You gave YOURSELF! You, my Jesus, want 'me' and 'my burden', so that it won't be *my* burden anymore, but *ours*: Yours and mine. "*Come to me!*" You said. That's a command. Like a mother to her child when he tries to do something on his own: 'Ask for help!' A yoke was a wooden crosspiece fastened over the necks of two animals and attached to the plough or cart that they pulled. Yokes were never made to balance. They were always made heavier on one side than the other. In that way, they would put a weak bullock alongside a strong bullock; the light end would rest on the weak ox, the heavier end on the stronger one. That's why the yoke is easy and the burden is light, because the Lord's yoke is made after the same pattern, and the heavy end is upon His shoulder.

On one occasion, St Josemaría had a very crucial meeting. A young student, José María González Barredo, commented to him, "*Father, you have a critical meeting in half an hour, and still, you are so much at ease!*" Immediately St Josemaría replied quite simply, "*And why should I be anxious? I am a son of God now... and in half an hour.*" Mary, my Mother, Comforter of the afflicted, always remind me to share my burden with your Son, so that it stops being *mine* and becomes *ours*.

Friday 15th week in ordinary time
Friday 18th July
Mt 12:1-8

At that time Jesus went through the grain fields on the sabbath; his disciples were hungry, and they began to pluck heads of grain and to eat. But when the Pharisees saw it, they said to him, "Look, your disciples are doing what is not lawful to do on the sabbath." He said to them, "Have you not read what David did, when he was hungry, and those who were with him? ...For the Son of man is lord of the sabbath."

The Pharisees (they seem to always hunt in a pack) were obsessed with the things that 'could not' be done, but had no concern about the ones that 'should' be done. The seventh day of the week was meant to be especially devoted to God, but for them it was a day to 'avoid doing things'. Instead of doing things for God, it was a day to do nothing at all.

But we know that the only really important thing on Sundays is the Holy Mass. Yet some may excuse themselves from going to Mass because it's their birthday - but then they should go to Mass and thank God for it! Or because some relatives come to visit - then bring them along to thank God for your family! Everything that we can enjoy on Sundays has been provided by Him, so how could we justify enjoying ourselves on Sunday... while leaving Him out of it? It would be like asking a friend to organise your party and, when everyone and everything is ready, kicking him out!

In the year 304 AD, a group of 49 Christians were found guilty of having illegally celebrated Sunday worship at Abitinae, a Roman town in Africa. The priest Saturninus was interrogated and he held firm even under torture. His example was followed by all the others, both men and women, including four children. One of them, Emeritus, declared that they had met in his house. When he was asked why he had violated the emperor's law, he replied, "*Sine Dominico non possumus*" - without the Lord we cannot live, meaning the Holy Eucharist that the emperor had declared illegal, but in which they had chosen to participate even at the cost of being tortured and sentenced to death.

Holy Mary, Mother of the Eucharist, help me never to haggle over my attendance and punctuality at Holy Mass.

Saturday 15th week in ordinary time
Saturday 19th July
Mt 12:14-21

The Pharisees went out and took counsel against him, how to destroy him. Jesus, aware of this, withdrew from there. And many followed him, and he healed them all, and ordered them not to make him known. This was to fulfil what was spoken by the prophet Isaiah: "Behold, my servant whom I have chosen, my beloved...He will not wrangle or cry aloud, nor will any one hear his voice in the streets; he will not break a bruised reed or quench a smouldering wick, till he brings justice to victory."

Jesus withdrew from there, and when He had healed '*them all*', He ordered them not to say anything. It looks like He was playing hide and seek! Some people wonder why God is not more visible, easier to find... But that is the prophecy: "*He will not wrangle or cry aloud, nor will any one hear his voice in the streets*".

Pope Benedict XVI told the rabbinical story of Jehel, a little boy, who comes running into the room of his grandfather, the famous Rabbi Baruch. Big tears are rolling down his cheeks. And he cries, "*My friend has totally given up on me. He is very unfair and very mean to me.*" "*Well, could you explain this a little more?*" asks the master. "*We were playing hide and seek,*" answers the little boy. "*I was hiding so well that he could not find me. But then he simply gave up and went home. Isn't that mean?*" You see? The most exciting hiding place has lost its excitement because his friend stops searching for him. The rabbi caresses the boy's face, himself with tears in his eyes. And he says, "*Yes, this is not nice. But look, it is the same way with God. He is in hiding, and we do not seek him. Just imagine! God is hiding, and we people do not even look for him.*"

God is in hiding. He waits for us to set out in search of Him: "*May you seek Christ; may you find Christ; may you love Christ*" (St Josemaría). That's what we do when we pray with the Gospel and help other people search for Him in the Gospel, because we can be sure that as soon as they find Him and listen to His Word, they will definitely love Him...

St Josemaría taught that "*we always go, and return, to Jesus through Mary.*" The best way to find the Son is to search for Him with the Mother. She knows perfectly where to find Him.

Sixteenth Sunday in Ordinary Time
Sunday 20th July
Lk 10:38-42

Now as they went on their way, he entered a village; and a woman named Martha received him into her house. And she had a sister called Mary, who sat at the Lord's feet and listened to his teaching. But Martha was distracted with much serving; and she went to him and said, "Lord, do you not care that my sister has left me to serve alone? Tell her then to help me." But the Lord answered her, "Martha, Martha, you are anxious and troubled about many things; one thing is needful. Mary has chosen the good portion, which shall not be taken away from her."

Martha wasn't idle. She was doing lots of things. As a matter of fact those things were also necessary. But they were not the 'priority', they weren't 'prior'. First things first. Mary was in prayer, listening to Our Lord, and that was more important than anything else. Get this: *Prayer is not one more thing to do. Prayer is what you do when you stop doing 'anything else'*. If we don't pray, all we do is written in water.

"*First, prayer; then, atonement* [sacrifice]; *in the third place, very much 'in the third place', action,*" wrote St Josemaría. When you sketch a plan of action you should put prayer first. For whatever intention: to bring a friend to God, to change your ways, to overcome your vices, to change the atmosphere or even the world, prayer is always the priority. After prayer and sacrifice then comes action, which can't be neglected either. St Augustine once said "*pray as though everything depended on God. Work as though everything depended on you.*"

A young girl had fallen in love with the wrong guy. She had made up her mind to leave university and go to live with him. Her dad tried every argument to make her realise her mistake, but all to no avail. Eventually the father broke the news to the mother. Immediately she said, "*Let's fix this mess,*" and putting on her coat, she left the house. In the evening the father had a phone call from his daughter. Everything was solved. She had understood her folly and broken up with that guy. The father turned to his wife and asked, "*Did you talk to her?*" "*I didn't talk to her.*" she answered, "I talked to God... and God talked to her." *She had spent the whole afternoon in prayer before the Tabernacle... First things first! Mary, my Mother, may I learn from you to always put prayer first.*

Monday 21st July
Mt 12:38-42

The Pharisees said to Jesus, "Teacher, we wish to see a sign from you." But he answered them, "An evil and adulterous generation seeks for a sign; but no sign shall be given to it except the sign of the prophet Jonah. For as Jonah was three days and three nights in the belly of the whale, so will the Son of man be three days and three nights in the heart of the earth. The men of Nineveh will arise at the judgment with this generation and condemn it; for they repented at the preaching of Jonah, and behold, something greater than Jonah is here.

Do you remember the story of Jonah? God asked him to go to Nineveh to preach repentance. God was counting on him to bring those souls back to Him. Jonah's reaction was immediate: he ran the other way! He didn't want to complicate his life. Something similar happened with those Pharisees who heard Our Lord preaching, but decided not to complicate their lives either.

The salvation of all in Nineveh depended on Jonah. God didn't have a 'Plan B'. If Jonah didn't go, the people of Nineveh would have had no chance. When, during the conclave of his election, Pope Benedict XVI understood that he was going to be elected, as he explained later, he prayed to Our Lord saying, "*Don't do this to me! You've got younger and better men, with altogether more vigour and more strength who could step up to this task.*" This is a very understandable reaction. What would you do if you were there? But then, the Pope continued explaining, a cardinal (we don't know who he was but we are very grateful to him) "*wrote me:* 'If the Lord should now tell you, 'Follow me,' then remember what you preached. Do not refuse. Be obedient' *...This touched my heart. The ways of the Lord are not comfortable, but we were not created for comfort, but for greatness, for good. So in the end, all I could do was say 'Yes'. I am trusting in God.*"

God has a plan. He follows us up step by step. Maybe sometimes we have told Him to leave us alone - as if He was a beggar! But *He always comes back.* Jonah said 'Yes' in the end and the people of Nineveh were given a chance to be saved. Through the intercession of Our Mother, I also want to say 'Yes' to God's plans for the sake of many other souls who depend on me.

St Mary Magdalene
Tuesday 22nd July
Jn 20:1-2,11-18

Now on the first day of the week Mary Magdalene came to the tomb early, while it was still dark, and saw that the stone had been taken away from the tomb... she turned round and saw Jesus standing, but she did not know that it was Jesus. Jesus said to her, "Woman, why are you weeping? Whom do you seek?"

St Mary Magdalene is an important saint. Pope Francis has raised her memorial to the dignity of a liturgical Feast, like one more Apostle. We know a few things about her. St Luke records that she was a notorious sinner but she came to weep at His feet. And that was the turning point of her life, because Jesus brought her innocence back to her when He said, "*her sins, which are many, are forgiven, for she loved much.*" Throughout history, great sinners have become great saints. Not because their sins were unimportant, but because they "*loved much.*"

Be certain of this: your sins are not a hindrance to your holiness. They weren't to St Peter, St Paul, St Matthew, St Augustine, St Dimas (the '*Good*' thief), St Thomas Becket... and so many thousands of saints. Sins are not a hindrance but an opportunity for holiness. No matter how many or how awful our sins are, nor how rotten and putrid our miseries, once they are forgiven in the Sacrament of Confession, they become a first class manure for the tree of sanctity. With the water of our love and the rays of God's grace, the tree of our sanctity will grow and give much fruit.

How much Mary loved her Master! She wept out of repentance at His feet one day. She wept again at the entrance of the tomb, looking for Jesus even after His death. A week before that day she was pouring her best perfume on the tired feet of Jesus. And when most of His disciples abandoned Him on Good Friday, she was next to Our Lady at the feet of Jesus once more, now nailed to the Cross. God could easily forgive those sins because He could easily feel her deep love.

Mary, Mother of Mercy, may I always come back to your Son. May I learn from Mary to repent and to love; may I be able to hear Jesus' voice one day saying that my sins have been forgiven... '*because I've loved much.*'

Wednesday 23rd July
Mt 13:1-9

Jesus said: "A sower went out to sow. And as he sowed, some seeds fell along the path, and the birds came and devoured them. Other seeds fell on rocky ground, where they had not much soil, and immediately they sprang up, since they had no depth of soil, but when the sun rose they were scorched; and since they had no root they withered away. Other seeds fell upon thorns, and the thorns grew up and choked them. Other seeds fell on good soil and brought forth grain, some a hundredfold, some sixty, some thirty. He who has ears, let him hear."

"He who has ears, let him hear." Jesus said that many times. He wasn't talking about the actual visible ears but about hearing God's voice, understanding His Word and following It. For Jesus, 'hearing' and 'obeying' God's voice come together. The seed is His Word. Some hear It but soon forget about It or the thorns of sin 'choke them' and never give fruit. To give fruit we need the courage to hear Him and do what He wants.

Reason moved Kimberly Hahn, a Presbyterian mother, to become a Catholic, but her heart resisted with all its might. One day her father asked her: "*Kimberly, do you pray the prayer I say every day? Do you say: "Lord, I will go where you want me to go, I will do what you want me to do, I will say what you want me to say, and I will give up what you want me to give up?*" She explained that she didn't dare to say it for fear of having to become a Catholic. "*Kimberly*" he replied, "*You do not tell the Lord where you want or do not want to go ... If you cannot recite this prayer, then ask God for the grace to say it, until you finally have the strength to say it out loud. Open your heart to him: you can trust Him.*" For 30 days she prayed: '*Lord, give me the grace to say this prayer.*' Finally she managed to say it and everything changed. "*My heart was thumping*" she writes, "*Now I was free to study and understand, to begin to examine things once again, but this time, with a sense of joy. Very well, Lord, I have realised that these were not the plans for my life, but that Your plans are better for me. What do You want to do with my heart? In my life? In our family?*" It is then that the seed can start to give fruit. Let us ask Our Mother to be able to say that prayer, to listen to God's voice and obey His Will.

St Bridget, religious, Patron of Europe
Wednesday 23rd July
Jn 15:1-8

I am the true vine, and my Father is the vinedresser...Abide in me, and I in you. As the branch cannot bear fruit by itself, unless it abides in the vine, neither can you, unless you abide in me. I am the vine, you are the branches. He who abides in me, and I in him, he it is that bears much fruit, for apart from me you can do nothing...If you abide in me, and my words abide in you, ask whatever you will, and it shall be done for you. By this my Father is glorified, that you bear much fruit, and so prove to be my disciples.

Fruitfulness depends on the unity of branch to stalk. There is a massive difference between a branch that is attached to the vine and one that is not. The latter is just a stick. That's the secret of the saints' fruitfulness. They are united to Christ. Holiness is like a blood transfusion. The Blood is Christ's Most Precious Blood. And as you know, blood is vital, it's necessary for 'life' (that's the etymology of 'vital'). Blood is not just about oxygen. Certainly it transports oxygen to the parts of the body and oxygen is 'vital'. It keeps you 'alive' - just as God does with us. But blood also transports nutrients, and those are necessary for growth. This is like grace. God's grace makes us grow in holiness. Another function of blood - sometimes overlooked – is the immune system. It reaches every part of the body through the blood. A blood transfusion can give a sick person antibodies to overcome an infection.

Union with Christ has these same effects in our spiritual life: He keeps us alive, He gives us His grace to grow in holiness, He heals our spiritual diseases (vices, miseries, weaknesses...) and, on top of that, He makes us give fruit. St Bridget is one more example of this union. What could a 40-year-old widow mother of 8 children do? She became the first woman ever to found a religious Order: the Brigittines. She can be called the Patroness of Failures. She never had the Pope return to Rome, nor managed to make peace between France and England; she never saw any nun in the habit that Christ had shown her... But her order spread swiftly throughout Europe. Today she is Patroness of Europe. How did her life give so much fruit? Because she was united to Our Lord. May Our Mother unite us to her Son to be fruitful as well.

Thursday 24th July
Mt 13:10-17

The disciples said to him, "Why do you speak to them in parables?" And he answered them, "To you it has been given to know the secrets of the kingdom of heaven, but to them it has not been given. For to him who has will more be given, and he will have abundance; but from him who has not, even what he has will be taken away...blessed are your eyes, for they see, and your ears, for they hear. Truly, I say to you, many prophets and righteous men longed to see what you see, and did not see it, and to hear what you hear, and did not hear it."

We are privileged people. Think: How many of your age are friends of God in your country? Or how many have been taught that Jesus Christ longs for their love and prayer, or that their prayer can be powerful? Probably not many. But you are among them. *'Why me?'*, you might wonder. Because He wants *you*. Then... why doesn't He give the same to everyone? It seems as if God isn't fair because to those who already have, He says, 'more will be given'...

Some people are convinced that saints were given more grace than the rest of us. But that is not true. God gives to everyone the favours of His grace. Nevertheless, saints receive more... because they ask for more, they want more, they insist more, they beg for more; "*at all times and in everything, they sought for everything in God...and in God they got everything.*" Eventually, the common features of saints are 'the mouth of a beggar' and 'the hands of a thief'.

"*A saint is a glutton who is filled with God by emptying himself. A saint is a poor man who makes his fortune plundering the coffers of God. A saint is a weak man who has walled in God and in Him he builds his fortress... A saint is one who washes his miserable filth at the mercy of God. A saint is a coward who becomes striking and brave, shielded by God's power... A saint is such an ambitious person that he is only satisfied owning an ever bigger portion of God... A saint is a man who takes everything from God, a thief who even steals from God the love he needs to be able to love Him. And God loves to be looted by his saints. That's the joy of God. And that is the secret business of the saints*" (P. Urbano, The Man of Villa Tevere). Mary, with your help, may I 'loot' from God the love and virtues I need to become a saint.

St James, Apostle
Friday 25th July
Mt 20:20-28

Then the mother of the sons of Zebedee came up to him, with her sons, and kneeling before him she asked him for something. And he said to her, "What do you want?" She said to him, "Command that these two sons of mine may sit, one at your right hand and one at your left, in your kingdom." But Jesus answered, "You do not know what you are asking. Are you able to drink the cup that I am to drink?" They said to him, "We are able."

To drink from the same cup was a sign of trust and intimacy. Good friends would drink from the same cup. And the meaning was not just to share drink, but to share destiny. If the cup was poisoned, they were both poisoned. If someone was able to drink from his friend's same cup, it meant that he was ready to go with him faithfully and follow the same fate.

We don't know many things about St James. But we do know one important feature of his character: he was fiercely loyal. When You, my Jesus, asked him and St John if they were able to drink Your cup, they didn't hesitate. In Latin the response is just one word: "*Possumus!*" - "*We can.*" The beautiful lesson of loyalty here is that they didn't know what the cup might contain... and they didn't care. They said 'Yes' to whatever might come, as long as they could be with You. You, Lord, had promised them persecutions... never mind: *Possumus!* They might have to go to preach the Gospel far away from home... they couldn't care less: *Possumus!* They might end up dying at the hands of persecutors... but it didn't matter to them at all as long as they could be with You: *Possumus!*

Eventually St John did accompany You, Lord, beside the Cross, but James didn't. He failed! He told You that he would always be with You, but when You needed him most he didn't come. Yet failures aren't a problem when there is repentance and love. And James did love You. He was the first Apostle killed for Your Name (*Acts* 12:2); so he fulfilled his promise in the end.

Holy Mary, Virgin Most Faithful, help me to be always ready to say 'Yes' to your Son unconditionally... to whatever, whenever, wherever, however, as long as I can always stay with Him.

Saturday 16th week in ordinary time
Saturday 26th July
Mt 13:24-30

"A man sowed good seed in his field; but while men were sleeping, his enemy came and sowed weeds among the wheat, and went away. So when the plants came up and bore grain, then the weeds appeared also. And the servants of the householder came and said to him, 'Sir, did you not sow good seed in your field? How then has it weeds?' He said to them, 'An enemy has done this.' The servants said to him, 'Then do you want us to go and gather them?' But he said, 'No; lest in gathering the weeds you root up the wheat along with them. Let both grow together until the harvest.'"

Why is there so much evil in the world? The answer is given by Jesus, the *"enemy has done this."* Then, why doesn't God pull it out? Because since the sin of our First Parents, good and evil grow together. You can't pull out evil without risking the removal of goodness too, because they are intertwined. The best things in life are a mixture of good and suffering. The way to happiness is paved with difficulties. Why does your father take you to the dentist if he knows that you are going to suffer? Because the result will be a great improvement in your teeth. Why does God allow us to suffer? For the very same reason.

Lovers suffer. Parents suffer for their children and spouses for their beloved and friends for their friends because they love. We can't do what Buttercup in the film 'The Princess Bride' did: she chose not to love so that she didn't have to suffer any more. A heart that doesn't love is already 'dead'. A heart that doesn't beat for anyone doesn't beat at all. But love gives power to persevere, to savour the bitter with the sweet. Saints are saints because they never gave up. St Teresa of Avila explained that those who want to be saints *"must have a great and very determined determination to persevere until reaching the end, come what may, happen what may, whatever work is involved, whatever criticism arises, whether they arrive or whether they die on the road, or even if they don't have courage for the trials that are met, or if the whole world collapses."* And St Josemaría wrote, *"What is the secret of perseverance? Love. Fall in Love, and you will not leave Him."* Mary, Virgin Most Faithful, help me to persevere.

Seventeenth Sunday in Ordinary Time
Sunday 27th July
Lk 11:1-13

He was praying in a certain place, and when he ceased, one of his disciples said to him, "Lord, teach us to pray, as John taught his disciples." And he said to them, "When you pray, say: "Father, hallowed be thy name. Thy kingdom come. Give us each day our daily bread; and forgive us our sins, for we ourselves forgive every one who is indebted to us; and lead us not into temptation."

When you pray with the Gospel, imagine the scene and try to be one more character in it. This one could have been more or less as follows: Jesus and His disciples had been sleeping in the open air. When the apostles started waking up they noticed that Jesus wasn't there. '*Where is He?*' someone asked. '*There! He is praying,*' answered another. As they were clearing their heads and rubbing their eyes and someone was grilling a fish on the fire, someone else, - maybe John, who had his eyes always on the Master - said, '*I wonder how He prays? ... John the Baptist taught us to pray, do you remember Andrew?*' '*Yeah!*' answered Andrew, '*I'm also curious to know what Jesus says in His prayer...*' By then Jesus was walking back towards them. He sat by the fire, smiling, knowing that they wanted to ask something but didn't dare. He might have looked at John and said '*What is it?*' "Lord, teach us to pray, as John taught his disciples!" And then Jesus taught them. So simple: talk to God as to your Father. You and I have to learn to pray as well, so we ask Him to teach us. He responds with His Gospel: take it and read it!

"*Open the Holy Gospel,*" St Josemaría taught, "*but don't just read it: live it. My advice is that, in your prayer, you actually take part in the different scenes of the Gospel, as one more among the people present...Live your life close to Christ. You should be another character in the Gospel, side by side with Peter, and John, and Andrew... In this way (and I know many perfectly ordinary people who live this way) you will be captivated like Mary was, who hung on every word that Jesus uttered or, like Martha, you will boldly make your worries known to him, opening your heart sincerely about them all no matter how little they may be.*" Mary, my Mother, let me be at your side, to see your Son as you see Him and to listen to Him as you do.

Monday 17th week in ordinary time
Monday 28th July
Mt 13:31-35

Jesus said, "The kingdom of heaven is like a grain of mustard seed which a man took and sowed in his field; it is the smallest of all seeds, but when it has grown it is the greatest of shrubs and becomes a tree, so that the birds of the air come and make nests in its branches." He told them another parable. "The kingdom of heaven is like leaven which a woman took and hid in three measures of flour, till it was all leavened."

You, Lord, want to teach us to be patient; to value the importance of the little things that always begin small, like a seed. You want to encourage us when we evangelize and do our apostolate, and fruits take their time to appear. You teach us not to lose heart when souls take their time to respond to the grace of the Gospel.

The Chinese bamboo plant starts from a tiny seed. Once it's planted, very little seems to happen during the first year. Only a tiny shoot pokes out of the ground. In the second year you water and fertilize and protect it... and nothing happens. In the third, fourth, fifth years, nothing happens.

Finally, during the sixth year, the Chinese bamboo plant begins to grow. In fact, it grows 90 feet tall in just 6 weeks! The roots (that you couldn't see) were growing all the time, and now allow the stalk to grow.

The seed grows underground even if you don't see it. The leaven is transforming the flour from the inside, slowly, without anyone noticing it. And your apostolate with your friends to bring them to Jesus is working always, regardless of what you see. We should never lose heart; we should never give up! The seed is there, and is growing anyway. One day it will shoot up!

"In the moments of struggle and opposition lift up your apostolic heart: listen to Jesus as he speaks of the grain of mustard-seed and of the leaven. And say to him: 'Explain the parable to me.' And you will feel the joy of contemplating the victory to come: the birds of the air lodging in the branches of your apostolate, now only in its beginnings, and the whole of the meal leavened" (St Josemaría).

Mary, Our Hope, teach me to be patient and never lose hope.

St Martha, Mary and Lazarus
Tuesday 29th July
Jn 11:19-27

When Martha heard that Jesus was coming, she went and met him, while Mary sat in the house. Martha said to Jesus, "Lord, if you had been here, my brother would not have died. And even now I know that whatever you ask from God, God will give you."

Jesus loved Martha, her sister Mary and her brother Lazarus. He was always welcome in their home. Bethany was a place where Jesus felt at ease. The Gospel explains how, after the death of Lazarus, Jesus went to Bethany and Martha ran to meet Him. And with all the familiarity of a good friend, she complains about Him being too late. She was absolutely certain that if Jesus had been there He could have saved Lazarus.

That confidence is the fruit of a personal relationship with Jesus in our prayer. *"Have you seen the affection and confidence with which Christ's friends treat him? In a completely natural way the sisters of Lazarus 'blame' Jesus for being away: 'We told you! If only you'd been here!' Speak to him with calm confidence: 'Teach us to treat you with the loving friendliness of Martha, Mary and Lazarus, as the first twelve treated you'"* (St Josemaría).

Martha, Mary and Lazarus are a good example of what real friendship with Jesus means. If we failed to have a personal relationship with Jesus, real friendship, including real dialogues with Him... we would be wasting our lives. Jesus Christ didn't come to the world just to make tables and chairs... He came to make friends. Don't you see? He is begging for your friendship.

But, in my prayer, how should I address Him? Exactly as you do your best friend. Sometimes we have time to chat for a while. Those delightful conversations help a friendship to grow. At other times we can only say to Him, '*I have something to tell You, but not now... I'll call you later!*' And so, you prepare your next time of prayer. Now and then there's only time for a short 'WhatsApp': '*I'm in a pickle right now. Need help!*' Sometimes just a smile at Him is all you can manage. Good friends have their ways of communicating with each other. And Jesus loves all those details of affection! May Martha teach us the lesson. May Our Lady help us to become true friends of God.

Wednesday 17th week in ordinary time
Wednesday 30th July
Mt 13:44-46

"The kingdom of heaven is like treasure hidden in a field, which a man found and covered up; then in his joy he goes and sells all that he has and buys that field. Again, the kingdom of heaven is like a merchant in search of fine pearls, who, on finding one pearl of great value, went and sold all that he had and bought it."

Vocation is the treasure that Jesus talks about, the precious pearl. God has made us for a definite purpose. He has a mission for all of us. But the treasure is hidden and we have to find it. And the process of finding it takes time. It is like searching for Jesus in the dark of night amongst a crowd. Slowly the dawn brings a bit of light and we can distinguish better. At some point we have a hunch: He is there. It has to be Him. But we are still not sure. The sun rises little by little and at some stage we start being sure: it's Him! Then, with the light of the sun, everything makes sense. Nothing has changed but everything has changed. The crowd is the same, Jesus was there all the time... but now I see Him.

Vocation is that: when everything makes sense at last. Have you ever seen the colonnade in Saint Peter's Square? It consists of four series of columns which seem like a forest of trees planted there by chance. But there are two points, marked on the ground with a circle, from where everything makes sense. From there, the four series of columns seem to align themselves and become a single column. The alignment of those columns is a symbol of what vocation brings to our lives. At first, everything is in confusion, until we find the 'spot' where everything that surrounds us falls into place. That spot is our vocation. And that is why it is worthwhile to give everything to get it... because everything is 'nothing' without it.

Our Lord explains that the man, *"in his joy...goes and sells all that he has"* to get it. And if we make that leap of faith, if we give everything in order to follow Him, we can say to Him, '*Here you are, Lord! Everything that I am, everything that I have, everything that I can do... I put everything at Your Feet to become what You want me to be, to go where You want me to go, to do what You want me to do and fulfil my mission, the one You thought up for me before the creation of the world.*' Mary, my Mother, make my prayer come true!

Thursday 31st July
Mt 13:47-53

"The kingdom of heaven is like a net which was thrown into the sea and gathered fish of every kind; when it was full, men drew it ashore and sat down and sorted the good into vessels but threw away the bad. So it will be at the close of the age. The angels will come out and separate the evil from the righteous, and throw them into the furnace of fire; there men will weep and gnash their teeth...Therefore every scribe who has been trained for the kingdom of heaven is like a householder who brings out of his treasure what is new and what is old."

The Church works like a huge net, thrown into the sea and gathering all kinds of fish. She was entrusted to fishermen and they were commanded to go and catch 'all' men. They were not asked to select but to go, like a net, gathering all they could: just and sinners, wise and ignorant, Jews and gentiles, free men and slaves, rich and poor, powerful and weak... Everyone! The Church is not the Church of the rich, or the Church of the poor, but the Church of all mankind. Everyone has a soul that needs to be saved and brought back to Jesus.

The apostle can't be fussy when selecting the people he wants to bring to the shore where Jesus is waiting. The commandment was clear: "*Go into all the world and preach the gospel to the whole creation...*" to "*everyone.*" The mission of the disciples of Jesus is to save all men, not to judge them. As St Teresa said, if we waste our time judging them we "*don't have time to love them.*"

Christians are like the fibres woven into the net of the Church: all united to one another, we collect souls for God. Together, we are the net. Once St Mother Teresa received a letter from a man who wrote that, on the preceding afternoon, he planned to commit suicide. Then, quite by accident, he came across a biography of Mother Teresa. Bored and with nothing else to do, he started to read it. As he read, he gradually began to discover a new interest in life and, as he finished it, he decided to begin life anew. The Christian example of that woman, until then unknown to him, brought him back to God.

Holy Mary, Mother of the Church, may I also be an instrument to 'catch' souls for your Son.

August

Friday 17th week in ordinary time
Friday 1st August
Mt 13:54-58

Coming to his own country Jesus taught them in their synagogue, so that they were astonished, and said, "Where did this man get this wisdom and these mighty works? Is not this the carpenter's son? Is not his mother called Mary? And are not his brethren James and Joseph and Simon and Judas? And are not all his sisters with us? Where then did this man get all this?" And they took offense at him.

For these people, wisdom was something you achieved in rabbis' schools. At the age of 12, Jesus had astonished those who were in the Temple by His wisdom and questions. And many saints in the history of Christianity have had the same effect. Because the common sense of saints is the Holy Spirit's gift of Wisdom.

St John Mary Vianney is a good example of a wise soul. He struggled during his years in the seminary because he didn't have enough intellectual capacity for the studies. Once ordained, he had to wait several months before receiving the authority to hear confessions because, as they reported, '*He lacked sufficient knowledge for the office.*' As soon as he was granted permission, the '*ignorant*' priest was soon visited from all over France by bishops, priests and thousands of religious and lay people seeking his advice.

One fine day an atheist came to try and prove to everyone that the Curé of Ars was an ignorant peasant and his superstition (our Faith) was nonsense. He came to him in the presence of other people in the sacristy and said, "*Father, I haven't come for Confession; I've come to argue.*" "*I don't know how to argue,*" replied the saint. "*But if you need some consolation, you can kneel here.*" "*But, Father,*" the man insisted sarcastically, "*I told you that I don't believe in God or in priests and, therefore, in Confession. It's all nonsense.*" "*I see,*" answered the holy priest. "*An eight-year-old boy, with his catechism, knows more than you. I thought I was ignorant. You know even less. Let me explain it to you.*" By the end of the sentence the man was on his knees. A few minutes later, converted, he was praying in tears in front of the Tabernacle. When they asked St John Vianney where he got all his wisdom, he answered that it wasn't 'his'; he "borrowed it from the Holy Spirit." Mary, Spouse of the Holy Spirit, help me to obtain the divine Gift of Wisdom.

Saturday 17th week in ordinary time
Saturday 2nd August
Mt 14:1-12

Herod had seized John and bound him and put him in prison, for the sake of Herodias, his brother Philip's wife; because John said to him, "It is not lawful for you to have her." And though he wanted to put him to death, he feared the people, because they held him to be a prophet.

John spoke up. He could have kept silent and saved his life. '*Anyway*', he could have thought, '*is Herod going to change by any chance, just because I tell him off?*' There are martyrs who have given their lives for the sacrament of the Eucharist; others, for being priests. St John the Baptist is the martyr of marriage. He didn't say, '*In my opinion, it's probably not such a good idea for you to have your brother's wife*'. Rather, he said things straight. And it didn't matter that it was the king he was speaking to. St John Fisher and St Thomas More acted in the same way with another king. Martyrs never compromised the truth, not even to save their lives.

We have to call *a spade a spade*; and a sin a sin. We have to be witnesses to the truth even when we face difficulties. In defending the truth, like St John the Baptist, Christians have to follow the words of Jesus: "*have no fear of them; for nothing is covered that will not be revealed or hidden that will not be known...everyone who acknowledges me before men, I also will acknowledge before my Father who is in Heaven*" (*Mt* 10:26).

Roma Ligocka tells a story of an incident that happened in communist Poland when she was a young girl during a summer camp. One day they were all singing songs together and at one point the leader started a revolutionary song that was offensive to God. Suddenly one of the girls, in tears, stood up petrified. "*Why don't you sing with us?*" asked the leader. "*I do not sing against God*," she answered in a small but firm voice. Silence. The camp leader intoned a new song. No one spoke anymore about it. But Ligocka explains how something had changed; something that shook her convictions and expanded her horizons. That night she discovered that "*there are people who have the courage to stand up and say 'No'.*"

My Mother, Queen of Martyrs, give me the courage to stand up for the truth.

Eighteenth Sunday in Ordinary Time
Sunday 3rd August
Lk 12:13-21

"The land of a rich man brought forth plentifully; and he thought to himself, 'What shall I do, for I have nowhere to store my crops?' And he said, 'I will do this: I will pull down my barns, and build larger ones; and there I will store all my grain and my goods. And I will say to my soul, Soul, you have ample goods laid up for many years; take your ease, eat, drink, be merry.' But God said to him, 'Fool! This night your soul is required of you; and the things you have prepared, whose will they be?' So is he who lays up treasure for himself, and is not rich toward God."

Jesus is warning us against covetousness, the desire to possess and keep more and more things. For in the end we will all die, like the man in the parable, and we won't be able to take our possessions with us. Tutankhamun tried to... and his tomb has been looted already. Those who are anxious about material things are never satisfied. They don't find peace and, worse of all, they don't find God. The story of the rich young man reminds us of it: he preferred his fields and cows and sheep over God.

For Christians, poverty of heart is a virtue. It allows us to fly high to God, because we can't fly if we are loaded with things. Have you ever seen the majestic flight of an eagle that can soar high in the sky without beating its wings? That is not just because of its wingspan. It is mainly because of the lightness of its body. Jesus wants us to fly high and so He wants us free from materialism and greed.

These are a few ways in which St Josemaría used to practice the virtue of poverty: 1. He never used anything as if it were 'his' possession; for instance, he never put his name in the books he used. He never said 'my room', but 'the room I use'. 2. He never kept anything he didn't need or use; for instance, he got rid of his watch because he was always accompanied by Bl Álvaro, who had one. 3. He never complained if he didn't have something he needed; Bl Álvaro comments that in 40 years at his side he *never* heard a complaint. 4. When he could choose, he chose the worst for himself... There were many more poverty habits of St Josemaría, but maybe we can try first with these few tips ourselves…

Mary, my Mother, you can teach me about poverty. Help me to be detached from material things...

Monday 18th week in ordinary time
Monday 4th August
Mt 14:13-21

Now when Jesus heard this, he withdrew from there in a boat to a lonely place apart. But when the crowds heard it, they followed him on foot from the towns. As he went ashore he saw a great throng; and he had compassion on them, and healed their sick. When it was evening, the disciples came to him and said, "This is a lonely place, and the day is now over; send the crowds away to go into the villages and buy food for themselves." Jesus said, "They need not go away; you give them something to eat." They said to him, "We have only five loaves here and two fish." And he said, "Bring them here to me."

I love to see You, my Jesus, always 'on call'. You had left for a lonely place, but souls came searching for You anyway. I imagine You exhausted, trying to rest, and Your disciples protecting You from the people, saying *'Come on! Leave Him alone for a while, for goodness' sake! He hasn't slept for ages. He needs to rest as well.'* But You looked upon each person that had come; You knew how much they had searched for You; You, Lord, knew what they needed better than they did and You always had compassion on them. I want to imitate You, Lord, and be always on call when souls need me. I can't give in to tiredness and put things off because we will never know for sure if we will have another opportunity to help someone.

To be a good Christian 24/7, always on duty, is very demanding. It's exhausting! But it fills us with true joy. For the salvation of souls and in order to relieve people's suffering we should be ready to do anything, anytime. There is not a second to waste! Bl Alvaro del Portillo once told how he went one day to visit St John Paul II at a rather late hour of the evening. While he was awaiting the Pope's arrival, he heard the Holy Father's steps approaching down the corridor, sounding as though he was dragging his feet. Obviously, the Pope was very fatigued. Bl Alvaro exclaimed: "*Holy Father, how tired you are!*" The Pope looked at him and, with a firm and friendly voice, replied: "*If I were not tired at this hour of the day, it would be a sign that I hadn't fulfilled my duty.*"

We will have a whole eternity to rest, but only a few years to save souls... Mary, my Mother, don't let me waste even a second of my life; help me to serve your Son and all souls!

Tuesday 18th week in ordinary time
Tuesday 5th August
Mt 15:1-2.10-14

The disciples approached and said to Jesus, "Do you know that the Pharisees took offence when they heard what you said?" He answered, "Every plant that my heavenly Father has not planted will be uprooted. Let them alone; they are blind guides of the blind. And if one blind person guides another, both will fall into a pit."

There is a sketch about two blind people who meet at the traffic lights. Casually, one of them bumps into the other. They both think someone is volunteering to help them cross the street. "*May I?*" one of them asks, grabbing the other's arm. "*By all means!*" replies the other, gratefully. And without another word they both jump onto the tarmac with confidence. You can hear some car skids and crashes whilst the two oblivious blind men happily chat about the weather until they reach the other side safely and say goodbye. There is no problem being blind if you seek assistance. The real danger is when the assistant is another blind person who doesn't know he's blind. That was the problem with the Pharisees.

John Newton (1725-1807) started his career as a slave trader at the age of 11. During a storm when he was 23, thinking the ship might sink, he prayed for mercy and survived. Later on, whilst aboard a slave vessel bound for the West Indies, he became ill with a violent fever; he asked for God's mercy and again his prayers were heard. Despite this, he continued his involvement in the Slave Trade for many years. It took him a long time to realise the gravity of his sin, but once he **saw** it, he fought with all his might to change public opinion and eradicate slavery. His heartfelt sorrow is expressed in his most popular hymn: "*Amazing grace! How sweet the sound, that sav'd a wretch like me! I once was lost, but now am found, was blind, but now I see.*"

In the spiritual life, there are blind people who ignore their blindness, which is especially serious when innocent lives depend on them. We should never lose hope in their recovery and never give up praying for them. The 'amazing' Grace of Our Lord can still heal that blindness - as St Paul so effectively testifies. Mary, my Mother, Star of the Sea, I ask you to intercede for those blind people who desperately need the light of Christ.

The Transfiguration of the Lord
Wednesday 6th August
Lk 9:28b-36

Jesus took with him Peter and John and James, and went up on the mountain to pray. And as he was praying, the appearance of his countenance was altered, and his raiment became dazzling white. And behold, two men talked with him, Moses and Elijah, who appeared in glory and spoke of his departure, which he was to accomplish at Jerusalem. Now Peter and those who were with him were heavy with sleep, and when they wakened they saw his glory and the two men who stood with him. And as the men were parting from him, Peter said to Jesus, "Master, it is well that we are here".

On Mount Tabor, Peter, James and John saw Jesus as they had never seen Him before. They were awe-inspired by this vision and surely, if they had had an *iPhone* there, they would have taken several *selfies* to put on *Insta* with the title '*Awesome!*' They wouldn't want to forget Jesus as radiant as He was then. So much so that Peter, filled with consolation, said, "*Lord, it is well that we are here.*" Those same three Apostles also saw Jesus in Gethsemane, but in a very different fashion. Jesus was suffering indescribable moral pain, sweating blood as He thought about His Passion. The same Jesus, but not as they would love to remember Him. On Mount Tabor they didn't want to leave. In the Garden of Gethsemane they didn't want to stay. So when Jesus was arrested they all fled.

Friends are meant to be friends always, for better or for worse. You, Lord, are also searching for friends who will stick with you through thick and thin; friends who are reliable, constant; friends who would go with You to Mount Calvary as well as to Mount Tabor; friends, Lord, that You can count on whether it's Tabor or Calvary, sunny or rainy, cold or hot, whether they are tired or energized.

We all have ups and downs. We have days when we find it easy to pray and others when it is a struggle; days when everything seems tiresome, when we don't feel like praying, when we don't fancy going to Mass or saying the Rosary. Those are the moments when we prove that we are real friends of God. Holy Mary, my Mother, help me understand that "*it is well*" for me to be with Jesus anywhere, anytime, no matter what; help me to be constant in accompanying Him with my prayer even when it becomes harder.

Thursday 7th August
Mt 16:13-23

Jesus began to show his disciples that he must go to Jerusalem and suffer many things from the elders and chief priests and scribes, and be killed, and on the third day be raised. And Peter took him and began to rebuke him, saying, "God forbid, Lord! This shall never happen to you." But he turned and said to Peter, "Get behind me, Satan! You are a hindrance to me; for you are not on the side of God, but of men."

Striking words of Our Lord. Literally a couple of verses before, in the same Gospel, Jesus was saying to Peter: "*you are Peter, and on this rock I will build my Church, and the powers of death shall not prevail against it. I will give you the keys of the kingdom of heaven.*" Jesus was going to give Peter the keys of the kingdom, but first he had to learn a lesson about gaining souls for God: 'No pain, no gain.' Suffering is a means of paying for souls.

Today we can consider the life of St John Mary Vianney as a clear example of this. When he was appointed to look after Ars, a village with just over 350 inhabitants, he prayed, "*Lord, grant me the conversion of my parish; I am willing to suffer whatever You wish, for my entire life.*" He certainly suffered. To all the sufferings of his life, scorn, physical ailments - especially when he was old - poverty and persecution, he added his own mortifications. He made the resolution never to enjoy the fragrance of a flower, never to taste fruit nor to drink, even only a few drops of water, during the height of the summer heat. He would not brush away a fly that annoyed him. When on his knees he would not rest his elbows on the kneeling bench. He never showed any dislike. He mortified his curiosity: thus he never expressed so much as a wish to see the recently invented railway which passed by Ars at a distance of a few kilometres. One meal sufficed him for the whole day. He normally ate only a little black bread and one or two potatoes boiled in water.

During an exorcism a demon once lamented that hell had lost 80,000 souls due to St John Vianney's prayers and sacrifices alone. Not because of his words... but his prayers and sacrifice. That's the secret of the apostle: to save souls we have to suffer for them. Mary, Queen of the Apostles, help me to be generous in sacrifice.

Friday 18th week in ordinary time
Friday 8th August
Mt 16:24-28

Jesus told his disciples, "If any man would come after me, let him deny himself and take up his cross and follow me. For whoever would save his life will lose it, and whoever loses his life for my sake will find it. For what will it profit a man, if he gains the whole world and forfeits his life? Or what shall a man give in return for his life?"

Everyone yearns for happiness. People strive to acquire what they think will make them happy. But some get their priorities wrong and set their hearts on false ambitions: getting into this or that university, getting this degree, getting that job, getting this salary or just getting the iPhone X Plus...! Today Jesus wants you to ask yourself: *'What is the most important investment I can make with my life?'* Some have more interest in getting into university than getting into Heaven, are more concerned about becoming a lawyer than becoming a saint, and put more effort into getting a life than getting a 'Life', an eternal One.

The most important investment you can make is giving everything to God. It's a win-win situation. It's like a roulette wheel that, instead of having 2 colours (red and black) and 37 figures, it has the figure 'red 1' in all the sections. There is no way you can lose. You wouldn't bet only one pound and keep all the rest of your money for later. Would you not rather put everything on 'red 1'? To become a saint you have to invest everything you have, everything you are, as St Thérèse of Lisieux put it, "*You cannot be half a saint. You must be a whole saint or no saint at all*." Loss and gain: you give everything to God (and therefore you lose it for a while) and then He can give you the prize. St Teresa of Avila said that "*those who risk all for God will find that they have both lost all and gained all*."

On the inside cover of a secondary school Bible it was written: "*Dear Jesus, that's it. No more messing around. From now on, I'm all in. Love, Anna.*" From now on, no more delay - the sooner I give, the sooner I will be given, and then I won't have to regret, as St Augustine did, all the time I have wasted: "*Late have I loved You, O Beauty ever ancient, ever new. Late have I loved You!*" Mary, my Mother, help me to follow your example and give everything to God.

Saturday 18th week in ordinary time
Saturday 9th August
Mt 17:14-20

A man came up to him and kneeling before him said, "Lord, have mercy on my son...I brought him to your disciples, and they could not heal him." And Jesus answered, "O faithless and perverse generation, how long am I to be with you? How long am I to bear with you? Bring him here to me." And Jesus rebuked him, and the demon came out of him, and the boy was cured instantly. Then the disciples came to Jesus privately and said, "Why could we not cast it out?" He said to them, "Because of your little faith. For truly, I say to you, if you have faith as a grain of mustard seed, you will say to this mountain, 'Move from here to there,' and it will move; and nothing will be impossible to you."

That man brought his son to be healed by the disciples. Imagine the Apostles, who have done this before, approaching the poor boy one after another, trying to heal him with different prayers and actions: '*Let me try! Let me try!*' but nothing happened. Picture also the disappointment of that father who, after having put his trust in those men, couldn't see any change in his son's state. But when Jesus came, He complained about the lack of faith of all of them, including the father. That boy was the innocent victim of the lack of faith of those around him.

It is a responsibility that I need to consider as well: my lack of faith will have many consequences in the lives of others. People erroneously think that if they have more money, time or talent, more knowledge or opportunities, then they could do more, bigger and better things. But saints prove that to do great things you only need faith; just a tiny amount like a mustard seed is enough.

Bishop Mullor came to see St John Paul II in order to present his resignation. But the Pope wanted to appoint him Nuncio. The bishop's mother had a chronic illness and he wanted to care for her. "*Is that the problem?*" asked the Pope, and he continued, "*Let's pray the Hail Mary.*" After the prayer the Pope said, "*Solved! Any other problems?*" Sure enough, when the bishop came home his mum was fine. "*God is the same as always. It is men of faith that are needed: and then, there will be a renewal of the wonders we read of in the Gospel. Ecce non est abbreviata manus Domini, God's arm, his power, has not grown weaker!*" (St Josemaría). Virgin Mary, increase my faith!

St Teresa Benedicta of the Cross, virgin and martyr
Saturday 9th August
Mt 25:1-13

"Then the kingdom of heaven shall be compared to ten maidens who took their lamps and went to meet the bridegroom. Five of them were foolish, and five were wise. For when the foolish took their lamps, they took no oil with them; but the wise took flasks of oil with their lamps...Watch therefore, for you know neither the day nor the hour."

Those virgins were praised, not because they were good but because they were 'wise'. This is the chosen Gospel for the feast of St Edith Stein. She was born of Jewish parents in 1891. By the age of 14 she stopped believing in God: "*I consciously decided, of my own volition, to give up praying*", she said years later. She made philosophy her life career and became an influential philosopher. She had her first experience of faith when, visiting Frankfurt Cathedral one day, she saw a woman with a shopping basket kneeling for a brief prayer. "*This was something totally new to me. In the synagogues and Protestant churches I had visited, people simply went to the services. Here, however, I saw someone coming straight from the busy marketplace into this empty church, as if she was going to have an intimate conversation. It was something I never forgot.*"

God was using these episodes to plant the seed of conversion in her heart. During the summer of 1921 she spent several weeks with a friend and her family. One evening Edith picked up an autobiography of St. Teresa of Avila and spent all night reading it. "*When I had finished the book, I said to myself: This is the truth.*" She converted, was baptised and a few years later she became a Carmelite nun. Then the Nazis started their persecution. "*I felt that those who understood the Cross of Christ should take it upon themselves on everybody's behalf.*" Edith Stein was arrested by the Gestapo on 2 August 1942. Her last words to be heard in the convent were: "*Come, we are going for our people.*" It was probably on 9 August that she died in the gas chamber of Auschwitz. In her words, "*things were in God's plan which I had not planned at all. I am coming to the living conviction that...nothing happens by chance and that the whole of my life, down to every detail, has been mapped out in God's divine providence and makes complete and perfect sense in God's all-seeing eyes.*" Mary, Queen of Martyrs, St Edith Stein, pray for us!

Nineteenth Sunday in Ordinary Time
Sunday 10th August
Lk 12:32-48

"Where your treasure is, there will your heart be also. Let your loins be girded and your lamps burning, and be like men who are waiting for their master to come home from the marriage feast, so that they may open to him at once when he comes and knocks. Blessed are those servants whom the master finds awake when he comes."

Our Lord wants His disciples to be always ready to meet Him each day in the many people who need us. Have you heard of the French expression *'l'esprit d'escalier'*? It can be translated as "staircase wit" and refers to the situation when you come up with the perfect reply too late, when you have already left the room and have reached the bottom of *the stairs*... How many times has it occurred to you that *'I could have said something'*, *'I could have helped there'*, *'I could have asked about his illness...'* By then, it's too late. We're thinking about other things; probably about *our own things*. Our heart is full of self.

Consider *Gollum* absorbed in the ring and repeating to himself, "*My Precioussss.*" We, like *Gollum*, can be so absorbed with our own concerns, ambitions, possessions and comforts, that we miss the opportunity to meet Jesus in other people who need us. Where we have our treasure, we have our heart. And it also works the other way round: If we put our heart into serving others, they become our treasure.

A man popped by to see his friend. When the friend opened the door and saw him, he was overwhelmed with gratitude: "*Thank goodness you came, I was on the brink of disaster!*" For an hour the host explained all his worries and concerns until the visitor had to leave. When they were at the gate, the host recalled the purpose of his friend's visit. "*Wait a second!*" he said, "*You came to visit me for something else, I guess. Sorry, with so much talking, I haven't asked you. What was it?*" The visitor smiled and said, "*There is not much time to explain now. I just came to tell you that I have cancer. I have a couple of months to live.*" You may imagine the distress of his friend. He was so wrapped up in his personal problems that he wasn't aware that his friend, thin and pale, came to him looking for comfort and left without it. Mary, may I be always ready to recognise Jesus in those who need me.

Monday 19th week in ordinary time
Monday 11th August
Mt 17:22-27

The collectors of the half-shekel tax went up to Peter and said, "Does not your teacher pay the tax?" He said, "Yes." And when he came home, Jesus spoke to him first, saying, "What do you think, Simon? From whom do kings of the earth take toll or tribute? From their sons or from others?" And when he said, "From others," Jesus said to him, "Then the sons are free. However, not to give offence to them, go to the sea and cast a hook, and take the first fish that comes up, and when you open its mouth you will find a shekel; take that and give it to them for me and for yourself."

Everyone was asked to pay half a shekel for the support of the Temple. When they came to Peter and asked him if Jesus paid the tax, Peter didn't say, '*Oh, let me ask Him!*' or '*Well, yes, sometimes He does...*' St Peter knew Jesus and didn't hesitate for a second; he said 'Yes', Jesus pays taxes. Maybe he was unsure about *how* Jesus was going to pay, but he didn't doubt that Jesus would pay.

Strictly speaking, God didn't have to pay taxes for *His Temple*, so why did He? As He says, "*not to give offence to them.*" In other words, not to give bad example. When Jesus went to be baptised by St John, the Baptist was a bit confused; why would the Messiah want to be baptised by me? And Jesus gave a similar answer: let's give an example that people will follow. Many times Jesus did things He wasn't obliged to do, to give us good example.

Jesus could have avoided paying taxes, as we can sneak on to the train without paying or illegally download programmes, films and songs... but He gave us a good example that we should follow. In 2010 two 8-year-old boys found a bag on a bus containing more than 15,000 dollars in cash. Immediately they went to the police to find the owners. A police officer, teasing, said to them, "*You could have kept the money!*" One of the boys said, "*We wish! But it is not ours.*" "*But no one would know*", replied the officer. To which the other boy answered, "*God would! And the owner would. And we would as well...*" The right thing is the right thing even if nobody is looking at us. Let us ask Our Lady, Mirror of Justice, to intercede for us so that we may follow the example of her Son and practise the virtue of justice, even if only God sees.

Tuesday 19th week in ordinary time
Tuesday 12th August
Mt 18:1-5, 10, 12-14

The disciples came to Jesus, saying, "Who is the greatest in the kingdom of heaven?" And calling to him a child, he put him in the midst of them, and said, "Truly, I say to you, unless you turn and become like children, you will never enter the kingdom of heaven. Whoever humbles himself like this child, he is the greatest in the kingdom of heaven. "Whoever receives one such child in my name receives me."

The disciples were discussing how to be greater. Jesus gave them the clue: humility makes us great. As St John of the Cross explains, "*To be taken with love for a soul, God does not look on its greatness, but the greatness of its humility.*" That's what He saw in Mary. Humility is necessary for holiness. St Augustine wrote that the way to God is, "*in the first place, humility; in the second place, humility; in the third place, humility...*"

Only humble souls know how to serve God. If we don't serve God we are good for nothing. The greatest saints have been the most humble ones, those who have been good instruments of God: Mary, Joseph, John the Baptist... On February 18th 1988, Blessed Alvaro went to Boston. As soon as he arrived there, he went to St Joseph's cemetery to visit the tomb of the Servant of God Fr Joseph Muzquiz who had been ordained with him and whom he loved dearly. But Blessed Alvaro was not accustomed to the tombs in the United States. At the gravesite, a bit confused, he asked, "*But... where is he buried?*" "*Right underneath you, Father,*" they told him. Blessed Alvaro smiled and said, "*Just like in every moment of his life, a foundation!*" We too are called by God to be humble 'foundations'. In fact, St Josemaría used to teach that, in order to serve others, we should put our hearts on the floor as soft carpets for others to walk on.

Not everyone has to struggle in every single virtue, but every single person (with the exception of Jesus and Mary) needs to struggle with pride. If you have time for a little bit of 'homework', you can take to your prayer Point 263 of St Josemaría's book *Furrow*; it will give you ideas for your examination of conscience.

Holy Mary, Handmaid of the Lord, help me to become a soft carpet for others, a humble instrument in the Hands of God.

Wednesday 13th August
Mt 18:15-20

If your brother sins against you, go and tell him his fault, between you and him alone. If he listens to you, you have gained your brother. But if he does not listen, take one or two others along with you, that every word may be confirmed by the evidence of two or three witnesses. If he refuses to listen to them, tell it to the church; and if he refuses to listen even to the church, let him be to you as a Gentile and a tax collector.

God, as a loving Father, corrects His children because He loves them and wants them to improve. And to make sure that His children get the corrections, He asked brothers to correct each other. This practice is called fraternal correction and has been a tradition in the Church since the very beginning. Everyone needs corrections because we are not saints but we want to be. And everyone means *everyone*.

Among the recommendations given by St Paul to the Christians at Corinth is to "*exhort one another*"; and he gave a good example of it. The Apostles had had the first Ecumenical Council and decided that the converts to Christianity who did not belong to the Jewish tradition didn't have to follow Jewish customs, like eating meat with traces of blood in it. St Peter and St Paul were having lunch in Antioch-on-the-Orontes. We don't know the menu, but they may have served, among other things, roasted rabbit, pork steak and eel from Orontes (the river crossing Antioch). St Peter was surrounded by Christians; some of them were Jews who had come with him, along with gentiles who lived there in Antioch. Then St Peter was unsure whether or not he should follow the Jewish tradition and have only the salad and the fruit, not to disappoint them. St Barnabas saw it... and did the same. The Christians from Antioch were a bit offended by this behaviour. But St Paul put his foot down and didn't hesitate to correct St Peter himself.

St Peter could have protested: '*I'm the prince of the Apostles!*' or '*Look who's talking, you stoned St Stephen!*' But he was humble instead and accepted the correction. He wasn't perfect, but he wanted to be. Mary, my Mother, you can teach me to be humble and accept all the corrections that will help me become better.

Thursday 14th August
Mt 18:21-19:1

Peter said to him, "Lord, how often shall my brother sin against me, and I forgive him? As many as seven times?" Jesus said to him, "I do not say to you seven times, but seventy times seven. Therefore the kingdom of heaven may be compared to a king who wished to settle accounts with his servants. When he began the reckoning, one was brought to him who owed him ten thousand talents; and as he could not pay...the servant fell on his knees, imploring him, 'Lord, have patience with me, and I will pay you everything.' And out of pity for him the lord of that servant released him and forgave him the debt.

You remember the rest of the story, don't you? That man who had been forgiven found a fellow friend who owed him 100 denarii and didn't want to forgive him. You see? Despite having been forgiven 10,000 talents (60,000,000 denarii), he couldn't forgive 100 denarii! Eventually his master claimed the 10,000 talents back because he didn't forgive his fellow friend. We say that in the *Our Father* every day, "forgive us our trespasses as we forgive", meaning *'forgive us only if we forgive; do with us as we do with others.'* Because what God has to forgive us is, like in the parable, at least a hundred times more than what we will have to forgive other people.

St. Pius X was a good example of mercy and forgiveness. When he was bishop of Mantua, a merchant of this city wrote a pamphlet full of calumnies against him. To those who advised him to prosecute the fellow, the future Pope replied, "*That unhappy man needs more prayer than punishment*." But forgiveness went beyond words. After a while, the merchant went bankrupt. Creditors prosecuted him without mercy. When he had lost everything, an anonymous hand came to his aid: the bishop of Mantua himself. He summoned an elderly woman dedicated to works of charity and, through her, he sent an envelope with the money that the man needed to avoid prison. He wanted to remain unknown, giving only this message, "*Tell him that this money comes from the most merciful Lady, that is, the Virgin of Perpetual Help.*"

Mary, Most Merciful Lady, help me to forgive everything always and to forget the actions of those who have offended me in any way; empty my heart of grudges and fill it up with love.

The Assumption of Our Lady
Friday 15th August
Lk 1:39-56

And Mary said, "My soul magnifies the Lord, and my spirit rejoices in God my Saviour, for he has regarded the low estate of his handmaiden. For behold, henceforth all generations will call me blessed; for he who is mighty has done great things for me, and holy is his name. And his mercy is on those who fear him from generation to generation. He has shown strength with his arm, he has scattered the proud in the imagination of their hearts."

Indeed God has done "*great things*" for you, Most Beautiful Mother! He has given you what He never gave anyone else. You are the Humble Woman who can humiliate the mighty Lucifer. The devil was created so powerful but now, poor thing, he trembles at the mere sound of your Name. You are the Humble Handmaid of the Lord now, together with your Son and like Him, with your body and soul in Heaven.

A lady was dying in the East End of London. Over her bed there hung a beautiful picture of Our Lady. The young doctor attending to her wasn't Christian. With no intended malice, just out of simple ignorance, he asked, "*Well, madam, who is the film star over the bed?*" "*Film star?*" she said. "*That's the Virgin Mother.*" "*Virgin and Mother?*" repeated the doctor, perplexed. "*Why, there never was such a Mother!*" "*Ah, doctor,*" she replied, "*there never was such a Son!*" That's why God did "*great things for her.*" She had to be the Mother of God and that's 'quite something'. And if she is good enough for Jesus... she is good enough for us.

We look at you today, my Mother, enthroned beside your Son, surrounded by all the angels and saints who are dazzled by your beauty. There you are in Heaven, body and soul, to help your children. I imagine you looking at me: what child of yours would not go to you for help? What would you not do for your children? There was a dramatic representation of the Passion of Jesus in a little town. The character of Judas, after his betrayal, was reciting his role: "*Where can I go? Everything is lost now!*" A little girl exclaimed in a loud voice from the back, "*Fool! Fool! Go to Mary!*" Of course! Where else could we go, my Mother, if we ever lost sight of your Son? May I never be a fool; may I always go to you!

Saturday 19th week in ordinary time
Saturday 16th August
Mt 19:13-15

Children were brought to him that he might lay his hands on them and pray. The disciples rebuked the people; but Jesus said, "Let the children come to me, and do not hinder them; for to such belongs the kingdom of heaven." And he laid his hands on them and went away.

Children sometimes look forward to growing up and becoming independent. But Jesus wants us to become children and remain *dependent* on the Father. He doesn't want us to lose our '*innocence*' because innocent children don't hesitate to ask their parents for whatever they need. They rely on their mum and dad for everything, big or small. They never forget that they are children, or who their father is. They know they can do nothing important but 'mum and dad' can do everything. They're never afraid because they know that their parents are there for them.

St Thérèse of Lisieux explained her 'Little Way' to get close to God with these words: "*We no longer have to take the trouble of climbing stairs because an elevator has replaced these. I wanted to find an elevator which would raise me to Jesus, for I am too small to climb the rough stairway of perfection. I searched, then, in the Scriptures and I read these words: "Let the children come to me." I felt I had found what I was looking for... The elevator which must raise me to heaven is Your arms, O Jesus! And for this I had no need to grow up, but rather I had to remain little and become this more and more.*" And St Josemaría teaches, "*My friend, if you want to be great, become little. To be little it is necessary to believe as children believe, to love as children love, to give yourself up as children give themselves up... to pray as children pray.*"

Quino, an Argentinian caricaturist, has a funny sketch in which a little boy, called Guille, is in his father's arms. It is cloudy but the child wants to see the sun, so he asks Daddy to bring it to him. The father smiles and replies, "*But that's impossible! How can I bring you the sun?*" "*You can't?*" little Guille asks his dad. Then, disappointed, he pushes his father's face away and says, "*Kindly put me down, sir.*" (As if saying 'I don't know you anymore'). God never disappoints. He can bring the sun - and does so every day - to His children. Mary, my Mother, help me to become a trustful child.

Twentieth Sunday in Ordinary Time
Sunday 17th August
Lk 12:49-53

Jesus said, "Do you think that I have come to give peace on earth? No, I tell you, but rather division; for henceforth in one house there will be five divided, three against two and two against three; they will be divided, father against son and son against father, mother against daughter and daughter against her mother."

This is a rather shocking statement. Didn't Jesus say "*Blessed are the peacemakers, for they shall be called sons of God*" (Mt 5:9)? Didn't the Angels say upon His birth, "*Glory to God in the highest, and on earth **peace** among men...*" (Lk 2:14)? Yes. That's right. But there are two kinds of peace. When Jesus said, "*Peace I leave with you; my peace I give to you; not as the world gives do I give to you*" (Jn 14:27), He makes the point that the peace that He offers is not the same quietness that the world can offer.

Old Simeon said about Baby Jesus that He would be a sign of 'contradiction' (*Lk* 2:34). Like all the prophets before Him, Jesus challenges people to denounce injustice and wrongdoing, calling them to repentance and conversion. Jesus leaves no one indifferent. Those challenges disturb peace; however, division is created not by Jesus but by the reaction of His listeners. As Jesus declared, "*He who is not with me is against me*" (Lk 11:23).

"*Faith is not a decorative or ornamental element,*" explains Pope Francis. "*Faith means choosing God as the criterion and basis of life, and God is not empty, God is not neutral, God is always positive, God is love... [His] peace is not neutrality, compromise at all costs. Following Jesus entails giving up evil and selfishness and choosing good, truth and justice. And this indeed divides. However, it is not Jesus who creates division! He establishes the criterion: whether to live for ourselves or to live for God and for others; to be served or to serve; to obey one's own ego or to obey God. Even among Jesus' relatives there were some who did not share His way of life (Mk 3:20-21). His Mother, however, always followed him faithfully, keeping the eyes of her heart fixed on Jesus. And in the end, thanks to Mary's faith, Jesus' relatives became part of the first Christian community (Acts 1:14). Let us ask Mary to help us too to keep our gaze firmly fixed on Jesus and to follow Him always, even when it costs what it may.*"

Monday 20th week in ordinary time
Monday 18th August
Mt 19:16-22

And behold, one came up to him, saying, "Teacher, what good deed must I do, to have eternal life?"...If you would enter life, keep the commandments..." The young man said to him, "All these I have observed; what do I still lack?" Jesus said to him, "If you would be perfect, go, sell what you possess and give to the poor, and you will have treasure in heaven; and come, follow me." When the young man heard this he went away sorrowful; for he had great possessions.

"*He went away sorrowful*" writes St Matthew, who saw the scene with his own eyes. That boy had everything that was needed. When Jesus asked Him to keep the commandments, he wasn't satisfied. He was more ambitious than that. '*I do that already,*' he said, '*what else can I do?*' He was good but wanted to be perfect! He wanted to move forward in generosity with God. He wanted to do more. We are all born with great desires. We are born for greatness. Jesus loved the fellow's answer and saw a man who could do so much!

'Well,' Jesus explained, '*if you want to be perfect... you can still do one more thing.*' Imagine the expectation of the boy after that sentence - he came to find out exactly that: 'what *else* can I do?' and it seems that he was ready to do whatever it took to be more generous with God. If you knew that the only obstacle between you and happiness were easy to remove, wouldn't you like to know exactly how to remove it? So the young lad was told, '*Your possessions are the only obstacle. Get rid of them and it's done!*' But he didn't expect that. He had probably imagined many things Jesus could ask for, but he didn't expect *that* one. He had a sort of '*clause*', as if saying to Jesus, 'You can ask me anything... except *this*'. Some people, like this fellow, are ready to give God 'some things' but not 'everything'.

It's not good to bargain with God, to want to save something for ourselves. To '*buy*' God you need to pay *your very last penny*. A little sick child got a tiny young rabbit; the child was delighted with it, and when he was praying with his mother he said, "*Jesus, I offer You my eyes, my ears, my tongue, my heart, in a word, my whole being*"; he had a moment of remorse and added, "*well, except my little rabbit.*" Mary, my Mother, help me to give God everything, including any '*little rabbit*' I might have saved for myself.

Tuesday 19th August
Mt 19:23-30

Jesus said to his disciples, "Truly, I say to you, it will be hard for a rich man to enter the kingdom of heaven. Again I tell you, it is easier for a camel to go through the eye of a needle than for a rich man to enter the kingdom of God." When the disciples heard this they were greatly astonished, saying, "Who then can be saved?" But Jesus looked at them and said to them, "With men this is impossible, but with God all things are possible."

Some people's only ambition is to possess more things. That's all they live for and all they spend their lives doing. This temptation has always existed and it has always destroyed people. Greed is the disordered love of riches, and often takes the form of consumerism. Advertising companies spend billions feeding our appetites for things to buy, even if we don't need them. It's as if *'he who dies with the most toys wins.'*

Our life is made rich not by the amount of things we have, but by what we have in our heart. Hearts were created to love persons, not things. If you put things into it, it gets corrupted. The bait that the enemy uses to catch men is, many times, greed. African hunters have a clever way of trapping monkeys. The trap has a hole just big enough for a monkey's hand to pass through. Inside they leave an orange. The monkey slips its hand through the small hole, grasps the orange, and tries to pull it through the hole. Of course, the orange won't come out; it's too big for the hole. But the monkey never thinks about dropping the orange. As long as it keeps its fist wrapped around the orange, the monkey is trapped.

The same happens to those rich people who have their hearts attached to things: toys, smartphones, gadgets, clothes... That heart, wrapped up in many things, will never pass through the narrow gate of Heaven. They may remind us of Gollum, that unhappy creature in 'The Lord of the Rings' who lives obsessed with his *"precious."* Do you remember? As a miserable slave of the ring, he ends up dragged down into the fire by that 'treasure'.

Holy Mary, my Mother, help me to live always detached from things; to have my heart attached only to God, my Lord.

Wednesday 20th week in ordinary time
Wednesday 20th August
Mt 20:1-16

For the kingdom of heaven is like a householder who went out early in the morning to hire labourers for his vineyard. After agreeing with the labourers for a denarius a day, he sent them into his vineyard...And about the eleventh hour he went out and found others standing...He said to them, 'You go into the vineyard too.' And when evening came...those hired about the eleventh hour came, each of them received a denarius. Now when the first came, they thought they would receive more; but each of them also received a denarius.

They were idle because they didn't have any work. That morning those people thought, 'If by the end of the day I can get one denarius, I will be happy.' They found an employer who offered them work and promised to pay them a denarius. And that's what they got. But they weren't happy. They would have been happy if they hadn't seen the others getting the same money. They lost their happiness because they started comparing and judging the others...

The world is full of these sorts of ungrateful people whose happiness depends not on what they get, but on getting *more than* others. They are like children unwrapping Christmas presents who, instead of being happy with what they have got, they look at what the others have got and check if they've got more or less than them. *Comparisons steal joy.* When you compare, you transform everything into a competition. And you always risk being the loser.

Today Jesus refers to those who will go to Heaven even if they convert after a long sinful life; the same Heaven as those who have been good Christians their entire lives. The fellows in the parable thought they *deserved* their denarius: Eternal Life. But eternal happiness is an undeserved '*gift*'. Imagine that you organise your birthday party and one of your friends says to you, *'Don't invite many... so each one of us will have more cake!'* Would you have a party with three friends just for that mean reason? No. You would probably just leave that selfish guy out of it. Heaven is a great party and God is like the 'cake'. We can never run out of God in Heaven. There is plenty for everyone! Our joy, on the contrary, would be to share that 'cake' with many people we love. Holy Mary, Queen of the Apostles, help me to bring many souls to the Party.

Thursday 21st August
Mt 22:1-14

The kingdom of heaven may be compared to a king who gave a marriage feast for his son, and sent his servants to call those who were invited to the marriage feast; but they would not come. Again he sent other servants, saying, 'Tell those who are invited, Behold, I have made ready my dinner, my oxen and my fat calves are killed, and everything is ready; come to the marriage feast.' But they made light of it and went off, one to his farm, another to his business.

How sad! They didn't want to come to the wedding feast! It wasn't a conference, a lecture or a retreat, but a wedding feast. They were supposed to enjoy themselves there. Consider this: a) it's the king's feast, and is always an honour to be invited; b) they don't have to pay for a ticket to get in, the king covers the cost; c) he is a wealthy host - that feast was going to be amazing; d) even if they didn't come, the party was fantastic anyway - the king didn't need them. It promised to be a great celebration: food, drink, many guests, music, spectacular entertainment... They didn't bother to figure out what they would find there. They just thought about themselves and never knew what they had missed.

But the one reason why they didn't go was that '*they didn't love the king.*' That's how some people behave with God. He has prepared a banquet for us and covered the cost. He wants us to join the party and be merry. But many can't be bothered to come because getting there is a bit troublesome. If only they knew what they were missing!

Holy Mass is the real King's banquet. Going to Mass can be demanding but there is just one reason to miss It: lack of love for the King. Imagine that you spend weeks preparing for your birthday party and when you invite your friends they turn down the invitation because they don't like chocolate cake or because 'so and so' is not coming, or because they may have to take the bus to get there... They obviously don't love you. They don't care about your friendship. The same with the Holy Mass: the reason for coming to Mass is not because of the priest, the music or because my friends are coming; rather we go to Mass just because we love the 'Host of the Banquet'. Holy Mary, Mother of the Eucharist, pray for us!

The Queenship of the Blessed Virgin Mary
Friday 22nd August
Lk 1:26-38

The angel Gabriel said, "Hail, full of grace, the Lord is with you!" But she was greatly troubled at the saying, and considered in her mind what sort of greeting this might be. And the angel said to her, "Do not be afraid, Mary, for you have found favour with God. And behold, you will conceive in your womb and bear a son, and you shall call his name Jesus. He will be great, and will be called the Son of the Most High; and the Lord God will give to him the throne of his father David, and he will reign over the house of Jacob for ever; and of his kingdom there will be no end."

Hail, Holy Queen! Mother of Mercy, hail, our life, our sweetness and our hope! Hail, Mother of the King of Kings, Queen of Angels, Queen of Patriarchs, Queen of Prophets, Queen of Apostles, Queen of the Universe, Queen Mother... my Mother! What will you not do for your children?

In the old days the mother of the king was called the Queen Mother. She would sit on the king's right, trusted as a confidante and advisor. The mother of King Solomon, for instance, assumed that role and when people wanted something from the king, they would ask her to intercede before Solomon (1 *Kgs* 2:19). The Queen Mother has a real power of intercession for her children. She cares about us and spends her time in Heaven telling God good things about us.

A ten-year-old boy who was a paralytic went to Lourdes to pray for a miracle. During Benediction with the Blessed Sacrament he was in his wheelchair close to the aisle where the procession was passing by. Staring at Jesus in the monstrance and pointing upwards with his index finger, the boy said in a loud voice, "*If you don't heal me I'll tell Your Mother!*" At the end of the ceremony when the monstrance passed by the boy, again, the priest was surprised to hear the same prayer: "*Sure I will... I'll tell Your Mother!*" But he was all the more surprised when suddenly, to the amazement of the whole congregation, the boy stood up - completely healed. What good mother is there who wouldn't listen to her child in need?

My Mother, Queen of all Saints, Queen of the Family, Queen of Peace! I love you, because you always listen to your children and the King of Kings always listens to you.

Saturday 23rd August
Mt 23:1-12

Jesus said: "The scribes and the Pharisees sit on Moses' seat; so practice and observe whatever they tell you, but not what they do; for they preach, but do not practice. They bind heavy burdens, hard to bear, and lay them on men's shoulders; but they themselves will not move them with their finger. They do all their deeds to be seen by men."

The difference between Jesus and the other rabbis was that Jesus walked the talk. The scribes and Pharisees knew the theory very well. They knew and taught what had to be done... by others. Therefore people didn't follow them. You see? In the army, the usual voice of command is 'Forward!', 'Charge!' or 'Attack!' when troops are sent to engage in combat. In the current army of Israel the officer says instead: "*Follow me!*", because he goes in front of his men.

How powerful is the example of the Saints, more powerful than their words. British journalist Malcolm Muggeridge was an agnostic for most of his life and a Communist sympathiser during his early years. In November 1982, he explained in 'The Times' the reasons for his conversion to the Catholic Faith. He was captivated by the faithfulness of the Church to her moral teachings. He was impressed by the fact that, many times, the Church was fighting alone in her defence of moral values. But the real push to his conversion was given by a small nun, St Teresa of Calcutta, who was 'living the Gospel in real life'. "*Words cannot express how much I owe her,*" he said in an interview. "*She showed me Christianity in action. She showed me the power of love. She showed me how one loving person can start a tidal wave of love that can spread to the entire world.*"

We will never fully realise until we arrive in Heaven all the good that God can do with our good example as Christians in the middle of the world. We could have a whole encyclopaedia full of stories about conversions to our Faith that started with the example of a good Christian. With our clean lives, our work well done, our love and concern for others, our eagerness to serve, to promote peace (in a word, to live the Gospel) we can bring people close to God. Holy Mary, Virgin Most Prudent, help me to embody the Gospel in my daily life, to become a living Gospel for my relatives and friends.

Twenty-first Sunday in Ordinary Time
Sunday 24th August
Lk 13:22-30

Someone said to Jesus, "Lord, will those who are saved be few?" And he said to them, "Strive to enter by the narrow door; for many, I tell you, will seek to enter and will not be able...There you will weep and gnash your teeth, when you see Abraham and Isaac and Jacob and all the prophets in the kingdom of God and you yourselves thrust out...behold, some are last who will be first, and some are first who will be last."

When they asked Jesus if those being saved were many or few, Jesus didn't give a number, but a warning. It is not going to be easy. The door is narrow. Many will try to get through but will not be able. Jesus said it not to frighten His disciples, but to encourage them; just as a teacher who announces that there will be an exam is not threatening the pupils but encouraging them to study. Those who feel threatened are the ones who haven't studied.

Jesus' warning is about those who are very confident that they will get through that narrow gate. As if we could buy the ticket to Heaven with 'our own money'. With our holy lives we can ask God for the ticket but not pay for it. The ticket has been paid for by Jesus on the Cross. Heaven is a gift. You see? It is God who helps us to get through the narrow gate, but He needs our co-operation. What we can do is always small, but God needs that in order to help us to enter Heaven.

We have an obligation to remind people that God is committed to seeing us in Heaven. He just needs our commitment to let Him do it. No one is allowed to despair. God "*desires all men to be saved and to come to the knowledge of the truth*" (1 Ti 2:4). He wants to save everyone with all His might, with all His Blood, with all His Heart, but they have to want to be saved. Our mistakes don't matter. Only His Mercy matters. A catechist was explaining the story of Judas and how he hanged himself. Then he asked one of the children, "*If you had betrayed Jesus, would you hang yourself?*" "*Of course!*" replied the child to the astonishment of the catechist. "*I would hang myself*", continued the child, "*from the neck of Jesus to beg forgiveness!*" Mary, Mother of Mercy, help me to bring many to the gates of Heaven; Jesus will push them in.

Monday 21st week in ordinary time
Monday 25th August
Mt 23:13-22

"But woe to you, scribes and Pharisees, hypocrites! Because you shut the kingdom of heaven against men; for you neither enter yourselves, nor allow those who would enter to go in. Woe to you, scribes and Pharisees, hypocrites! For you traverse sea and land to make a single proselyte, and when he becomes a proselyte, you make him twice as much a child of hell as yourselves."

Our Lord showed infinite compassion towards all kinds of sinners. He could forgive every sin. But here was a group of sinners with whom He was very harsh. Dealing with hypocrites, Jesus pulled no punches. Isn't God Merciful with every sinner? Why was He so severe with hypocrites? For one single reason: they didn't consider themselves sinners. God can forgive every sinner as long as they recognise their sins. Like an alcoholic, they can only solve the problem when they realise they *have* a problem.

When little St Josemaría felt embarrassed trying new clothes, his mother used to tell him, "*Josemaría, you should only be ashamed of sinning.*" There is no shame in confessing our sins. There is a story of a priest who found a devil messing around among the people waiting in the queue of his confessional. The priest asked him, "*What are you doing here, you wretch?*" "*I took from them their shame of sinning,*" the evil spirit replied, "*now I'm giving it back to them, so that they feel ashamed of confessing.*"

A teacher had had a terrible year with a particular class. He'd kept a record of all the misdemeanours - more than 200! Towards the end of the year he was reading the list of offences and thinking about a proportionate punishment for the pupils. Suddenly a thought struck him. Next to every incident of misbehaviour was a name. There was not a single record without the name of the offender next to it. Then he realised that every time he asked, "*Who did this?*" someone always admitted the offence. Every single time! Not even once did the responsible pupil remain silent or blame someone else. 'They were rascals,' the teacher thought, but '*honest rascals.*' How could he punish them? In the same way, God always forgives those who admit their guilt with sorrow. Holy Mary, Refuge of Sinners, help me to be always sorry for my sins and never delay my confession.

Tuesday 21st week in ordinary time
Tuesday 26th August
Mt 23:23-26

"Woe to you, scribes and Pharisees, hypocrites! For you tithe mint and dill and cumin, and have neglected the weightier matters of the law, justice and mercy and faith; these you ought to have done, without neglecting the others. You blind guides, straining out a gnat and swallowing a camel! Woe to you, scribes and Pharisees, hypocrites! For you cleanse the outside of the cup and of the plate, but inside they are full of extortion and rapacity. You blind Pharisee! First cleanse the inside of the cup and of the plate, that the outside also may be clean."

Jesus reproaches the guile and hypocrisy of the Pharisees. They were only worried about what people saw or thought about them. They were masters of 'deception', of disguise, of making everyone think well of them. They made life difficult for everyone with their impositions, but didn't care about the law of God. They thought they could fool people but they couldn't fool God.

Saints have never been worried about what people thought about them. Their only concern was about what God thought about them. And so they never lost their peace when others said or did all kinds of things against them - as Jesus himself said would happen. On the contrary, saints were always at ease, for they knew that doing the Will of God often clashes with doing the will of people.

In August 1642 two soldiers escorted an eighty-six-year-old priest along Bianchi Street to the prisons of the Inquisition. His name was Joseph of Calasanz, founder of the Religious Order of the Piarists. He had been arrested suddenly on a false accusation - with no time even to take his hat with him. He walked, stooped and shaky, but very calm. So calm that during the interrogation he fell asleep! Eventually he was removed from the Institution he had founded and died soon afterwards. Fortunately, a few years later everything was put right: the slander was revealed, the Piarists became a religious order and he became *Saint Joseph of Calasanz*.

Mary, my Mother, help me to live detached from the opinion of others; and only be concerned about what my Father God thinks of me.

Wednesday 27th August
Mt 23:27-32

Woe to you, scribes and Pharisees, hypocrites! for you are like whitewashed tombs, which outwardly appear beautiful, but within they are full of dead men's bones and all uncleanness. So you also outwardly appear righteous to men, but within you are full of hypocrisy and iniquity.

When You, Lord, denounced the hypocrisy of the Pharisees, You mentioned the things that they were doing: they fasted (twice a week, actually), they gave a tenth of all their possessions (not bad)... The problem was not the things they did – as each of them was very good. The problem, says the Gospel, was 'within', because they would do that to "*outwardly appear righteous to men.*"

Their intention is what made them hypocrites. They didn't give alms for the sake of the poor but to be seen and admired. Everything they did was to make people think they were holy men. But what we read about You, Lord, is quite different. We find often in the Gospel that You asked people not to say anything about Your miracles. When You prayed, You'd go to a lonely place. You didn't show off Your virtues because You didn't do things in order to be known, recognised, praised or admired. Virtue is usually very silent.

A man and his son were walking on a cobblestone pavement when they heard a horse and cart coming. Over the noise of the horse's hooves they heard the clattering of the cart. The father said: '*That cart is empty*'. When the cart came into view the boy saw that his dad was right. '*How did you know it was empty?*' asked the boy. '*When a cart is very noisy it's always empty*', replied the wise father, '*when it's heavily loaded there is not much clattering*'. The same happens with the lives of the Pharisees: much clattering, but empty lives. But those saints who are 'heavily loaded' with virtue are discreet and silent.

The life of Our Lady and that of St Joseph, were lives full of virtue and for that reason, really silent. Mary, my Mother, St Joseph, my father and lord, help me to avoid the clattering of those who only want to attract attention and to be praised; help me to rectify my intention and to do everything only for the Glory of God.

Thursday 21st week in ordinary time
Thursday 28th August
Mt 24:42-51

Who then is the faithful and wise servant, whom his master has set over his household, to give them their food at the proper time? Blessed is that servant whom his master when he comes will find so doing. Truly, I say to you, he will set him over all his possessions.

A faithful steward is a reliable one. He can be trusted to do what he has to do. He acts at any time as he would if his master were watching him. Saints have always lived with that sense of presence of God. They acted always as if God were watching because, precisely: God is always there.

A skinny boy loved football. In every training session, he eagerly gave everything he had, but he was very small. At all the games he sat on the bench and hardly ever played. His father was always in the stands cheering, nevertheless. The boy never missed training or any games but remained a bench-warmer for more than four years. One day he went to see the coach to tell him that his father had died. "*Is it all right if I miss practice today?*" he asked. The coach, moved, granted his permission and asked him to take the week off. "*And don't even plan to come back for the play-off on Saturday.*" But that Saturday, during the game, suddenly the boy appeared at half-time in his football gear. "*Coach, please let me play. I've just got to play today,*" he said. But they were losing and the coach didn't want his worst player on the pitch in this close play-off game. Finally, feeling sorry for the kid, the coach let him go on. Before long, the coach, the players and everyone in the stands could not believe their eyes. The boy was playing amazingly well. He had given a push to the whole team and they were now leading the match. He even scored and they won the game in the end. "*Kid, I can't believe it. How did you do that?*" the coach asked as soon as he met up with him. "*Well, you knew my dad died,*" answered the boy, "*but did you know that he was blind? He came to all my games, but today was the first time he could see me play, and I didn't want to let him down!*"

Mary, my Mother, may I never forget that my Father God is always looking at me; help me to make Him feel proud, to never let Him down.

The Passion of St John the Baptist
Friday 29th August
Mk 6:17-29

Herod had sent and seized John, and bound him in prison for the sake of Herodias, his brother Philip's wife; because he had married her. For John said to Herod, "It is not lawful for you to have your brother's wife." And Herodias had a grudge against him, and wanted to kill him. But she could not, for Herod feared John, knowing that he was a righteous and holy man, and kept him safe. When he heard him, he was much perplexed; and yet he heard him gladly.

It's surprising that Herod was glad to hear St John reprimanding him, isn't it? He was putting the truth across. But that can be done in many ways. The truth doesn't have to be harsh, cruel or rude. We tend to imagine St John shouting at Herod for his immoral life but that couldn't be the case if the king "*heard him gladly*" as we read in the Gospel. It's interesting also to see that St John did take the trouble to admonish Herod. For most of the Jews Herod was a '*hopeless case*'. Why bother to yell at such a wicked king? Because *everyone* can change. Great sinners have become great saints.

In the film 'Batman Begins' (2005), Bruce Wayne had done many wrong things in the past. His loyal butler, Alfred, wants to encourage him with a lesson his father gave to him: "*Why do we fall, sir?*" asks Alfred. And he himself gives the answer: "*So that we can learn to pick ourselves up.*" Bruce smiles at his faithful butler and asks, "*You still haven't given up on me?*" And Alfred's reply also comes with a smile: "*Never!*" Just like the faithful Alfred, God never gives up on anyone.

Doctor Bernard Nathanson was responsible for over 75,000 abortions; a '*hopeless case*'. But God touched his heart one day when he saw a group of pro-life people praying for him and for the unborn children. He thought about what he was doing and changed radically. He became the most well-known pro-life supporter and converted to Catholicism. He died at the age of 84, having spent the rest of his life defending the unborn, speaking the truth boldly - like the Baptist - and changing and saving many lives. Many would have given up on him... but not God. God had a great plan for him. Holy Mary, Refuge of sinners, help me to speak the truth with courage and with love, without giving up.

Saturday 21st week in ordinary time
Saturday 30th August
Mt 25:14-30

"A man going on a journey called his servants and entrusted to them his property; to one he gave five talents, to another two, to another one, to each according to his ability...But he who had received the one talent came forward, saying, 'Master, I knew you to be a hard man, reaping where you did not sow, and gathering where you did not winnow; so I was afraid, and I went and hid your talent in the ground. Here you have what is yours.'"

The man who received one talent "*was afraid,*" and thus, he did nothing. He was afraid to risk and lose. Fear paralyses people. What really offended the master of the parable wasn't that he didn't get more talents, but that he didn't even try! God is a Father. No father or mother on earth could ever be disappointed if they saw their children trying their best. All that God asks His children is to try hard. God will help us provided that we try our best.

Wishing to encourage her young son's progress on the piano, a mother took her boy to a Paderewski concert. After they were seated, the mother spotted an old friend in the audience and walked down the aisle to greet her. Seizing the opportunity, the little boy decided to explore the concert hall. He went through a door marked 'No Admittance', found a piano and started practising there. When the mother returned to her seat, the child was missing. As the curtains parted and the spotlights focused on the stage, she saw in horror her child sitting at the keyboard, innocently picking out '*Twinkle, Twinkle Little Star.*' Suddenly, the great piano master made his entrance, quickly moved to the piano, and whispered in the boy's ear, "*Don't stop. That's it. Keep it up. Give me your best.*" Then leaning over, Paderewski reached down with his left hand and began a melodic bass part. Soon his right arm reached around to the other side of the child, adding a running '*obbligato*'. Together, the old master and the child transformed what could have been an embarrassing situation into a wonderful symphony. That's what Our Father God does with our efforts. We just need to keep playing the best we can, without giving up, and He transforms our efforts into a masterpiece. There is no fear. We can't disappoint Our Father if we try our best. Our Lady will encourage us to try to give our best, however little it seems to be.

Twenty-Second Sunday in Ordinary Time
Sunday 31st August
Lk 14:1, 7-14

"When you give a dinner or a banquet, do not invite your friends or your brothers or your kinsmen or rich neighbours, lest they also invite you in return, and you be repaid. But when you give a feast, invite the poor, the maimed, the lame, the blind, and you will be blessed, because they cannot repay you. You will be repaid at the resurrection of the just."

Generosity is about giving without expecting anything in exchange... Giving until it hurts. When we give in that way, we are not just helping others; we are helping - first of all - ourselves. We are the first beneficiary of our virtue of generosity.

There was a woman who as a child was crippled by polio. She became angry with God and was mean to everyone around her. By chance one day she came into contact with members of a parish who showed her a lot of love. She returned to that parish every Sunday and her frozen heart started warming up. The parish started a campaign to raise funds for refurbishment. The woman surprised everyone by announcing that she was giving $45,000 to the parish. Her family was stunned. When they asked her where she was going to get all that money, she told them that since her childhood she had been saving bit by bit in order to buy a handicapped van with a lift. Her parish was now more important to her than her dream van. She said, *"I am so thankful that God healed me of my crippled heart! I can walk now... in the way of His Son. I need my parish more than I need that van."*

When a group of people heard of her sacrifice and experienced her radiant joy in her new-found freedom, together they bought her a lift-van anyway. They remained anonymous... and when she was presented with her new van there was a note on it from these parishioners that simply said, *"Thank you for showing us how to walk with Jesus."*

Our generosity can change many things, but first of all it changes ourselves. The giver's heart changes with every gift. If someone decides to give up clothes, for instance, the more clothes they give, the emptier the wardrobe. In the spiritual life is exactly the opposite: the more we give up, the more our heart is filled up. Then, once our hearts are changed, we can change the environment. Mother, Virgin Most Generous, you can teach me to take after you, to be generous, until it hurts.

September

Monday 22nd week in ordinary time
Monday 1st September
Lk 4:16-30

And he came to Nazareth, where he had been brought up; and he went to the synagogue, as his custom was, on the sabbath day. And he stood up to read; and there was given to him the book of the prophet Isaiah...And he began to say to them, "Today this scripture has been fulfilled in your hearing"...When they heard this, all in the synagogue were filled with wrath. And they rose up and put him out of the city, and led him to the brow of the hill on which their city was built, that they might throw him down headlong. But passing through the midst of them he went away.

Jesus came to preach the Good News but they didn't like what they heard or they didn't like Him. The fact is that something had got into them. When we don't like what we hear, for example our neighbour's music, we can shut the windows or go for a walk but we don't try to throw the neighbour off a cliff (even if we are tempted to think about it...)

Sometimes people react in that way. You want to offer them help or share your faith and they go '*up the wall.*' When Jesus was a baby Simeon said that He would be a "*sign of contradiction*" and that the "*hearts of many would be revealed*" (Lk 2:35). And some hearts turn violently against the truth of the Gospel.

Just like in the life of Jesus, many saints have had to fight against a similar violent persecution. But Jesus didn't answer back or panic. The Gospel says that "*passing through the midst of them He went away.*" And saints and all Christianity will always do the same thing, '*pass through*' the midst of those who do not want to hear us, without answering back, without panicking, and '*go away*' to try in another place.

"*The truth that sets us free cannot be kept to ourselves; it calls for testimony, it begs to be heard. In our own time, the price to be paid for fidelity to the Gospel is no longer being hanged, drawn and quartered but it often involves being dismissed out of hand, ridiculed or parodied. And yet, the Church cannot withdraw from the task of proclaiming Christ and his Gospel*" (Pope Benedict XVI). Mary, Queen of the Apostles, with your help, may I never waver when having to witness to the Truth.

Tuesday 22nd week in ordinary time
Tuesday 2nd September
Lk 4:31-37

A man who had the spirit of an unclean demon cried out with a loud voice, "Ah! What have you to do with us, Jesus of Nazareth? Have you come to destroy us? I know who you are, the Holy One of God." But Jesus rebuked him, saying, "Be silent, and come out of him!" And when the demon had thrown him down in the midst, he came out of him, having done him no harm. And they were all amazed and said to one another, "What is this word? For with authority and power he commands the unclean spirits, and they come out."

Your Word, Jesus, has authority and power. It can rebuke every evil. That unclean spirit had maybe bound that poor man for many years and everyone had failed to cast it out. Perhaps that devil was at ease there until he met You face to face. And that was the end of it! The power of Your Word! At times the enemy tries to convince me that I will always be lazy or proud or selfish... But I know that's not true. You, Lord, can heal my miseries in one go.

Son of one of the wealthiest noble families in England, Philip Howard (1557-1595) could afford any pleasure he liked - and he liked them all. At court he was a notorious playboy, gambler and fop. In 1581, he went to the Tower of London to hear a debate between several Anglican ministers and a prisoner, the Jesuit priest St. Edmund Campion. Although the ministers were armed with books and assistants, Father Campion was alone and had only his memory to rely on, yet he did so well in the debate that the government cancelled it before a verdict was rendered. Inspired by Father Campion, Howard was reconciled with his wife and they both returned to the Catholic faith. When they tried to leave the country secretly for the Continent, where they could practice Catholicism freely, they were stopped and Howard was imprisoned in the Tower of London. He died there 10 years later. The power of the Word of God changed him in one go.

God's Word can cast out my bad tendencies, my laziness and love of comfort, and help me to start anew; I should never forget that You can do everything. Mary, my Mother, help me to prepare for the new academic year so that over the next few months I become, with the Grace of your Son, the person He wants me to be.

Wednesday 22nd week in ordinary time
Wednesday 3rd September
Lk 4:38-44

When the sun was setting, all those who had any that were sick with various diseases brought them to him; and he laid his hands on every one of them and healed them...And when it was day he departed and went into a lonely place. And the people sought him and came to him, and would have kept him from leaving them; but he said to them, "I must preach the good news of the kingdom of God to the other cities also; for I was sent for this purpose."

What a wonderful day! The sunset found Jesus attending to hundreds of people queuing to be healed at the door of St Peter's house in Capernaum. The weary Apostles were happy to help the people, organising lines and calming down the anxious crowd which was pressing in around Jesus. The evening came and there He was... *still* laying His hands "*on every one of them.*" And when the sun rose, exhausted as He was after a long day and a long night, Jesus left for a lonely place to pray. But people didn't want Him to leave. Maybe even the Apostles preferred to stay there: the mob was coming to Him, 'why should they go'? Yes, probably it was lovely and more comfortable to be at Peter's house. But Jesus wasn't content with serving only those who sought Him. His Will was to go "*to the other cities also*" and seek more souls.

We, like Jesus, can't be content with just helping those around us. Jesus told us to *go* "*to the whole world,*" not to stay with the same souls and in the same place. We have to search souls out and get out of our comfort zone to bring them to Christ. One day the Bishop of Madrid, Leopoldo Eijo y Garay (1878-1963), was told of a dying person in hospital who didn't want to go to Confession. In order to put off the nun who was insisting that he should receive the sacrament, he said that his sins were so many that he would need to confess them to a bishop. As soon as the bishop heard about it he took a taxi and went to the hospital straightaway. You can imagine the face of that sick person when the bishop entered the room and said with a smile, "*Let's get down to business. Where do we start?*"

Mary, Queen of the Universe, bury deep in my heart the sentiment that where souls are concerned, nothing is too much trouble. Everyone is worth all the Blood of Jesus.

Thursday 4th September
Lk 5:1-11

While the people pressed upon him to hear the word of God, he was standing by the lake of Gennesaret. And he saw two boats by the lake; but the fishermen had gone out of them and were washing their nets. Getting into one of the boats, which was Simon's, he asked him to put out a little from the land. And he sat down and taught the people from the boat.

Contemplating this text of the Gospel, St Josemaría used to point out that Jesus didn't ask for permission to get into Peter's boat. We can imagine the scene: Peter had been working the whole night with his partners but caught nothing. He was tired and frustrated. Getting close to the shore he saw a great crowd; they were pressing upon a Rabbi who was teaching them. Who was that Man? Why were there so many? Why was He preaching on the shore instead of in the synagogue? As Peter's boat drew near he could hear the Voice of that Rabbi and see His Face. Who was that captivating Man?

Imagine the surprise on Peter's face when, as soon as he and his companions touched the shore, Jesus jumped into his boat without saying a word! That's how Jesus jumps into our lives. All of a sudden, you find Him in your boat. When someone told St Josemaría how God entered his life with no warning, he replied, "*I didn't think God would get hold of me the way he did, either. But, let me tell you once again, God doesn't ask our permission to complicate our lives. He just gets in: and that's it!*"

The key moment came later when Jesus asked Peter to "*put out a little from the land*" because He wanted to teach the people from that 'platform': Peter's place of work. Once Jesus jumps into our lives, He asks for permission then, to use your boat, your life, your work, to reach out to many others. And from the platform of your work well done, your Christian life, your good example, He can teach many and 'jump' into others' lives.

Peter never forgot the day when Jesus jumped into his boat. Peter and James and John, who were also there, fell in love with this Rabbi that day, at the end of which they "*brought their boats to land, they left everything and followed him*"... forever. Mary, Queen of the Apostles, help me to follow their generous example.

Friday 22nd week in ordinary time
Friday 5th September
Lk 5:33-39

Jesus told them a parable: "No one tears a piece from a new garment and puts it upon an old garment; if he does, he will tear the new, and the piece from the new will not match the old. And no one puts new wine into old wineskins; if he does, the new wine will burst the skins and it will be spilled, and the skins will be destroyed. But new wine must be put into fresh wineskins'."

In the old days they didn't store wine in bottles which were far too expensive. They used containers made of animal skin, particularly convenient for transportation, as they could be carried easily, were lightweight, and would occupy less and less space as the liquid was consumed. However, wineskins had to be treated with care, since the leather became worn over time and could easily rupture, especially if filled with unfermented ('new') wine.

Over the years, the Pharisees had begun resisting more and more any 'new' approach to Divine Revelation to the one they already held. They thought they 'knew' everything and therefore they expected nothing 'new'. But Jesus came to preach the Good '*News*' and the Pharisees weren't ready to receive it, like old wineskins that can't retain new wine: they leaked, they broke and they spilled everything.

Nowadays, some people (like the Pharisees) aren't ready to receive the Word of God. Jesus wants to speak to them and change their lives but they are not receptive. They don't want to know. They don't like anything new. They are comfortable as they are. They may even pray; they come, tell their story and leave; but they don't listen to God. Like the tale of a lady who was praying about her vocation; maybe God wanted her to become a nun, but she wasn't very keen on the idea. She would go to the chapel and pray in front of a statue of Our Lady holding Baby Jesus, and repeat again and again, "*Should I become a nun or a wife?*" One day the Baby Jesus opened His mouth and replied, "*A nun, my dear.*" And the unhappy lady, a bit upset, replied, "*Be quiet, Child! I'm talking to Your Mother...*" She obviously didn't want to know.

Mary, my Mother, may I learn from you to listen to God and to do what He wants me to do.

Saturday 22nd week in ordinary time
Saturday 6th September
Lk 6:1-5

On a sabbath, while he was going through the grainfields, his disciples plucked and ate some heads of grain, rubbing them in their hands. But some of the Pharisees said, "Why are you doing what is not lawful to do on the sabbath?"

We often come across the complaints of the Pharisees: that "*Your disciples eat without washing their hands*", that "*they eat with publicans*", that "*they are plucking ears of grain on a Sabbath*", that "*Your disciples eat and drink whilst we are fasting*"... Moaning, complaining, whining all the time! Thinking about people like them, St Josemaría wrote, "*Long face, rough manner, ridiculous appearance, unfriendly attitude. Is that how you hope to inspire others to follow Christ?*"

But with You, Jesus, it was very different. You were drawing people to Yourself like iron to a magnet with your welcoming smile; that is how I imagine You, Lord. That's what we can see in the lives of your saints.

Saint Teresa of Calcutta talked many times about the "*power of the smile.*" She said, "*We shall never know all the good that a simple smile can do.*" During her life, people felt attracted to her joy and deep smile but very few knew that for almost 50 years she was suffering interior darkness and loneliness. She often asked those who knew about it to pray for her, so that she would never lose her smile: "*There is in my soul*" she wrote, "*such deep longing for God - so deep that it is painful - a constant suffering - and yet not wanted by God - empty - no faith - no love - no zeal. Souls hold no attraction - Heaven means nothing - and yet this torturing longing for God. Pray for me please that I keep smiling at Him in spite of everything.*"

You, Lord, need smiling apostles; disciples who keep smiling in the midst of our trials and difficulties; disciples who are not naïve, unable to see the terrible things that happen in the world... but who have put our trust in You and radiate that smile to the world as a witness to our faith. Mary, Cause of our Joy, may your children never lose that welcoming smile that draws people to your Son.

Twenty-Third Sunday in Ordinary Time
Sunday 7th September
Lk 14:25-33

"Which of you, desiring to build a tower, does not first sit down and count the cost, whether he has enough to complete it? Otherwise, when he has laid a foundation, and is not able to finish, all who see it begin to mock him, saying, 'This man began to build, and was not able to finish.'"

We are now at the beginning of the new academic year. This coming year will involve lots of classes and study and works and papers... and the norms of our 'plan of life'... So many things! That is why it's so important to do what Jesus suggests today in the Gospel, "*sit down and count the cost.*" 'Well begun is half done', says the proverb. We need to plan the year right now, at the beginning. Your timetable, your study, your plan of life. This building is different for each person. There is no standard plan for everyone. You have to prepare yours in prayer, in dialogue, negotiating with God.

A football player has a training plan. He knows the exercises he has to practise more, which are different from other football players. He knows that some days he has to train particular groups of muscles and rest others. The success of the whole season depends on his training plan. But football players don't just plan the exercises. They plan their resting periods as well. It's the perfect balance between exercise and rest that allows them to be fit for the matches. They also care much about their diet. An important part of their training too is tactical preparation and the concentration before each match. On September 22nd 2015, Bayern Munich was playing against Wolfsburg. Lewandowski was on the bench during the first half whilst his team was losing 1-0. He started playing in the second half. In 6 minutes he scored the first goal; 58 seconds later the second. Two minutes later, the third. Another two minutes on and he volleyed home a fourth. It took him three more minutes to add his fifth, with a brilliant acrobatic volley. When asked afterwards about his performance he just said that he had prepared for that match as always, 'conscientiously'.

How important is the preparation before the game! Let's plan our academic year conscientiously as well. My timetable for my plan of life (my prayer, Holy Mass, spiritual reading...), for study, time for leisure as well and sport... Mary, my Mother, I entrust to your intercession the new academic year that we now begin.

The Nativity of Our Lady
Monday 8th September
Mt 1:18-23

Now the birth of Jesus Christ took place in this way. When his mother Mary had been betrothed to Joseph, before they came together she was found to be with child of the Holy Spirit; and her husband Joseph, being a just man and unwilling to put her to shame, resolved to send her away. But as he considered this, behold, an angel of the Lord appeared to him in a dream, saying, "Joseph, son of David, do not fear to take Mary your wife, for that which is conceived in her is of the Holy Spirit; she will bear a son, and you shall call his name Jesus."

Today is the birthday of Our Mother, Mary. On our mother's birthday we, as good children, try to offer her a present. In order to make the right choice of gift, you have to put yourself in your mother's place and think what she would love to have. And we know that, much more than material things, mothers long for affection, thoughtfulness. They love to have their children around and to see them happy. That's always the best gift for a mother and Mary is very much Our Mother.

Little children offer little things... but with great love. Blessed Álvaro told a story that can help us to pray today. During the month of May, an African Catholic family lived the custom of offering something special to Our Lady every day. At the end of the day, each member of the family would leave a note with their offering under a small image of Mary. The offerings were very simple: to study better, help a younger brother or sister, do their jobs, pray with more attention and devotion... One day, however, the boy (who was about 12 years old) had a horrible day: he was especially lazy that day and was told off in school, he was disobedient, he had a few fights at home, he didn't finish his homework... and, finally, he was sent to bed without dinner. His mother thought he wouldn't dare to leave a note that day. But before she went to bed she checked and was surprised to see his note at the feet of Our Lady. She never read those notes, but that day she felt curious to know what he had written. This is what the note said: *"I'm sorry, Mother. I've done everything wrong today."* His mother was moved and so was Bl Álvaro when telling the story. And, surely, so was Our Lady. Because mothers know that, even if we have nothing else to offer, *contrition is a great present*. Happy Birthday, Mother!

Monday 23rd week in ordinary time
Monday 8th September
Lk 6:6-11

On another sabbath, when he entered the synagogue and taught, a man was there whose right hand was withered. And the scribes and the Pharisees watched him, to see whether he would heal on the sabbath, so that they might find an accusation against him. But he knew their thoughts, and he said to the man who had the withered hand, "Come and stand here." And he rose and stood there. And Jesus said to them, "I ask you, is it lawful on the sabbath to do good or to do harm, to save life or to destroy it?"

The man didn't ask for the miracle but Jesus saw him and reacted as the scribes and Pharisees expected Him to. When it comes to people in need, Jesus is very predictable: He is always ready to help. The scribes and Pharisees didn't care at all about that man. They were obsessed with the things that 'could not' be done and forgot to do the things that 'should' be done. They were the *'omissions men'*.

Some people are like them: they haven't hurt anyone, but they just couldn't care less. It is not what they do that condemns them; it is what they don't do. Just like the man in the Gospel, many people today are in need also. They need money, sometimes. But more often it is another kind of help that they need: attention, affection, advice, understanding, or even a simple smile...

On September 2nd 1827 a humble French lady was travelling from Milan to Lyon with her family. She was pregnant and gravely sick when she knocked at the door of a parish. Given her state, the priest took her to the hospital but she wasn't admitted because she was a foreigner. He tried other hospices but no one wanted to help. After a long agony, the lady died in his arms. There and then, he understood the need of such people: the helpless, the destitute, orphans, mentally ill people... And he started housing and caring for them all. That priest became St Giuseppe Benedetto Cottolengo. Today there are hospices of St Cottolengo all around the world. And it all started with the sad story of a lady whom no one wanted to help... Mary, Mother of Mercy, teach me to see the needs of others, as you did at the wedding feast in Cana, and to be always ready to help those in need.

Tuesday 23rd week in ordinary time
Tuesday 9th September
Lk 6:12-19

He went out to the mountain to pray; and all night he continued in prayer to God. And when it was day, he called his disciples, and chose from them twelve, whom he named apostles; Simon, whom he named Peter, and Andrew his brother, and James and John, and Philip, and Bartholomew, and Matthew, and Thomas, and James the son of Alphaeus, and Simon who was called the Zealot, and Judas the son of James, and Judas Iscariot, who became a traitor

If Jesus knew that Judas was going to betray Him... why didn't He choose someone else?' The truth is that when Jesus called him, Judas must have had a beautiful soul. He was a fine young man, full of energy, practising his faith sincerely. Don't forget that Judas was able to leave everything to follow Jesus. He was a generous young lad. One day he was entrusted with carrying the money bag, paying the expenses of the group and giving money to the poor. There wasn't much money in that bag, anyway. But that clinking of the coins in his pocket started one day to bother him. Maybe one day he took just one little copper to quench his thirst with a glass of wine. Another day two coppers for a bite… never anything big, no. But venial sins make the sinner weaker and blinder. He still loved Jesus... within limits. One day they offered him thirty pieces of silver if he led them to Jesus. All would be fine - he thought - Jesus will escape as He always has done before. Thus, repeated venial sins made it so easy for Judas to justify his evil doings.

We can also betray Our Lord if we don't fight against venial sins and defects: swearing, gossiping, laziness, procrastination, wasting time, vanity in front of the mirror, sarcasm, cheating... On one occasion St John Paul II was meeting a Bishop who got carried away and suddenly used a rude word. A bit embarrassed, the Bishop immediately apologised. But after a short while another swear word came out. He apologised again, "*Sorry, Holy Father. I'm like that when I get carried away.*" St John Paul II didn't hesitate and replied, "*If you are like that, then... change!*" There is no excuse. We can always change and overcome our defects. It's necessary to struggle against venial sin to avoid having to struggle with mortal sins. Mary, my Mother, help me to abhor venial sin.

Wednesday 23rd week in ordinary time
Wednesday 10th September
Lk 6:20-26

Jesus lifted up his eyes on his disciples, and said: "Blessed are you poor, for yours is the kingdom of God. "Blessed are you that hunger now, for you shall be satisfied. "Blessed are you that weep now, for you shall laugh. "Blessed are you when men hate you, and when they exclude you and revile you, and cast out your name as evil, on account of the Son of man! Rejoice in that day, and leap for joy, for behold, your reward is great in heaven; for so their fathers did to the prophets."

I can see You, Lord, explaining to Your disciples that they were blessed when they were poor or suffered hunger, blessed for weeping and for being hated and excluded on Your account. You explained that being poor and hungry, hated and persecuted is a sign of being 'with' You and of being 'like' You... And to be with You, my Jesus, is itself a blessing.

The example of St. Peter Claver can help us to pray. He was a Spanish Jesuit priest. While studying in Majorca, he decided to go to the Indies and save 'millions of perishing souls.' In 1610, he landed at Cartagena (Colombia), which received 10,000 slaves every year. He dedicated himself to serving the slaves and fighting for the abolition of the slave trade. In his time the great majority of people thought slavery to be a good and profitable thing for society so only a few opposed it. Fewer still stood up for those slaves whom St Peter saw as the 'people of the beatitudes': rejected, abused, hungry... Boarding the slave ships as they entered the harbour, he would hurry to serve them, care for the sick and catechise them as well; it is estimated that he personally baptised around 300,000 people.

We Christians are called to persevere and never give up in defending the innocent victims of injustice, even when everyone thinks the opposite (think about abortion, for instance). Today St Peter is a universal hero but in his time he was a revolutionary. Pope Francis is calling us today to be rebels against injustice and to defend those outcasts of society who are the present-day 'men of the beatitudes'.

Let's ask Our Lady, Mother of Mercy, to help us to be merciful as Pope Francis is asking us to be.

Thursday 11th September
Lk 6:27-38

"But I say to you that hear, Love your enemies, do good to those who hate you, bless those who curse you, pray for those who abuse you. To him who strikes you on the cheek, offer the other also...And as you wish that men would do to you, do so to them...Judge not, and you will not be judged; condemn not, and you will not be condemned; forgive, and you will be forgiven; give, and it will be given to you...For the measure you give will be the measure you get back."

Many people are convinced that the "*golden rule*" is '*don't do to others what you wouldn't like to be done to you.*' And so, if you don't like people poking a finger in your eye, you don't poke a finger in their eye; if you don't like people calling you names... you don't call them names; if you don't like people using your stuff without permission, you don't use their things without permission either... fair enough! But that is *not* the '*Golden Rule.*'

Because Jesus didn't say, '*Don't do to them what you don't like to be done to you.*' He said instead, "*And as you wish that men would do to you, do so to them.*" He didn't speak about things to avoid doing to others, but about things to do to others. And in order to live the *Golden Rule* we need to keep our eyes open to the needs of others. Then we will see what many don't see: that people need each other. St John Henry Newman described a gentleman as someone who "*has his eyes on all his company,*" who pays attention to the needs of others and is always ready to help.

A mother was talking with a young priest about one of her children: "*He doesn't need to be told to do anything. Whenever he sees something he can do he doesn't hesitate for a second to do it. He lets me rest.*" Apparently, when that child was around, his entire family was at ease. That could be good food for prayer, couldn't it? Am I the kind of child, brother, sister, student or friend who lets people rest? Do people like to be around me? Do I live the *Golden Rule*?

Mary, Mother of Fair Love, with your intercession, may I become the kind of person who makes people feel at ease, one of those I would love to have always around me.

Friday 23rd week in ordinary time
Friday 12th September
Lk 6:39-42

He also told them a parable: "Can a blind man lead a blind man? Will they not both fall into a pit? ...Why do you see the speck that is in your brother's eye, but do not notice the log that is in your own eye? Or how can you say to your brother, 'Brother, let me take out the speck that is in your eye,' when you yourself do not see the log that is in your own eye? You hypocrite, first take the log out of your own eye, and then you will see clearly to take out the speck that is in your brother's eye.

How easily we see defects in others! How difficult it is to see our own mistakes! How ready we are to correct others and help them to improve! How slow we are to accept our own failures and amend them! We are sometimes like the boy who failed his maths exam. He gave the report to his dad who obviously wasn't happy at all: "*This can't be: it's unacceptable!*" the dad said, "*It deserves severe punishment!*" "*You are quite right, dad,*" replied the boy, "*it DOES deserve SEVERE PUNISHMENT! I couldn't agree more. And... I know where the teacher lives!*"

Some people don't know themselves or their defects but are, nevertheless, always ready to correct others about anything. They are 'professional critics' who always analyse everyone except themselves. The story is told of a nit–picking arts professor who was guiding his students around an art gallery. He was criticising all the portraits they were finding: the style was poor, the model inappropriate, the colours messed up... The man stopped in front of a full-length portrait of an old man. He smiled in disdain and started criticising it: "*What a ridiculous lanky fellow! Look at the disproportion of the big nose and ears in a small head; do you see the slovenly clothes and lack of taste...*" Someone interrupted him, "*Professor! This is not a portrait, sir... it's a mirror!*"

St Augustine said that we often see in others the reflection of our own defects. We need to examine ourselves to spot our faults and try to correct them. Once we strive to correct our own mistakes we won't get annoyed with the shortcomings of others and we will be able to help them improve... Mary, my Mother, help me to see those aspects that God wants me to change and obtain for me from Heaven the grace I need to change them.

Holy Name of the Blessed Virgin Mary
Friday 12th September
Lk 1:39-47

In those days Mary arose and went with haste into the hill country, to a city of Judah, and she entered the house of Zechariah and greeted Elizabeth. And when Elizabeth heard the greeting of Mary, the babe leaped in her womb; and Elizabeth was filled with the Holy Spirit and she exclaimed with a loud cry, "Blessed are you among women, and blessed is the fruit of your womb! And why is this granted me, that the mother of my Lord should come to me? For behold, when the voice of your greeting came to my ears, the babe in my womb leaped for joy. And blessed is she who believed that there would be a fulfilment of what was spoken to her from the Lord."

Your children never get tired of blessing you, Mother. *"Blessed are you among women, and blessed is the fruit of your womb!"* We celebrate your birthday on the 8th, and your Most Holy Name today because, as good children, we enjoy praising you and celebrating with you before the whole of creation today: *"Blessed be the name of Mary, Virgin and Mother."*

It's a powerful name which leaves no one indifferent. Devils flee from it, angels rejoice on hearing it, saints smile at it, the Holy Souls in Purgatory find relief in it and Jesus... Jesus... well, HE LOVES IT! He was the first to venerate that Holy Name and pronounce it with pride when people asked Him who He was: *"I am the Son of Mary."* Mary! Those four letters are an aspiration in themselves. Let's use that name - 'Mary' - to give thanks, to say sorry, to ask for help... let's say it in times of temptation to get help, in times of distress to be comforted, in times of doubt to get answers, in times of joy to rejoice with her and in times of suffering to find relief. Let's pronounce this name like St Joseph, with great affection and love, like the saints who were most in love with Our Lady. Let's keep that name on our lips and we will keep our Mother in our hearts. Let us say it again and again: *"Blessed be your name, Mary, Virgin and Mother."*

"O name of Mary! Joy in the heart, honey in the mouth, melody to the ear of Her devout children!" said St. Anthony of Padua. *"O most sweet name! O Mary, what must thou thyself be, since thy name alone is thus amiable and gracious"* (Bl Henry Suso). Let us use this name - 'Mary' - frequently as an aspiration, for God and the entire Heaven exult in it.

Saturday 23rd week in ordinary time
Saturday 13th September
Lk 6:43-49

"For no good tree bears bad fruit, nor again does a bad tree bear good fruit; for each tree is known by its own fruit. For figs are not gathered from thorns, nor are grapes picked from a bramble bush. The good man out of the good treasure of his heart produces good, and the evil man out of his evil treasure produces evil; for out of the abundance of the heart his mouth speaks. "Why do you call me 'Lord, Lord,' and not do what I tell you?"

When we do what Our Lord wants us to do, then He can bear fruit in us. Fruit that will always be disproportionate with our doings. Saints were never obsessed with the fruit of their work. They were only interested in doing what God wanted them to do. When St Thérèse of Lisieux died, she wasn't well known, not even by some of the nuns that lived in the same convent. She never left the convent. She died at the age of 24 not having accomplished any 'great deed' in her life. Yet she is now a Doctor of the Church and her "Story of a Soul" still changes thousands of lives.

'Do you want to be a saint?' asked St Josemaría, *'Do what you ought and put your heart into what you are doing.'* The first fruit will be our own holiness. But much more fruit will come. Because holiness is fruitful. Luis Ruiz Suarez was born in 1913. He became a Jesuit in 1930 and in a few months the Republican government of Spain expelled the Jesuits from the country. He ended up in China. He was imprisoned for a while, expelled to Hong Kong, went back to Macao and there started working for the refugees and the poor. He was nicknamed "Luk Ngai" in Cantonese, "Father of the Poor". When he died in 2011, at the age of 97, he was in charge of 145 leper colonies, hospices for mentally disabled people, HIV and AIDS patients and schools for poor children. When he was 90 years old a journalist asked him if he had thought about retirement. In an outburst of laughter he lost his false teeth. Another journalist mentioned to him that his name wasn't as well-known as Mother Teresa's. *"Who cares if they know me?!"* he answered quickly. *"The important thing is that they know Jesus. I do all this for God. He knows!"*

Let us ask Our Lady to help us to give fruit, the fruit that God expects from us, even if only He sees it.

The Exaltation of the Holy Cross
Sunday 14th September
Jn 3:13-17

No one has ascended into heaven but he who descended from heaven, the Son of man. And as Moses lifted up the serpent in the wilderness, so must the Son of man be lifted up, that whoever believes in him may have eternal life. For God sent the Son into the world, not to condemn the world, but that the world might be saved through him.

On one occasion, when the people of Israel were in the desert, they faced the curse of a multitude of snakes which bit and killed many of the Israelites. They prayed to the Lord and He ordered Moses to make a bronze serpent and lift it up on a pole. Those who looked at it were healed from the poison of the serpents. The Holy Cross of Our Lord has real healing power. Such a simple sign means a lot to us. Every crucifix reminds us of God's Love for each one of us. Every crucifix is like a label with the price of our ransom paid by Jesus with His Blood. Lovers carry with them a picture of their beloved. A father has in his wallet a picture of his wife and children. Good Christians should also carry a crucifix in their pockets.

The crucifix is an effective weapon against the poison of the enemy. The devil has been described as a roaring lion to be feared. But in the presence of a crucifix, the lion becomes a tame cat. In times of difficulty, in times of temptation or when we suffer setbacks of any kind, having a crucifix at hand which we can kiss or caress becomes the most valuable instrument.

To kiss the crucifix is a great act of love and can also be a great act of contrition. One day St Josemaría went to assist a man who was dying in hospital. He was a gipsy who had been a great sinner. After his Confession, when St Josemaría gave him his crucifix to kiss, that contrite gipsy started to shout, and no one could stop him, "*I can't kiss Our Lord with this filthy, rotten mouth of mine!*" St Josemaría was moved by that act of contrition and answered him, "*But listen: very soon you are going to embrace him and give him a big kiss, in Heaven!*"

Mary, Mother of Sorrows, teach me to meditate on the Cross and keep me always close to your Son, close to you, on Calvary.

(Good advice from St Josemaría: *get a pocket crucifix and carry it with you always.*)

Monday 24th week in ordinary time
Monday 15th September
Lk 7:1-10

A centurion had a slave who was dear to him, who was sick and at the point of death. When he heard of Jesus, he sent to him elders of the Jews, asking him to come and heal his slave...And Jesus went with them. When he was not far from the house, the centurion sent friends to him, saying to him, "Lord, do not trouble yourself, for I am not worthy to have you come under my roof; therefore I did not presume to come to you. But say the word, and let my servant be healed."

We use these words during the Holy Mass before we receive Holy Communion: "*Lord, I am not worthy.*" St John Vianney explained that if Jesus had taken into account our 'worthiness', He would never have instituted the Eucharist. But He took into account only His love for us. Ordinarily we can only receive Him once a day but our desire would be to receive Him many times. According to St. Thomas Aquinas and St. Alphonsus Liguori, the value of a spiritual communion can be as great as Holy Communion itself. It depends, obviously, on the internal dispositions. If God can unite Himself to souls with a piece of bread, would it not be possible for Him to do the same with a strong desire? St. Teresa of Jesus wrote: "*When you do not receive communion and you do not attend Mass, you can make a spiritual communion, which is a most beneficial practice; by it the love of God will be greatly impressed on you.*" St. John Vianney taught, "*If we are deprived of Sacramental Communion, let us replace it by spiritual communion, which we can make every moment...when we cannot go to the church, let us turn towards the tabernacle; no wall can shut us out from the good God.*"

In 1975 the Communist Army took control of Vietnam, sending numerous bishops and priests to prison. Many disappeared, leaving no trace. A prisoner described what he found once in a cell he was moved to. It had been used by a priest who disappeared. On the wall, with a loose stone, the priest had drawn a huge Host and a Chalice. Presumably, unable to say Mass, he had spent a long time there in 'adoration', longing for the Eucharist. Lord, I know I'm not worthy, but I wish to receive You "*with the purity, humility and devotion with which your most holy Mother - my Mother - received you, with the spirit and fervour of the saints.*"

Our Lady of Sorrows
Monday 15th September
Jn 19:25-27

Standing by the cross of Jesus were his mother, and his mother's sister, Mary the wife of Cleophas, and Mary Magdalene. When Jesus saw his mother, and the disciple whom he loved standing near, he said to his mother, "Woman, behold, your son!" Then he said to the disciple, "Behold, your mother!" And from that hour the disciple took her to his own home.

After the Feast of the Holy Cross we look at Our Lady at the foot of Jesus Crucified. If we hold our Mother close to us and stand by her Son's Cross, we will learn something great from her. Consider that Mary wasn't hysterical in her grief or shouting back at those who tortured her Son. The Gospel does not mention whether she spoke encouraging words to Jesus as He was dying. It only says that she "*was standing by the Cross.*" She was in a place where she could be seen by Jesus. And there she contemplated her Son in agony. What great comfort she gave to Jesus just by being there with Him!

Bear in mind that Our Lady was not there out of a sense of duty. Rather, she knew that for Jesus it was important to look down and find the lovely face of His Mother; to let Him know that He wasn't left alone. Until the end of time that is the place of Our Lady: at the foot of the Cross, close to her Son, co-redeeming with Him. That's where we find her constantly. Every Christian who suffers finds Mary always beside him or her. Because this Mother cannot ever abandon her children, and even less in time of suffering. By the bed of a sick child you find the mother. She may not say anything, but her presence comforts the child. Since that day on Calvary, it's impossible for a Christian to suffer alone. If we suffer, we are with Jesus on the Cross. And if we are there we will see Mary at our side.

As we try to learn from Mary how to pray, we see that prayer does not always imply words. We can pray as Our Lady does, by looking at Jesus and contemplating Him on the Cross. Love doesn't always need words. In fact, many times it needs no words.

Mary, Mother of Sorrows, may I be a comfort for Jesus as He looks down from the Cross and finds you, His Mother, and me, holding your hand, "*standing by the Cross.*"

Tuesday 24th week in ordinary time
Tuesday 16th September
Lk 7:11-17

As he drew near to the gate of the city of Naim, behold, a man who had died was being carried out, the only son of his mother, and she was a widow; and a large crowd from the city was with her. And when the Lord saw her, he had compassion on her and said to her, "Do not weep." And he came and touched the bier, and the bearers stood still. And he said, "Young man, I say to you, arise." And the dead man sat up, and began to speak. And he gave him to his mother. Fear seized them all; and they glorified God, saying, "A great prophet has arisen among us!" and "God has visited his people!"

God has certainly visited His people. That was sort of a visit. He came into the city exactly when He was needed. He saw the suffering of that widow and, the Gospel says, Jesus *"had compassion on her and said to her, 'Do not weep'."* And before anyone asked for help, He resurrected the young man. Jesus is the real picture of God, the Perfect Image of God: a compassionate God, a merciful God, a Lover more than a judge.

Some people still have a different picture of God. A good Christian who went to China to spread the Good News spent the first month of his stay learning the language, attending Chinese lessons in a public academy. One day the Chinese teacher pointed at a word and asked for the meaning. As the pupils were hesitating, she wanted to give a clue and said, *"What God is...?"* The Christian pupil suddenly understood the mistake. She was pointing at the word *'chastiser.'* Before anyone could answer, the young Christian asked his Guardian Angel for help and tried to find in the dictionary the word he had in mind. He found it at once and showed it to the teacher: *'Merciful.'*

We have the mission to spread the real picture of Our Lord. *"God's face is the face of a merciful Father,"* said Pope Francis. In the same way that Jesus approached this lady and said to her *"Do not weep,"* He gets closer to us. In moments of suffering, He is always closer than ever. We can understand that the tears of this lady didn't stop flowing. They were changed into tears of joy. That's what God does. Mary, Mother of Mercy, help me to show to the world the real face of God.

Wednesday 17th September
Lk 7:31-35

"To what then shall I compare the men of this generation, and what are they like? They are like children sitting in the market place and calling to one another, 'We piped to you, and you did not dance; we wailed, and you did not weep.' For John the Baptist has come eating no bread and drinking no wine; and you say, 'He has a demon.' The Son of man has come eating and drinking; and you say, 'Behold, a glutton and a drunkard, a friend of tax collectors and sinners!' Yet wisdom is justified by all her children."

That was a children's game in the time of Jesus. Some children would play music and others had to react appropriately. They had to adapt their dancing to the rhythm of the music that was played. This was Jesus' complaint against people who didn't react to His preaching. They didn't react to the teachings of St John the Baptist either. No one was good enough for such people. John the Baptist? 'Ah, well', they may have thought, 'too bizarre, dressed in camel skins and eating locusts and wild honey'. Jesus? 'Too rustic, just a carpenter, you know'...

They had a mental picture of the 'perfect prophet' they would follow, and no one could match that imaginary picture. Some live in that imaginary world where things and people never meet their expectations, and that serves them as an excuse not to listen to them. They don't want to complicate their lives by following Jesus. God sends everyone the help that they need, which may not be the help that they expect.

Some don't pray because they don't feel anything special when they pray. They have a mental picture of what prayer should feel like but they don't feel it! So they quit. And they even blame God for it because He doesn't 'give' them prayer. The truth is that in our prayer God is the Master and He plays the music He wants us to dance to. We need to ask God to teach us to pray as He wants us to pray and not as we would love to pray. I've no excuse for not reacting to God's promptings; no excuse for saying, *'I can't pray in this situation.'* Because I don't pray for my sake and my feelings, but for God's sake.

Mary, my Mother, Master of Prayer, teach me to pray.

Thursday 18th September
Lk 7:36-50

A woman of the city, who was a sinner...brought an alabaster flask of ointment, and standing behind him at his feet, weeping, she began to wet his feet with her tears, and wiped them with the hair of her head, and kissed his feet, and anointed them with the ointment...Jesus said to the Pharisee, "A certain creditor had two debtors; one owed five hundred denarii, and the other fifty. When they could not pay, he forgave them both. Now which of them will love him more?" Simon answered, "The one, I suppose, to whom he forgave more." And he said to him, "You have judged rightly."

I love Your forgiveness, my Jesus. I love it because I am a sinner as well. The more sins You forgive me, the more I love You. I love it that there is no sin that You won't forgive. I love it that there is no human 'misery' that can exceed Your Divine Mercy. I love reminding all sinners that You are looking for them more than they are looking for You. I give You thanks for Your Mercy, for You are more willing to forgive us than we are willing to be forgiven; and I beg You for millions of souls to be reconciled with You this year.

There is a crucifix in St Eulalia's parish in Majorca given by Pope Innocent to King James I. It's called the 'Christ of the miracles'. The story is told that a man who had led a very sinful life decided to change and went to Confession. This crucifix was hanging in front of the confessional – a silent witness to the man's Confession. But when the priest heard his sins he was scandalized and thought that he couldn't grant the man absolution. The poor sinner left the church, devastated. But a young man found him in tears at the gates of the church, approached him and said, "*Go back; try again!*" The man hesitated but the young fellow insisted so he gave in and went back to the confessional. The priest was surprised to see him back and was about to send him away for a second time when suddenly the right hand of the Christ on that Crucifix came away from the nail. Showing the priest the scar from the nail, Jesus said to him, "*Give him absolution. Look how much it has cost me!*"

Mary, Refuge of sinners, help me to be always grateful for your Son's Mercy; help me to remind everyone that Jesus has already paid for their sins, and so they just have to come to the confessional to '*cash in*' forgiveness.

Friday 24th week in ordinary time
Friday 19th September
Lk 8:1-3

Jesus went on through cities and villages, preaching and bringing the good news of the kingdom of God. And the twelve were with him, and also some women who had been healed of evil spirits and infirmities: Mary, called Magdalene, from whom seven demons had gone out, and Joanna, the wife of Chuza, Herod's steward, and Susanna, and many others, who provided for them out of their means

How much You, Lord, must have loved these women! They were always serving You, Jesus, in all You needed; making sure that You didn't lack anything. They spent their time and money on You. In actual fact, being God, You could have gone without any help; couldn't You? You are God. But You wanted to eat and to drink what they provided and to sleep in the houses to which You were invited. For some reason, Jesus, You like to be given things instead of taking them. And these women [notice: all of them *women*!] were generous enough not just to give You what You needed but to follow You to make sure that You *always* had what was needed; You lived on earth as if obliged to depend upon generous people.

You are now in the Tabernacle and that also obliges You to depend on us. Saints have always been generous with everything that related to You. Even when they were poor, they didn't spare anything to give You the best. St John Vianney is a good example of this. He was very poor. He always used to eat just three or four boiled potatoes a day. He slept on the floor and had only one cassock... He was very austere with himself. But when it came to spending money on You, Lord, in the Blessed Sacrament, he didn't calculate. He was famous in the markets of Lyon for always purchasing the best materials for his church. When they offered him different materials he would say: "*This is not good enough for God, I need the best!*" Also St Francis of Assisi, known for his poverty, wanted to send brothers throughout the world with precious chalices and ciboria for the Eucharist. At times, we may not be able to provide money, but we can always serve Jesus in many other ways with devotion and affection, like these women of the Gospel. Mary, Mother of the Eucharist, make me generous with your Son in the Tabernacle. May He never be lacking anything I can provide.

Saturday 24th week in ordinary time
Saturday 20th September
Lk 8:4-15

Jesus said in a parable: "A sower went out to sow his seed; and as he sowed, some fell along the path, and was trodden under foot, and the birds of the air devoured it. And some fell on the rock; and as it grew up, it withered away, because it had no moisture. And some fell among thorns; and the thorns grew with it and choked it. And some fell into good soil and grew, and yielded a hundredfold."

The seed is the Word of God that was sown everywhere. The sower didn't choose to cast the seed in just a few places, but everywhere. He sowed bountifully and without calculating because he knew that the rain would eventually come, and if he had tried to avoid the paths, rocks and thorns, maybe an important part of the field wouldn't have received seed. We are now sowers of the Word of God. With our Christian life, our prayer and our words, we bring the Good News to many people. We shouldn't be held back, thinking that this or that person might or might not understand - God will rain down His grace on everyone and He certainly wants everyone to be saved.

A Mexican architect called Bosco Gutierrez was held hostage in 1990 for 257 days. His captors put him in a small cell; they masked their faces and never talked to him. Being a good Christian, Bosco prayed a lot every day. He had a dream one night when he saw himself in hell. One of his masked captors in front of him was yelling, *"I am in hell because I was bad. Nobody told me I was wrong. And you... You are in hell because you didn't help me."* Bosco realized that his captors also had souls to be saved, so he started to pray especially for them. At Christmas, he told them he wanted to pray together with them. They opened his door a little and he saw all five captors ready to listen. He then read the Christmas story from the Bible, talked to them about the love of God and prayed a decade of the Rosary. At the end, one by one, they came forward and shook his hand. *"Can you imagine the happiness inside my soul?"* he said months later. *"It was the happiest Christmas I ever had."*

Mary, Queen of Apostles, help me to sow God's Word abundantly, so that It can reach out to everyone.

Twenty-Fifth Sunday in Ordinary Time
Sunday 21st September
Lk 16:1-13

"He who is faithful in a very little is faithful also in much; and he who is dishonest in a very little is dishonest also in much. If then you have not been faithful in the unrighteous mammon, who will entrust to you the true riches?"

"*He who is faithful in a very little is faithful also in much.*" Our faithfulness to God is shown in little things. If we aren't faithful in the little things, how can we be faithful in the big ones? It would be like wanting to be a martyr and give your life to God and, at the same time, being unable to get up on time out of laziness or complaining because the soup is cold or the Coke is warm... If you can't offer a little sacrifice, how could you ever offer a big one?

How important are little things! "*'Great' holiness consists in carrying out the 'little duties' of each moment,*" teaches St Josemaría. Our holiness won't probably depend on being able to die a martyr for Christ, but on being able to live daily for Christ. Martyrs are not holy because they were martyrs. They are martyrs because they were struggling for holiness before. Saints lived some extraordinary moments, but 99% of their lives were like yours: get up on time in the morning, tidy your room, be on time for class, study, do your jobs, pray, go to bed on time, smile at the inopportune friend, eat what you are given.

The enemy of our holiness is more powerful than us. We won't beat him by extraordinary things. It is by many little things that the victory will be ours (or rather, Christ's). Remember David and Goliath. That giant could not be beaten with swords, arrows or armies. He was stronger than all that. What defeated him was a small smooth pebble. Do you remember 'The Hobbit'? All the hopes were pinned on that little 'halfling'. When Galadriel asks Gandalf why he chose a hobbit, the wizard replies, "*Saruman believes it is only great power that can hold evil in check, but that is not what I have found. I found it is the small everyday deeds of ordinary folk that keep the darkness at bay. Small acts of kindness and love.*" The building of our holiness is made out of many 'little' bricks. Mary, my Mother, teach me to be faithful in the little things that your Son is asking from me at each moment, to "*do what I ought and concentrate on what I am doing*" as St Josemaría taught.

Monday 25th week in ordinary time
Monday 22nd September
Lk 8:16-18

"No one after lighting a lamp covers it with a vessel, or puts it under a bed, but puts it on a stand, that those who enter may see the light. For nothing is hid that shall not be made manifest, nor anything secret that shall not be known and come to light. Take heed then how you hear; for to him who has will more be given, and from him who has not, even what he thinks that he has will be taken away."

When we illuminate a room that has been dimly lit for a while, we discover dust and cobwebs that have been accumulating there. The inhabitants of that room may not like to know that they've been living in such a place, but that doesn't change the truth: the dust and cobwebs are real. St John Paul II wrote an encyclical called *'The Splendour of Truth'*, because when truth shines it gives light. When we share the Truth of the Gospel we are giving light. *"I am the Truth,"* said Jesus. And the brightness of this Truth can't be hidden. Someone compared the truth to a lion. A lion doesn't need to be defended. It just needs to be unleashed. It can defend itself.

There is an 'urban legend' about the encounter of a battleship with another vessel. This is the transcript of the radio conversation… **Battleship**: *"Please divert your course 15 degrees to the North to avoid a collision."* **Voice from the other side**: *"I recommend you divert your course 15 degrees to the South to avoid a collision."* **Battleship**: *"This is the Captain of an aircraft carrier. I repeat, divert your course."* **Voice**: *"Hi, Captain, this is Frank. I repeat, you divert your course."* **Battleship**: *"This is the Captain. We are accompanied by three destroyers, three cruisers and numerous support vessels. I demand that you change your course, or countermeasures will be undertaken to ensure the safety of this ship."* **Voice**: *"Well Captain. I'm here alone with my dog… surprised to see your fleet heading straight for my lighthouse. Your call."*

Truth gives light, like the lighthouse. And it stands firm, founded on solid ground: God Himself. Like the sun, it can't be hidden. It can't be put out. It can't be shaken. It prevails. The splendour of God's Truth gives light to every soul. Christians give light wherever they are. Mary, Lady of Light, help me to share this Light with those around me.

Tuesday 25th week in ordinary time
Tuesday 23rd September
Lk 8:19-21

Then his mother and his brethren came to him, but they could not reach him for the crowd. And he was told, "Your mother and your brethren are standing outside, desiring to see you." But he said to them, "My mother and my brethren are those who hear the word of God and do it."

Again Jesus reminds His disciples that to listen is not enough. Some people had no problem listening to Jesus. Their difficulty was in doing what Jesus said. The Pharisees, for example, listened to the reading of the Bible and very often we find them listening to Jesus' preaching. You can listen to the Word of God as you listen to the rain falling. But it's not just about listening, it's about acting. Jesus Christ doesn't need spectators, but actors.

Our Lady was following Jesus and listening to Him. Apparently, that day there were so many people that His Mother had to wait outside. Someone mentioned Our Lady to Jesus and He used her example to teach a lesson: Mary listened to God's Word but she also did God's Will. When we pray we come to 'listen' to Him and to 'do' what He tells us to do. Do I want to DO what Jesus wants? When I pray, do I tell Jesus that He can count on me for whatever He wants me to do?

It's very comfortable to listen but not necessarily want to DO anything. The '*audience*' of a movie never changes the script. We have to be ready to give everything to God. There is the story of a hen and a pig who lived together on a farm. The hen suggested giving the farmer a surprise. "*Why don't we give him something special for breakfast today?*" she asked. "*We could give him fried eggs and bacon.*" But the pig wasn't very enthusiastic about the idea. "*It's not fair,*" said the pig. "*You only lay the eggs, but I have to commit my life for his breakfast!*" And the pig was right. The hen only had to co-operate with laying eggs; the pig, however, had to die to produce the bacon. Some Christians are happy co-operating, giving some time or some things to God, but not their lives. They are spectators but they are not willing to give their lives in the fulfilment of the Will of God. Mary, Virgin Most Faithful, teach me to listen and to obey the Word of your Son.

Wednesday 24th September
Lk 9:1-6

And he called the twelve together and gave them power and authority over all demons and to cure diseases, and he sent them out to preach the kingdom of God and to heal. And he said to them, "Take nothing for your journey, no staff, nor bag, nor bread, nor money; and do not have two tunics. And whatever house you enter, stay there, and from there depart. And wherever they do not receive you, when you leave that town shake off the dust from your feet as a testimony against them." And they departed and went through the villages, preaching the gospel and healing everywhere.

Jesus gave them power and taught them to rely on nothing else. So they were to take nothing for the journey, "*no staff, nor bag, nor bread, nor money...*" In order to spread the Good News, Saints (like the Apostles) were to rely on nothing else but grace, the power given by the Holy Spirit to those who want to become His apostles.

One day St Josemaría went to see Manuel Valdes, a young medical student who was in bed with a painful throat infection. Sitting at his bedside, St Josemaría began explaining to him the importance of the new apostolate he was planning to do with his help, to reach out to many university students. Listening to him, the patient was wondering how the priest planned to do all that. Since he was unable to speak, he took a piece of paper and wrote, "*But...what about the means?*" St Josemaría took that same piece of paper and wrote, "*They are the ones that Peter and Paul had, and Dominic and Francis, and Ignatius and Xavier: the Crucifix and the Gospel. Are they insufficient for you?*"

Do you see? In order to spread the Word you just need the Word. The Holy Spirit needs instruments, you and me. But we need no more instruments than the gifts and fruits of the Holy Spirit. When St Josemaría sent people to start the apostolic work in a foreign country he used say to them, "*My children, I'm sorry I can't give you any material help. I give you the best I have: a crucifix, a picture of Our Lady and my blessing.*" Nothing else is needed but the apostolic zeal that the Paraclete places in the hearts of His apostles. Mary, Spouse of the Holy Spirit, Queen of the Apostles, help me to grow in apostolic zeal and to trust in the means that God sends me.

Thursday 25th September
Lk 9:7-9

Herod the tetrarch heard of all that was done, and he was perplexed, because it was said by some that John had been raised from the dead, by some that Elijah had appeared, and by others that one of the old prophets had risen. Herod said, "John I beheaded; but who is this about whom I hear such things?" And he sought to see him.

If Herod sought to see Jesus... why didn't he go to Him? Everybody knew where to find Jesus. As king of Judea, Herod had everything he could wish for; what would a powerful and rich king want from a poor Rabbi who had nothing except a few disciples? The fact is that the tetrarch's house was full of things but his heart was empty; and as Pope Francis says, *"The emptier a person's heart is, the more he or she needs things to buy, own and consume."*

We are attracted by God like iron to a magnet, and nothing on earth will stop that attraction. God made us to be happy, and the only real and complete happiness can be found in Him: *"You made us, Lord, for Yourself and our hearts are restless until they rest in You"* (St. Augustine). Trying to satisfy our longing for happiness with things is like scratching itchy skin; it may relieve the discomfort for a few seconds, but the burning feeling eventually only gets worse. God wants to fill your heart up with His Love, but if a heart is full of 'junk' there is no room in it for God's Love.

A young boy explained his conversion in an interview. When he was young his parents and grandparents had given him everything he wanted and more - tablet, smartphone, video games; he explained that he *"had more gadgets in his room than the NASA research centre."* But he wasn't happy. For his birthday, not knowing what to give him (since he had everything already), a family friend bought him a good edition of the Gospels. He was amused at the idea but he decided to read it, out of curiosity. There he found Jesus Christ, and was so fascinated by His Life and Death... that he changed his life and is now studying to become a priest. *"I was looking for Him,"* he said, *"but I didn't know it; I was trying to find God but I had so much junk in front of me that I couldn't see Him!"* Mary, my Mother, *"may I seek Jesus, may I find Jesus, may I love Jesus."* (St Josemaría)

Friday 26th September
Lk 9:18-22

Now it happened that as he was praying alone the disciples were with him; and he asked them, "Who do the people say that I am?" And they answered, "John the Baptist; but others say, Elijah; and others, that one of the old prophets has risen." And he said to them, "But who do you say that I am?" And Peter answered, "The Christ of God."

Many people had different opinions about Jesus because each one had a different relationship with Him. The entire Gospels give us an accurate description of Jesus written by God Himself. And yet different readers can see Jesus in different ways. For that reason the Holy Spirit comes to assist us when we read the Gospel so that we know Jesus, the 'real' Jesus Christ that walked on earth two thousand years ago and not just an "opinion" of Jesus.

The Apostles transmitted what they saw. Then the early Christians transmitted what they heard from the Apostles. Some of those things were put in writing and became the New Testament. Some other things were never written, just transmitted from generation to generation. That's what we call *Tradition*. Tradition allows us to understand the Gospels appropriately and know the 'Real Jesus' rather than my 'opinion' about Jesus.

In 1865 missionary priests were allowed to go to Japan after more than 250 years of prohibition and persecution of Christians. Some people who lived in Urakami (a village near Nagasaki) received a French priest, Bernard Thadee Petitjean, and confessed to him that their families had kept the 'Kirishitan' (Christian) faith all that time without priests. But they wanted to ask three questions: 1) Where is your wife? "*I have no wife*," said the priest; 2) Do you have a Mother in Heaven? "*The Virgin Mary is my Mother*," he replied; and 3) Do you follow a bishop dressed in white? "*Yes, I follow the Pope.*" They were satisfied with the answers, explaining that three centuries before, the priests told them that other priests would come one day and, in order to make sure that they were the successors of the Apostles, those questions had to be asked.

Mary, Mother of the Church, help me to read the Gospel with the same Spirit with which it was written; to see Jesus as you, Mother, saw Him.

Saturday 25th week in ordinary time
Saturday 27th September
Lk 9:43b-45

But while they were all marvelling at everything he did, he said to his disciples, "Let these words sink into your ears; for the Son of man is to be delivered into the hands of men." But they did not understand this saying, and it was concealed from them, that they should not perceive it; and they were afraid to ask him about this saying.

The Apostles were afraid to ask Jesus about His Passion and we can understand why. It's not pleasant to talk about the suffering and death of those you love. And they loved Jesus as much as we do (or even more). They "*did not understand this saying*", the Gospel tells us. They could not understand why Jesus insisted so many times on such a gloomy thought. But Jesus was adamant that they should keep it in mind, and for that reason He says, "*Let these words sink into your ears*" - as if saying 'don't you ever forget this'.

It could well be that the Apostles were afraid of the Cross. That's wrong. The only people who have reason to fear the Cross are the devil and his followers, because the Cross is now the instrument of our salvation. Today I ask You, Lord, that I may never feel afraid of the Cross or of suffering because the Cross is an instrument of salvation. It hurts; it certainly does. A dentist may conduct painful procedures in order to deal with tooth decay or an infection. You don't go to the dentist to suffer, but to have your dental problems solved. It may involve pain, but that is part of the process of healing. A person who avoids the dentist for fear of suffering will suffer even more when his tooth gets infected.

On 7th February 1945 the Communist soldiers arrived at the Franciscan Monastery in Siroki Brijeg. They said, "*God is dead, there is no Pope, no Church, no need of you*", and asked them to remove their habits. The Franciscans refused. One angry soldier took the Crucifix and threw it on the floor. He said, "*you can now choose either life or death.*" Each of the Franciscans knelt down, embraced the Crucifix and said, "*You are my God and my All.*" The thirty Franciscans were all killed and their bodies burned. They are known as the Thirty Franciscan Martyrs of Siroki Brijeg. Mary, Queen of Martyrs, may I never be afraid of the Cross, for it is there that I find your Son.

Twenty-Sixth Sunday in Ordinary Time
Sunday 28th September
Lk 16:19-31

"There was a rich man, who was clothed in purple and fine linen and who feasted sumptuously every day. And at his gate lay a poor man named Lazarus, full of sores, who desired to be fed with what fell from the rich man's table; moreover the dogs came and licked his sores. The poor man died and was carried by the angels to Abraham's bosom. The rich man also died and was buried; and in Hades, being in torment, he lifted up his eyes, and saw Abraham far off and Lazarus in his bosom..."

We remember the story well. The rich man was condemned, not because he had too much, but because he shared nothing. He didn't have mercy on Lazarus. Generosity is attractive. Lack of generosity is repulsive. Saints have been always ready to give. To become a saint it doesn't matter how much we have. It matters how much we give. Venerable María del Carmen González was 9 years old when she died. One day a beggar rang the doorbell. She opened the door, asked the beggar to wait and brought him all her pocket money. Then she said to the beggar, *"Now you ring again and my mum will open and give you some more."*

Children can teach great lessons about generosity because they don't calculate much nor worry about the future. Like that other girl who was given her pocket money upon leaving the church on Sunday. She went straight to a beggar at the church door and gave him the lot. Her mum was very proud and so, when they had walked for about a hundred yards, she gave the girl the pocket money again. But the girl ran back to the same beggar and gave him that as well! Mum was very pleased but a bit concerned. So, instead of rewarding her generosity with more money, she bought her an ice cream. But you can guess what she did with the ice cream too!

Being merciful does not always imply giving money. We can give comfort, attention, dedication, affection, time, help. Even a smile is great alms for those who need it. Those around you, specially your family, always need you for something.

Mary, Virgin Most Merciful, teach me to be generous with those around me.

Gabriel, Archangel, Alternative: Michael or Raphael
Monday 29th September
Jn 1:47-51

Jesus said to Nathanael, "Because I said to you, I saw you under the fig tree, do you believe? You shall see greater things than these." And he said to him, "Truly, truly, I say to you, you will see heaven opened, and the angels of God ascending and descending upon the Son of man."

One of those Angels that Nathanael could see ascending and descending from Heaven was you, dear St Gabriel. Only to you could God entrust the most important of missions; only you could deliver the greatest message in history.

It is probably not very theological to say that Angels can get nervous, but if that were possible, this would be the most appropriate time to be anxious. The salvation of mankind depended on it. Dear Gabriel, had you ever thought that Mary could say 'No'? Because, in fact, she could have said 'No' to her mission. Mary was perfectly free.

We might think that Our Lady was 'far too holy' to say 'No'. However, the magnificence of it is that Mary, the second Eve, could have said 'No' to God but she said "*Yes*" instead. Otherwise, the most important decision that a human person ever took in history would have been just 'inevitable'. As if God was forcing us: 'I will redeem you, whether you like it or not!' Yes, Our Lady was holy, but she still found the message difficult: "*How can this be?*" she asked St Gabriel. The Archangel reassured her. She didn't have to do anything special, the Holy Spirit would do it. She just had to accept. And thank goodness she accepted, because St Gabriel wasn't given a 'plan B', in case Mary said 'No'.

Today God still sends His messages through His Angels. Millions of people are given the chance to accept God's plans for them; you and I, the divine mission that God has entrusted to us. Like Our Mother, we are certainly free to say 'Yes' or 'No'. But there is an alarming thought that should help us to be generous and say 'Yes': God has no 'Plan B'. What I fail to do will remain undone for eternity. Mary, Queen of Angels, help me to be generous and say a big 'YES' to whatever God has prepared for me, because if I accept, God will do all the rest.

St Michael, Archangel, Alternative: Gabriel or Raphael
Monday 29th September
Jn 1:47-51

Jesus said to Nathanael, "Because I said to you, I saw you under the fig tree, do you believe? You shall see greater things than these." And he said to him, "Truly, truly, I say to you, you will see heaven opened, and the angels of God ascending and descending upon the Son of man."

Many people have no experience of the power of the Angels and Archangels. If we knew how mighty they are and how willing to help us, we would ask them for their intercession many times during the day. Today we celebrate the feast of the three Archangels whose names we know: St Michael, St Gabriel and St Raphael. St Michael is mentioned in the Book of Daniel, in the Epistle of St Jude and in the Book of Revelation, where it describes the battle fought by the Archangel Michael and his host against 'the dragon' (the devil) and all his evil angels, defending all the friends of God. He is a really powerful protector against the snares of the devil.

The 'dragon' fears him. The devil himself told St John Marie Vianney that St Michael was protecting him at the door of his church. Rather than assault him, all the devil could do was to yell and insult him. St Padre Pio also recommended devotion to him. He said, *"You will need the help of St Michael, living in this world."*

On October 13, 1884, after celebrating Mass, Pope Leo XIII was found staring blankly. A moment later, he suddenly snapped back, went to his office and composed the Prayer to St. Michael. Supposedly, he had had a vision in which he heard a guttural voice, the voice of Satan in his pride, boasting to Our Lord, *"I can destroy your Church."* As a reaction to that vision, Pope Leo asked for this prayer to St Michael to be said after Holy Mass throughout the universal Church: *St. Michael the Archangel, defend us in battle: be our defence against the wickedness and snares of the devil. May God rebuke him, we humbly pray. And do you, O prince of the heavenly host, by the power of God thrust into hell Satan and all the evil spirits who prowl about the world for the ruin of souls. Amen.*

We are still fighting this constant battle with the devil and his angels and for that reason we should ask for protection from this powerful Archangel very often. Mary, Queen of Angels, remind me to have recourse to St Michael the Archangel.

St Raphael, Archangel, Alternative: Michael or Gabriel
Monday 29th September
Jn 1:47-51

Jesus said to Nathanael, "Because I said to you, I saw you under the fig tree, do you believe? You shall see greater things than these." And he said to him, "Truly, truly, I say to you, you will see heaven opened, and the angels of God ascending and descending upon the Son of man."

Angels are ascending and descending from Heaven in order to assist us in many ways. The story of St Raphael summarises all the missions that an Angel can be entrusted with by God. His story is told in the Book of Tobit. Tobit was a very good man, known for his works of mercy such as burying the abandoned bodies of some people who had died. For this and other things, he suffered persecution. On top of those sufferings, he even became blind. We are also told the story of Sarah, a young woman who had married seven times, but each of her husbands died on their wedding night. Both Tobit and Sarah felt miserable. God heard their prayers and sent Raphael on a mission to help them.

Tobit had to send his only son, Tobias, on a long trip to recover their money. Before sending him off, he instructed his son on how to live a good life and asked him to find a good companion. It is then that St Raphael (introducing himself as Azarias) joined young Tobias on his journey.

It's a long story (you may want to read it) but the gist of it is that God solves all the problems they prayed for and even a few more. (Spoiler alert!) With the help of St Raphael, Tobias recovered his money; Sarah got rid of the spell and happily married Tobias himself; Tobias got back home safe and sound with his new wife and, finally, even Tobit recovered his sight. Towards the end, Tobit raised the question of the Archangel's wages. Tobias felt he should receive half of the money they had recovered. It is then that the Archangel revealed who he was and that '*Angels earned no salary*'. Instead of money, he asked them to '*praise God forever.*' After reading the story, you may also feel like asking St Raphael to be your companion on this journey of life. Don't miss the opportunity today!

Mary, Queen of Angels, remind me to have recourse to these three powerful Archangels: Michael, Gabriel and Raphael.

Tuesday 26th week in ordinary time
Tuesday 30th September
Lk 9:51-56

Jesus set his face to go to Jerusalem. And he sent messengers ahead of him, who went and entered a village of the Samaritans, to make ready for him; but the people would not receive him, because his face was set toward Jerusalem. And when his disciples James and John saw it, they said, "Lord, do you want us to bid fire come down from heaven and consume them?" But he turned and rebuked them. And they went on to another village.

Those people wouldn't receive Jesus because they didn't like any pilgrim who was heading for Jerusalem. That wasn't nice. No wonder James and John felt offended and resentful towards them. Our Lord rebuked them and went on to another place. He didn't dwell on the offence or say anything against those people. In fact, He was planning to give His Life for them as well. But their time had not yet come. Resentment, animosity and rancour are all at odds with Christianity. *"What a great gift the Lord has given us in teaching us to forgive!"* Pope Francis tells us.

Resentment is like an infection in our hearts. It damages our soul and prevents us from finding peace. On the contrary, when we show forgiveness, we help the offender to reconsider what they did. Around the year 1929, a worker covered in lime got on a tram and approached a young priest, St Josemaría, who was dressed in his cassock. Taking advantage of the tram's rough movements, the worker intentionally bumped into him and stained his cassock amidst the smiles and silence of some passengers who had witnessed the scene. St Josemaría turned and, with a smile full of affection, told the worker, *"My son, let us finish this,"* and gave him a hug, dirtying his cassock completely.

As St Josemaría put it, we should '*drown evil in an abundance of good*'. Thus Jesus prayed for those who crucified Him. And today, in the midst of Christian persecution, we still have the same answer for those who do us any evil. We pray for those who kill Christians, those who insult us, threaten us, ridicule us, laugh at us - and we love them. They show what they have in their hearts, and we, with God's Grace, show them what we have in ours. Mary, Help of Christians, help me always to repay evil with good.

October

Wednesday 1st October
Lk 9:57-62

As they were going along the road, a man said to him, "I will follow you wherever you go"...To another he said, "Follow me." But he said, "Lord, let me first go and bury my father." But he said to him, "Leave the dead to bury their own dead; but as for you, go and proclaim the kingdom of God." Another said, "I will follow you, Lord; but let me first say farewell to those at my home." Jesus said to him, "No one who puts his hand to the plough and looks back is fit for the kingdom of God."

Jesus was walking along the road. He was calling new disciples and some others were approaching Him and volunteering to follow Him too. But some wanted to follow Him only after first setting out their own conditions. It's as if they were trying to negotiate their vocation with God: '*I will follow You, Lord, but... not now, maybe later*' or '*OK, but I have to study this degree*', or '*live in this city*' or '*have this job*' or '*get married.*'

Our vocation is non-negotiable. A fiancé can't say to his beloved: '*OK. I'll marry you but only if I can still live in my parents' house.*' God thought about my vocation for all eternity. He made me, exactly as I am, in order to fulfil my mission. I am still free to accept it or not, to say 'Yes' or 'No' to my vocation. But I can't take some parts from it like a child who discards the vegetables on his plate because he only likes the steak. We can always do other things with our life; even good things. But the best is always doing what I was meant to do. St Teresa of Calcutta is a good example of generosity. At the age of 18 she became a missionary. She entered the convent of the Sisters of Loreto in India and lived there happily for 18 years. But then God asked her to leave that life and start a new congregation to serve the poor and destitute. For a long time she experienced only difficulties, from the Loreto Sisters, the bishop, the authorities... She could easily have settled in her convent and left this new calling. Who would know that she was saying 'No' to God? She would still be a nun. No one could tell. No one but God and herself. But she was generous and left everything to follow God's Will and we can now see the fruit.

Mary, my Mother, do not allow me to present God with conditions. Help me to say a definitive and generous 'Yes'.

The Holy Guardian Angels
Thursday 2nd October
Mt 18:1-5, 10

Jesus said to his disciples, "Truly, I say to you, unless you turn and become like children, you will never enter the kingdom of heaven. Whoever humbles himself like this child, he is the greatest in the kingdom of heaven. Whoever receives one such child in my name receives me; See that you do not despise one of these little ones; for I tell you that in heaven their angels always behold the face of my Father who is in heaven."

A good father will never send his child alone on a dangerous road with threatening robbers on the prowl. On our way to Heaven we are threatened by the devil and Our Lord, the Best of Fathers, won't allow us to walk on our own. Think about it: Such a majestic, beautiful and powerful creature has been assigned only to me; I don't share my Guardian with anyone else. He is no 'second-hand' Angel. He waited for millions of years until I was born and is now faithfully at my side fulfilling this mission: leading me to Heaven.

St Josemaría saw God's providence in the fact that Opus Dei was born on the feast of the Guardian Angels. He recommended keeping up a daily conversation with our Guardian Angel, asking him for help many times during the day and greeting other people's Angels as well. One day, he received the visit of his very good friend archbishop Marcelino Olaechea, accompanied by his secretary. St Josemaría greeted him and then asked him playfully, "*Marcelino, let's see if you can guess - whom did I greet first?*" The archbishop replied, "*You greeted me first.*" "*No,*" St Josemaría said, "*I greeted the VIP first.*" Archbishop Olaechea, understandably perplexed, replied, "*But of the two of us, my secretary and me, I am the 'VIP'.*" Then the saint explained, "*No, the VIP is your Guardian Angel.*" Let's be good friends with the Guardian Angels of our relatives and friends.

St John Vianney suggested that if we find it difficult to pray, we should "*hide behind our good Angel and charge him to pray in our stead.*" A little girl preparing for her First Holy Communion gave the priest a wonderful lesson: "*Since I'm so little*" she explained, "*I ask my Guardian Angel during the Mass to fly to the Altar and kiss Jesus on my behalf.*" Mary, Queen of Angels, help me to keep my Guardian Angel busy the whole time. My Guardian Angel, intercede for me!

Friday 26th week in ordinary time
Friday 3rd October
Lk 10:13-16

"Woe to you, Chorazin! woe to you, Beth-saida! for if the mighty works done in you had been done in Tyre and Sidon, they would have repented long ago, sitting in sackcloth and ashes. But it shall be more tolerable in the judgement for Tyre and Sidon than for you. And you, Caperna-um, will you be exalted to heaven? You shall be brought down to Hades."

It is hard to hear these words from You, Our Merciful Lord. It doesn't quite sound like You. I understand that it is not You who want to condemn them; it was them who didn't want to be saved. It wasn't You, Lord, who didn't knock at their door; it was them who didn't open. You want to save everyone but some stubborn sinners refuse to be saved. As St Augustine put it: "*God who created you without you, will not save you without you.*" These people were free to accept You, and freely decided to reject You.

It's not sin but the obstinacy of sin that condemns people. It is the insanity of remaining in our sin and not wanting to make amends. This insanity could be named '*insinnity*': the obstinacy of remaining in our sins. Our mission, in order to save souls, is to encourage those sinners to keep trying to fight against their sins and to atone for them. We are all sinners. The only difference is that some sinners keep fighting and some others have given up. *Discouragement* is the devil's great speciality. The enemy spends his energy trying to convince us to give up: '*You will never get rid of these sins*' he suggests in your ear. '*This is too hard for you*', '*There is no point in going to Confession: you will need to confess the same sin again in no time...*' Sound familiar?

A medical doctor was giving a lesson to his students. They entered a ward crowded with patients and he asked: "*Which one of these do you think should receive attention first? Who do you think is in the worst state?*" After they had given their different opinions, he gave the right answer: "*Do you see that man with flies on his face? If he has given up shooing the flies away, it's because he has given up on himself.*" We have this mission among our friends and relatives today, to assist those sinners who have given up and encourage them. Mary, my Mother - their Mother - Refuge of sinners, 'help me to help them'.

Saturday 26th week in ordinary time
Saturday 4th October
Lk 10:17-24

The seventy returned with joy, saying, "Lord, even the demons are subject to us in your name!" And he said to them, "I saw Satan fall like lightning from heaven. Behold, I have given you authority to tread upon serpents and scorpions, and over all the power of the enemy; and nothing shall hurt you. Nevertheless do not rejoice in this, that the spirits are subject to you; but rejoice that your names are written in heaven."

The Eagles' was a school football team. The players were very good friends but not very skilful. They had lost all their matches. That is, until the toughest fixture – against the best team that season. For some strange reason, the 'best team' didn't manage to bring a full team, and according to the rules, forfeited the match 3–0. Nevertheless, the 'best team' still wanted to play on, just for fun, even though the Eagles had won the match. Their team was very good. Even with 4 fewer players, they still scored one goal after another. But every time they scored, the Eagles' keeper (whose sense of humour was better than his goalkeeping) would shout out at the top of his voice, "*You can score as many goals as you want... BUT YOU HAVE LOST THE MATCH!*"

As disciples of Jesus, we need to remember that God has given us authority "*to tread upon serpents and scorpions*" and the first serpent is the devil. He spends his time tempting us and may win some victories every now and then. He can get us to do something wrong, make mistakes or commit sins. But when he manages to make us fall into temptation we will go quickly to Confession and remind him of this: 'you may have scored... BUT YOU HAVE LOST THE MATCH!' because Jesus has already won.

Do you see the power of Confession? It can take a while for the devil to tempt us and make us stumble and fall; but it takes 10 seconds for the priest to give absolution and destroy all the enemy's work. A saint is a simple soul treading upon the enemy with God's Feet, just as we do in Confession.

Mary, Handmaid of the Lord, you who crushed the serpent's head, help me to '*rejoice*' always, because my name is written in Heaven, written in red with the Blood of Jesus Christ!

Twenty-seventh Sunday in Ordinary Time
Sunday 5th October
Lk 17:5-10

"Will any one of you, who has a servant ploughing or keeping sheep, say to him when he has come in from the field, 'Come at once and sit down at table? Will he not rather say to him, 'Prepare supper for me, and gird yourself and serve me, till I eat and drink; and afterward you shall eat and drink? Does he thank the servant because he did what was commanded? So you also, when you have done all that is commanded you, say, 'We are unworthy servants; we have only done what was our duty.'"

"Duty" is linked to the word "due". The definition of the word *'justice'* is *"giving to everyone what is their due."* If you buy an ice-cream, you give the ice-cream seller his due, the cost of the ice-cream. When you pay him, you are not doing him a favour but giving him 'his due'. We have a good sense of justice when people owe us something. Imagine you lend your phone to your friend to call home because his ran out of battery. Then you ask him if you can borrow his pen for a second and he says, *'No way! If you forgot yours it's not my fault.'* It doesn't seem very reasonable, does it?

Think about your parents. Your mum gave birth to you. Then your parents nurtured you, fed you, dressed you, cleaned you, taught you... For countless nights they woke up several times in the middle of the night to hold you, feed you or change you. For countless hours your mum has been cooking for you, washing your clothes, tidying your room, making your bed, driving you home... Who paid for the bed that you use, your food, your clothes, your games, your house, your books, your education...? And so, when one good day mum asks you to clear the table, tidy your room (which is not yours really, it's your parents'), make 'your' bed... do you think you are entitled to claim some kind of 'reward' in exchange?

Now think about God: Everything you have, you are, you enjoy, everyone in your life (parents, siblings, friends…), - EVERYTHING! – has been given to you by God. Don't you think that going to Mass or saying your prayers or struggling to be a good child of His, is the least that He deserves? We don't expect any 'reward' from Him: He has rewarded us already beyond measure. Our 'duty' is to be grateful and to love Him with all our hearts. Mary, my Mother, may I be a 'dutiful' child of God.

Monday 27th week in ordinary time
Monday 6th October
Lk 10:25-37

A lawyer asked Jesus, "who is my neighbour?" Jesus replied, "A man was going down from Jerusalem to Jericho, and he fell among robbers, who stripped him and beat him, and departed, leaving him half dead. Now by chance a priest was going down that road; and when he saw him he passed by on the other side. So likewise a Levite, when he came to the place and saw him, passed by on the other side. But a Samaritan, as he journeyed, came to where he was; and when he saw him, he had compassion, and went to him and bound up his wounds, pouring on oil and wine; then he set him on his own beast and brought him to an inn, and took care of him. And the next day he took out two denarii and gave them to the innkeeper, saying, 'Take care of him; and whatever more you spend, I will repay you when I come back.'"

The story of Jesus explains perfectly who 'my neighbour' is. We find it easier to feel compassion for those people we see in the news, in a far distant country, than for those who live next door to us, or even under the same roof. It's easier to give way to a stranger in the street than to our sister at home; to give up our seat to someone we don't know on the train than to help our mother at home... Who's your neighbour? Look around: *They are! Don't you see them?*

A woman explained a lesson her dad taught her. One night at dinner her mother placed a plate of jam and a piece of *extremely burnt* toast on the table. The girl waited to see if her dad was going to say something. But he just ate his toast and asked his daughter about her day. The girl heard her mum apologising and never forgot her dad's reply: "*Sweetie, I love burnt pieces of toast.*" Later that night, she went to say good night to her dad and, joking, she asked him if he really liked burnt pieces of toast. He put his arm around her shoulder and said: "*Your mum put in a very long day at work today and she was very tired and still made dinner for us. Besides, burnt toast never hurt anyone but a harsh or careless word can!*"

Who is your neighbour? Look around; be attentive and you will see your neighbour in the person sitting in front of you at breakfast, on the train, in class, at sports, in the streets... Be alert, for God notices how you treat His children! Mary, my Mother, teach me to love my 'neighbour' as you do, for they are your children too.

Tuesday 27th week in ordinary time
Tuesday 7th October
Lk 10:38-42

A woman named Martha received him into her house. And she had a sister called Mary, who sat at the Lord's feet and listened to his teaching. But Martha was distracted with much serving; and she went to him and said, "Lord, do you not care that my sister has left me to serve alone? Tell her then to help me." But the Lord answered her, "Martha, Martha, you are anxious and troubled about many things; one thing is needful. Mary has chosen the good portion, which shall not be taken away from her."

You, Lord, knew that house very well. Bethany was the place where You could rest and be among friends. That day there were more guests in the house than usual and You were teaching them. But Martha was a bit anxious: so many people, so much to do, people sitting on the floor, plates and cups and food all over the place... In actual fact, she was doing something good and even necessary. But You praised Mary – the one who apparently wasn't doing anything – and not Martha.

Serving You is a good thing. But Martha was missing something better. The choice was not between a 'good' thing and a 'bad' thing, but between a 'good thing'... and a 'better' one. To listen to You is the best we can do 'for You'. It would have been better for Martha to prepare everything in advance and so, when You arrived, she could spend the rest of the evening just listening to You and enjoying Your presence: in prayer.

When we go to church something of this sort can happen. Some people can't see the wood for the trees. A priest asked some First Holy Communion children, *"What do you like most about the church?" "The songs,"* said one. *"Your stories in the homily"* said another. *"The beautiful pictures, that lovely chapel, the flowers, praying together..."* added the others. A little girl finished the brainstorming session with the one word the priest was waiting for: *"Jesus!"*

Some people, like Martha, could miss a conversation with God when going to church, getting distracted with all the other things that surround God. Let's not miss the point. Let's not miss God. Holy Mary, Mother of Jesus and my Mother, how many hours you spent listening to your Son... teach me to do the same!

Our Lady of the Rosary
Tuesday 7th October
Lk 1:26-38

The angel said to Mary, "Hail, full of grace, the Lord is with you!" But she was greatly troubled at the saying, and considered in her mind what sort of greeting this might be. And the angel said to her, "Do not be afraid, Mary, for you have found favour with God. And behold, you will conceive in your womb and bear a son, and you shall call his name Jesus.

The month of October is the special month of the Rosary. We all love to be reminded of the things that make us happy. A mother, for instance, may love a particular song that reminds her of her first date with her husband or the birth of her child. The song may not be the best song ever, but she loves it. And Mary loves to be reminded that she is the Mother of God, that the Lord is with her, that she is blessed, full of grace...

A man once told a priest that he preferred to say other prayers. To which the priest answered, "*God sent not His prophets, but His Immaculate Mother to Fatima to tell us, not just once but six times, that we had to say the rosary every day. If a mother sends her child to the shop for a bottle of milk and he comes back instead with ice cream, is she pleased? In a way, ice cream is better than milk, but it is not what she asked for.*" In that Most Holy Home in Nazareth, do you think that Our Lady had to ask for anything twice? If we want in any way to be like Jesus, we must do what His Mother asks.

Sister Lucia who was present at the apparitions of Our Lady of Fatima, said, "*In these last times in which we live, the Most Holy Virgin has given a new power to the recitation of the Holy Rosary. There is no problem that cannot be solved by the Rosary; no matter how difficult it is, whether temporal or above all, spiritual, in the personal life of each one of us, of our families, of the families of the world, or of the religious communities, or even of the life of peoples and nations.*" When Our Lady appeared in Lourdes to St Bernadette, the girl pulled out her rosary. As Bernadette prayed out loud, the Virgin passed the beads of her rosary between her fingers in silence (it wouldn't make any sense for Our Lady to pray to herself, but she did recite the Glorias with her). How nice it is, Mary, Queen of the Most Holy Rosary, to pray the Rosary with you.

Wednesday 8th October
Lk 11:1-4

He was praying in a certain place, and when he ceased, one of his disciples said to him, "Lord, teach us to pray, as John taught his disciples." And he said to them, "When you pray, say: "Father, hallowed be thy name. Thy kingdom come. Give us each day our daily bread; and forgive us our sins, for we ourselves forgive every one who is indebted to us; and lead us not into temptation."

When we speak to a particular person amongst a group of people we pronounce their name; a mother at table with several of her children will say, '*Mike, how was your day?*' or '*Sarah, how was your exam?*' Our Lord's lesson is very clear: when you talk to God, say "*Father*". We are to talk to God as children to their father. How simple is that?! Even a baby can do it!

Ever since that day no human being can say, honestly: '*I don't know how to pray.*' It would be like saying, '*I don't know how to talk to my father or my mother.*' Who taught you to talk to your mum and dad? Have you ever seen an advertisement: "*Now you can learn to talk to your dad. With our method, even you can!*"? Nonsense. You may not know how to talk in public or how to address the Pope or the King, but you certainly know how to talk to your dad. You don't need an appointment to talk to him (neither with your Father God). You don't need to introduce yourself or to be introduced. You don't need a special vocabulary to talk to your mother; you do it in your 'mother tongue' (as with your Father).

You don't need long speeches. Think of a baby: sometimes just a word will do. The baby says '*wa-ha*' and mum gives him water. Sometimes you don't even need words. When there is good mutual knowledge, a gesture, a look can communicate enough. Your Father God loves those conversations. He loves your prayer, your words, your requests, your complaints, your apologies, your looks, your visits, your time... He loves you so much! So, don't say that you don't know how to pray. That doesn't wash. "*You say that you don't know how to pray? Put yourself in the presence of God, and once you have said, 'Lord, I don't know how to pray!' rest assured that you have begun to do so*" (St Josemaría). Mary, Master of prayer, teach me to talk to my Father God.

Thursday 9th October
Lk 11:5-13

And he said to them, "Ask, and it will be given you; seek, and you will find; knock, and it will be opened to you. For every one who asks receives, and he who seeks finds, and to him who knocks it will be opened. What father among you, if his son asks for a fish, will instead of a fish give him a serpent; or if he asks for an egg, will give him a scorpion? If you then, who are evil, know how to give good gifts to your children, how much more will the heavenly Father give the Holy Spirit to those who ask him!"

Jesus can't lie: "*every one who asks receives*." And 'every one' means *everyone*. But we need to ask for it. It's not enough to need something; neither is it enough that Jesus knows what we need; it's not even enough that Jesus wants to give us what we need... We need to *ask* for it.

There is a story of a man who died. As his Guardian Angel was leading him towards the gates of Heaven, the Angel said to him, "*Come! First I have something to show you!*" Curious, the man followed him to a huge storehouse that had his name written on a banner over the entrance. There he saw lots of things, material and spiritual, that he would have loved to get when he was on earth. "*This was exactly what I needed before my wedding!*," complained the man. "*And that*," he continued saying, "*if I had had that on the day I started working!*" One after another, in front of him was all that he had needed during his life. He felt frustrated and asked his angel: "*But why? Why didn't you give me these things when I needed them?*" The angel looked at him with a bit of disappointment on his face and answered: "*Why? Why didn't you ask for them?*"

It would be sad to discover in Heaven that God had some gifts, spiritual and material graces, ready for us but we never got them because we never asked for them. Saints are the people who have asked for more. They were like beggars always asking for everything. They never stopped praying because they knew that God loves giving His children what they need. At any time and in every situation they turned to God for all their needs and from Him they got everything they needed. Mary, Help of Christians, help me to never stop praying, never give up asking for what I need.

Friday 27th week in ordinary time
Friday 10th October
Lk 11:15-26

Jesus said to the Jews: "If Satan is divided against himself, how will his kingdom stand? For you say that I cast out demons by Be-elzebul...But if it is by the finger of God that I cast out demons, then the kingdom of God has come upon you. When a strong man, fully armed, guards his own palace, his goods are in peace; but when one stronger than he assails him and overcomes him, he takes away his armour in which he trusted, and divides his spoil. He who is not with me is against me, and he who does not gather with me scatters."

Lucifer (which means 'morning star') was one of the top angels in glory, wisdom and power. But he thought he could fight against God and, obviously, he was wrong. Then he decided to fight against the children of God. Such a powerful angel against humans was a very one-sided war. He thought he was like the strong man of the parable, fully armed and with his goods undisturbed. But if the devil thought that he could overcome men, he was wrong again, because God became a man and that 'stronger Man' defeated him.

There is a tale of a few ants that were having a banquet over the skin of an elephant while the elephant was sleeping. Suddenly, the elephant got up and with a quick shake sent them off. All but one. One ant found itself hanging on to a hair under the elephant's mouth. From the ground the other ants started calling up to him, "*Come on! Don't give up! It's almost yours. Smother it with your bare hands!*" The devil has less chance of defeating God than that ant had of smothering the elephant...

If we are united to Christ we are safe. And precisely for that reason the enemy will always try to separate us from Him. You see? The enemy thought he could fight against us, and indeed we are no match for him, but he trembles at the Name of Jesus, he trembles at the name of Our Lady, and "*he trembles and flees at the sight of your Guardian Angel*", as St John Bosco taught. Do you see the whole picture? A good Christian is shielded behind Jesus, Our Lady, St Joseph (who is called "Terror of the demons"), St Michael the Archangel, your Guardian Angel... It is certainly a one-sided battle: the enemy has no chance. Mary, Queen of Angels, let me be always shielded by you.

Saturday 27th week in ordinary time
Saturday 11th October
Lk 11:27-28

As he said this, a woman in the crowd raised her voice and said to him, "Blessed is the womb that bore you, and the breasts that you sucked!" But he said, "Blessed rather are those who hear the word of God and keep it!"

The most beautiful thing ever said of Our Lady was what Jesus said of her: she was always ready to hear the Word of God, to keep it and follow it. It was in prayer that Mary heard the Word of God, His Will for her; there she got the grace she needed to carry it out. 'Prayer': the best way to make decisions in our lives. *"Never make a decision without stopping to consider the matter in the presence of God,"* said St Josemaría; a very sound piece of advice.

During our life we will have to make decisions about many issues: reading, good use of time, studies, family, friends, career. God made us for happiness, for greatness - and He knows how to get it. Our paths are all different and personal, so we need to discover the Will of God for us. We need to ask for light to see His Will. We need to want to hear His Word: We need to pray, to talk to God.

The Russian author, Gorki, tells the story of a thinker who decided to rest for a few days in a monastery. His name was written on the door of his room. At night he couldn't sleep and decided to take a stroll through the impressive cloister. When he came back he discovered that there wasn't enough light to find his room; all the doors around the cloister looked alike; all had names on them but he couldn't read them. He didn't want to wake the monks so he spent the night wandering along the huge, dark corridor. With the first light of dawn he at last saw the door of his room and realised that he had passed in front of it a hundred times that night without recognising it. Like the man in the story, we need light to see which door to open. And that light comes with prayer.

We need to be souls of prayer. Not just souls who say prayers, but souls who pray, who have a personal conversation with God. Mary, Virgin most Faithful, as Jesus blessed you for hearing His Word and for keeping It, you can be my Teacher of prayer. I want to talk to God like you did in your Home in Nazareth, like you do now in Heaven. Mary, teach me to pray.

Twenty-eighth Sunday in Ordinary Time
Sunday 12th October
Lk 17:11-19

As Jesus entered a village, he was met by ten lepers, who stood at a distance and lifted up their voices and said, "Jesus, Master, have mercy on us." When he saw them he said to them, "Go and show yourselves to the priests." And as they went they were cleansed. Then one of them, when he saw that he was healed, turned back, praising God with a loud voice; and he fell on his face at Jesus' feet, giving him thanks. Now he was a Samaritan. Then said Jesus, "Were not ten cleansed? Where are the nine? Was no one found to return and give praise to God except this foreigner?"

It's interesting to see that Jesus missed a bit of gratitude from these lepers. They came to be healed. They made a long journey, suffered a lot, called out to Jesus for healing and Jesus healed them. After that only one came back. Jesus didn't perform the miracle to be thanked, but He did miss the lepers' appreciation. *"Were not ten cleansed? Where are the other nine?"* How easily we can 'use' God like this: We ask Him to do something for us and when He gives it, we take it for granted. How many gifts of God we can take for granted: your life, your family, your talents, your health, the fact that you can read, talk, listen, see, walk...

There is a story of a father of a poor family with many problems who started asking God for help. God put an Angel in charge to look after that family and immediately the situation started to change: financially all was sorted out, his children stopped using drugs, they began to go to Mass on Sunday and to be generous collaborators of charities. They had everything they wanted... but they weren't happy. When the man was on his deathbed, the Angel appeared before him and asked, *"Have you and those you love been happy?"* *"No,"* answered the desolate old man, *"We have everything and are incomparably better off than before... but we still are not happy. Why?"* The Angel replied, *"I have given you all you asked for. But there is a most important gift that you never requested: the gift of gratitude. You learned how to give, how to share your things with others. But you never learned to be grateful. And without gratitude, you take everything for granted, you don't enjoy what you have as gifts; without gratitude there is no happiness."* Mary, Cause of our Joy, teach me to be grateful.

Monday 28th week in ordinary time
Monday 13th October
Lk 11:29-32

When the crowds were increasing, he began to say, "This generation is an evil generation; it seeks a sign, but no sign shall be given to it except the sign of Jonah. For as Jonah became a sign to the men of Nineveh, so will the Son of man be to this generation...The men of Nineveh will arise at the judgment with this generation and condemn it; for they repented at the preaching of Jonah, and behold, something greater than Jonah is here."

Sometimes in our prayer we can think what it would be like to travel back in time and be able to hear Jesus 2,000 years ago preaching in Jerusalem; to see Him healing people, walk with Him along the roads of Judea, spend time chatting with Him. Wouldn't it be great? Well the fact is that many people heard Him, saw Him and walked and talked with Him and yet they didn't want to be His disciples. They saw the Son of God made man but that was not enough for them – they wanted a sign!

Someone said that mediocrity could be defined as being in front of 'greatness' and not recognising it. Those contemporaries of Our Lord stood before the greatness of the Son of God and many didn't realise it. Or maybe they realised at the beginning but later they got used to Him, took His miracles and Words for granted... Too bad to get used to having God in the midst of us.

Lucy, a four-year-old girl, went for the first time to her grandparents' country house. At night, when everything was dark outside, she suddenly came running in from the garden, stormed into the lounge where the grown-ups were having coffee and started shouting to her mum, "*Come! Come, mum!*" and pulling her hand, the girl urged her to stand up and follow her out to the garden. Mum rushed out behind the child, fearing that something was wrong. Once in the garden, Lucy pointed at the sky with her little finger: "*Look!*" There, the startling sight of millions of blinking stars covering the whole sky had the child dumbstruck; and the mum as well.

Mary, Mother of the Eucharist, with your help, may I never get used to having your Son in the Tabernacle and being able to see Him, talk to Him... eat Him! There is Someone greater than Jonah there.

Tuesday 28th week in ordinary time
Tuesday 14th October
Lk 11:37-41

A Pharisee asked him to dine with him; so he went in and sat at table. The Pharisee was astonished to see that he did not first wash before dinner. And the Lord said to him, "Now you Pharisees cleanse the outside of the cup and of the dish, but inside you are full of extortion and wickedness. You fools! Did not he who made the outside make the inside also? But give for alms those things which are within; and behold, everything is clean for you."

How quick that Pharisee was to judge Jesus! How quick some people are to jump to conclusions, just because someone else doesn't seem to live up to their standards. The Pharisee had invited Jesus to dine with him, and was already judging Jesus before the dinner had even started. He thought Jesus was neglecting the tradition of the elders by not washing His Hands, when in fact it was he, the Pharisee, who had failed to live charity by judging and condemning Jesus in his mind.

An old lady who had been mugged was behind the two-way mirror contemplating a few suspects in the police line-up. Police officer: "*Madam, can you identify the man who robbed you?*" Granny: "*Most certainly.*" Police: "*Are you sure?*" Granny: "*Absolutely. It was the small guy dressed in red.*" Police: "*That's... that's a fire extinguisher, madam.*" Granny: "*Really? Well, now, you make me doubt...*" Moments before, the old lady had been most certain that the fire extinguisher should go to prison.

Like the Pharisee and the old lady, many people are absolutely certain of their judgements... and yet, on many occasions they are wrong. Jesus was very clear: "*Judge not, and you will not be judged; condemn not, and you will not be condemned*" (Lk 6:37). The problem with this sin against charity is that it is an 'internal sin'. No one sees it, but it damages us as does any other sin. And because it's not seen, many people don't fight against it. It's not totally invisible, though, because those who have this critical spirit are like Ebenezer Scrooge in Charles Dickens' *A Christmas Carol*: a miserable grouch who is never happy with anyone or anything.

Mary, Our Lady of Charity, help me to love people and not waste time judging them.

Wednesday 15th October
Lk 11:42-46

"But woe to you Pharisees! For you tithe mint and rue and every herb, and neglect justice and the love of God; these you ought to have done, without neglecting the others. Woe to you Pharisees! For you love the best seat in the synagogues and salutations in the market places."

The tithe was a requirement of the Law in which all Israelites were to give 10% of everything they earned and grew to the temple. Pharisees were very diligent about paying that. They didn't have any problem '*doing*' or '*giving*' things. Their problem was that they had neglected "*justice and the love of God.*"

Apparently they thought that God could be satisfied with things. They didn't consider that God doesn't need 10% of anything because He OWNS everything already. God is not an employer. God didn't create men to "work for Him". God created us to LOVE Him. God doesn't want our things. He wants our hearts. The only 'gift' with which we can satisfy Him is 'love'.

You remember the story of Cain and Abel. The Book of Genesis says that "*Cain brought to the Lord an offering of the fruit of the ground, and Abel brought of the firstlings of his flock and of their fat portions.*" But God loved Abel's offering and rejected Cain's. Why? Certainly it has nothing to do with God not liking vegetables or preferring meat. It wasn't the *thing* that was offered. It was the *love* with which it was offered. Maybe Cain was just fulfilling his duty. But Abel loved God and wanted to offer Him the best he could.

When we go to Mass, say our prayers, work and study or we offer up some sacrifice, we need to make sure that we aren't just fulfilling our duty: we are loving God. Kissing your grandma, for example, can be just a duty (grandchildren are supposed to kiss grandmas) or a real act of affection. Think of a bride asking her groom: '*Do you love me?*' and the newly-married man, distracted, looking at his phone, waving a hand and replying, '*Yeah, yeah, whatever!*' Mary, my Mother, help me to put my heart into everything that I do for God, to do everything for the right intention; teach me, Mother, to love God with everything I am and everything I do.

Thursday 16th October
Lk 11:47-54

"Woe to you lawyers! For you have taken away the key of knowledge; you did not enter yourselves, and you hindered those who were entering."

These 'lawyers' shouldn't be confused with modern-day solicitors or barristers. They were called 'lawyers' because they were in charge of teaching the 'Law of Moses'. They studied the Bible and knew everything about it; but apparently they weren't practising it or teaching it properly to the people. They knew the Scripture but they didn't know God. They read the Bible but didn't know Its Author. They spoke *about* God but they never spoke *with* God. If they had spent less time talking *about* God and more time talking *to* God they would have recognised Jesus as the Son of God and the Messiah they were expecting. They weren't men of prayer.

St Teresa of Avila is a good teacher of prayer. She became a nun at the age of 20. For more than 20 years she lived in the Monastery but didn't pray properly. She certainly said prayers… but didn't have a personal dialogue with God. Visitors often popped into the monastery, distracting her from her duties and maintaining frivolous and vain conversations. One day she saw a picture of Jesus scourged and wearing the crown of thorns; she felt sorry for her waste of time, for not loving Jesus as she should. Teresa fell on her knees in tears and implored Jesus to change her life. And Jesus heard her prayer.

Those dialogues with God changed her life and she changed the world. Fully in love with God, she wrote remarkable teachings on prayer and how to talk to God. "*For prayer,*" she said, "*is nothing else than being on terms of friendship with God.*" She taught that all that was needed was for people to look upon Jesus as He is represented in the Gospel, and to talk to Him: "*This friendly conversation will not be much thinking but much loving, not many words but rather a relaxed conversation with moments of silence as there must be between friends.*"

Holy Mary, Mother of God, teach me to talk to your Son as friends do!

Friday 28th week in ordinary time
Friday 17th October
Lk 12:1-7

Jesus began to say to his disciples, "Do not fear those who kill the body, and after that have no more that they can do. But I will warn you whom to fear: fear him who, after he has killed, has power to cast into hell; yes, I tell you, fear him! Are not five sparrows sold for two pennies? And not one of them is forgotten before God. Why, even the hairs of your head are all numbered. Fear not; you are of more value than many sparrows."

We are used to hearing Jesus say "*Do not fear*", but this is the first (and last) time in which we hear Him say "*fear*": fear the enemy who can cast us into hell. "*Yes, I tell you, fear him!*" Jesus said. And if Jesus had left the explanation there it would have sounded a bit scary. But then He went on: God does not forget sparrows, so "*Fear not; you are of more value than many sparrows.*" That's better! '*Fear not*' sounds more like Jesus.

The enemy has power. That's a fact. So we shouldn't be imprudent or too self-confident with him. He is like a *tram*: we aren't scared of trams but we are prudent and never step on its tracks when the tram is close. We are also careful with the devil. Jesus, though, has comforted us with His Words: "*fear not*" because God loves us more than the rest of creation.

In actual fact, it is the enemy who lives in fear. Have you ever seen one of those dogs that start barking at you loudly from a distance and, when you get close to it, the frightened dog runs away? This 'powerful angel' trembles in fear when the Holy Name of Jesus is pronounced. Like insects when we use mosquito repellent, the devil runs away when we invoke Our Lady, St Joseph, St Michael or our Guardian Angel, or we kiss our crucifix, hold the Rosary or use holy water. If we are prudent and stay close to Our Lord, the enemy can tempt us - but we have nothing to fear.

The enemy got his victory with Adam and Eve in paradise. But, ever since Jesus died on the Cross, he has been running away in fear. You, Virgin most Powerful, have crushed the head of the serpent who appears often represented with the apple stuffed in his mouth. Your children fear nothing if they are close to you, Mother.

St Luke, Evangelist
Saturday 18th October
Lk 10:1-9

After this the Lord appointed seventy others, and sent them on ahead of him, two by two, into every town and place where he himself was about to come. And he said to them, "The harvest is plentiful, but the labourers are few; pray therefore the Lord of the harvest to send out labourers into his harvest."

These 72 disciples couldn't be more different from one another. They weren't a set of apostles in uniforms with written speeches to be read in a particular tone of voice, all in the same way. They were all different and had different talents, different accents, different ways of expressing themselves. They were not an army of clones or robots because God needs free and genuine disciples, not impersonators. St Paul explains that God called some to be *"apostles, some prophets, some evangelists, some pastors and teachers..."*

St Luke was a physician. He wasn't a skilful rhetorical speaker or a wise Scripture scholar. He was a faithful companion of St Paul on his trips, absorbing his teachings on their missionary journeys. There is something he was good at: writing. He was inspired by the Holy Spirit to write his Gospel and the Book of the Acts of the Apostles. He researched the life and preaching of Our Lord, carefully interviewing witnesses who were still living and collating all the necessary material. Almost half of the content of his Gospel is not to be found in the other Gospels. To him we owe, for instance, the account of Jesus' Infancy that he probably gathered from Our Lady.

Luke had that talent: he could write very elegant Greek. God didn't need two St Pauls or two St Peters to spread the Gospel; He needed one Paul and one Peter, and one Luke... and one you. He needs people with different talents but who put their gifts at the service of the Holy Spirit. The Gospel has to be spread throughout the world. Some will use pulpits, others can use websites, blogs, social media, radio stations, music, poems, novels, articles, paintings, films... There are so many different ways! You have your talents as well: what can you do?

Mary, Mother of the Evangelists, help me to put all my talents at the disposal of the Holy Spirit so that He can spread the Gospel effectively everywhere.

Twenty-ninth Sunday in Ordinary Time
Sunday 19th October
Lk 18:1-8

Jesus told them a parable, to the effect that they ought always to pray and not lose heart. He said, "In a certain city there was a judge who neither feared God nor regarded man; and there was a widow in that city who kept coming to him and saying, 'Vindicate me against my adversary.' For a while he refused; but afterward he said to himself, 'Though I neither fear God nor regard man, yet because this widow bothers me, I will vindicate her, or she will wear me out by her continual coming.'" And the Lord said, "Hear what the unrighteous judge says. And will not God vindicate his elect, who cry to him day and night? Will he delay long over them? I tell you, he will vindicate them speedily. Nevertheless, when the Son of man comes, will he find faith on earth?"

Jesus wants us to pray without losing heart. But this Gospel passage finishes with a reproach for the lack of faith. Many people don't pray because they don't expect their prayers to be answered. For some, prayer is the last resort. After trying everything and finding that nothing succeeds, then the only thing left is to pray. A doctor had a reputation of being incompetent. After a check-up his patient asked, "*Is it something serious, doctor?*" The doctor replied, "*We are in the hands of God, madam*" and left the room. The woman turned to the nurse and said, "*Is it that bad?*" The nurse smiled at the lady and answered, "*Believe me, madam: it's way better to be in the hands of God than in the hands of this doctor!*"

It is definitely way better to be in the Hands of God than in the hands of men, but people lack trust in those Divine Hands. If we had faith in the power of prayer we could turn the world upside down in a tick. The founder of an orphanage undergoing financial hardships came to St John Mary Vianney to seek advice. He was considering the idea of attracting public opinion by using the press to make, as he said "*a bit of noise.*" The holy priest of Ars replied, "*Instead of making noise in the newspapers, go and make noise in front of the Tabernacle.*" It's a good piece of advice. Let's trust in the power of prayer. The world needs more Christians praying on their knees than creating websites or typing posts and tweets.

Mary, Help of Christians, help me to never give up on prayer; to have faith in the power of prayer.

Monday 29th week in ordinary time
Monday 20th October
Lk 12:13-21

Jesus told them a parable, saying, "The land of a rich man brought forth plentifully; and he thought to himself, 'What shall I do, for I have nowhere to store my crops?' And he said, 'I will do this: I will pull down my barns, and build larger ones; and there I will store all my grain and my goods. And I will say to my soul, Soul, you have ample goods laid up for many years; take your ease, eat, drink, be merry.' But God said to him, 'Fool! This night your soul is required of you; and the things you have prepared, whose will they be?' So is he who lays up treasure for himself, and is not rich toward God."

You know how the pharaohs of Ancient Egypt used to be buried surrounded by all their treasures. It only served to ensure that their graves would be plundered and their treasures taken away. *"For what will it profit a man, if he gains the whole world and forfeits his life?"*

A man who was travelling to the Middle East went to visit a holy hermit who lived in a cave with nothing other than was necessary. The man, surprised at his poverty, exclaimed, *"Where is your furniture?"* The wise hermit answered, *"And where is yours?"* "But", replied the traveller, *"I am on a journey. I don't intend to live here!"* "So am I," answered the holy man, *"just on my way to Heaven. I don't intend to live on earth for ever!"*

Everyone has an ambition. As Mother Angelica explained once, some people don't spare any effort to become a banker or a physicist; they would devote their whole lives to being able to add letters like MD, PhD, MBA, at the end of their names. Some people will do anything to gain honours, esteem, fame or money... But all our titles, diplomas, qualifications and credentials will be useless to get into Heaven. The only worthwhile ambition is to add **'St'** before our names: to become *saints*. To become St Thomas, St Charles, St Catherine, St John Capistrano, St ... (fill the gap with your name). We should spare no effort to attain it, because that will be the only achievement that will last for ever!

Mary, my Mother, help me make it my great ambition to gather a great treasure in Heaven by loving God on earth.

Tuesday 29th week in ordinary time
Tuesday 21st October
Lk 12:35-38

"Let your loins be girded and your lamps burning, and be like men who are waiting for their master to come home from the marriage feast, so that they may open to him at once when he comes and knocks. Blessed are those servants whom the master finds awake when he comes; truly, I say to you, he will gird himself and have them sit at table, and he will come and serve them. If he comes in the second watch, or in the third, and finds them so, blessed are those servants!"

Have you ever been caught red-handed doing something you were not supposed to do? It's an awkward feeling, isn't it? Do you remember Adam and Eve embarrassed, trying to hide themselves after their sin? 'Awkward historical moment': where could you hide from God?

But of course, if we were always doing what we ought to do we wouldn't need a hiding place, would we? This is called 'unity of life'. *Unity of life* is that feature of lives of the saints which ensured they were always doing the right thing, because they realised that God is always with them. If your mum, your dad, your teacher or priest was there with you, how would you behave? Well, God is there. He is not like a busybody watching you through CCTV cameras all the time to know what you are doing. He is a Father who has an eye on His children because He loves them. If I could remember that God is always at my side, watching what I do, He would surely be proud of me. One day, suddenly, time will be over and we will go to meet Him as we are... as we have been.

In the year 79 AD, Pompeii, a roman city in Naples, was buried under 4 to 6 metres of lava and ash in the sudden eruption of Mount Vesuvius. It was so sudden that most of the 11,000 inhabitants had no chance to run away. When the place was discovered in 1599, archaeologists realised that the exact size and position of people, dogs and objects could be recovered just by filling holes they found in the lava with plaster and removing the lava once the plaster set: the sentinel was at his post, a dog wandering in the streets, some people sleeping, a mother protecting her baby. How will God find me at the end of my life? Mary, my Mother, help me to be always ready like a faithful servant.

Wednesday 22nd October
Lk 12:39-48

Jesus said to his disciples: "that servant who knew his master's will, but did not make ready or act according to his will, shall receive a severe beating. But he who did not know, and did what deserved a beating, shall receive a light beating. Every one to whom much is given, of him will much be required; and of him to whom men commit much they will demand the more."

This is the same as saying: "*Do not compare yourself with anyone else because you are not anyone else*". It's a very natural thing. When your mother asks you to clear the table, you check if your brother is also doing something. When you are told to load the dishwasher, you make sure that your sister also has a job to do. And when we do something wrong, we try to excuse ourselves by immediately pointing out others' wrongdoings.

Comparisons are often used just to excuse ourselves. Like the boy who was asked by his dad if he had passed the last exam he had taken. "*I didn't pass, Dad,*" said the boy, "*but I was top of those who didn't!*" What consolation would it be to fail to enter Heaven but be top of the list of those left outside?

God doesn't give the same talents to everyone because He doesn't entrust the same mission to everyone. From some individuals He expects more because He gives them more. And you are on the list of the privileged ones. Not many people know that they can talk to God (like you do); not many know what you know about God; not many have had the Christian formation that you have. Some people still don't know what sin is, but you do. For that reason God will demand more from you than from others. The enemy loves it when we compare ourselves to others because that way we are being less demanding on ourselves. Others are not expected to give as much as you are expected to give, because they are not you. This would be like Leo Messi playing football in a school team. Surely you couldn't demand from the other boys what you would expect from him. And if he spent his life playing in that team it would be a waste of his talents. God has given you great talents also. He wants you close to Him. Mary, my Mother, don't allow me to waste my talents, to waste my life!

Thursday 23rd October
Lk 12:49-53

"I came to cast fire upon the earth; and would that it were already kindled! I have a baptism to be baptised with; and how I am constrained until it is accomplished!"

The fire of God's Love, like any big fire, spreads on contact: one tree ignites the next one and that sets the next ablaze. A tiny spark can set a whole forest alight. That's what a soul in love with God can do and what Jesus is longing for. But those who want to set the world on fire with the Love of God may have to fight many battles. All saints have had to struggle against the resistance of those who hate that fire because they hate the light: the light of the Gospel. Saints are strong, they are ready for the spiritual battle. As Peter Kreeft says: *'God has made saints out of sinners, but never out of wimps.'*

St John Paul II is a good example. Karol was born in Wadowice, Poland, on May 18, 1920. His elder sister Olga had died before his birth. His mother died when he was 9. His only brother Edmund also died when he was 12 and eventually his father passed away during WWII when he was 20. He had no family left. The Nazi occupying forces closed his university and young Karol had to work in a quarry and in the Solvay chemical factory for 5 years. During that time, aware of his call to the priesthood, he began studying courses in the clandestine seminary of Krakow. Many of his friends were killed. When he became a priest the communists spied on him. At the age of sixty, an assassin shot him and he nearly died. As an old man, he suffered from an intestinal tumour, a femur fracture and the debilitating Parkinson's disease that rendered him immobile, distorted his physical appearance, and finally took away his ability to speak.

It doesn't look like the story of a powerful man. However, he changed the world with the fire of the love of God that he had in his heart. St John Paul inspired many countries in Eastern Europe to turn away from Communism; his zeal for the Gospel took him on apostolic trips all over the world. Neither illnesses, Nazis, communists nor bullets could stop that flame because it's a divine Fire! Saints are not made out of wimps. Mary, Queen of all Saints, help me to be strong and reliable, so that I can serve your Son to spread this divine Fire.

Friday 24th October
Friday 29th week in ordinary time
Lk 12:54-59

He also said to the multitudes, "When you see a cloud rising in the west, you say at once, 'A shower is coming'; and so it happens. And when you see the south wind blowing, you say, 'There will be scorching heat'; and it happens. You hypocrites! You know how to interpret the appearance of earth and sky; but why do you not know how to interpret the present time?"

The world, like the masterpiece of an artist, is marked by the signature of its Creator. We receive the gifts of God and can take them for granted: our lives, our family, the world, our intelligence, friends... everything! But some people do not bother to find out where all these come from and why they have been granted to them.

In Jules Verne's novel '*Mysterious Island*' he writes about a group of men shipwrecked on an unknown island. They believed themselves to be alone but at critical moments they received help: a toolbox; a rope hanging from a rock; enemies exterminated... However, they didn't know where it came from. One night, finding themselves lost at sea after an exploration, they saw a bonfire from afar that served as a beacon to guide them. This fire saved their lives. The seafarers believed that the fire had been lit by their leader, who had remained on land. But later they discover that it wasn't him. The main character of the novel tries to find the mysterious helper, but some others don't care who provides that help; they just benefit from it without asking questions. As in Verne's novel, some people see the world but don't bother to ask 'Who made it?' After all, 'nothing comes from nothing'. If we find a football in the jungle we wonder how it ended up there; we need an explanation because we know that footballs don't grow on trees. A human soul - capable of loving and thinking - is to the material universe what a football is to a jungle.

Towards the end of the adventure, the main character says: "*What I do know is that a beneficent hand has constantly protected us since our arrival on the island, that we all owe our lives to a good, generous, and powerful being.*" He did not stop searching and eventually he found his benefactor. Mary, Mother of the Creator, help men to encourage everyone never to stop looking for the reason behind everything, searching for the Truth.

Saturday 29th week in ordinary time
Saturday 25th October
Lk 13:1-9

Jesus told this parable: "A man had a fig tree planted in his vineyard; and he came seeking fruit on it and found none. And he said to the vinedresser, 'Lo, these three years I have come seeking fruit on this fig tree, and I find none. Cut it down; why should it use up the ground?' And he answered him, 'Let it alone, sir, this year also, till I dig about it and put on manure. And if it bears fruit next year, well and good; but if not, you can cut it down.'"

Nothing was missing from the tree (sun light, soil, water, care...) except fruit. It had everything it needed to give fruit except determination. It decided to produce leaves, to grow and give shade... but no more than that. It wanted all the advantages of being in the vineyard without all the responsibilities that were expected of it. It wanted to do part of it, but not everything. Our Lord also has been patient with us. If we don't give the fruit that He expects from us, He prunes us like a tree (although unlike a tree, we find this painful) and He gives us more graces (fertiliser) so that we can start bearing fruit. Because He chose us to give fruit, fruit of holiness - and we have all we need to bear that fruit. No one else can be blamed for my lack of holiness: neither the devil, nor the environment, nor any other circumstance: *If I am not 'holy' it's just because I don't 'wholly' want to be.*

During a catechism class the teacher was explaining to the children that if they wanted to become saints, they had to pray every day. "*Every single day?*" asked one of the boys. "*Why, of course,*" replied the teacher, "*Do you want to be a saint?*" "*Yes,*" answered the boy. "*But without overdoing it!*" This boy should have heard St Thérèse of Lisieux saying, "*You cannot be half a saint. You must be a whole saint or no saint at all*".

It's time to make up your mind. You are now talking to God. If you want to be a saint tell Him right now because He is looking for volunteers. Decide! Because 'indecision' is a 'decision' already. "*Do not be satisfied with mediocrity*" (St John Paul II). "*Why don't you give yourself to God once and for all... really... NOW!*" (St Josemaría). Mary, Queen of all Saints, help me to give fruits of holiness, because I 'wholly' want to be 'holy'.

Thirtieth Sunday in Ordinary Time
Sunday 26th October
Lk 18:9-14

"Two men went up into the temple to pray, one a Pharisee and the other a tax collector. The Pharisee stood and prayed thus with himself, 'God, I thank thee that I am not like other men, extortioners, unjust, adulterers, or even like this tax collector. I fast twice a week, I give tithes of all that I get.' But the tax collector, standing far off, would not even lift up his eyes to heaven, but beat his breast, saying, 'God, be merciful to me a sinner!' I tell you, this man went down to his house justified rather than the other; for every one who exalts himself will be humbled, but he who humbles himself will be exalted."

Poor man! This is what we mean by the expression '*holier-than-thou*'. This Pharisee, haughty and proud, self-sufficient and self-satisfied, was presenting before God his "*decorations*", his many "*merits*". How ridiculous! He seems to think that God, like a teacher, is satisfied if you do your homework. He seems to think that he could 'buy' Heaven with his works. It seems that he was convinced that he 'deserved' Heaven. Pride, conceit, contempt, critical thoughts, but specially, lack of love for God and others, are sins. He was a sinner but didn't know it. All his works, done without love, were as useless as a chocolate teapot, like sewing without thread.

We should examine ourselves to see if we have a bit of this attitude as well: '*I thank You, Lord, because I'm not like my friends who cheat in exams, or don't go to Mass on Sundays. I go to Mass twice a week, I pray the rosary with my family and even use the iPray* almost *every day. I tidy my room once a week and do the dishwasher when I'm told...*' Be aware that St Peter will not be very impressed with your list of 'merits' the day you meet him at the gates of Heaven, because he will also have a list with all your sins (that one which the Pharisee forgot to bring to his prayer). We will get to Heaven, not by 'how much we did' but by 'how much we loved'. An mp3 player can say prayers ('*mp3 prayer*'), but it can't love. We can do both things at the same time.

It's by the Mercy of God that we will enter Heaven. All the things we have done will help us if - and only if - we did them out of love. Mary, Mother of Fair Love, may I learn from you to do everything for Love, out of love.

Monday 30th week in ordinary time
Monday 27th October
Lk 13:10-17

Now he was teaching in one of the synagogues on the sabbath. And there was a woman who had had a spirit of infirmity for eighteen years; she was bent over and could not fully straighten herself. And when Jesus saw her, he called her and said to her, "Woman, you are freed from your infirmity." And he laid his hands upon her, and immediately she was made straight.

For eighteen years that lady couldn't fully straighten herself; she couldn't look up to Heaven or the beauty of the landscape; she could only see the ground and her own feet. She couldn't look at people's faces... only at their feet. Eighteen years of misery. Until Jesus laid His Hands upon her and changed her life. How many people walk around the world like that: just looking down at the earth and never up to Heaven. That is what sin does. If we don't go to Confession we have to carry our sins on our shoulders. And sin weighs us down like a heavy burden bending our back over and preventing us from looking up.

The sacrament of Confession frees us from that burden and allows us to look up, filling us with real joy. What joy the lady in today's Gospel experienced when she found herself released from suffering after 18 years! A simple touch of Jesus made the change. A simple absolution from the priest is enough to make that change no matter how long the problem has been going on. What a joy to be forgiven! And how that joy attracts other souls to go to Confession!

A lady once went into the confessional and started making her Confession when, after a few minutes, she realised... that there was no priest on the other side of the grille! When she saw that she was talking alone, she had a fit of laughter and left the confessional planning to come another time. When the following day she went back to the church, another lady stopped her and said: *–'I need to thank you. Today I went to Confession for the first time in a long time. I couldn't bring myself to do it... but yesterday I saw you coming out of the confessional so happy, so cheerful that I decided to come to Confession as well!'* Luckily she didn't know the whole story. Holy Mary, Mother of Mercy, with your intercession, may many sinners be able to experience the joy of God's Mercy.

Sts Simon and Jude, Apostles
Tuesday 28th October
Lk 6:12–19

Jesus went out to the mountain to pray; and all night he continued in prayer to God. And when it was day, he called his disciples, and chose from them twelve, whom he named apostles; Simon, whom he named Peter, and Andrew his brother, and James and John, and Philip, and Bartholomew, and Matthew, and Thomas, and James the son of Alphaeus, and Simon who was called the Zealot, and Judas the son of James, and Judas Iscariot, who became a traitor.

Jesus prayed the whole night. He prayed for the new Apostles He was going to call that day. They were going to be given great responsibilities. Jesus had many disciples but only twelve Apostles. He was surrounded by thousands but only these twelve were given special missions. That doesn't mean that the other disciples were just 'second class'. In a family too there are no 'second class' members, but neither do they have the same roles and responsibilities. A football team with 11 players in the same position would never work. When Jesus chose His Twelve, no one came to complain to Him because they hadn't been chosen or because they were better than Peter or joined Him before Matthew... '*NOBODY has a right to be chosen for a particular vocation*'.

God calls some to be priests, or to a celibate life in the middle of the world, or to be nuns or friars or fathers or mothers... God made them and knows what He made them for. We can, of course, turn down God's proposal and do something else with our talents. Bl Álvaro used an interesting example. Imagine that a chair is free and decides that it doesn't like people sitting on it, so it wants to be a hanger! Upside down and attached to the wall, it insists that 4 coats can be hung on it at a time. Sure, but the carpenter who made it wouldn't approve of the change. If the carpenter wanted a hanger, he could easily make one (with 4 or 16 hooks if necessary); what's more, everyone who saw it would think '*Why is that chair upside-down and hanging on the wall?*' We know 'what' it is, regardless of what it thinks it is. You and I have a vocation. We can certainly do different things with our talents and our lives, but the Carpenter knows what He made us for. Mary, Queen of the Apostles, help me to follow your Son where He wants, as St Simon and St Jude did... until the end.

Wednesday 29th October
Lk 13:22-30

Someone said to Jesus, "Lord, will those who are saved be few?" And he said to them, "Strive to enter by the narrow door; for many, I tell you, will seek to enter and will not be able. When once the householder has risen up and shut the door, you will begin to stand outside and to knock at the door, saying, 'Lord, open to us.' He will answer you, 'I do not know where you come from.' Then you will begin to say, 'We ate and drank in your presence, and you taught in our streets.' But he will say, 'I tell you, I do not know where you come from; depart from me, all you workers of iniquity!' There you will weep and gnash your teeth"

How many times has your mum told you that *you should not open the door to strangers*? You don't allow a stranger to join you for dinner, use your toilet or spend the night in your house, not even to join your birthday party. Even if the stranger says: '*I am a friend of your friend*' or '*We played football together in the park; do you remember?*' or '*We ate together at the Smiths' barbecue*' or '*I'm also an Arsenal supporter.*' To that person you should reply what your mum taught you: '*Sorry, but I don't know you.*'

In September 2012 a girl organised a party for her 16th birthday. By mistake she left the 'Facebook event invitation' open. On the day of the party up to 600 riot police officers were forced to break up the crowd after more than 3,000 turned up to the party! You see? You open the door for your friends, but you shouldn't for strangers! The same with Jesus. He tells us how some people will come to Him and say '*We ate and drank in your presence... you taught in our streets!*' but Jesus will reply: '*Maybe, but I don't know you*'. We could update the dialogue saying, '*we were there at Mass most Sundays!*' or '*we said grace at meals*' or '*I prayed the Angelus in school!*' But they would get the same reply: '*Sure, but I don't know you*'.

Jesus opens the door to His friends. Friends know each other, they talk to each other, they count on each other: they love each other. God wants to be your Friend. And for friendship to grow you need time, dialogue ... prayer! Does Jesus know you well? It depends on what you say in your prayer. It's very important to answer this question honestly: Is Jesus your Friend? Mary, Most Gracious Advocate, help me to be good friends with your Son.

Thursday 30th October
Lk 13:31-35

Some Pharisees came, and said to him, "Get away from here, for Herod wants to kill you." And he said to them, "Go and tell that fox, 'Behold, I cast out demons and perform cures today and tomorrow, and the third day I finish my course. Nevertheless I must go on my way today and tomorrow and the day following; for it cannot be that a prophet should perish away from Jerusalem'."

I love to see that You, Lord, are never intimidated by any authority on earth: Herod?! "*Go and tell that fox...*" that God writes His own agenda and no authority in the world will change His programme! And so it will be with all the 'Herods' of history, whatever name they use. Because You, Jesus, have a mission and when it comes to saving souls, no Herod, no king, president or mayor on earth can stop You.

And we, Your disciples, will have to do the same if someone tries to prevent Your Name from being known. We will have to remind those who prefer You, my Jesus, to be silent in public life, that they don't decide Your schedule. You, Lord, choose when to speak and when to be silent…

After the Ascension of Our Lord, when the Apostles were brought before the Sanhedrin for preaching and healing in the Name of Jesus, the authorities told them, "*We strictly charged you not to teach in this name, yet here you have filled Jerusalem with your teaching and you intend to bring this man's blood upon us.*" But the apostles were not intimidated and Peter answered, "*We must obey God rather than men.*" The Pharisees didn't like the answer so the Acts of the Apostles (5:40–42) explains that they beat the Apostles, reminded them of the warning again and let them go. But the next verse proves that they didn't follow the advice: "*Then they left the presence of the council, rejoicing that they were counted worthy to suffer dishonour for the Name. And every day in the temple and at home they did not cease teaching and preaching Jesus as the Christ*". And they didn't stop... not until they were killed. Even from Heaven, with Our Lady, Queen of the Apostles, they keep encouraging us to be faithful and to '*tell that fox*' that wants to silence Christ - whoever he may be - that God writes His own agenda!

Friday 31st October
Lk 14:1, 7-11

He told a parable to those who were invited, when he marked how they chose the places of honour, saying to them, "When you are invited by any one to a marriage feast, do not sit down in a place of honour, lest a more eminent man than you be invited by him; and he who invited you both will come and say to you, 'Give place to this man,'...For every one who exalts himself will be humbled, and he who humbles himself will be exalted."

The most subtle sin is pride. That was the sin of Lucifer and the one he taught to Adam and Eve. Lucifer was magnificent but he didn't recognise that everything he had was a gift from God and preferred to do his own will rather than God's Will. And God can only work with humble instruments like Our Lady and St Joseph... That's how saints became 'powerful': with the power of humility.

St John Vianney was the dunce of his class and found it very difficult to learn Latin. In 1812 he went to the seminary and was bottom of the class due to his poor Latin; but when they examined him again in French he was still bottom of the class. For that reason he was asked to leave after five months. He was taught theology privately in French and eventually was ordained at the age of 29. The bishop allowed him to say Mass, but didn't give him permission to hear Confessions or to preach, thinking that he wasn't yet ready. After three years he was appointed to Ars, a village with just over 300 inhabitants, most of them not practising the Faith. He began to pray and offer sacrifices for them.

In 1827 pilgrims (including bishops!) started coming to Ars seeking St John Mary Vianney for Confession and to hear him preach. From 1830 until his death in 1859, four hundred people came each day. By 1855 there was a daily service of two horse buses between Lyons and Ars, and two other buses met the Paris train at Villefranche. The railway station in Lyons even had a special ticket office for people going to Ars... No one in France was more famous than this humble priest. The power of humility!

Holy Mary, Handmaid of the Lord, teach me to be humble like your Son, like you, like the saints, so that I can be effective in bringing souls to God.

November

All Saints
Saturday 1st November
Mt 5:1-12a

Seeing the crowds, he went up on the mountain, and when he sat down his disciples came to him. And he opened his mouth and taught them, saying: "Blessed are the poor in spirit, for theirs is the kingdom of heaven. Blessed are those who mourn, for they shall be comforted. Blessed are the meek, for they shall inherit the earth...Blessed are you when men revile you and persecute you and utter all kinds of evil against you falsely on my account. Rejoice and be glad, for your reward is great in heaven."

"*Rejoice,*" says Our Lord, "*for your reward is great in heaven.*" Today we celebrate a great feast. It's the feast day of all those who are in Heaven whose names we don't know. Heaven is packed with saints. We know the names and lives of many saints. We know of some Popes, bishops and priests; we know of some virgins and martyrs and some heroic mothers and fathers and girls and boys... but there are millions more that we don't know anything about: teachers, shop assistants, housewives, athletes, gardeners and soldiers, children, teenagers, youngsters and old people, sick and healthy, black and white, tall and short, blonde and ginger... from all countries, from all ages, from all trades, from every walk of life.

As a matter of fact in the future this will surely be *our own feast day*. If we allow God to make us saints, we will celebrate the feast of all saints in Heaven. And there they are, worshipping God, perpetually and completely happy with a joy that we, here on earth, can't even imagine. There we will discover how much love, happiness and joy a human heart can take. There we already have an army of intercessors who watch out for us, supporting, encouraging and helping us with their prayers.

When a climber has finally reached the summit of a mountain, the ascent is easier for the remaining roped team that comes behind. From up there, he encourages them, points out the difficulties and warns of the dangers: '*Be careful of those rocks. Watch out!*' '*On the right you'll find a place to hang on to*'; '*Look ahead!*' Saints from Heaven are encouraging us today: '*Come on! You can do it!*' Mary, Queen of All Saints, during this month I want to help the Holy Souls get into Heaven from Purgatory with my prayers and sacrifices!

All the Faithful Departed
Sunday 2nd November
Mk 15:33-39, 16:1-6

And when the sixth hour had come, there was darkness over the whole land until the ninth hour. And at the ninth hour Jesus...uttered a loud cry, and breathed his last...And very early on the first day of the week they went to the tomb when the sun had risen...And entering the tomb, they saw a young man sitting on the right side, dressed in a white robe; and they were amazed. And he said to them, "Do not be amazed; you seek Jesus of Nazareth, who was crucified. He has risen, he is not here; see the place where they laid him."

November is traditionally an especially important month to pray for those in Purgatory. Many visit the graves of the departed today. It's only normal: If you saw a boy being carried away by the current of a river and drowning, and you could save him by just stretching out your hand and grabbing him, wouldn't you help? As long as he lived he would always remember what you had done for him; and you could be sure that he would always be happy to help you in any way he could. Well, the Holy Souls in Purgatory are in a river of suffering right now and you can definitely help them to get out of there with your prayer. Like the boy in the river, they can't do anything for themselves. They suffer and pray an awful lot but can't offer those prayers for themselves. Only we and the saints in Heaven can pray for them and help them to get into Paradise. If we do this, the Holy Souls will be tremendously grateful. They will remember for all eternity that it was our prayers that helped them to enter Heaven. And here on earth we will feel their powerful intercession. This is a *win–win* situation: we pray for them, they pray for us.

One day St Padre Pio had an apparition of a Holy Soul in Purgatory asking for prayers to go to Paradise. St Padre Pio promised to offer the Mass on the following day for him. When that soul heard that he had to wait he cried, "*Cruel!*" Then he wept and disappeared. "*That complaint,*" said St Pio, "*produced in me a wound to the heart that I have felt and I will feel my whole life. In fact I would have been able to immediately send that soul to Heaven but I condemned him to remain another night in the flames of Purgatory.*" Mary, Mother of the Holy Souls, use my prayers and sacrifices to help your children get into Heaven.

Monday 3rd November
Lk 14:12-14

Jesus said also to the man who had invited him, "When you give a dinner or a banquet, do not invite your friends or your brothers or your kinsmen or rich neighbours, lest they also invite you in return, and you be repaid. But when you give a feast, invite the poor, the maimed, the lame, the blind, and you will be blessed, because they cannot repay you. You will be repaid at the resurrection of the just."

Generosity is giving without expecting anything back. A holy priest explained it very well to an old lady. She wanted to pay him for having brought Holy Communion to her when she was sick. The priest said, "*Please, don't. Please don't pay me. Let Jesus pay me instead,*" and with a smile he added, "*He's rich. He pays much more!*" Generous people know how to give love, understanding, thanks or material help without ever asking to be loved, understood, thanked or helped themselves. They give and forget that they have given. They never think about what they can get, but about what they can give. And the more they give, the happier they are and the closer God is to them. Those who are generous with others can be generous with God. Love is the reason to give and the reward as well. We give out of love; we give because we love; whatever it is that we give, it's always love that we are giving.

The joy of the lover is to love. The joy of the generous giver is to give. They always wonder what else they can give. '*If God gave Himself entirely*', they argue, '*why shouldn't I give myself entirely also?*' They want to give 'everything' and God will repay them with 'everything'. Bishop Eijo y Garay had an interview with Bl Álvaro before his ordination. Álvaro del Portillo had been one of the most brilliant students in his university; he had great intellectual talents and enormous professional prestige as an engineer. The Bishop asked him, '*But, Álvaro, do you realise that you will lose your "personality"? You will go from being a prestigious engineer to becoming just one more priest*'. '*Know, your Excellency,*' replied Bl Alvaro, '*that I gave my "personality" to Our Lord many years ago.*' He didn't have money or possessions to give, but he could give his career, his prestige, his personality! When you give to God... you just give everything. Mary, Mother Most Generous, teach me to give without counting the cost.

Tuesday 31st week in ordinary time
Tuesday 4th November
Lk 14:15-24

Jesus said, "A man once gave a great banquet, and invited many; and at the time for the banquet he sent his servant to say to those who had been invited, 'Come; for all is now ready.' But they all alike began to make excuses...Then the householder in anger said to his servant, 'Go out quickly to the streets and lanes of the city, and bring in the poor and maimed and blind and lame.' And the servant said, 'Sir, what you commanded has been done, and still there is room.' And the master said to the servant, 'Go out to the highways and hedges, and compel people to come in, that my house may be filled. For I tell you, none of those men who were invited shall taste my banquet.'"

When the banquet was ready, the man sent his servant to let the guests know that it was time to come. He didn't go himself but sent his servants. Nowadays we don't have servants to deliver an invitation to a banquet or party, but people still send out invitations by post or email. It's a matter of courtesy, as well as respect: it allows a guest to choose freely, rather than feel obliged to accept an invitation so as not to appear ungrateful.

The parable represents Our Lord's invitation to go to Heaven. And for that invitation He uses servants to tell people that God has invited them to an eternal banquet with Him. It's interesting to consider that the servant fulfilled his duty faithfully and when some declined the invitation he didn't stop. He went to find more guests; and later still, even more. He didn't get discouraged.

God continues to need servants who will invite people to the Heavenly banquet. He is asking you and me to go to the "*highways and hedges*" of the world to bring people to Him. A French priest, Fr. Michel Quoist (1918-1997) imagined Jesus speaking to us like this: "*Son*", Jesus says, "*out of all eternity, I chose you. I need you. I need your hands to continue to bless, I need your lips to continue to speak, I need your body to continue to suffer, I need your heart to continue to love, I need you to continue to save; stay with me*".

Well, Lord, here I am. You can count on my hands, my lips, my body, my heart; You can count on me to help You save souls! And I also want to finish my prayer today asking for help for the Holy Souls in Purgatory.

Wednesday 31st week in ordinary time
Wednesday 5th November
Lk 14:25-33

Now great multitudes accompanied him; and he turned and said to them, "If any one comes to me and does not hate his own father and mother and wife and children and brothers and sisters, yes, and even his own life, he cannot be my disciple. Whoever does not bear his own cross and come after me, cannot be my disciple ... So therefore, whoever of you does not renounce all that he has cannot be my disciple.

To follow You, Lord, is demanding. You invite us to be ready to give everything, to bear the cross and to follow You, to be faithful to You come what may, through thick and thin. Those who have decided to follow You closely, my Jesus, should certainly not expect a lot of support from the world.

St Charles Borromeo was the Archbishop of Milan. He was the victim of a systematic attack from those who didn't accept the reforms of the Council of Trent. He suffered slanders, insults, threats and was even shot a couple of times. In one of the shootings, the bullet was stopped by the crucifix the bishop was wearing. But the second one was fired at the saint from a distance of four or five metres as he was kneeling at the altar of his chapel. Believing himself mortally wounded, St. Charles calmly finished his prayers and offered his life to God, thanking Him for allowing him to die for His Church. Miraculously he survived. The Lord wanted St. Charles to continue His labours on earth for 15 more years before allowing him to take his just reward in Heaven.

In 1857, archaeologists discovered a graffito in Rome from 200 AD scratched into the plaster on a wall near the Palatine Hill. It ridicules a Christian boy called Alexamenos. The blasphemous image mocks the crucifixion of Jesus, representing Him with the head of a donkey. Beneath the cross a text says, "*Alexamenos worshipping his god*". We don't know who this Alexamenos was, but we know that he was the object of mockery for being a Christian. And we know something else, because in the next chamber archaeologists found another inscription in a different hand reading "*Alexamenos fidelis*" - Latin for 'Alexamenos is faithful'.

Mary, my Mother, make me as faithful as St Charles; as Alexamenos...

Thursday 6th November
Lk 15:1-10

The Pharisees and the Scribes murmured, saying, "This man receives sinners and eats with them." So he told them this parable: "What man of you, having a hundred sheep, if he has lost one of them, does not leave the ninety-nine in the wilderness, and go after the one which is lost, until he finds it? ...I tell you, there is joy before the angels of God over one sinner who repents."

The Pharisees were surprised that Jesus "*received sinners and ate with them*." And not just that: He loved them, He searched them out, He helped them to come back to God, He taught them how to love God... He even died for them. That's one of the things I love most about You, Lord: You never give up on anyone.

Fr. O'Malley was asked to attend to a patient in hospital who was dying. He travelled for 30 miles through a severe storm, past flooded streets with trees and power lines falling all around him. The name of the patient was Tom; he was an alcoholic who had been in prison for many years and had no interest in confessing his sins to a priest. Fr O'Malley tried to convince him to go to Confession for a while until the man stopped him, "*No priest can convince me. I have done something in my life that God wouldn't want to forgive.*" The priest insisted that God would love to forgive all sins committed by all sinners. But then Tom told his story:

"*Thirty-two years, two months and eleven days ago, I was working on the railway. That day the whole crew was drunk. Someone had to go out and push the switch for the train to go northbound. I was so drunk that I pushed the switch in the wrong direction. At 45 miles per hour the freight train slammed into a passenger car at the next crossing and killed a young man, his wife, and their two daughters. I have had to live with that all of my life,*" Tom explained. There was a moment of silence as Tom's confession of this tragedy hung in the air. After what seemed like an eternity, Fr. O'Malley gently put his hand on Tom's shoulder and said very quietly. "*I know God can forgive you, son, because I can. In that car were my mother, my father and my two sisters.*"

Mary, Mother of Mercy! How great is your Son's Love for sinners! How much He loves to forgive all men! Help me, Mother, to spend my life in thanksgiving.

Friday 31st week in ordinary time
Friday 7th November
Lk 16:1-8

Jesus said to the disciples, "There was a rich man who had a steward, and charges were brought to him that this man was wasting his goods. And he called him and said to him, 'What is this that I hear about you? Turn in the account of your stewardship, for you can no longer be steward'...So, summoning his master's debtors one by one, he said to the first, 'How much do you owe my master?' He said, 'A hundred measures of oil.' And he said to him, 'Take your bill, and sit down quickly and write fifty.'...for the sons of this world are more shrewd in dealing with their own generation than the sons of light."

This corrupt steward didn't feel guilty for having been dishonest. His only concern was not to lose his livelihood. So when it came to getting the approval of others in order to get a new job, he just had to be a bit 'more dishonest'. It didn't worry him that it involved cheating and stealing...Some people don't mind sacrificing the truth for the sake of their own comfort; in order to avoid upsetting people they don't hesitate to hide the truth. When the High Priest asked Jesus if He was the Son of God, Jesus knew what was going to happen to Him if He said the truth. And He still told the truth. Many saints have given their lives defending the truth.

Honest people don't bargain with half-truths. It is said that one day, Dionysius I of Syracuse, who thought himself to be a gifted poet, was reading some of his verses to a wise man called Filoxenus. The man criticised his verses and Dionysus sent him to prison. After a few days, trying to give him a second chance, the tyrant asked for Filoxenus to be brought into his presence and read him a few more verses he had composed. The only words of the wise man were addressed to the soldiers, *"Please, take me to prison again."*

St Maximilian Kolbe said, *"No one in the world can change Truth. What we can do and should do is to seek truth and to serve it when we have found it."* God is Truth and we love the Truth. And even if the Truth gets us in trouble, the proverb says, *'honesty is always the best policy.'* For the truth is the truth, even if no one believes it. And a lie is a lie, even if everyone believes it.

Holy Mary, Mirror of Justice, help me to always stand up for the Truth.

Saturday 8th November
Lk 16:9-15

Jesus said to his disciples, "No servant can serve two masters; for either he will hate the one and love the other, or he will be devoted to the one and despise the other. You cannot serve God and mammon."

Mammon' means greed or material wealth. You can't love God and material riches. That would be a bit like supporting both teams in a football match. It is interesting that Jesus speaks about serving *mammon* rather than 'having' possessions, because riches can enslave people. It isn't a matter of just having wealth.

There was a wealthy man, a landowner who owned a mansion overlooking a beautiful valley. But despite his wealth, he was deeply dissatisfied with life: he was possessed by his possessions. In the gate lodge at the entrance to his estate lived John, his farm manager. John was a man of simple faith; he was a regular church-goer and often the landowner would notice John's family on their knees in prayer at night. One morning the wealthy man was gazing out over the beautiful valley saying to himself, "*It is all mine*" when John came to see him: "*Sir,*" said John hesitantly, "*last night I had a dream, and in it the Lord told me that the richest man in the valley would die tonight at midnight. I felt you should know.*" The landowner dismissed him, but John's words kept bothering him, so much so that he took out his car and went to the local doctor for a complete check-up. He was in good health, said the doctor, nothing to be worried about. When he came back it was past midnight and he was still very much alive. "*Silly old John...upset my whole day...him and his dreams!*" Passing by the gate lodge he saw John's daughter in tears. "*Sir,*" she said, "*Daddy died at midnight.*" The landowner froze as it was suddenly made clear to him who was the richest man in the valley.

Our Lord once talked to St. Thomas Aquinas from a Crucifix and said, "*You have spoken well of me, Thomas, what should be your reward?*" To which St Thomas replied, "*Nil nisi te, Domine.*" (Nothing but you, O Lord.)

Mary, Mother of the Eucharist, may I always remember that my wealth is the Real Presence of Your Son in the Eucharist: Jesus alone is enough for me!

Dedication of the Lateran Basilica
Sunday 9th November
Jn 2:13-22

Jesus went up to Jerusalem. In the temple he found those who were selling oxen and sheep and pigeons, and the money-changers at their business. And making a whip of cords, he drove them all, with the sheep and oxen, out of the temple; and he poured out the coins of the money-changers and overturned their tables. And he told those who sold the pigeons, "Take these things away; you shall not make my Father's house a house of trade."

We are not used to seeing Jesus so upset: making a whip of cords, driving people and animals out of the Temple, pouring out coins and overturning tables...Jesus, who was patient and loving with everyone, including sinners, is angry today because of that lack of respect for God in His own Temple. Today is the anniversary of the dedication of the Basilica of St John Lateran (the Cathedral of the Pope), in 324, and is a good day to reflect on this.

Imagine going to the cinema and stuffing yourself with popcorn and fizzy drinks but without actually watching the film! That's what happened when people came to the Temple but didn't care about God. Still today, some can go to church and talk to everyone they meet except to God. Some people forget that the "house of God" is a house of prayer.

God is Really Present in our churches, but some people regard the Tabernacle as they would a nice painting or a statue. Jesus once lamented to St. Faustina, "*How painful it is to Me that souls so seldom unite themselves to Me in Holy Communion,*" He said, "*I wait for souls, and they are indifferent toward Me. I love them tenderly and sincerely, and they distrust Me. I want to lavish My graces on them, and they do not want to accept them. They treat Me as a dead object, whereas My Heart is full of love and mercy. In order that you may know at least some of My pain, imagine the most tender of mothers who has great love for her children, while those children spurn her love. Consider her pain. No one is in a position to console her. This is but a pale image and likeness of My love.*" Mary, House of Gold, may I always comfort your Son in the Tabernacle, during the Holy Mass, with my presence and my prayer.

Monday 32nd week in ordinary time
Monday 10th November
Lk 17:1-6

Jesus said to his disciples, "Take heed to yourselves; if your brother sins, rebuke him, and if he repents, forgive him; and if he sins against you seven times in the day, and turns to you seven times, and says, 'I repent,' you must forgive him."

Fraternal correction is an obligation of charity: to help someone to be holier by pointing out some mistake or defect they may have. A good athlete always wants to improve. If by changing the length of his stride or by doing a particular exercise, he can run faster, wouldn't he be very grateful to be told about it? In the same way, saints have always been very grateful when they have been corrected. St Josemaría, for instance, was always very grateful when people corrected him and wrote down the corrections to improve. When the Holy See approved the Statutes of Opus Dei, the Vatican didn't agree with allowing the members of the Work to correct the Founder, since (according to traditional custom) "*a superior cannot be corrected by his subordinates*". But St Josemaría stuck to his guns, arguing that he shouldn't be deprived of the 'work of mercy' which was being corrected by others. Eventually they agreed a compromise: approval was given to his having two guardians or aides who would live close to him, advising and correcting him - Bl Alvaro and Father Javier Echevarría.

But in order to be corrected we need to be humble, and that is not easy. One day, St Josemaría confided to a group of young ladies: "*Don Alvaro corrected me today. It was hard to accept it. So much so that I went to the oratory for a moment. Once there, I said, 'Lord, Alvaro's right and I'm wrong.' But after a second, I said, 'No, Lord, this time I am right. Alvaro doesn't let me get away with a single thing, and that doesn't seem like affection but cruelty.' And then I said, 'Thank you, Lord, for placing my son Alvaro near me, who is so fond of me that he doesn't let me get away with a single thing!'*" Then, deeply moved and full of affection, he turned toward Bl Alvaro, who had been listening in silence, smiled at him, and said, "*God bless you, Alvaro, my son!*"

Mary, Our Lady of Charity, teach me to help others be holy by practising fraternal correction.

Tuesday 11th November
Lk 17:7-10

"Will any one of you, who has a servant ploughing or keeping sheep, say to him when he has come in from the field, 'Come at once and sit down at table? Will he not rather say to him, 'Prepare supper for me, and gird yourself and serve me, till I eat and drink; and afterward you shall eat and drink? Does he thank the servant because he did what was commanded? So you also, when you have done all that is commanded you, say, 'We are unworthy servants; we have only done what was our duty'."

Four young men needed batteries and a cable for their speakers. They went to the store and found what they were looking for, but there wasn't anyone there – no employees, no cashier. After waiting for a while they realised that no one was coming out to help them, so they left the money for their purchase on the counter and left. What happened, it turns out, was that the store was actually closed; the lock on the door had malfunctioned. This incident was recorded by a security camera and broadcast on national news. When the youths were interviewed on TV and asked about it, they said that they '*had just done the right thing*'. It's surprising that 'honesty' can be a piece of news!

Doing the right thing is our duty. We don't expect something in exchange for every good action that we do, as if we were 'negotiating' with God: I will only do something if God rewards me. We are not God's employees. We are His children. Imagine asking your mum: '*what will you give me if I make my bed?*' She could just remind you that it is not 'your' bed, actually: '*I've given you the bed*', she could say, '*the linen, the pyjamas, the room and the house; the food you eat, the clothes you wear...and the life you live*'. Our mothers deserve our obedience.

It's the same with every good action: When you do good, when you help others, *you've only done your duty*. When you resist temptations to sin, forgive those who offend you, when you are faithful, kind, and compassionate, when you keep all the commandments from one to ten, in all their depth and breadth... you've only done your duty; for Our Father God deserves as much from His Children. Mary, my Mother, help me always to do the right thing just because God deserves it.

Wednesday 12th November
Lk 17:11-19

As Jesus entered a village, he was met by ten lepers, who stood at a distance and lifted up their voices and said, "Jesus, Master, have mercy on us." When he saw them he said to them, "Go and show yourselves to the priests." And as they went they were cleansed.

"*Show yourselves to the priests.*" We all have sins and we can all be made clean by going to Jesus. All the saints (except Our Lady) had to be forgiven. All of them had committed sins and needed to ask for forgiveness. And they were all forgiven. Jesus can touch a leper and cure him; He can touch a sinner and make him a saint. And Jesus can decide to do it the way He wants, because He is God.

Jesus could have chosen a different way: He could have said: '*Dig a hole, say your sins there and bury them*' or '*Go to this wall and tell your sins there*'. And yet, a wall doesn't hear, a wall doesn't understand, a wall doesn't console, a wall doesn't encourage, a wall doesn't guide you. But a man can do all that. "*Show yourselves to the priests,*" He says.

Many saints went to Confession as often as once a week, like St Josemaría, St Padre Pio, St John Paul II, St Faustina, St Teresa of Calcutta, St Francis and so many others... not because they were saints, but because they were sinners. Thank You, Lord, for the Sacrament of Confession; thank You because You always forgive all sins, and forgive everything completely; thank You for Your priests.

"*Go to confession to the Blessed Virgin, or to an angel; will they absolve you? No. Will they give you the Body and Blood of Our Lord? No. The Holy Virgin cannot make her Divine Son descend into the Host. You might have two hundred angels there, but they could not absolve you. A priest, however simple he may be, can do it; he can say to you, "Go in peace; I pardon you." Oh, how great is a priest!*" (St John Mary Vianney) "*Priests have received a power which God has given neither to angels nor to archangels. It was said to them: 'Whatsoever you shall bind on earth shall be bound in heaven; and whatsoever you shall loose, shall be loosed.'*" (St John Chrysostom)

I pray through your intercession, Holy Mary, Mother of Priests, that there will be an abundance of priests - of holy priests!

Thursday 32nd week in ordinary time
Thursday 13th November
Lk 17:20-25

"The kingdom of God is not coming with signs to be observed; nor will they say, 'Lo, here it is!' or 'There!' for behold, the kingdom of God is in the midst of you." And he said to the disciples, "The days are coming when you will desire to see one of the days of the Son of man, and you will not see it. And they will say to you, 'Lo, there!' or 'Lo, here!' Do not go, do not follow them...But first he must suffer many things and be rejected by this generation."

We are coming close to the end of the liturgical year. During these days the Gospel of the Mass will be reminding us of the Second Coming of Our Lord and describes some of the things that will happen beforehand. One of them is the confusion caused by false prophets. The devil is an expert liar who tries to sow confusion among Jesus' disciples.

In a transatlantic sailing race one team employed the strategy of pretending to be their opponents' shore team, sending them misleading information on their radios. The ploy worked, since the other boats naturally followed their instructions and found themselves thoroughly lost. But the following year something very different happened. The teams didn't trust any radio instructions and so chose not to follow any...so they got lost again!

The devil does the same: he spends most of his energy sowing disunity and mistrust in the Church, mistrust in the Pope for '*something*' he '*is reported*' to have said; mistrust in that priest because he did something wrong once, mistrust in that Catholic institution or society because one of its members misbehaved. The devil loves those doubts which he sows abundantly among Christians. But let's keep it clearly in mind, and also spread the word, that we can't fight effectively if we are divided.

Our Lord predicted that many people would come and mislead His disciples. That happens every day in some media. But as St John Henry Newman wrote, *"Ten thousand difficulties do not make one doubt."* If ever we see difficulties amongst some Christians, we shouldn't distrust the Church. People may make mistakes, but God knows what He is doing. Mary, Mother of the Church, may I be an instrument of unity.

Friday 14th November
Lk 17:26-37

Jesus said to his disciples, "Whoever seeks to gain his life will lose it, but whoever loses his life will preserve it. I tell you, in that night there will be two in one bed; one will be taken and the other left. There will be two women grinding together; one will be taken and the other left."

A paradox is a statement that seems self-contradictory or absurd but in reality expresses a truth. Jesus explains that those who are concerned about their happiness will lose it. If you want to enjoy life, you have to suffer; if you want to win, you have to lose; if you want to live, you have to die. Only those who give themselves to others can really keep their life; only those who use their freedom to serve God become really free.

Human beings long for happiness. God created us in such a way that only love makes us happy. Some people forget this and try to achieve happiness in many different ways: money, pleasure, vengeance, hatred, drugs... All those alternatives have something in common: they never satisfy the human heart. Human hearts can't be fooled. As a plane only flies on fuel and you can't make it run on milk, so our heart runs on love and nothing else can make it fly. Saints have always been the happiest people in the world, for they have known how to love God and others the most. Many people still don't understand how St Teresa of Calcutta, who spent her life serving the poor in the slums of that city and undergoing many spiritual hardships, could be happier than all the rich men in the world put together.

A man went to hell in a dream and found many miserable people trying to eat their food with very long spoons, so long that they couldn't put them into their mouths and were starving in front of a table covered with food. Then he visited Heaven and saw the exact same scene, except he saw everyone beaming with joy because each person was using the long spoon to feed the person opposite them. A loving concern for the welfare of others meant everyone was fed. By giving everything, everyone received all they wanted. Mary, Queen of All Saints, help me to remember that only by giving everything will I get everything; and only by giving myself to the full will I be fully happy.

Saturday 32nd week in ordinary time
Saturday 15th November
Lk 18:1-8

Jesus told them a parable, to the effect that they ought always to pray and not lose heart. He said, "In a certain city there was a judge who neither feared God nor regarded man; and there was a widow in that city who kept coming to him and saying, 'Vindicate me against my adversary'...And he added, "will not God vindicate his elect, who cry to him day and night? Will he delay long over them? I tell you, he will vindicate them speedily. Nevertheless, when the Son of man comes, will he find faith on earth?"

Faith. It's all a matter of faith. Jesus wants us to "*pray and not lose heart*", to never give up. God never stops listening to our prayer but He wants us to persist *faith*-fully until our prayers are answered. He said this in many different ways: "*Truly, truly, I say to you, if you ask anything of the Father, he will give it to you in my name*" (Jn 16:23); "*Ask, and it will be given you*" (Mt 7:7); "*every one who asks receives*" (Lk 11:10); "*whatever you ask in prayer, you will receive, if you have faith*" (Mt 21:22). Sometimes Jesus takes His time to answer us because persisting is a proof of our faith. If we pray little we get little. If we pray much, we get much.

From the time he was a baby, you could tell he was headed for trouble. He was a rebel all his life. He didn't like study (particularly Greek, he explained later); he had all kinds of problems with chastity, stealing, keeping bad company, telling lies... He wrote many years later that he did this "*for the only reason that it was forbidden*". And his mother, Monica, suffered with all this and she prayed; she prayed a lot; she prayed for more than 30 years for him without ever giving up, even when she saw her son going off the rails.

And her persevering prayer was rewarded. St Monica's son changed his life. You may have heard of him: St Augustine, bishop, Doctor of the Church, one of the most brilliant minds in Christian history; but first of all he was a great saint. St Monica's prayer changed the course of Christianity, since St Augustine brought about the conversion of many thousands throughout history. What would have happened if St Monica had given up? Mary, Comfort of the Afflicted, may I never let up on prayer. (*Half way through November you can renew your resolution to pray for the Holy Souls in Purgatory*).

Thirty-Third Sunday in Ordinary Time
Sunday 16th November
Lk 21:5-19

And as some spoke of the temple, how it was adorned with noble stones and offerings, Jesus said, "As for these things which you see, the days will come when there shall not be left here one stone upon another that will not be thrown down... Take heed that you are not led astray; for many will come in my name, saying, 'I am he!' and, 'The time is at hand!' Do not go after them. And when you hear of wars and tumults, do not be terrified; for this must first take place, but the end will not be at once...Nation will rise against nation, and kingdom against kingdom; there will be great earthquakes, and in various places famines and pestilences; and there will be terrors and great signs from heaven. But before all this they will lay their hands on you and persecute you, delivering you up to the synagogues and prisons, and you will be brought before kings and governors for my name's sake. This will be a time for you to bear testimony...You will be delivered up even by parents and brothers and kinsmen and friends, and some of you they will put to death; you will be hated by all for my name's sake. But not a hair of your head will perish. By your endurance you will gain your lives."

It is worth reading these words of Our Lord, a prophecy which comes not from a prophet but from the Son of God Himself. When you read the prophecy a couple of times you realise that we are too familiar with the theme today. Jesus explains what will happen, what people will do to Christians. But He also explains what He is expecting from us: "*This will be a time for you to bear testimony,*" He said. And the word 'testimony' in Greek is '*martyria*'.

When persecutions started in Mexico in the 1920s, many Christians were martyred for their Faith. St José Sánchez del Río was 14 years old when he was tortured and killed for refusing to renounce his faith. When he was 13 his mother had tried to convince him to stay at home and not put his life at risk; but he answered her, "*Mamá, it has never been easier to earn Heaven as now.*" The words of this 13-year-old boy who died a martyr can feed our prayer today also, since we currently see in our world many of the things prophesied by Our Lord, and we are asked to "*bear testimony.*" With our "*endurance*" we will earn Heaven, for it has never been easier.

Mary, Queen of Confessors, may I never be afraid to confess my faith with my life.

Monday 33rd week in ordinary time
Monday 17th November
Lk 18:35-43

As he drew near to Jericho, a blind man was sitting by the roadside begging and hearing a multitude going by, he inquired what this meant. They told him, "Jesus of Nazareth is passing by." And he cried, "Jesus, Son of David, have mercy on me!" And those who were in front rebuked him, telling him to be silent; but he cried out all the more, "Son of David, have mercy on me!"

This blind man was probably there every day. But that day something caught his attention: a stir in the air, the sound of a chattering crowd approaching. Accustomed to the usual daily movements of pedestrians, he knew something different was afoot and he asked what was going on. There and then he was told that Jesus was passing by. And he didn't need any further explanations. He wasn't going to miss the opportunity of his life. And he didn't miss it. St Augustine once wrote, "*Timeo Iesum transeuntem et non revertentem*" ['I fear Jesus will pass by and will not come back'.] Jesus has planned from all eternity to encounter each person one day so that they may find Him, but not everyone is ready: some people see Jesus and don't recognise Him.

There is a story of a woman who found a letter in her letter box signed by Jesus, saying, "*Tomorrow I will visit you.*" The woman went to buy groceries for a special meal for Jesus and herself, and prepared everything for the next day. As she was waiting, someone knocked at the door. She opened it and was disappointed to find a beggar standing there asking for something to eat. She said that she was waiting for someone else and was ready to dismiss him when it occurred to her to give him her part of the dinner. She kept Jesus' portion and gave him her own. It was getting late when someone knocked at the door again. She opened it expecting to see Jesus but it was a lady with a baby asking for food. After hesitating for a moment and thinking that it was now too late for Jesus to come, she gave the lady and her baby the rest of the dinner. The following morning another note was in her letter box. Signed by Jesus, it read, "*Thank you for the dinner yesterday; everything was delicious!*"

Mary, Mother of God, don't allow me to let Jesus pass by without stopping Him and inviting Him into my life.

Tuesday 33rd week in ordinary time
Tuesday 18th November
Lk 19:1-10

He entered Jericho and was passing through. And there was a man named Zacchaeus; he was a chief tax collector, and rich. And he sought to see who Jesus was, but could not, on account of the crowd, because he was small of stature. So he ran on ahead and climbed up into a sycamore tree to see him, for he was to pass that way. And when Jesus came to the place, he looked up and said to him, "Zacchaeus, make haste and come down; for I must stay at your house today."

We know a few things about Zacchaeus: he was a wealthy tax-collector, he didn't have many friends in Jericho and he was short. We also know he couldn't care less what people thought about him. It is hilarious: try to imagine a wealthy banker dressed in an expensive suit, up a tree, like a child, in the middle of the street! We know that he wanted to see Jesus so badly that nothing could stop him.

What we don't know is why he wanted to see Our Lord; was it curiosity? Was he trying to change his life? Did someone else bring him there? We don't know. But none of that mattered to Jesus. This story tells us about Jesus' love for sinners. The conversion of Zacchaeus began with him trying to see Our Lord. A little effort on his part was all it took, and Jesus did the rest. Zacchaeus probably wasn't expecting to change his life that day. He just wanted to see Jesus.

Yet Jesus wanted to see *him* even more. It was Jesus who came to *him*. He had planned that encounter from all eternity. Our Lord stopped and, setting His eyes on him, full of love, He said: "*Zacchaeus, make haste and come down; for I must stay at your house today.*" Like Bartimeus in yesterday's Gospel, Zacchaeus didn't miss his opportunity.

God loves sinners '*as they are*' but He '*refuses*' to leave them '*as they are*'. He goes in search of them and He expects a sign from them, a gesture, a token of interest...and then He can pour down His grace over the sinner. And just as Jesus sets His eyes on Zacchaeus, He sets His eyes on you and me as well, and invites us to converse with Him. Mary, Refuge of Sinners, bring to my ears often the soft Voice of your Son who says to me: '*make haste and come down from your world; for I must talk to you today.*'

Dedication of the Basilica of St Peter and St Paul
Tuesday 18th November
Mt 14:22-33

In the fourth watch of the night he came to them, walking on the sea...And Peter answered him, "Lord, if it is you, bid me come to you on the water." He said, "Come." So Peter got out of the boat and walked on the water and came to Jesus; but when he saw the wind, he was afraid, and beginning to sink he cried out, "Lord, save me." Jesus immediately reached out his hand and caught him, saying to him, "O man of little faith, why did you doubt?"

Peter could have gone as far as he *wanted*, as far as he *trusted*. From the first step he was aware that it wasn't his sandals but Jesus who made him walk on the water. Whilst Peter trusted, he walked. When he *mistrusted*, he sank. It's not difficult to trust for a little while when you can still reach the boat by stretching out your hand, at a 'safe' distance, with no risks. What is difficult, and what God demands, is that we trust *only* Him and never waver.

A lifejacket would seem safe, but it would be safer to trust Jesus, Who loves you more than you love yourself. If it is God Who asks for it and He stays at your side all the time, what can be safer? To become a saint is even more difficult than to walk on water. But the essence is the same: God can make it happen if we trust. Saints understood it clearly: you go as far as you trust.

By November 1942, less than a dozen young ladies had joined Opus Dei. During a meeting with three of them, St Josemaría unfolded a piece of paper on the desk. On it there was a sketch of what he thought God was asking for around the world: rural schools, university students' residences, clinics, vocational training centres for women in various areas, bookshops... Speechless, the three ladies were astonished. They felt inexperienced, without means, without resources, absolutely incapable. St Josemaría understood their feelings and commented, "*Given all this, you can react in one of two ways. Either to think that it's very nice but impossible, unrealizable or to **trust** in the Lord that, if He asks for all this, He will help us to make it happen...Dream and your dreams will fall short!*" Fortunately they decided to trust and those dreams are now a reality. They trusted and walked as far as Jesus wanted to take them. Holy Mary, my Mother, Arc of the Covenant, teach me to trust.

Wednesday 19th November
Lk 19:11-28

Jesus said to his disciples, "A nobleman went into a far country to receive a kingly power and then return. Calling ten of his servants, he gave them ten pounds, and said to them, 'Trade with these till I come.'"

The master gave each of his servants something to trade with until he came back. He gave them the money and instructions, but made no mention of the time of his return. He didn't give any indication about how much time they had to trade and make their talents bear fruit, because the time is 'NOW'.

Some people waste their time planning to do things in the future and never manage to do them. Some want to become souls of prayer, or to be holy, or to do the Will of God, or to change the world... And they plan it; they think about it; they consult people and devise a course of action... But they never do it: 'I will give this to God', 'I will do this for God', 'I will go to Confession'... As St Augustine reminds us: "*God has promised you 'forgiveness', but He has not promised you 'tomorrow'*". Saints were saints because they never left anything for tomorrow; because they didn't know if they would have 'tomorrow'. They didn't plan to be holy. They 'tried' to be holy. They didn't plan to be friends with Jesus: they 'tried' to become His friends. They knew that talents don't last forever.

A man was given a very expensive bottle of vintage wine and he decided to store it in the cellar, waiting for a very special occasion. But no occasion was ever 'special enough' for him. His daughter's wedding came but he thought: 'Not special enough. There are many weddings'. His 50th wedding anniversary came but he thought: 'Next year it will be 51, which is even better than 50'. Time passed and he never found a special occasion. Eventually he died and after his funeral his children decided to open the bottle, but the wine had gone off already and had to be thrown away. Too much waiting! What a waste!

Let's not make God wait to start to become holy: this is the moment, today is the day, the time to be holy is now! *Hodie, nunc!* is the Latin for "today, now!" Mary, Virgin Most Faithful, don't allow me to procrastinate.

Thursday 33rd week in ordinary time
Thursday 20th November
Lk 19:41-44

And when he drew near and saw the city he wept over it, saying, "Would that even today you knew the things that make for peace! But now they are hid from your eyes. For the days shall come upon you, when your enemies will cast up a bank about you and surround you, and hem you in on every side, and dash you to the ground, you and your children within you, and they will not leave one stone upon another in you; because you did not know the time of your visitation."

We all remember Jesus' great sorrow on Good Friday in Gethsemane. But many have forgotten His tears over Jerusalem. The authorities of Jerusalem had been given every opportunity to repent and change their ways, but they didn't take advantage of them. God sent them prophets but they wouldn't listen to them and killed them. Eventually God sent them His Son; but again they wouldn't listen to Him. And God wondered what else He could do...and He wept.

We should meditate on the Tears of God. It's a hard thing to see a father weeping for his children who are destroying their life. Like a mother and a father, God sheds tears for His children because He loves us. Think about it slowly: We make God suffer and even cry. Many people ask God for comfort and consolation, but who comforts God? Who consoles Him?

During the apparitions of the Angel of Fatima to the three shepherds (Lucia, St Jacinta and St Francisco) he brought them Holy Communion and said: "*Take and drink the Body and Blood of Jesus Christ, horribly outraged by ungrateful men. Make reparation for their crimes and console your God.*" The Angel's words, "*Console your God,*" burned themselves into Francisco's heart. He sought to be the consoler of 'the Hidden Jesus' in the Tabernacle and by praying the Rosary. "*How beautiful God is, how beautiful!*" he said, "*But He is sad because of the sins of men. I want to console Him, I want to suffer for love of Him*" (St Francisco Marto died at the age of 10). How do I console God and suffer for love of Him? The Angel said to the shepherds in Fatima, "*The Hearts of Jesus and Mary are attentive to your prayers.*" Mary, Our Lady of Fatima, you and your Son are attentive to my prayer, remind me often that *'I' can console GOD!* Holy Souls, help me to comfort Him.

Friday 33rd week in ordinary time
Friday 21st November
Lk 19:45-48

And he entered the temple and began to drive out those who sold, saying to them, "It is written, 'My house shall be a house of prayer'; but you have made it a den of robbers." And he was teaching daily in the temple. The chief priests and the scribes and the principal men of the people sought to destroy him; but they did not find anything they could do, for all the people hung upon his words.

Apparently some people didn't go to the temple to pray, but to buy and sell animals for sacrifices. That wasn't the original plan. In Sacred Scripture they could read: "*My house shall be a house of prayer*". Some of the people of Jerusalem did many things in the temple but prayer wasn't one of their priorities.

We are also 'temples of God' Who lives in us. This house of God is called to be a 'house of prayer' and so we should try to be souls of prayer. We can be busy in our lives with lots of things and we often find it difficult to do them all. For that reason we have our list of 'priorities' and a list of other less urgent things. Prayer should be our top priority.

Many people don't pray because they say that they don't find time for it. The fact is that until you are convinced that prayer is the best use of your time, you will not find time for your mental prayer. Our conversation with God is the most important time of the day. The real priority. And the more things we have to do, the more we need that time of prayer. One day St John Paul II was praying in his chapel. A secretary interrupted his prayer, requesting his attention to solve a very important issue. St John Paul asked him to wait a while and kept praying. After a few minutes the secretary insisted, "*Holy Father, this is an urgent matter.*" "*I know,*" said the Pope, "*Just a minute!*" But the secretary insisted that it was 'very urgent'. The Pope looked serious and said, "*If it's urgent I need to pray much; if it's 'very urgent' then I need to pray 'very much'!*"

Let's set our time of prayer as a priority, the best investment of our time. Mary, Teacher of Prayer, help me to devote some time each day to talking to God. Holy Souls in Purgatory, please also help me; if you do... I promise to pray for you.

Saturday 33rd week in ordinary time
Saturday 22nd November
Lk 20:27-40

There came to him some Sadducees, those who say that there is no resurrection, and they asked him a question...Jesus answered them: "that the dead are raised, even Moses showed, in the passage about the bush, where he calls the Lord the God of Abraham and the God of Isaac and the God of Jacob. Now he is not God of the dead, but of the living; for all live to him."

The Sadducees didn't believe in life after death. For them death was the end. But Jesus explained to them that God identified Himself to Moses as the God of Abraham, Isaac and Jacob and it didn't mean that He was a God of 'corpses', but that He was *still* the God of Abraham, Isaac and Jacob, for they were *living* in His presence. It is clear that there is life after death because God doesn't make mistakes and if He created us to love, it means that we should love forever, because real love lasts for ever.

When we die we are judged and our soul enters into its proper state: Heaven, Purgatory or Hell. But when the present world finishes there will be the Universal Judgement and then the world and everything in it will be restored. We ourselves will resurrect to a new life. All that is corrupted in the world will be restored. Then a new body will be given to us, a glorious one, perfect and incorruptible. Michael Faraday was a famous British scientist born in 1791. One day a pupil of his dropped a silver cup into a jar of *nitric acid*; being highly corrosive, the acid dissolved the silver cup and it disintegrated into thousands of tiny grains of silver, like sand floating in a glass of water. Faraday came to the rescue and put some salt into the jar. This made the grains of silver precipitate to the bottom; the famous London scientist took the grains out and used them to have the cup refashioned into one more beautiful than it had been before. It was the same cup, made of the same silver, but better. So it will be with the risen bodies of the saints.

Mary, Queen of Heaven, there with your radiant and glorious body, you always watch over your children. I ask for your intercession to be able to join you and the whole crowd of Saints and Angels...There I will meet my loved ones again; and I will greet the Holy Souls in Purgatory that I have helped with my prayers.

Our Lord Jesus Christ, King of the Universe
Sunday 23rd November
Lk 23:35-43

And the people stood by, watching; but the rulers scoffed at him, saying, "He saved others; let him save himself, if he is the Christ of God, his Chosen One!" The soldiers also mocked him, coming up and offering him vinegar, and saying, "If you are the King of the Jews, save yourself!" There was also an inscription over him, "This is the King of the Jews."

Jesus is King of the Universe. King of the entire creation. But His Kingship is not obvious. He was crowned by Pilate on the Cross. He was killed on the day of His Coronation; but He rose from the dead. And over the years many people who proclaimed His Kingship have been killed as well. Where was their King when they died? If He is King... why is there so much evil in His Kingdom? What is the King of the Universe doing about it?

J.R.R. Tolkien once referred to God as a great Composer. At the beginning of time He composed the most beautiful music. Knowing our instruments and our skills, He composed a perfect piece of music for His creatures to interpret. But we are free. We can follow the score as we like. The devil and many other skilled angels decided not to follow the score and made up their own melody to increase their own glory. The discordant noise of the devil and all evildoers clashed with the original composition and there was a violent war of sound. But that didn't stop God. He is Almighty: He is the Perfect Composer. God knows what the devil and his followers are going to play; so He has arranged a new score that wraps all that noise in a more beautiful composition and the result is even more harmonious than before. But you and I need to play that new score for Him; we, with our Christian life, have to play His 'symphony' the best we can. When we work, when we pray, when we help people and serve others, even when we rest and have a nice time, we are playing that 'symphony' the best we can, and we are making Jesus King of our lives. With our Christian lives we will show that Jesus is King. And all those who don't want Jesus to reign will have to wake up to the Truth: Jesus is *King* and His Kingdom will have no end. Today, with Mary, Mother of the King, Queen of the Universe, we pray with all creation: *Long live Christ the King!*

Monday last week in ordinary time
Monday 24th November
Lk 21:1-4

He looked up and saw the rich putting their gifts into the treasury; and he saw a poor widow put in two copper coins. And he said, "Truly I tell you, this poor widow has put in more than all of them; for they all contributed out of their abundance, but she out of her poverty put in all the living that she had."

Today's Gospel brings to our consideration the virtue of generosity. Jesus was moved when He saw that poor lady giving out of her poverty all that she had. It's easy to give away toys and clothes that we no longer use. And we can have that attitude with Our Lord sometimes: giving Him the remains of our time: to pray 'if I have time', to go to Mass 'if I have nothing else to do', to say the Rosary 'if I can fit it in on the train or on the bus'... Consistency in your life of prayer, in your Holy Mass, in your time for God is the best proof of your generosity towards Him. Because if we are not constant and we only pray when we 'have time' or when we 'feel like praying', we can't become intimate friends with Him.

It is difficult to be consistent. It is especially difficult if we don't see the changes that our dialogue with Jesus produce in us. But even if we don't see the effects, God is acting in our souls when we spend time with Him. It is like sunbathing. If you are exposed to the sun's rays, you get tanned. You may not notice it much, but when you meet your friends again after a while they notice and ask you: *'Where have you been?'*

A man published a letter in a newspaper announcing that he had decided to stop going to Sunday Mass. He argued his position saying, *"During my life I have gone to Sunday Mass more than 1,800 times but can't recall any homily or see any effect in my life."* The following day another man published a letter in the same newspaper stating that he had decided to stop eating. He wrote, *"My wife has been feeding me three times a day for 35 years (38,325 meals) and I can't recall any particular meal or see where all those tons of food are now."* Just because we can't see the effects of our prayer doesn't mean there aren't any. Mary, my Mother, help me to be consistent in giving my time to God, unworried about the results, convinced that God is changing my life anyway.

Tuesday last week in ordinary time
Tuesday 25th November
Lk 21:5-11

Jesus said, "As for these things which you see, the days will come when there shall not be left here one stone upon another that will not be thrown down." And they asked him, "Teacher, when will this be, and what will be the sign when this is about to take place?" And he said, "Take heed that you are not led astray; for many will come in my name, saying, 'I am he!' and, 'The time is at hand!' Do not go after them".

In recent times we have seen an attempt to build a Godless society. But for centuries people have tried to replace God's law with their own. There has been no shortage either of people (and whole societies) that have tried to hide God from public life, attempting to replace the worship of God with the worship of dictators or governments. This shouldn't surprise us – Jesus warned us about it.

Many authoritarian regimes have made it a priority to root out God and religion from people's hearts. But they have never succeeded because God is anchored in the human heart as a necessity for our happiness. In places where Christians have been slain, religion forbidden and believers persecuted, God has always remained the same.

For over 34 years communists had attempted to abolish religion and build an atheistic society in Poland. From 1945 the regime started circulating anti-religious propaganda, persecuting practising Christians. But in 1979 St John Paul II visited his country for the first time as Pope. Two months before the Pope's arrival, Polish communists took steps to restrain the enthusiasm of the people. They also issued instructions to the Polish media to censor and limit the Pope's comments and appearances. But when the Holy Father got up on the stage and started preaching, millions of people started singing at the tops of their voices: "*We want God! We want God! We want God!*" The Pope tried to continue but the shouting went on, "*We want God!*" and it didn't stop for fifteen minutes! What a moment in modern history! Don't you hear the hearts of today's men and women shouting the same: '*We want God! We want God! We want God!*'? Mary, Mother of God, I also hear the Voice of your Son shouting, '*I want women! I want men! I want you!*'

Wednesday last week in ordinary time
Wednesday 26th November
Lk 21:12-19

Jesus said, "they will lay their hands on you and persecute you, delivering you up to the synagogues and prisons, and you will be brought before kings and governors for my name's sake. This will be a time for you to bear testimony...You will be delivered up even by parents and brothers and kinsmen and friends, and some of you they will put to death; you will be hated by all for my name's sake. But not a hair of your head will perish. By your endurance you will gain your lives."

There is a time for testimony and when it comes, the disciples of Jesus have to be steadfast. Jesus warned about difficulties but also promised His assistance. Rather than try to hide away when our time for testimony comes, all Jesus asks of us is to 1) trust Him: "*not a hair of your head will perish*"; and 2) not give up: "*By your endurance you will gain your lives.*" That's the example we have received from the Apostles, from martyrs, confessors, popes, bishops and priests and millions of lay people as well; saints who never flinched, never hesitated, never took a step back.

Jesus asked His disciples for perseverance and Christians have always tried to be faithful. The Hill of Crosses in northern Lithuania, for instance, has come to signify the peaceful endurance of Lithuanian Catholicism despite the repeated threats it faced over time. When the country rebelled against the Russian Empire and families couldn't locate and bury the bodies of their deceased, they decided to put crosses on that Hill. During the years 1944 -1990 Lithuania was occupied again by the Soviet Union. The Soviets worked hard to remove new crosses and bulldozed the site several times. At night Lithuanian people would come, replace them and add a few more. There were 50 crosses at the beginning of the last century. In 1990, when Lithuania became independent from the Soviet Union, there were 55,000 crosses. Today there are more than 400,000. A memorial plaque inscribed with the words of St John Paul II reads: "*Thank you, Lithuanians, for this Hill of Crosses which testifies to the nations of Europe and to the whole world the faith of the people of this land.*"

Holy Mary, Help of Christians, through your intercession and the intercession of the Holy Souls - for whom I pray now - may we always trust God and never give up.

Thursday 27th November
Lk 21:20-28

Jesus said to his disciples, "great distress shall be upon the earth and wrath upon this people; they will fall by the edge of the sword, and be led captive among all nations; and Jerusalem will be trodden down by the Gentiles, until the times of the Gentiles are fulfilled...And then they will see the Son of man coming in a cloud with power and great glory. Now when these things begin to take place, look up and raise your heads, because your redemption is drawing near."

Towards the end of the liturgical year the Gospel insists on hope. Our Lord explains what we should expect: persecutions, wars, catastrophes of all kinds... But then He reminds us that we need to *"raise our heads because our redemption is near." "Raise your heads,"* Jesus is telling us, *'don't look down, don't get discouraged by everything that goes on around you, don't be afraid; raise your heads, look to Heaven, keep your sights on God... don't lose heart, don't lose hope!'*

We need to raise our heads and look at Jesus Christ on the Cross. His Body nailed to the wood teaches us to be faithful; His wounded Skin shows us the price of our sins; His open Side gives us an insight into the Love of His Sacred Heart for us; His Head pierced by multiple thorns reminds us to keep our heads up... Raise your head and look at the Pierced God and you will understand that the disciple has to follow the Master; that there is only one way to show your love: through suffering.

Father Francesco Bressani was an Italian Jesuit who arrived in North America in 1642 as a missionary. One day he and a recently converted man were captured and tortured for the Faith. It was a slow and drawn-out martyrdom lasting for several weeks. The Jesuit wrote to his Superior: *"I have no more than one entire finger; six times they burned my hands, over eighteen times they have applied fire and hot iron on my body and forced me to sing during the ordeal."* When they started to torture his companion, the convert said, *"Father Bressani, I can't take this anymore, I see I'm going to waver: Quick, quick, Father, show me your hands – they tell me how to love God..!"* Mary, Mother of the Crucified, help me to keep my head up and to look at Him! He teaches me to suffer and to love.

Friday last week in ordinary time
Friday 28th November
Lk 21:29-33

And he told them a parable: "Look at the fig tree, and all the trees; as soon as they come out in leaf, you see for yourselves and know that the summer is already near. So also, when you see these things taking place, you know that the kingdom of God is near. Truly, I say to you, this generation will not pass away till all has taken place. Heaven and earth will pass away, but my words will not pass away."

Jesus often spoke about the Kingdom of God. Some people think that the Kingdom will come at the end of time, but that's not what Jesus referred to. He said that the Kingdom of God was like a mustard seed: it grows slowly, unseen for a long time. He also compared it to someone who scatters seed on the ground and the enemy comes and sows weeds among the wheat (*Mt* 13).

Jesus said that the Kingdom was like yeast that a woman took and mixed in with three measures of flour until all of it was leavened (*Mt* 13:33). We Christians are the leaven that is transforming the world from within. He also compared the Kingdom to a king settling accounts with his servants, to a landowner hiring labourers, to the wise bridesmaids who were ready... The Kingdom of God is already in the world; Jesus is King (don't forget!) and therefore He 'has' a Kingdom.

Often great kingdoms started as a small patch of land and a bunch of people with a strong leader who became their king and together, little by little, they conquered grounds. Gradually some of their enemies quit, others joined their army, while others ran away. Sometimes the king and his army lost ground for a while and were defeated in battle, but the soldiers stood by their king faithfully and eventually recovered the land again.

Don't you see this battle happening within you? Don't you feel Jesus fighting to conquer your heart? Don't you remember that His Kingdom will have no end? The kingdom He is longing to conquer is each and every person's heart. But for Him to conquer my heart I need to fight to control it and then I need to surrender it to the King. Mother, remind me to pray every day, many times: '*Your Kingdom come!*' so that my Jesus can conquer my heart, be the only King of it and rule it with His Love.

Saturday last week in ordinary time
Saturday 29th November
Lk 21:34-36

"But take heed to yourselves lest your hearts be weighed down with dissipation and drunkenness and cares of this life, and that day come upon you suddenly like a snare; for it will come upon all who dwell upon the face of the whole earth. But watch at all times, praying that you may have strength to escape all these things that will take place, and to stand before the Son of man."

Jesus asks us to be on our guard because one day He will come to take us to Heaven and we need to be ready. And the best way to be always ready is to do what we are supposed to do and do it as we should. "*Do you really want to be a saint?*" St Josemaría teaches, "*Carry out the little duty of each moment: do what you ought and concentrate on what you are doing.*" That would mean to live our life as someone who knows that Life is eternal.

Christians are not afraid of death or of the future, any more than an athlete is afraid of a race. They train for it. We, however, prepare ourselves for eternal Life. On days when the athlete is tired and thinks about giving up, he can think about the race, about the prize. When things get difficult for us we also keep our mind on Heaven.

Saints tried to live their lives as if they might die at any moment. In this way, whenever God came to call them to Heaven they were ready. Usually they made an examination of conscience at night, asking for forgiveness for that day's failures and help for the following day's struggle to love and be more holy. That examination of conscience, finished with a good act of contrition, could make up for all the failures of their day. Thus they were always ready. They were constantly doing what they had to do, as they should do it. If they failed, an act of contrition put things right again.

St Charles Borromeo was relaxing one day playing chess with some priests. One of them asked the others what they would do if they were told by an angel that they would die within the hour. Some priests said they would pray and go to Confession in order to get ready. St Charles replied that he would continue his game of chess - for that was precisely what he should be doing at that time. Mary, Mother of Divine Grace, help me to do always what I should do at each moment.

Day 1 of the Novena to the Immaculate Conception
First Sunday of Advent
Sunday 30th November
Mt 24:37-44

"As were the days of Noah, so will be the coming of the Son of man. For as in those days before the flood they were eating and drinking, marrying and giving in marriage, until the day when Noah entered the ark, and they did not know until the flood came and swept them all away, so will be the coming of the Son of man... Watch therefore, for you do not know on what day your Lord is coming."

Advent starts with the invitation of Our Lord to be alert, to "*watch at all times.*" We don't know when He will come. We don't know which day will be our last. But for those who are ready it doesn't matter when that day comes. Have you ever been so well prepared for an exam that you didn't mind when it was going to take place? You knew the subject so well that you had no worries at all. The same happens with the saints and their encounter with God at the end of their lives.

Saints lived their lives in the presence of God. That means they tried to never forget that God was there, present in their lives. Therefore they didn't try to be holy only when someone was watching, but 'all the time'. We should remember this: **Saints are made when no one is watching.** Saints try to be holy 'all the time'.

Cardinal Mermillod of Geneva was known for his love for the Eucharist. Many people converted just by listening to his preaching. He used to spend long hours at night in prayer before the Blessed Sacrament. One night he prostrated himself, as usual, before the Tabernacle. After a while he heard a noise. To his great surprise, the door of the confessional opened and a lady walked out. The astonished bishop asked: "*What are you doing here at this hour, Madam?*" "*Your Excellency*," replied the woman, a little breathless, "*I am not a Catholic. I have been listening to your preaching over the last few months. I heard what you said about the real Presence of the Blessed Sacrament. I was convinced by your arguments but one doubt remained in my mind, and that is 'if you really believe what you preach'. So I hid myself in the Church to see if you walked the talk.*" The woman converted because the priest was holy always, even when no one was watching. Mary, Mother of Grace, help me this Advent to behave always as your good child and God's.

December

Day 2 of the Novena to the Immaculate Conception
Monday 1st week of Advent
Monday 1st December
Mt 8:5-11

The centurion said, "Lord, my servant is lying paralysed at home, in terrible distress." And he said to him, "I will come and heal him." But the centurion answered him, "Lord, I am not worthy to have you come under my roof; but only say the word, and my servant will be healed..." When Jesus heard him, he marvelled, and said to those who followed him, "Truly, I say to you, not even in Israel have I found such faith."

Those words are repeated every day in Mass before Holy Communion as a reminder of the faith of this centurion and the faith with which we should approach and adore Our Lord really present in the Eucharist with His Body, Blood, Soul and Divinity. Our Lord praised the faith of that centurion... could he praise yours and mine?

During the Spanish Civil War Bl Álvaro del Portillo was sent to prison for being a Christian. Eventually he was released. With two friends, he decided to enlist in the army and get sent to the front in order to cross over into the safe part of the country. Miraculously, the three of them ended up in the same regiment, same battalion, same company, and same platoon! Knowing that they risked their lives, Bl Álvaro managed to get a few Consecrated Hosts that he kept in his wallet in order to receive Holy Communion. When night fell they went for a walk with the Eucharist to do a 'Visit to the Blessed Sacrament'. *"We are living intensely the strength and truth of the Gospel story of the disciples of Emmaus: 'Were not our hearts burning as we walked with Him?'"*

Before going to bed one of them went for a walk carrying the Blessed Sacrament away from possible profanity and blasphemies until everyone was asleep. On October 9 they walked 25 miles. *"Uphill and downhill slopes..."* Bl Álvaro continues, *"turns to one side or other, canyons, stream, small ports, paths that lead nowhere, bushes that conceal men, shouting, wind, profanity, night noises, worn-out shoes. A Roman bridge? More. And even more. Stops, soldiers who are lost, boys who swear not to continue...And Our Lord with us; affection, trust, appreciation, mutual words of encouragement...What a long walk for the others! Yet how short is the hike for us!"* How short is this stroll of life when we are with Our Lord.

Mary, Mother of the Eucharist, increase my faith!

Day 3 of the Novena to the Immaculate Conception
Tuesday 1st week of Advent
Tuesday 2nd December
Lk 10:21-24

In that same hour he rejoiced in the Holy Spirit and said, "I thank thee, Father, Lord of heaven and earth, that thou hast hidden these things from the wise and understanding and revealed them to babes; yea, Father, for such was thy gracious will. All things have been delivered to me by my Father; and no one knows who the Son is except the Father, or who the Father is except the Son and any one to whom the Son chooses to reveal him."

God reveals Himself and the secrets of His Wisdom to whoever He chooses. The 'wise and learned' try to find the truth without God, but... how can you seek the truth without *the* 'Truth'? History is full of saints who have been very simple, had no university degrees or didn't even know how to write and yet they knew God better and did more for the conversion of the world than many theologians. Children with wisdom and composure that defied the people of their times.

On 13th August 1917 the three shepherds of Fatima were put in prison with common criminals to scare them into revealing the secret that Our Lady commanded them to keep. When one of the prisoners advised the little shepherds to tell the administrator the secret, St Jacinta (who was 8 years old) said, "*Never, I'd rather die.*" And then she took off a medal and asked a prisoner to hang it up for her on a nail in the wall. Kneeling before this medal, they began to pray the rosary. Then the most amazing thing happened: the prisoners, all of them, one by one, knelt down and started praying with them! You can imagine the face of the administrator (who had put the children in prison to frighten them) when they got the whole bunch of criminals to pray the rosary on their knees.

Humility teaches us that there are mysteries that we don't understand. In fact, as St Josemaría used to say, "*If God fitted into this poor head of mine, my God would be very small.*" But even if God doesn't fit into our 'heads', He still fits into the 'hearts' of those who become like little children.

Advent is a special time to grow in spiritual childhood, to contemplate the coming of Our Lord with the eyes of a child. My Mother, during the Novena, help me to be like a child, and to know your Son better every day.

Day 4 of the Novena to the Immaculate Conception
Wednesday 1st week of Advent
Wednesday 3rd December
Mt 15:29-37

Jesus called his disciples to him and said, "How many loaves have you?" They said, "Seven, and a few small fish." And commanding the crowd to sit down on the ground, he took the seven loaves and the fish, and having given thanks he broke them and gave them to the disciples, and the disciples gave them to the crowds. And they all ate and were satisfied; and they took up seven baskets full of the broken pieces left over.

Jesus multiplies. Note that He didn't ask, '*How many* **spare** *loaves have you got?*' He asked about the total. They had seven and they gave seven, even if they thought they were few. They thought the fish were few and too small. But they gave it all anyway. And thanks to their generosity 4,000 people had something to eat. That's what Jesus does: He multiplies. You don't have to be very good at maths to know that, even if Jesus multiplies by a thousand, if you give zero, you get zero.

In our case we also need to consider the fact that whatever Jesus *asks* from you is something He actually *gave* you in the first place. Even if He were to ask for your life, remember that it was He who gave it to you. Imagine, for instance, that God gave you a car (and imagine you can drive!) You are test-driving your car and enjoying it when all of a sudden you see Jesus hitchhiking at the side of the road. Would you pick Him up? (Remember that He had given you the car!) He deserves to be allowed in. Don't you agree?

Now imagine that He asks you to take Him to the supermarket, just a short diversion from your route. Remember that you were just test-driving the car, not going anywhere in particular. Would it not be the right thing to do? This is an image of Jesus asking us to let Him into our lives. Since He gave our lives to us He can rightly expect us to give them back. And if He asks us to change our original plan we can be sure that His plan is going to be better than ours.

But there is an even more generous attitude, and a more relaxing approach: give Jesus the key of the car and tell Him: '*You drive! Take me wherever You want us to go.*' Then enjoy the trip: enjoy your life with Him.

Mary, my Mother, may I never leave Jesus as co-pilot of your life: May I let Him drive and give Him what He asks for!

Day 5 of the Novena to the Immaculate Conception
Thursday 1st week of Advent
Thursday 4th December
Mt 7:21.24-27

"Not everyone who says to me, 'Lord, Lord,' shall enter the kingdom of heaven, but he who does the will of my Father who is in heaven. "Everyone then who hears these words of mine and does them will be like a wise man who built his house upon the rock; and the rain fell, and the floods came, and the winds blew and beat upon that house, but it did not fall, because it had been founded on the rock."

The warning is clear: "*Not everyone who says to me, 'Lord, Lord,' shall enter the kingdom of heaven.*" It is not about saying 'Lord, Lord', but about *doing* His Will. It is not about saying that you believe, love or hope, but about proving it with deeds. It is not enough for a man to say to a woman, '*I love you*'. She wants to *see* it. They tell of a boy who wrote to his girlfriend: "*In order to see you I would walk a hundred miles; I'd cross a lava pit barefoot, sail a raft through a terrifying hurricane, swim across shark-infested waters... That's how much I love you! P.S: Tomorrow, as long as it's not raining, I'll cross the road and pop in to see you.*" Not much love here, is there?

When we love God people can see it. Blessed Engelmar Unzeitig (1911 - 1945) was ordained a priest on 6 August 1939. The Gestapo arrested him on 21 April 1941 for defending Jews in his sermons and sent him to the Dachau concentration camp without a trial on 8 June 1941. While there, he served all prisoners in his role as pastor; he even studied Russian in order to administer to the Eastern Europeans. In the autumn of 1944 he volunteered to care for victims of typhoid but he soon contracted the disease himself. From prison he wrote to his sister: "*God's almighty grace helps us overcome obstacles ...love doubles our strength, makes us inventive, makes us feel content and inwardly free. If people would only realise what God has in store for those who love Him!*" He died of the disease on 2 March 1945 and became known as the "Angel of Dachau". Those were real deeds of love. St Josemaría wrote "*There is a story of a soul who, on saying to our Lord in prayer, 'Jesus, I love you,' heard this reply from heaven: 'Love means deeds, not sweet words.' Think if you also could deserve this gentle reproach*" (St Josemaría). Mary, Mother Immaculate, through your intercession during the Novena, may I also be able to prove my love for God with deeds.

Day 6 of the Novena to the Immaculate Conception
Friday 1st week of Advent
Friday 5th December
Mt 9:27-31

As Jesus passed on from there, two blind men followed him, crying aloud, "Have mercy on us, Son of David" ...Jesus said to them, "Do you believe that I am able to do this?" They said to him, "Yes, Lord." Then he touched their eyes, saying, "According to your faith be it done to you." And their eyes were opened. And Jesus sternly charged them, "See that no one knows it." But they went away and spread his fame through all that district.

It all depended on their faith: since the power of Jesus has no limit, the only limit is our faith. Maybe if the two blind men had only had 'a bit' of faith they would have changed from blind men to one-eyed men... or short-sighted men with myopia... But they had lots of faith and Jesus could heal them completely. The only limit on miracles is our faith. If someone complains that there are not as many miracles today as there were in the past, we should help that person to consider that perhaps there is not as much faith today as there was in the past.

There is the story of a rural church in the middle of a farming community that organised a special Mass to pray for rain. A drought had hit the area and their harvest was at risk. Almost the entire village was there at Mass, joining in the prayers for rain. After the Gospel, the priest opened the homily expressing his amazement, *"This is strange!"* he said. *"Two hundred people praying for rain... and no one brought an umbrella!"* It is obvious that they were not expecting God to answer their prayers straight away. Sometimes we can suffer from the same lack of faith. We ask Our Lord for many things but, deep down, we don't expect Him to answer our prayers at once. Maybe we even pray with resignation, as if we don't expect God to hear our prayers. But He does. God always does.

When the Apostles saw that their faith was not even the size of a mustard seed, they asked Jesus: *"Increase our faith!"* (*Lk* 17:5). St Josemaría used to write a sentence on the first page of his liturgical calendar, as a motto for the entire year. On New Year's Day of 1970 he wrote: *"Beata Maria intercedente, fortes in fide!"* ("Through the intercession of Blessed Mary, may we be strong in the Faith.") Why not use his motto for these days of the Novena?

Day 7 of the Novena to the Immaculate Conception
Saturday 1st week of Advent
Saturday 6th December
Mt 9:35-10:1.5a.6-8

And Jesus went about all the cities and villages, teaching in their synagogues and preaching the gospel of the kingdom, and healing every disease and every infirmity. When he saw the crowds, he had compassion for them, because they were harassed and helpless, like sheep without a shepherd...And he called to him his twelve disciples and sent them out, charging them, "go to the lost sheep of the house of Israel. And preach as you go, saying, 'The kingdom of heaven is at hand.' Heal the sick, raise the dead, cleanse lepers, cast out demons. You received without paying, give without pay.

Jesus had compassion on the crowd and in order to help and relieve them, His loving Heart decided to send them His disciples. That's what Jesus did: He had pity on them and sent them His Apostles. And the Apostles received very clear instructions: to preach and to "*heal the sick, raise the dead, cleanse lepers, cast out demons.*" They had been given that power for free and were asked to put it at the service of those who needed it.

That's what God does: He gives people talents to serve others. You and I have been given something that many others may need; that's the purpose of our talents and gifts. Have you heard the story of the man who saw a little girl begging in the streets? He was upset and indignant with God, and said to Him, "*God! Why do you allow this girl to have to beg for a living? Why don't you do something?*" To his surprise, he heard the voice of God replying, "*But I HAVE done something! I put YOU there!*"

We are a gift to others. But a proper 'gift' has to be 'given'. We have to give ourselves to others *completely*! If you fill a large cask with wine and leave other casks half full, your wine would spoil only in the latter instance. Wine is well preserved if the cask is full of wine and sealed with no air inside it. On the other hand, those casks that are half-full can turn sour, because wine becomes vinegar when it comes into contact with air. Something like that happens with the soul. Giving oneself only partially ends up corrupting our friendship with Jesus. We can ask ourselves today: Do I put my talents at the service of others? Do I give myself completely to those around me? I ask you, my Mother: help me to be generous in giving myself to others.

Day 8 of the Novena to the Immaculate Conception
Second Sunday of Advent
Sunday 7th December
Mt 3:1-12

In those days came John the Baptist, preaching in the wilderness of Judea, "Repent, for the kingdom of heaven is at hand." For this is he who was spoken of by the prophet Isaiah when he said, "The voice of one crying in the wilderness: Prepare the way of the Lord, make his paths straight...I baptise you with water for repentance, but he who is coming after me is mightier than I, whose sandals I am not worthy to carry; he will baptise you with the Holy Spirit and with fire."

St John the Baptist is called the 'precursor', because he prepared the people of Israel for the imminent coming of Jesus. And he was so effective because he was humble. When they asked him who he was, he didn't say, 'I am John, son of Zachary of the priestly tribe of...' On the contrary, St John said, "*I am the voice of one crying in the wilderness.*" The voice, like an envelope, is forgotten. The content of the message is the important thing.

He prepared the first disciples of Jesus, sending his own followers to go with Jesus instead of following him. He was the 'voice'; Jesus was the Word of God! When they met Jesus, He made them Apostles. Humility is a feature of the true Apostle. A witness, a precursor, has the humility to bring people to Jesus and then move aside and let Him transform them. That's what we are: precursors, witnesses to Jesus for our friends and relatives. Our mission is to bring souls to Him and He will make of them whatever He wants or needs.

In actual fact, not everyone followed St John the Baptist. Some thought that he was mad. But he didn't care. He gave witness anyway. Bl Dominic Barberi, who received many souls into the Catholic Church in England, had that same humility that made his apostolate effective. People laughed at him, insulted him and pelted him with mud and stones. Dominic never retaliated – he picked up the stones, kissed them and often put them into his pocket as someone who collects precious stones. He was unperturbed and often stood and recited the rosary for his opponents. In time he won them round and Catholicism was revived in England thanks to his persevering witness to Jesus Christ. Mary, Queen of Confessors, help me during this Novena to become a precursor for many souls.

The Immaculate Conception of Our Lady
Monday 8th December
Lk 1:26-38

The angel Gabriel said to Mary, "Hail, full of grace, the Lord is with you! ...Do not be afraid, Mary, for you have found favour with God. And behold, you will conceive in your womb and bear a son, and you shall call his name Jesus. He will be great, and will be called the Son of the Most High; and the Lord God will give to him the throne of his father David, and he will reign over the house of Jacob for ever; and of his kingdom there will be no end."

Friday, 8th December 1854, was a cloudy day. At 8am a solemn liturgical procession entered St Peter's Basilica where Bl Pius IX celebrated Holy Mass. After the singing of the Gospel the Cardinal dean prostrated at the feet of the Pontiff asking him for the decree. From this moment to the end of the *Te Deum*, sung after the Mass, and on a signal from a cannon fired from the Castel Sant'Angelo, for a period of one hour all the bells of Rome rang out together to celebrate a day which, as Mgr. Campana writes, "*will be remembered until the end of time as one of the most glorious days in history.*"

But something else happened that no one had foreseen. During the solemn promulgation a ray of sun opened its way through the clouds and across the stained glass windows to illuminate the face of the Pope, all covered in tears. Everyone saw that light but nobody could ever explain how the sunlight could reach the place where the Pontiff was. The Holy Father interpreted this sunbeam as a heavenly confirmation of the dogma.

At the end of a gifted violinist's concert, when people in the audience were leaving the theatre they found a lovely little girl approaching them and asking, "*Did you like it?*" When they answered affirmatively, she replied with satisfied pride in her eyes, grinning from ear to ear, "*She is my mum!*" And we can feel today just like that child, as millions of Angels and Saints and Holy Souls and people contemplate the Immaculate Conception, the supreme masterpiece of Almighty God, the most beloved, the most admired, revered, cherished, esteemed, impressive, extraordinary, magnificent, sublime creature... Rejoice: *She is your Mother!*

Blessed be your purity, may it be blessed for ever, for no less than God takes delight in such exalted beauty...

Tuesday 2nd week of Advent
Tuesday 9th December
Mt 18:12-14

"What do you think? If a man has a hundred sheep, and one of them has gone astray, does he not leave the ninety-nine on the mountains and go in search of the one that went astray? And if he finds it, truly, I say to you, he rejoices over it more than over the ninety-nine that never went astray. So it is not the will of my Father who is in heaven that one of these little ones should perish."

How much God loves sinners. He calls them "*those little ones*" because they are His children and He is looking for them. His Will is that not one of them is lost. As Pope Francis explained, "*God never tires of forgiveness*," He never gives up, He always goes in search of sinners to bring them back to Him. And in this task of bringing souls to Himself He relies on us, His apostles of the 21st century. If we stop going in search of sinners they may have no other chance.

The enemy is adamant in discouraging God's apostles. The devil tries with all his energies to obstruct our apostolate, to dissuade us from trying again to bring sinners back to God, to demoralise us and interfere with our mission. But souls depend on us. Many souls depend on our struggle never to give up.

For a while St John Vianney suffered the temptation of leaving his parish and retiring to a place where he could devote himself to prayer. But one day he had a very interesting conversation with the devil. The evil spirit talked to him through a possessed lady and insulted him: "*How you torment me! You 'Vilain crapaud noir!*" (the devil called him "*ugly black toad*"). And then, furious with the saint, the devil continued, "*You are a miser of souls. You rob me of all you can...You are a liar! You said, a long while ago, that you wished to depart from this place, and here you still remain. What do you mean by that? Why do you not retire and rest, as others do? You have worked long enough...You talked of retiring into solitude. Why do you not do so?*" So desperate was he to get rid of the saint that he was actually imploring him, like a little child, '*please, please, please... go away!*' Because that is the only way the enemy can manage to get his way: when we give up on God's plan. Mary, Gate of Heaven, help me to never quit going in search of those souls that need to be brought back to your Son.

Wednesday 10th December
Mt 11:28-30

"Come to me, all who labour and are heavy laden, and I will give you rest. Take my yoke upon you, and learn from me; for I am gentle and lowly in heart, and you will find rest for your souls. For my yoke is easy, and my burden is light."

For some the demands of being a disciple of Jesus are too much. They feel overwhelmed with all their responsibilities: '*I have to pray, to offer sacrifices, to finish my work, do my jobs, to live charity with this person, to read, to...*' They feel like they are doing more than everyone else. They are anxious, stressed, harassed, worried, frenetic... they spend the day complaining and don't find time for God. There is a rule we can follow to know whether a burden comes from God or not: its weight. If it is from God, He helps us to carry it.

There is a joke about a tough man, very strong, who was helping his mother to move house, taking the furniture to a neighbouring one. A wardrobe didn't fit in the lorry. Being just one mile away, his mum told him to ask his brother for help and between them both to take it to the new house. After half an hour the lady saw her husky son approaching the house alone, staggering and sweating beneath the wardrobe. She opened the door and blurted out, "*Didn't I tell you to ask your brother for help?*" "*But he **is** helping,*" replied the son, "*he is inside holding the hangers!*"

Sometimes we are like that. The burden is heavy because we don't know how to accept it and we don't ask Our Lord for help; but Our Lord never sends us anything we can't cope with. His yoke is *easy*, He says. Have you seen those ladies carrying heavy burdens on their heads? The secret is in the 'balance'. In our lives, to cope with all our responsibilities, the secret is also 'balance': balance between prayer and action.

Those burdens, taken for and with Jesus, become opportunities to sanctify ourselves. Complaining about your burdens would be like a bird complaining about the weight of its wings! Wings are a lovely burden for an eagle, for they allow it to soar! Mary, my Mother, may I never complain about the burden that God puts on my shoulders but rather, give thanks to Him and use that to soar to the heights of holiness.

Thursday 2nd week of Advent
Thursday 11th December
Mt 11:11-15

"Truly, I say to you, among those born of women there has risen no one greater than John the Baptist; yet he who is least in the kingdom of heaven is greater than he. From the days of John the Baptist until now the kingdom of heaven has suffered violence, and men of violence take it by force."

Our Lord warned us that Christian life is a 'struggle'. It is a struggle to do your prayer, to say the Rosary, to go to Mass, to make good use of your time, to work hard and with perfection, to offer up sacrifices... It is a struggle because we have to "*take it by force.*" Our struggle for holiness is a real battle against the enemy; he never gives up, but nor do we.

To win this war we need to know the enemy well. In a war, if you know your opponent's strategy, their best soldiers, weapons and moves, their weak and strong points... you can plan your strategy better. And our enemy in this war for holiness has very predictable moves and obvious weak points. Think about the times he has beaten you: it has always happened in the same 'ways'. For example, you start wasting time and temptation comes; you stop doing what you should be doing or you start thinking about yourself or criticising someone else interiorly and you find yourself in temptation. When you allow these things to happen, you've already opened the door to the enemy; you are fighting now behind the enemy lines.

On the contrary, if you fight against those things, the enemy always finds the door well shut. You are fighting on your own ground and the enemy has to comply and fight where you want, not where he wants. If we struggle to make good use of our time, if we stop thoughts of vanity or criticism of others, if we are doing what we should be doing all the time, if we are looking for new sacrifices to offer, new people to help, new good things to do... the enemy has no chance. It is like playing a football match in the opponent's half - they will never score and will let in goals one after another. Whilst the enemy has to defend himself, he can't attack. And he has to defend when we spend the whole day struggling to do what we have to do, pray as we have to pray, help whoever we should help and try all the time to become a saint.

Friday 12th December
Mt 11:16-19

"But to what shall I compare this generation? It is like children sitting in the market places and calling to their playmates, 'We piped to you, and you did not dance; we wailed, and you did not mourn.' For John came neither eating nor drinking, and they say, 'He has a demon'; the Son of man came eating and drinking, and they say, 'Behold, a glutton and a drunkard, a friend of tax collectors and sinners!' Yet wisdom is justified by her deeds."

Jesus complained about those who are never satisfied with anything. St John the Baptist had been preaching for them and they wouldn't listen to him; maybe they thought he was too harsh or too radical or too rustic... Then came Jesus and they didn't like Him either. They were expecting someone different. This happened many times in the history of Israel: they were never happy with the prophets that God gave them or with the messages that Our Lord sent to them.

Have you heard the legend of Procrustes? He had an iron bed which all his victims 'had to' fit into. If a guest was shorter than the bed he would stretch him. And if the victim was longer than the bed he would cut off his legs... Some people can be a bit like Procrustes. Nothing ever meets their expectations. Not even God.

At the end of the day, it was just pride: *'St John didn't eat; Jesus ate too much...'* When people don't want to change their way of life they always make excuses. Imagine that a doctor tells a man to follow an uncomfortable diet to stay healthy. What would you think if that man refused to follow the diet, claiming that the doctor smokes or drinks too much? Excuses! He just doesn't want to follow the diet. Or if a man doesn't want to take the medicine because the doctor who prescribed it is a gambler? Some people who are not interested in going to Mass or confessing their sins, praying a bit more, giving money to the poor or lending a hand to their neighbours... they may try to accuse someone else of other vices to justify themselves and not do anything. Mary, Mother of Good Counsel, do not allow me to make excuses when your Son makes demands on me and when His plan doesn't coincide with my 'project'. Mother, teach me with your life that God can never ask too much of me.

Our Lady of Guadalupe
Friday 12th December
Lk 1:39-47

In those days Mary arose and went with haste into the hill country, to a city of Judah, and she entered the house of Zechariah and greeted Elizabeth. And when Elizabeth heard the greeting of Mary, the babe leaped in her womb; and Elizabeth was filled with the Holy Spirit and she exclaimed with a loud cry, "Blessed are you among women, and blessed is the fruit of your womb! And why is this granted me, that the mother of my Lord should come to me? For behold, when the voice of your greeting came to my ears, the babe in my womb leaped for joy. And blessed is she who believed that there would be a fulfilment of what was spoken to her from the Lord."

As you will remember, this Gospel text comes after the visitation of the Angel Gabriel to Mary. He explained Our Lady's vocation to her and also what had happened to her cousin Elizabeth. Elizabeth and Zechariah were expecting a child (St John the Baptist) in their old age. Mary didn't hesitate for a second. She went *'with haste'* to help Elizabeth. No one asked for her, no one was expecting her. But she went anyway. She had her own personal problems as well, she was pregnant with the Son of God... but she went all the same. Because when it comes to serving, Mary doesn't hesitate.

How reassuring for her children to consider that *'it is a thing unheard of, that anyone ever had recourse to her protection, implored her help, or sought her intercession and was left forsaken.'* Even if we don't ask for help, she comes to our aid all the same.

On December 12th 1531, Juan Diego (an Indian convert) was going to the Church in order to bring a priest to his dying uncle. He was stopped by Our Lady, who had come to meet him on the road. She listened quietly to Juan's excuse for not having kept his appointment with her the day before. Then she said to him, *"Listen, put it into your heart, my youngest and dearest son, do not let anything afflict you and be not afraid of illness or pain. Am I not here who am your Mother? Are you not under my shadow and protection? Are you not in the crossing of my arms? Is there anything else you need? Let nothing else worry you, disturb you."* What comfort to be so loved by Our Lady! Mother, teach me to pray with the same confidence of a beloved child who talks to his beloved mother. Help me to trust you and if I forget to ask for help... come to help me anyway!

Saturday 2nd week of Advent
Saturday 13th December
Mt 17:9a.10-13

And as they were coming down the mountain, the disciples asked him, "Then why do the scribes say that first Elijah must come?" He replied, "Elijah does come, and he is to restore all things; but I tell you that Elijah has already come, and they did not know him, but did to him whatever they pleased. So also the Son of man will suffer at their hands." Then the disciples understood that he was speaking to them of John the Baptist.

It's astonishing how short-sighted people can be. They can have a prophet right in front of their faces and fail to recognise him. On one occasion Elijah gently brought a dead boy back to life for the sake of the widowed mother (1 *Kgs* 17:22) but they persecuted him all the same. St John the Baptist was famous, even King Herod heard him. But the people of Israel didn't recognise him either.

There was a famous tennis player who won a grand slam. Journalists and fans went to the airport to receive him on his arrival. But the loudspeakers at the airport announced that there would be an hour's delay due to bad weather. To keep the waiting crowd entertained, airport staff projected the recorded championship final on a big screen. The problem came when the plane landed twenty minutes ahead of schedule in another terminal where no one was actually expecting it to. Everyone was so absorbed in the tennis match that they missed the celebrity's arrival!

The people of Israel were awaiting the Messiah for centuries, imploring God to send Him soon and preparing themselves for that coming. And when He eventually came... they also failed to recognise Him. Still today, people are expecting Christmas... but not Christ; like celebrating a wedding and leaving the bride outside. They expect gifts... but not 'The Gift', the Son of God made man. They will celebrate the Birth of Jesus Christ... without Jesus Christ. To avoid this happening again, we have Advent. "*Advent is here. What a marvellous time in which to renew your desire, your nostalgia, your real longing for Christ to come - for him to come every day to your soul in the Eucharist. The Church encourages us: Ecce veniet! - He is about to arrive!*" (St Josemaría). Mary, Mother of God, help me to get ready for your Son's arrival.

Third Sunday of Advent. Gaudete Sunday
Sunday 14th December
Mt 11:2-11

Now when John heard in prison about the deeds of the Christ, he sent word by his disciples and said to him, "Are you he who is to come, or shall we look for another?" And Jesus answered them, "Go and tell John what you hear and see: the blind receive their sight and the lame walk, lepers are cleansed and the deaf hear, and the dead are raised up, and the poor have good news preached to them. And blessed is he who takes no offence at me."

Today is 'Gaudete Sunday'. Gaudete is the *imperative* form of 'rejoice'. We open the Mass today with the words of St Paul: "*Rejoice in the Lord always. I shall say it again: rejoice!*" (*Phil* 4:4). It is a command: rejoice, because God is coming. Rejoice, says the liturgy today, because our days of darkness are close to their end, dawn is nearly here! The sun is rising: the Son is coming.

St John was in prison. He knew his time was over and then sent his disciples to Jesus. The question they asked Jesus was a 'Yes-or-No' question. But Jesus didn't say, 'Yes' or 'No'. He said to them, 'Look around!' It is easy to recognise the effect of God's love: the blind seeing, the lame walking, the deaf hearing, lepers cleansed and dead people alive and kicking... You can imagine the blessedness in that atmosphere. That was the best of parties because where God is, there you find joy.

Venerable Monste Grases was diagnosed with bone cancer at the age of 17. In her pain she never stopped smiling. Such was her constant joy that her mother doubted if she had understood her illness properly: "*Montse, do you think you will get well?*", she asked her daughter. "*No, mum,*" Montse replied from her bed, "*but why don't you open the blinds - wide open - I need light and joy in the room. Why don't we sing something?*" Then she started singing. Mum cleared her throat and joined...but dad covered his face with the newspaper to hide his tears. Montse interrupted the song and said, "*Dad, I can't hear you. I want you joyful always.*" She died shortly after, with a smile on her face.

Mary, Cause of Our Joy, with the coming of your Son just around the corner, may I never lack joy: "*Don't be gloomy. Let your outlook be more 'ours', — more Christian.*" (St Josemaría)

Monday 3rd week of Advent
Monday 15th December
Mt 21:23-27

The chief priests and the elders of the people came up to him as he was teaching, and said, "By what authority are you doing these things, and who gave you this authority?" Jesus answered them, "I also will ask you a question; and if you tell me the answer, then I also will tell you by what authority I do these things. The baptism of John, whence was it? From heaven or from men?" And they argued with one another, "If we say, 'From heaven,' he will say to us, 'Why then did you not believe him?' But if we say, 'From men,' we are afraid of the multitude; for all hold that John was a prophet." So they answered Jesus, "We do not know." And he said to them, "Neither will I tell you by what authority I do these things."

We don't often see someone coming to You, Lord, with a question and going away without an answer, but of course, not everyone was ready to listen. There are people who pray and talk to You, Lord, but do not want to listen to Your Voice for fear that You may say something that can complicate their lives.

Prayer is a *dialogue*. A dialogue involves listening *and* talking. But we sometimes spend our prayer time asking for things, venting our problems or just getting distracted with a text or our own thoughts, never giving God time to reply. 'Silence' is an important part of our prayer. That's God's turn to speak. If we spend the whole time talking, God has no time to answer.

A young man made a long trip to visit a wise old priest and asked him to teach him to pray. The old priest lifted his index finger and said, "*Listen, my son...*" The lad quickly took a notebook from his pocket to start writing down his words. "*I'm listening Father. What else?*" said the youngster. "*There is nothing else. Just listen,*" replied the priest. To learn to pray, learn to listen. Our prayer is a dialogue where we talk *and* listen because God listens and talks as well. But remember that God is the main character here: "*What is essential is not what we say but what God tells us and what He tells others through us. In silence He listens to us; in silence He speaks to our souls. In silence we are granted the privilege of listening to His voice*" (St Teresa of Calcutta).

Mary, Master of Prayer, teach me to converse with God.

Tuesday 3rd week of Advent
Tuesday 16th December
Mt 21:28-32

"What do you think? A man had two sons; and he went to the first and said, 'Son, go and work in the vineyard today.' And he answered, 'I will not'; but afterwards he repented and went. And he went to the second and said the same; and he answered, 'I go, sir,' but did not go. Which of the two did the will of his father?" They said, "The first."

Both sons did something wrong. The first one wasn't ready to help at the beginning, but later he thought about his father, understood his duty and decided to do it. The second one was well disposed at the beginning. He knew he should help. He wanted to help. But when it was time to act...he just didn't. He wasn't a 'bad son', deciding not to obey; he did *want* to...but didn't do it. St Paul referred to this when he wrote: "*I do not do what I want, but I do the very thing I hate...For I do not do the good I want, but the evil I do not want is what I do*" (*Ro* 7:15,19). Laziness, for instance, has that effect. We want to do something but we start procrastinating and end up not doing it at all. We regret it, because we wanted to get it done but just didn't. How many people were determined to do something important in their lives and eventually couldn't bring themselves to do it!

One of the enemy's best strategies is not suggesting bad things for us to do, but persuading us to stop doing good things. They are called 'omissions'. We don't stop doing a good thing because we *decide not to do it*, but because we *never decide to do it*. When Our Lord talks about those who didn't enter Heaven, He explains that it wasn't because of what they *did*, but because of what they *didn't do*: "*for I was hungry and you gave me no food....*"

People don't fail exams because they intend to fail, but because they just don't study. Most people don't stop praying because they decide to quit, but because it's more comfortable not to pray. "*The world offers you comfort*", said Pope Benedict XVI, "*But you were not made for comfort. You were made for greatness.*"

Mary, Virgin Most Faithful, this child of yours was made for greatness; help me to reach the goal that your Son has for me. May I always do what He wants me to do, when He wants it done, as He expects it done... and always for love of God.

Wednesday 17th December
Mt 1:1–17

The book of the genealogy of Jesus Christ, the son of David, the son of Abraham. Abraham was the father of Isaac, and Isaac the father of Jacob, and Jacob the father of Judah and his brothers, and Judah the father of Perez and Zerah by Tamar, and Perez the father of Hezron,...Achim the father of Eliud, and Eliud the father of Eleazar, and Eleazar the father of Matthan and Matthan the father of Jacob, and Jacob the father of Joseph the husband of Mary, of whom Jesus was born, who is called Christ.

Today we start the second phase of Advent. The readings of the Mass now turn our attention to preparing for the Nativity of Our Lord. Today's Gospel is full of the names of Jesus' ancestors. Lots of these names are unfamiliar to us. Others are well-known patriarchs and saints. Still others are well-known sinners. Before Jesus, history is made up of a mixture of saints and sinners, many of them anonymous characters. God used them all to bring about His salvation.

God *'writes straight with crooked lines.'* He can use anyone He likes as an instrument. And when His marvellous deed happens, it's the Artist who gets the credit, not the instruments. You don't find a monument to Shakespeare's pen. It would be ridiculous if someone on the list of ancestors claimed to have brought about salvation; that, thanks to him or her, Jesus became a man or that without them, redemption wouldn't have been possible. God brought salvation. They had the 'honour' of being chosen to co-operate. That's all.

Pope John Paul I described a comic scene: imagine that during Jesus' entrance into Jerusalem, the donkey that He was riding on could think out loud. Seeing a crowd cheering, applauding and placing palm branches under its hooves, imagine the donkey looking around him with a big smile and starting to thank his audience, *'Thank you! Thank you very much! Thanks for coming!'* Hilarious! The same ridiculous scene would be repeated if we, instruments in the Hands of God, claimed credit for the marvellous works that God performs through us. If God chooses us to perform great things, we should never forget that we are just instruments. He is the Artist. Mary, Mother of God, help me to be grateful for the honour (the privilege!) of being God's instrument.

December 18
Thursday 18th December
Mt 1:18–25

Now the birth of Jesus Christ took place in this way. When his mother Mary had been betrothed to Joseph, before they came together she was found to be with child of the Holy Spirit; and her husband Joseph, being a just man and unwilling to put her to shame, resolved to send her away. But as he considered this, behold, an angel of the Lord appeared to him in a dream, saying, "Joseph, son of David, do not fear to take Mary your wife, for that which is conceived in her is of the Holy Spirit; she will bear a son, and you shall call his name Jesus, for he will save his people from their sins"...When Joseph woke from sleep, he did as the angel of the Lord commanded him.

To live Advent better we should look at this holy man: St Joseph. Our Lord could rely on him because he always did *'as the Lord commanded him'*. That's what made him such a great saint. He didn't say anything; we don't find a word of St Joseph's in the Gospels. But with his life he kept saying, *"Your Will be done!"*

It's impossible to read the life of St Joseph and not be deeply grateful to him. It's impossible to reflect on his life and not feel impelled to love him more each day. It's impossible to consider his faithfulness to both God and Mary and not be moved. It's impossible to approach St Joseph and not get close to his Son, Jesus. It's impossible to see his love for Jesus and Mary and not yearn for that same feeling. It's impossible to consider his silence before adversity and not long for that interior peace. It's impossible to imagine St Joseph working shoulder to shoulder with the Son of God and not wish to be able to work like that. It's impossible to see St Joseph surrounded by Jesus and Mary and not look forward to spending our Life like that. It's impossible to be fond of this saint and not become a saint yourself. It's impossible to be told that St Joseph is your father and not feel proud of it.

"To other Saints Our Lord seems to have given power to succour us in some special necessity - but to this glorious Saint He has given the power to help us in all. As He was subject to St. Joseph on earth - for St. Joseph, bearing the title of father and being His guardian, could command Him - so now in Heaven Our Lord grants all his petitions" (St Teresa of Avila). Mary, teach me to love your husband and grow in devotion to him over the coming days.

Friday 19th December
Lk 1:5–25

The angel said to Zechariah, "Do not be afraid, Zechariah, for your prayer is heard, and your wife Elizabeth will bear you a son, and you shall call his name John"...And Zechariah said to the angel, "How shall I know this? For I am an old man, and my wife is advanced in years." And the angel answered him, "I am Gabriel...and behold, you will be silent and unable to speak until the day that these things come to pass, because you did not believe my words."

Zechariah was a godly man. However, when the Archangel Gabriel confirmed that Zechariah's prayer *was heard*, he wasn't ready to believe it: "*How shall I know this?*" How can I be sure? Was it not enough to receive the visit of an Archangel? As Jesus complained to St Faustina, **"Distrust on the part of souls is tearing at My insides. The distrust of a chosen soul causes Me even greater pain; despite My inexhaustible love for them they do not trust Me."**

Many people find it difficult to make decisions out of fear: '*What if...?*' More than daydreaming, it is *day-nightmaring*. They are petrified by the thought of some potential future calamities that could happen. Then the safest route is not to take any route. But not to make any decision is already a *decision* - the decision not to trust in God.

One day Fr Lainez was quizzed by St Ignatius of Loyola. "*If God gave you the choice between going straightaway to Heaven or staying here on earth working for His Glory - but risking your salvation - what would you choose?*" Lainez answered quickly: "*I'd certainly choose the first: my salvation.*" Then St Ignatius replied: "*I'd rather choose the second. How could God allow my condemnation as a consequence of a previous act of generosity on my part?*" Risk is part of human life. We can't do anything at all if we don't take some risks. To walk you have to take the risk of lifting one foot and balancing all your weight on the other. But if you don't... you can't walk! And what if I make a mistake? Don't worry! If you make it out of trust in God, He knows how to turn that mistake into something good.

Mary, my Mother of God, help me to trust God more and to be daring in following His promptings.

Saturday 20th December
Lk 1:26-38

In the sixth month the angel Gabriel was sent from God to a city of Galilee named Nazareth, to a virgin betrothed to a man whose name was Joseph, of the house of David; and the virgin's name was Mary. And he came to her and said, "Hail, full of grace, the Lord is with you!" But she was greatly troubled at the saying, and considered in her mind what sort of greeting this might be. And the angel said to her, "Do not be afraid, Mary, for you have found favour with God. And behold, you will conceive in your womb and bear a son, and you shall call his name Jesus."

O, Gabriel, what a decisive moment in history! Among the millions of Angels it fell to you to deliver the most important message ever announced. How many centuries practising your lines! In this divine play that started millions of centuries ago we were all given lines; but yours, Gabriel, were the most important ever to be spoken by a creature (after those of Mary, of course). You had three parts in the play: one with Zechariah, one with Joseph (although this was only in his dreams) and the one that was every Angel's dream to deliver, your message to Mary.

How was it? Actually, how was *she*? Were you nervous? The salvation of the whole human race depended on the outcome of that conversation with Mary. What if your sudden appearance frightened her? What if your words wouldn't come out? What if you missed out a line? And what if...what if Mary said 'No'? But, of course, that couldn't happen...could it? Well, you, Gabriel, had centuries to prepare your lines, but not Mary. You had read the script millions of years ago, but Mary hadn't. You, Gabriel, were given your lines, but Mary wasn't. There were no lines for her in the script. There was a gap that only she could fill. All the Angels in Heaven knew the question. All the Archangels, patriarchs - and God Himself - knew your lines, Gabriel. And all of them waited eagerly for the reply. And that is the case for every vocation, for every mission that God gives men. Angels, Archangels, Saints and Holy Souls - and God Himself - know my calling and mission. What they don't know, what they are still waiting for, what history hasn't heard yet, is my reply.

Here it is: Holy Mary, through your intercession, be it done unto me according to God's Word!

Fourth Sunday of Advent
Sunday 21st December
Mt 1:18-24

Now the birth of Jesus Christ took place in this way. When his mother Mary had been betrothed to Joseph, before they came together she was found to be with child of the Holy Spirit; and her husband Joseph, being a just man and unwilling to put her to shame, resolved to send her away. But as he considered this, behold, an angel of the Lord appeared to him in a dream, saying, "Joseph, son of David, do not fear to take Mary your wife, for that which is conceived in her is of the Holy Spirit; she will bear a son, and you shall call his name Jesus, for he will save his people from their sins."

O, poor Joseph, my father and lord! What an agony for a heart like yours that loved so much! Your beloved wife, Mary, that wonderful creature who accepted your hand in marriage... O, how blessed you felt not so long ago when telling your family and friends that the daughter of Joaquim and Anne, the most beautiful, lovely, sensible, virtuous maiden in Nazareth was going to become your wife! O Joseph, how you would walk with your betrothed through the streets, your neighbours staring at you in awe; Mary radiant and you, Joseph, brimming with joy.

No man has loved his wife as you, Joseph, loved Mary. No man can understand the pain of your heart ripped apart at the news that Mary was expecting...and it was not your son! No man can understand the depth of your anguish, but God can. Because God knew that, in the whole of creation, only one man - one man alone! - could cope with this torment, and it was you, Joseph, son of David. The one who loves more can endure more suffering.

It was all a mystery for you, Joseph, since God still hadn't told you that the son of Mary...was to be your son! He would call you dad and hold your hand, Joseph. He would cry on your shoulder, kiss your face, hug your neck, pull your beard... He would live with you, sing with you, work with you, laugh with you, play with you, pray with you! Joseph: no man has suffered what you suffered, but no one was loved as you were loved by the Son of God, by the Mother of God, by us too. Blessed are you, Joseph; your pain had no equal, but neither your joy! Mary, spouse of Joseph, teach me to love your husband as you do, as Jesus wants me to love His father.

December 22
Monday 22nd December
Lk 1:46–56

Mary said, "My soul magnifies the Lord, and my spirit rejoices in God my Saviour, for he has regarded the low estate of his handmaiden. For behold, henceforth all generations will call me blessed; for he who is mighty has done great things for me, and holy is his name. And his mercy is on those who fear him from generation to generation. He has shown strength with his arm, he has scattered the proud in the imagination of their hearts, he has put down the mighty from their thrones, and exalted those of low degree."

Of course all generations would call you blessed, would they not? You are the Mother of God! Chosen from among millions to be the Mother of Jesus. And what did you say? *"He who is mighty has done great things for me."* It has all been God's doing. The only creature in the world who could boast about her gifts and talents, considers herself the *handmaid* of God. Blessed are you, Mother!

When our friends praise us for our deeds, we thank them for their kindness. When Elizabeth extols Mary, Mary glorifies God. Mary receives praise as a mirror receives light; she doesn't store it but makes it pass from her to God, to whom is due all praise, all honour and thanksgiving. It is above all a wonderful praise of Almighty God, an act of thanksgiving for the goodness of the Creator. The shortened form of Mary's song – the 'Magnificat' – is: *"Thank God."*

Mary's song has two notes: humility and joy. Her spirit rejoices because God has looked favourably on her humility. A box that is filled with sand cannot be filled with gold; a soul bursting with its own ego can never be filled with God. The emptier the soul is of self, the greater room in it for God. And Mary was all room, free space into which God could pour His Grace. God did great things in Mary because of her humility. He will hardly do great things in us if He doesn't also see our humility. Humility attracts the attention of God. *"It was the virtue which attracted the gaze of the Most Holy Trinity to his Mother and our Mother: the humility of knowing and being aware of our nothingness... 'Because he has looked graciously upon the lowliness of his handmaid' ...I am more convinced every day that authentic humility is the supernatural basis for all virtues! Talk to Our Lady, so that she may train us to walk along that path"*. (St Josemaría)

Tuesday 23rd December
Lk 1:57-66

On the eighth day they came to circumcise the child; and they would have named him Zechariah after his father, but his mother said, "Not so; he shall be called John." And they said to her, "None of your kindred is called by this name." And they made signs to his father, inquiring what he would have him called. And he asked for a writing tablet, and wrote, "His name is John."

They wanted to name the baby after his father, Zechariah, because that was what people did at the time. They were expecting Zechariah to do exactly what everyone else did. They didn't know the story behind the birth of St John. They didn't know what the Angel had revealed to Zechariah. They didn't know why he was dumb. Nevertheless, these busybodies wanted to name the baby after his father because that was 'what people did'. But God doesn't ask us to do 'what people do', He asks us to do His Will.

Zechariah had been dumb for nine months. In that period he had time to meditate upon the instructions of the Lord. So, when he had to do what the Angel had said, he didn't waste time writing explanations. He went straight to the point: "*His name is John;*" full stop! As if saying, 'Mind your own business'. And after he had obeyed, he recovered the use of his speech...

Some people (even relatives) expect us to do something because that is the custom or their project or because that's 'what people do'. But God doesn't follow the same pattern. The father of St Francis of Assisi didn't allow him to follow his vocation for a long time. But it didn't change the saint's resolution. The father of St Francis of Sales had already arranged a marriage for him when he revealed his intention to become a priest. The argument lasted for years. St Louis Bertran had to run away from home at the age of 18 because his parents wouldn't allow him to become a friar. Eventually the three of them managed to solve the problem and their parents felt proud of their holy children, but it took years and great suffering on both parts. It all happened because people had plans 'for others': for their children, their friends... Mary, Virgin Most Prudent, I pray that, through your intercession, many may understand how God's plans are always better and that they may help others to follow God's Will.

Christmas Eve
Wednesday 24th December
Lk 1:67–79

Zechariah said, "Blessed be the Lord God of Israel, for he has visited and redeemed his people, and has raised up a horn of salvation for us in the house of his servant David, as he spoke by the mouth of his holy prophets from of old, that we should be saved from our enemies, and from the hand of all who hate us; to perform the mercy promised to our fathers, and to remember his holy covenant, the oath which he swore to our father Abraham."

The natural response to the season we start tonight is to sing. Elizabeth sang the *Hail Mary*; Mary sang the *Magnificat*; Zechariah sang the *Benedictus*. A noted poet was once asked in an interview if he could explain one of his poems *'in ordinary terms.'* He replied with some feeling, "*If I could say what I meant in ordinary terms I would not have had to write the poem.*" Christmas is a song, a poem. The fulfilment of God's promise is the loveliest chant ever. Even Angels came to sing it. Because the Mystery of the Love of God lying on straw in a manger cannot possibly be spelled out *'in ordinary terms.'*

Tonight is Christmas again. God's Word will be there, in Person, as a newborn Baby, between His beautiful Mother (my Mother too) and Joseph, (her young, faithful and fearless husband), with an ox and a donkey, and you and me. A silent night. With a stillness that allows us to hear the song of Angels and accompany them. We start singing tonight and will carry on singing for the whole season, because there is no way to thank God for His Incarnation in just *'ordinary terms.'*

"*Again and again the beauty of this Gospel touches our hearts...Again and again it astonishes us that God makes himself a child so that we may love him, so that we may dare to love him, and as a child trustingly lets himself be taken into our arms. It is as if God were saying: I know that my glory frightens you, and that you are trying to assert yourself in the face of my grandeur. So now I am coming to you as a child, so that you can accept me and love me*" (Pope Benedict XVI). Mary, Mother of God, let me be at your side tonight, with Joseph, to contemplate your Baby-God.

The Nativity of the Lord
Thursday 25th December
Lk 2:1-14

Joseph went up from Galilee, from the city of Nazareth, to Judea, to the city of David, which is called Bethlehem, because he was of the house and lineage of David, to be enrolled with Mary, his betrothed, who was with child. And while they were there, the time came for her to be delivered. And she gave birth to her first-born son and wrapped him in swaddling cloths, and laid him in a manger, because there was no place for them in the inn. And in that region there were shepherds out in the field, keeping watch over their flock by night. And an angel of the Lord appeared to them, and the glory of the Lord shone around them, and they were filled with fear. And the angel said to them, "Be not afraid; for behold, I bring you good news of a great joy which will come to all the people; for to you is born this day in the city of David a Saviour, who is Christ the Lord. And this will be a sign for you: you will find a babe wrapped in swaddling cloths and lying in a manger."

Do you remember the holy eagerness of the patriarchs who sighed longingly for the coming of the Messiah? Blessed be our eyes because we see what many longed to see and never saw; we hear what many yearned to hear and never heard. Blessed are we who have seen God in a Baby, the Creator in swaddling cloths; blessed are we who have met the Redeemer in a manger; blessed are we who contemplate Mary holding Salvation in her arms; blessed are we who stare at Joseph kissing the Son of God (who is also his adopted Son); blessed are we who hear the Angels singing; blessed are we who see the shepherds adoring the Baby; blessed are we who have seen the promise fulfilled.

Feel blessed at Christmas: the wait is over, God is here; the devil trembles now in front of this Baby because, out of love for you, He has come to erase your sins.

Today then is a day for contemplating, listening, singing... and loving. "*Make your way to Bethlehem, go up to the Child, take him in your arms and dance, say warm and tender things to him, press him close to your heart... I am not talking childish nonsense: I am speaking of love! And love is shown with deeds. In the intimacy of your soul, you can indeed hug him tight!*" (St Josemaría). Mary, Mother of God and my Mother, show me the Baby!

St Stephen, first martyr
Friday 26th December
Mt 10:17–22

Jesus said to his disciples, "Beware of men; for they will deliver you up to councils, and flog you in their synagogues, and you will be dragged before governors and kings for my sake, to bear testimony before them and the Gentiles. When they deliver you up, do not be anxious how you are to speak or what you are to say; for what you are to say will be given to you in that hour; for it is not you who speak, but the Spirit of your Father speaking through you. Brother will deliver up brother to death, and the father his child, and children will rise against parents and have them put to death; and you will be hated by all for my name's sake. But he who endures to the end will be saved."

A day after the celebration of Our Lord's Birth we celebrate the death of the first martyr, St Stephen. He became the first Christian to be killed for his faith in Jesus Christ. Jesus warned his disciples of this persecution. In fact, that is a clear sign that you are on the right path: if you follow in Jesus' footsteps, you get what He got and you end up where He ended up. St Stephen gave witness to Jesus but they didn't accept his testimony. The Acts of the Apostles tells that they "*stopped their ears and rushed upon him.*" (7:57)

They couldn't refute anything. They just "*stopped their ears.*" But Stephen didn't compromise the truth. And for that reason he was killed fulfilling the prophecy that we read about in today's Gospel. They *thought* they had finished him. However, that was just the beginning. Do you remember Saul? Saul was a young man, full of zeal. He helped the executioners stone Stephen to death. Stephen died praying for his murderers.

Saul couldn't stand that Message; he covered his ears to stop hearing that Truth but the Truth came to him. From Heaven, St Stephen kept doing his job and eventually, the man who had been stoning him became St Paul, the Apostle, the man who changed the history of Christianity and spread that Message, that Truth all over the world. He would in turn also be killed for that same Truth.

Because the transforming work of martyrs doesn't finish when they die. That's just the beginning! Mary, Queen of Martyrs, help me to be steady in witnessing to that same Truth, namely, that God became a Man in Bethlehem to die for our sins in Jerusalem.

St John, Apostle and Evangelist
Saturday 27th December
Jn 20:1a, 2-8

Now on the first day of the week Mary Magdalene went to Simon Peter and the other disciple, the one whom Jesus loved, and said to them, "They have taken the Lord out of the tomb, and we do not know where they have laid him." Peter then came out with the other disciple, and they went toward the tomb. They both ran, but the other disciple outran Peter and reached the tomb first...

O, John, "*the one whom Jesus loved*"! How you loved that title! The 'Beloved'. You were still young when you started following St John the Baptist. You loved him and listened to him, thinking that he could be the one. But one memorable day he looked into your eyes with affection and said to you, '*I am not the One you are looking for, John. I am not the One who can quench your thirst for Love. I am not the One you should follow, the One that can give meaning to your life... the One that is worth living with and dying for...*' Then he pointed at Jesus, Who was passing by, '*He is the One you are looking for.*'

And you, John, jumped to your feet and followed Jesus. You never forgot that day, not even the time: "*it was about the tenth hour.*" And from that day on, always with Jesus. You were with Him from beginning to end. You heard Jesus preaching on the mount, by the sea, in the Temple, in the streets; you, John, saw His Glory on Mount Tabor during His Transfiguration; you saw Him multiplying loaves and fish, transforming water into wine; you saw Him acclaimed by the crowds. But there you were also, dear John, when He was despised by the leaders; when He was betrayed, rejected, deserted... there you were, John, when Jesus cried; when He bled; when He was tried, scorned, repudiated, scourged, insulted... and crucified.

You, John, were the youngest, but also the bravest. Because 'love gives courage'. Thank you, John, for loving Him so much; for your daring, for comforting Jesus when He needed you. That's why you were the Beloved, why Mary was entrusted to you; that's why you rested your head on Jesus' bosom...What a consolation it was for Our Lord to have you there, so young, so madly in love! John, teach me to love Jesus, to give myself to Him now, in my youth; to follow Him, to stand faithful beside the Cross, comforting Jesus... and taking Mary, as my Mother, into my home.

The Holy Family of Jesus, Mary and Joseph
Sunday 28th December
Mt 2:13-15, 19-23

Now when they had departed, behold, an angel of the Lord appeared to Joseph in a dream and said, "Rise, take the child and his mother, and flee to Egypt, and remain there till I tell you; for Herod is about to search for the child, to destroy him." And he rose and took the child and his mother by night, and departed to Egypt, and remained there until the death of Herod. This was to fulfil what the Lord had spoken by the prophet, "Out of Egypt have I called my son."

Jesus planned our Redemption from all eternity. To bring about the forgiveness of our sins and make us children of God He charted a course of action. Jesus wanted to come into the world without being noticed, without a house, without money, without a cradle, without possessions... but not without a *family*, a Holy Family. He didn't want us to be left without that Holy Family either and now Mary is our Mother, Joseph our father, Jesus our Brother and we... the privileged members of the Family of Nazareth.

Today's Gospel tells us about a painful experience for Mary and Joseph: the flight to Egypt. Families exist so that joys and sorrows can be shared, so that my joy can also be others' joy and my sufferings would never only be mine. Today the family is the main target of the enemy, because he knows, as St John Paul II said that *"as the family goes, so goes the nation and so goes the whole world in which we live."* So we have a battle to fight.

How can I change the world? What can I do for my community, my city, my country, for peace in the world? The answer is simple: love your family; love each of the members of your family, as they are, taking the bitter with the sweet. Family love is powerful. Family unity is a hammer blow on the devil's head! An army of families in which its members love each other, who share joys and sorrows, who pray together, who place God at the centre and holiness as the common goal. That army can change the world. Families are under attack but in this violent battle that we fight, family is also the weapon! Let us pray today for all the families of the world, especially for those that are suffering most. Mary, Queen of the Family, St Joseph, my father and lord, I entrust to you all the families of the world so that you may protect them, defend them, comfort them, fill them with supernatural love and bless them with unity.

Fifth day within the Nativity Octave
Monday 29th December
Lk 2:22-35

And when the time came for their purification according to the law of Moses, they brought him up to Jerusalem to present him to the Lord...Simeon took Jesus up in his arms and blessed God and said, "Lord, now lettest thou thy servant depart in peace, according to thy word; for mine eyes have seen thy salvation..." And his father and his mother marvelled at what was said about him.

The presentation of a firstborn Jewish child in the temple served two purposes; the first was the redemption of the first-born and the second was the purification of the mother. In this case, Jesus didn't need to be redeemed because He was God of the Temple; similarly, Mary didn't need purification because she was Immaculate from her Conception. Nevertheless, they went to fulfil the law. That's today's first lesson.

There Mary and Joseph were amazed at the things that were spoken about the Baby. At the end of this chapter, St Luke writes that Mary *"kept all these things in her heart."* Some of us are amazed at the number of things that our mothers can remember about us. How much mothers can store in their memory - in their heart - about each of their children! Things that they did, things that they said, things that they love, things that they fear and also things that they heard about them. Love increases our capacity to remember. Our Lady was filled with these memories.

Many years later St Luke came to ask Mary about Jesus in order to write his Gospels. He couldn't have found a better source! The heart of Mary was an archive of memories about Jesus. She stored them; she meditated on them; she spoke with Jesus about them; in time, she could understand them more and more. That is *mental prayer*: To take all these things written in the Gospels and meditate on them in your heart. Can you imagine the prayer of Mary when she remembered all these things? So should be your prayer and mine.

Mary, my Mother, during this season of Christmas you can give a boost to my mental prayer. With you, I'll take the Gospel as cherished memories about Jesus, I'll find Jesus there and get to know Him better and love Him more. *"May you seek Christ; may you find Christ; may you love Christ!"* (St Josemaría)

St Thomas Becket, bishop and martyr
Monday 29th December
Lk 22:24-30

A dispute also arose among them, which of them was to be regarded as the greatest. And he said to them, "The kings of the Gentiles exercise lordship over them; and those in authority over them are called benefactors. But not so with you; rather let the greatest among you become as the youngest, and the leader as one who serves."

Today's Gospel matches perfectly with the life of St Thomas Becket. He was born on St Thomas' feast day, 1119, into a good family. His education was outstanding, finishing his studies in the University of Paris. He is described as a strongly built, spirited youth, a lover of field sports, who seems to have spent his leisure time hawking and hunting. At the age of 24 he was given a post in the household of the archbishop of Canterbury. He studied canon law at the University of Bologna and was ordained deacon. The archbishop began to entrust him with many of his affairs. Among them he helped to get the approval of the Pope for the coronation of King Henry II, who appointed him Chancellor and chief minister at the age of 36. There he was at the top of his career. King Henry placed all his trust in him. So when, in 1161, Archbishop Theobald died, the King decided to make him the primate of England in order to have a friend in that office who could back up all his decisions.

Thomas was ordained a bishop and, although he was proud, strong-willed, and irascible, and remained so all his life, there was a transformation in him. From this day worldly grandeur no longer interested Thomas. He lived a life of penance, and his customary dress was a plain black cassock. He lived ascetically, spending much time in the distribution of alms, in reading and discussing the Scriptures, in visiting the infirmary, and serving the people of God with humility. The King saw he had lost his influence on Thomas since sacramental grace had taken over his soul. Eventually some of the King's knights killed Thomas in his Cathedral. Though far from a faultless character for most of his life, Thomas Becket had the courage to lay down his life to defend God's rights. He became, as today's Gospel describes, the *leader who serves*. Mary, Queen of Martyrs, through your intercession may the grace of Our Lord have the same effect on my soul.

Sixth day within the Nativity Octave
Tuesday 30th December
Lk 2:36–40

And there was a prophetess, Anna, the daughter of Phanuel, of the tribe of Asher; she was of a great age, having lived with her husband seven years from her virginity, and as a widow till she was eighty-four. She did not depart from the temple, worshipping with fasting and prayer night and day. And coming up at that very hour she gave thanks to God, and spoke of him to all who were looking for the redemption of Jerusalem. And when they had performed everything according to the law of the Lord, they returned into Galilee, to their own city, Nazareth. And the child grew and became strong, filled with wisdom; and the favour of God was upon him.

Anna was a holy woman. She was a soul of prayer and of penance. That made it possible for her to discover Jesus among all the people who visited the temple. She saw the Baby in the arms of Mary and she recognised Him. How many people were oblivious to the presence of God in their midst! How many passed by Mary, Joseph and Jesus and didn't recognise them. But Anna did.

To be able to recognise someone you need to know that person first. And we get to know Jesus in the Eucharist and in our daily conversation with Him. But after meeting Jesus and giving thanks to God, Anna didn't keep her joy to herself. The Gospel says that she "*spoke of him to all.*" She went around sharing her joy of having found Jesus and of knowing that our redemption had begun. She became the first 'apostle' to teach others about Jesus.

Anna didn't think it was enough to give thanks to God for having found the Messiah. She didn't think it was enough to tell a few people about it. The Gospel says she spoke about Him to *everyone*. In an interview with St Teresa of Calcutta someone asked her if she and her sisters talked about God with the sick and poor. "*Naturally!*" she replied; "*we teach them to pray, try to bring them to God through the sacrament of confession.*" The journalist made the point that we don't always have to talk about Jesus. The holy nun answered, "*What else do we have to talk about, then? We would not be missionaries if we didn't talk about Jesus. We would be acting for something… but we act for Someone!*" Mary, Queen of the Apostles, intercede for me that I can be daring enough to talk about your Son to everyone, with words and deeds.

Seventh day within the Nativity Octave
Wednesday 31st December
Jn 1:1-18

In the beginning was the Word, and the Word was with God, and the Word was God. He was in the beginning with God; all things were made through him, and without him was not anything made that was made. In him was life, and the life was the light of men. The light shines in the darkness, and the darkness has not overcome it...The true light that enlightens every man was coming into the world. He was in the world, and the world was made through him, yet the world knew him not. He came to his own home, and his own people received him not.

This reproach always strikes us: "*He came to his own home, and his own people received him not*". People waiting for Him for centuries, asking God to come and, when He came, they didn't receive Him! And what happened then can still happen in our life when Jesus shows up every day and we "*receive Him not.*"

A year has passed. 365 days have succeeded one another, opening to us thousands of opportunities to meet Jesus: in the Holy Mass, in the Tabernacle, in our prayer, in family life, at work, in the needy, the sick, the suffering... Not one day has passed this year in which you and I couldn't have grown in love...

Today is a *day of examination*. How have I made the most of each day to be holier, to grow in love with God? It's a *day of thanksgiving* for thousands of things that have gone well. 'Thank You, Lord.' It's also a *day of contrition* for our failures and sins: '*I am truly sorry, my Jesus.*' It's a *day of hope* because God grants us the grace to begin again and keep trying. That's what a father loves: that his children *keep trying* to be better.

A playful little girl came to kiss her dad, singing, "*Mirror, mirror on the wall, who's the best daughter of them all?*" The father, amused, said that she wasn't; "*Not yet,*" he added. The daughter looked serious, kissed him again and replied, "*I'm trying, dad. I'm trying hard!*" The father was moved and couldn't help thinking that he wasn't following his daughter's example: he wasn't trying to be the best father. Our Lady, my dear Mother, to you I entrust the new year that starts tomorrow: 365 opportunities for me to keep trying, seriously, to be a better child of Our Father every day, a better child of yours, Mother.

EXAMINATION OF CONSCIENCE

Some topics you could include on your examination

	1	2	3	4	5	6	7	8	9	10	11	12	13	14	15	16	17	18	19	20	21	22	23	24	25	26	27	28	29	30	31
Morning offering																															
Angelus																															
Prayer																															
Grace at meals																															
Rosary																															
Spiritual Reading																															
Night prayers																															
Examination at night																															
List of sacrifices																															
Heroic Minute																															

Common prayers

Visit to the Blessed Sacrament:

V/ *O Sacrament most holy! O Sacrament divine!*

R/ *All praise and all thanksgiving, be every moment Thine!*

Our Father, Hail Mary, Glory be...

[After repeating this three times, we repeat the aspiration 'O Sacrament most holy…' and then say the following Spiritual Communion]:

I wish, Lord, to receive You, with the purity, humility and devotion with which Your most holy Mother received You; with the spirit and fervour of the saints.

Angelus:

V/ *The Angel of the Lord declared unto Mary,*
R/ *And she conceived by the Holy Spirit. Hail Mary.*
V/ *Behold the handmaid of the Lord,*
R/ *Be it done unto me according to thy word. Hail Mary.*
V/ *And the Word was made flesh,*
R/ *And dwelt among us. Hail Mary.*
V/ *Pray for us, O holy Mother of God,*
R/ *That we may be made worthy of the promises of Christ.*

Let us pray.

Pour forth, we beseech Thee, O Lord, Thy grace into our hearts: that we, to whom the Incarnation of Christ, Thy Son, was made known by the message of an Angel, may by His Passion and Cross be brought to the glory of His Resurrection, through the same Christ our Lord. Amen.

Memorare:

Remember, O most gracious Virgin Mary, that never was it known that anyone who fled to thy protection, implored thy help, or sought thy intercession was left unaided. Inspired by this confidence, I fly unto thee, O Virgin of virgins, my mother; to thee do I come, before thee I stand, sinful and sorrowful. O Mother of the Word Incarnate, despise not my petitions, but in thy mercy hear and answer me. Amen.

Morning offering:

O Jesus, through the most pure heart of Mary, I offer you all the prayers, works, sufferings and joys of this day, for all the intentions of your Divine Heart. Amen.

Blessing before meals:

Bless us, O Lord, and these Thy gifts which we are about to receive from Thy bounty, through Christ our Lord, Amen.

Grace after meals:

We give you thanks, Almighty God, for all Your benefits, who live and reign, world without end. Amen.

Act of contrition:

O My God, because you are so good, I am very sorry that I have sinned against you, and by the help of your grace, I will not sin again. Amen.

Guardian Angel:

Angel of God, my Guardian dear, to whom His love commits me here, ever this day (or night) be at my side, to light and guard, to rule and guide. Amen.

Morning offering:

O Jesus, through the most pure heart of Mary, I offer you all the prayers, works, sufferings and joys of this day, for all the intentions of your Divine Heart. Amen.

Prayer to St. Michael:

St. Michael the Archangel, defend us in the day battle: be our defence against the wickedness and snares of the devil. May God rebuke him, we humbly pray. And do you, O prince of the heavenly host, by the power of God cast into hell Satan and all the evil spirits who prowl about the world fo the ruin of souls. Amen.

Holy Rosary:

In the name of the Father, and of the Son, and of the Holy Spirit. Amen.

The Apostles' Creed

I believe in God, the Father Almighty, Creator of heaven and earth; and in Jesus Christ, His only Son, our Lord; Who was conceived by the Holy Spirit, born of the Virgin Mary, suffered under Pontius Pilate, was crucified, died, and was buried. He descended into hell; the third day He arose again from the dead. He ascended into heaven, and sits at the right hand of God, the Father Almighty; from thence He shall come to judge the living and the dead. I believe in the Holy Spirit, the Holy Catholic Church, the communion of Saints, the forgiveness of sins, the resurrection of the body and life everlasting. Amen.

Then you can say one "Our Father", three "Hail Marys" and the "Glory be to the Father."

V. Thou, O Lord, wilt open my lips,
R. And my tongue shall announce thy praise.
V. Incline to my aid, O God.
R. O Lord, make haste to help me.

V. *Glory be to the Father, and to the Son, and to the Holy Spirit.*
R. As it was in the beginning, is now, and ever shall be, world without end. Amen.

After each decade say the following prayer requested by the Blessed Virgin Mary at Fatima:

"O my Jesus, forgive us our sins, save us from the fires of hell, lead all souls to Heaven, especially those in most need of your mercy."

The Joyful Mysteries *(recited Monday and Saturday)*
1. The Annunciation
2. The Visitation
3. The Birth of Our Lord
4. The Pr esentation
5. The Finding of the Child Jesus in the Temple

The Mysteries of Light *(recited Thursday)*
1. The Baptism of Jesus
2. The Wedding Feast at Cana
3. The Proclamation of the Kingdom and the call to Conversion
4. The Transfiguration
5. The Institution of the Eucharist

The Sorrowful Mysteries *(recited Tuesday and Friday)*
1. The Agony in the Garden
2. The Scourging at the Pillar
3. The Crowning with Thorns
4. The Carrying of the Cross
5. The Crucifixion and Death of Our Lord

The Glorious Mysteries *(recited Wednesday and Sunday)*
1. The Resurrection
2. The Ascension
3. The Descent of the Holy Spirit
4. The Assumption
5. The Coronation of the Blessed Virgin Mary

At the end of the fifth Mystery we say the Hail, Holy Queen:

Hail, Holy Queen, Mother of Mercy; Hail our life, our sweetness and our hope! To thee do we cry, poor banished children of Eve. To thee do we send up our sighs, mourning and weeping in this vale of tears! Turn, then, most gracious Advocate, thine eyes of mercy towards us, and after this, our exile, show unto us the blessed fruit of thy womb, Jesus. O clement, O loving, O sweet Virgin Mary.

V. Lord, have mercy	*R. Lord, have mercy.*
V. Christ, have mercy	*R. Christ, have mercy.*
V. Lord, have mercy	*R. Lord, have mercy.*
V. Christ hear us	*R. Christ graciously hear us.*

V. God the Father of heaven   R. have mercy on us.
V. God the Son, Redeemer of the world   R. have mercy on us.
V. God the Holy Spirit   R. have mercy on us.
V. Holy Trinity, one God   R. have mercy on us.

R. Pray for us

Holy Mary
Holy Mother of God,
Holy Virgin of virgins,
Mother of Christ,
Mother of the Church,
Mother of Mercy,
Mother of divine grace,
Mother of Hope,
Mother most pure,
Mother most chaste,
Mother inviolate,
Mother undefiled,
Mother most lovable,
Mother most admirable,
Mother of good counsel,
Mother of our Creator,
Mother of our Saviour,
Virgin most prudent,
Virgin most venerable,
Virgin most renowned,
Virgin most powerful,
Virgin most merciful,
Virgin most faithful,
Mirror of justice,
Seat of wisdom,
Cause of our joy,
Spiritual vessel,
Vessel of honour,

Singular vessel of devotion,
Mystical rose,
Tower of David,
Tower of ivory,
House of gold,
Ark of the covenant,
Gate of heaven,
Morning star,
Health of the sick,
Refuge of sinners,
Solace of migrants,
Comfort of the afflicted,
Help of Christians,
Queen of Angels,
Queen of Patriarchs,
Queen of Prophets,
Queen of Apostles,
Queen of Martyrs,
Queen of Confessors,
Queen of Virgins,
Queen of all Saints,
Queen conceived without original sin,
Queen assumed into heaven,
Queen of the most holy Rosary,
Queen of the family,
Queen of Peace.

V. Lamb of God, you take away the sins of the world,
R. Spare us, O Lord.
V. Lamb of God, you take away the sins of the world,
R. Graciously hear us, O Lord.
V. Lamb of God, you take away the sins of the world,
R. Have mercy on us. V. Pray for us, O holy Mother of God.
R. That we may be made worthy of the promises of Christ.

Let us pray:

O God, whose only-begotten Son, by his life, death and resurrection, has purchased for us the rewards of eternal life; grant, we beseech thee, that meditating on these mysteries of the most holy Rosary of the Blessed Virgin Mary, we may both imitate what they contain, and obtain what they promise, through the same Christ our Lord. Amen.

Prayer to Mary for Holy Purity

Blessed be your purity, May it be blessed for ever, For no less than God takes delight In such exalted beauty. To you, heavenly Princess, Holy Virgin Mary, I offer on this day My whole heart, life, and soul. Look upon me with compassion; Do not leave me, my mother.

Prayer to the Holy Spirit (St Josemaría)

Come, O Holy Spirit! Enlighten my mind to know your commands; strengthen my heart against the snares of the enemy; inflame my will... I have heard your voice, and I don't want to harden myself and resist, saying "Later..., tomorrow." Nunc coepi! Now I begin! In case there is no tomorrow for me. O Spirit of truth and wisdom, Spirit of understanding and counsel, Spirit of joy and peace! I want whatever you want. I want because you want, I want however you want, I want whenever you want.

Printed in Great Britain
by Amazon